ENMITY AND EMPATHY

ENMITY AND EMPATHY

Japanese Americans in Minnesota
during World War II

Ka F. Wong

MINNESOTA
HISTORICAL
SOCIETY PRESS

The publication of this book was supported through a generous grant from the June D. Holmquist Fund for Publications and Research.

mnhspress.org @mnhspress

The Minnesota Historical Society Press is a member of the Association of University Presses.

Manufactured in the United States of America.

10 9 8 7 6 5 4 3 2 1

♾ The paper used in this publication meets the minimum requirements of the American National Standard for Information Sciences—Permanence for Printed Library Materials, ANSI Z39.48–1984.

International Standard Book Number
ISBN: 978-1-68134-310-5 (paperback)
ISBN: 978-1-68134-311-2 (e-book)

Library of Congress Control Number: 2024948818

Contents

Enmity and Empathy

Stories of Japanese Americans in Minnesota during World War II

"Until Dec. 7, 1941, I thought I was a normal boy, a normal American. All of a sudden, I was dirty. All of a sudden, I was sinister. All of a sudden, I couldn't be trusted."—YOSH MURAKAMI

Known to his family and friends in Minnesota as "Yosh," Yoshiteru Murakami was fourteen years old on "the day of infamy," when Imperial Japan attacked Pearl Harbor. Following President Franklin D. Roosevelt's Executive Order 9066 on February 19, 1942, approximately 120,000 people of Japanese ancestry in total, nearly two-thirds of them American citizens, were uprooted from their homes and forced into ten incarceration camps in mostly desolate parts of the country. Remote locales like Minidoka in Idaho, Heart Mountain in Wyoming, Manzanar and Tule Lake in California, which held thousands of forcibly removed Japanese Americans behind barbed wire for the rest of the war, have since entered the lexicon of twentieth-century American history. Because of the perception of "public danger," all Japanese within varied distances from the Pacific coast were targeted. Unless they were able to dispose of or make arrangements for care of their property within a few days, their homes, farms, businesses, and most of their private belongings were lost forever.[1]

Born in San Pedro, California, Murakami, a teenage Nisei (second-generation Japanese American), was one of them. "We were assigned numbers, herded into a troop train and shipped to the Mojave Desert," he said. "For two years [in Manzanar], tar paper barracks with loosely constructed floors were the only homes and straw-filled bags covered with blankets the only beds for about 10,000 Japanese-Americans crowded into one square mile, surrounded by barbed-wire fences and sentry towers." In the candid words of Dillon S. Myer, director of the War Relocation Authority (WRA), the federal civilian agency that operated the incarceration and resettlement, these were "kid-glove concentration camps" even though they "gave the fancy name of 'relocation centers' to these dust bowls."[2]

The forcible eviction and imprisonment of Japanese Americans, according to the Congressional Commission on Wartime Relocation and Internment of Civilians, was "a grave injustice" shaped not by "military necessity" but "race prejudice, war hysteria, and a failure of political leadership." However, all the civil rights violations and abuses by the federal government were buried under the jingoistic banner of national security. The policy was summed up by John L. DeWitt, the wartime lieutenant general of the Western Defense Command and the Fourth Army: "A Jap's a Jap. They are a dangerous element, whether loyal or not."[3]

There was never the slightest proof of subversive activity by the Japanese American residents and citizens on the West Coast, but the removal needed no justification except fear. There was no wholesale incarceration of American residents who traced their ancestry to the two other foes either. "It would have been somewhat reasonable considering wartime conditions had equal treatment been accorded to other American enemies. But we wondered why we were behind barbed wire and not the Germans or Italians," Murakami asked. For the young Nisei, it was difficult to understand, especially in a nation proclaiming "freedom and justice" for all and the unalienable rights to life, liberty, and the pursuit of happiness. "We were herded away without due process of law," Murakami lamented. "What crime did we commit?"[4]

Murakami was not alone in feeling confused and conflicted. The battle for "freedom and justice" was fought on all fronts by different individuals and institutions. A main concern focused on the American-born youths like Murakami, whose rights to higher education were denied or abruptly cut short. There were reportedly 3,252 Nisei students enrolled in institutions of higher learning in California, Washington, and Oregon in 1941, with an additional 278 of them attending schools outside of the West Coast, although the number might have been underestimated. Instead of on college campuses

Civilian Exclusion Order No. 5

WESTERN DEFENSE COMMAND AND FOURTH ARMY
WARTIME CIVIL CONTROL ADMINISTRATION
Presidio of San Francisco, California
April 1, 1942

INSTRUCTIONS
TO ALL PERSONS OF
JAPANESE
ANCESTRY
LIVING IN THE FOLLOWING AREA:

All that portion of the City and County of San Francisco, State of California, lying generally west of the north-south line established by Junipero Serra Boulevard, Worchester Avenue, and Nineteenth Avenue, and lying generally north of the east-west line established by California Street, to the intersection of Market Street, and thence on Market Street to San Francisco Bay.

All Japanese persons, both alien and non-alien, will be evacuated from the above designated area by 12:00 o'clock noon, Tuesday, April 7, 1942.

No Japanese person will be permitted to enter or leave the above described area after 8:00 a. m., Thursday, April 2, 1942, without obtaining special permission from the Provost Marshal at the Civil Control Station located at:

> 1701 Van Ness Avenue
> San Francisco, California

The Civil Control Station is equipped to assist the Japanese population affected by this evacuation in the following ways:

1. Give advice and instructions on the evacuation.

2. Provide services with respect to the management, leasing, sale, storage or other disposition of most kinds of property including: real estate, business and professional equipment, buildings, household goods, boats, automobiles, livestock, etc.

3. Provide temporary residence elsewhere for all Japanese in family groups.

4. Transport persons and a limited amount of clothing and equipment to their new residence, as specified below.

Reprint by: Japanese American Citizens League
National Committee to Repeal the Emergency Detention Act
c/o Ray Okamura,
1150 Park Hills Road, Berkeley, Calif. 94708

(OVER)

Civilian Exclusion Order No. 5, April 1, 1942, "Instructions to all persons of Japanese Ancestry," issued by the Western Defense Command and Fourth Army and Wartime Civil Control Administration to Presidio of San Francisco, California. *Courtesy of Bill Doi* where they belonged, these young people were imprisoned in concentration camps.[5]

It was in Manzanar that Murakami discovered his talent for and interest in music. His teachers enthusiastically encouraged the Nisei to pursue his passion through higher education, yet he was "apprehensive" about leaving his family in confinement for the "hostile outside world." For most of the Nisei, departing for college meant a separation from everything they knew. Once they were released, they could never go back to the camps or their prewar homes. With the uncertainty of the war, the exile might well be for life.[6]

The outside world, as Murakami expected, was not particularly friendly to Japanese Americans. The attitude of higher education institutions toward accepting Nisei students at the time varied from open arms to closed doors. Many colleges and universities refused them admission mostly because of politics, which ignited a range of protesting voices from both Japanese Americans and sympathetic compatriots. As a result, the WRA, first headed by Milton S. Eisenhower—the younger brother of then General and later President Dwight D. Eisenhower and an academic administrator himself— and subsequently by Myer, quickly took up mitigating measures to encourage the Nisei's education. Notable endeavors included those by the National Japanese American Student Relocation Council (NJASRC), a privately organized and financed agency operated largely by volunteers from the American Friends Service Committee, more commonly known as the Quakers. The NJASRC was officially founded on May 29, 1942.[7]

The laborious efforts by the NJASRC and other activists to get Nisei students out of the camps became known as an "Underground Railroad" among those who worked on it during the early months of the war. Clearances to enroll Japanese American students required an overwhelming amount of paperwork and administrative procedures, such as completed questionnaires from the student applicants, testimonies from public officials vouching for community acceptance, institutional approvals from the Department of War, and background checks from the Federal Bureau of Investigation (FBI).[8]

Evidently, many higher education institutions preferred to avoid the potential "train wreck." Only about a quarter of schools would admit Japanese Americans to their campuses. Three months after the relocations began, the first passes to leave the camps were eventually granted. Murakami was among a total of eleven Japanese American students admitted to St. Olaf College in Northfield, Minnesota, between the spring of 1943 and the fall of 1944.[9]

The college journey for many Nisei students was neither swift nor smooth. Of those Japanese American students at St. Olaf, the majority stayed for a year or less; only Murakami and a couple of others actually graduated. The odds were stacked against them, from financial difficulties to wartime antagonism, bureaucratic inertia to the military draft. At the end of his sophomore year, Murakami answered the call of duty to serve as an interpreter in Japan. He returned to St. Olaf two years later in 1948, completed his degree in music and got married in 1951, then went on to become an outstanding music educator in the Northfield school system and Concordia College at Moorhead, among many other contributions to Minnesota during the decades to come. Over the course of the war, around four thousand Nisei students were able to leave the camps to pursue their dreams of higher education, and more than five hundred of them, like Murakami, chose the North Star State.

Besides the inflow of college students, the war also saw Minnesota become the new home to a resettled Japanese American community. In 1942, the Military Intelligence Service Language School (MISLS) was established at Camp Savage and moved to Fort Snelling after its expansion in 1944. Its purpose was to train soldiers as Japanese linguists to aid the US military effort. Accompanying the recruits came their families and friends, from nurses to trade workers to entrepreneurs.

While the extraordinary accomplishments of these Japanese Americans, together with those advocates who worked tirelessly for them, should be acknowledged, this was not a happily-ever-after story for them or the nation. The disastrous mistake should not have happened to begin with, and it should be a lesson to remember in the struggle for racial and social justice that continues to plague the country today. If history is a mirror of the past, what images can be seen in it? Where can Japanese Americans find themselves reflected and represented, if anywhere at all, in the mirror of Minnesotan history?[10]

Although the wartime imprisonment of Japanese Americans manifests a haunting and horrible past, many ordinary folks are indifferent if not ignorant about it. Perhaps it was just an outlier, an inevitable causality of war. Perhaps the incarceration was meant to protect the Japanese American population from wartime hostility. Perhaps people are unprepared to accept a crime committed against some of their fellow citizens under the watch of everyone.

Mainstream histories tend to avoid deep engagement with truly difficult moments. Those hard stories that evoke guilt or shame in members of the majority also make them recoil from learning more to get past those negative reactions. Perhaps because the confinement happened to a marginalized group, it stays in the margin. The Japanese American experience, therefore, has been shelved mostly inside an ethnic niche or added as minor footnotes in history books. Their incarceration is still a blurry visage in the American collective memory. Even those with knowledge about the events feel uneasy about its interpretation and implication.[11]

This is certainly not due to a lack of effort by activists and researchers. Over the years critical reviews of the forced removal and mass incarceration, including subsequent legal challenges, have revealed a concerted attempt to keep this historical lesson in the national discourse. Owing to the courageous incarcerees and various supportive organizations, accounts of trying removal experiences, terrible conditions in the camps, and their assiduous fight for freedom amid adversities have increasingly been shared with the public. Through books, films, documentaries, plays, artistic works, and museum exhibitions, among other media, the Japanese American incarceration has rightfully become a pivotal point in Asian American history.

Advocacy for justice has also made significant progress with the "redress movement." The passage of the Civil Liberties Act of 1988 offered both a national apology and monetary compensation, with individual payments of $20,000 to incarceration survivors. In Minnesota, for example, more than three hundred Japanese Americans received their redress checks by the fall of 1993.[12]

While the redress movement is a shining achievement for Japanese Americans in particular and the nation as a whole, ensuring civil liberties for all is a constant battle. The constitutionality of the incarceration remained intact for another two decades after the redress. It was not until 2018 that the *Korematsu v. United States* decision, in which a young Nisei man was convicted for his refusal to be imprisoned in 1944, was overturned by the Supreme Court. The reason why it took so long to denounce the unlawful past was in part due to racism, the assumption that people of color were often considered a threat to national security, and in part to the overall vagueness surrounding the entire subject of Japanese American wartime ordeals. To many, the Japanese American incarceration camps were at least not "hell holes of starvation or death" like those in Nazi Germany, a view which helped assuage the "national honor."[13]

The specter of prejudice, unfortunately, lives on to this day. As historian Greg Robinson argues, the "void of public knowledge" about the imprisonment allowed a "small but tenacious" circle of interest groups to exploit the aftermath of the September 11 crisis and the anxiety over immigrants of color among the mostly white populace. Noticeably, in the case of President Donald Trump's Executive Order 13769 that was first signed in 2017, otherwise known as the Muslim travel ban, some politicians rationalized and trivialized the Japanese American confinement for their own agenda.

The highest court upheld the travel ban, however. The decision "redeploys the same dangerous logic underlying Korematsu," dissenting Justice Sonia Sotomayor stated; instead of "formal repudiation of a shameful precedent," it merely replaces one devastating injustice with another. George Takei, the actor turned activist who was imprisoned as a child himself, warned that the bigotry and frenzy that the Japanese Americans endured in the 1940s still "continue to threaten the freedom and livelihoods of people whose voices have been suppressed."[14]

The unresolved past is bound to catch up with an uninformed present. Japanese Americans, or Asian Americans in general, have always been outsiders. The wartime tragedy of Japanese Americans on the West Coast did not materialize in a vacuum but emerged from a long list of anti-Asian immigrant policies and violence starting in the late nineteenth century. Scapegoating Asian Americans for the woes of the country is nothing new, from the Chinese Exclusion Act (1882) to the Rock Springs Massacre (1885) to the murder of Vincent Chin (1982). The rise of anti-Asian hate crimes during the pandemic in 2019–2020 is another alarming case in point. While many blame President Trump and his administration's use of racist rhetoric for the upsurge in violence, the Trump White House "didn't create this kind of discrimination and, indeed, hatred," Senator Mazie Hirono of Hawaiʻi pointed out; they only "called to the fore the kind of thinking that some people in our country have."[15]

She continued, "We have always been deemed 'the other,' the perpetual foreigners." In the war against the COVID-19 virus, Asian Americans once again became the targets of antagonism and attack—guilty solely because of their ethnic association. Without cleaning the dust of racism, ignorance, and misinformation from the mirror of history, the nation remains unable to see itself with clarity. The reflections are distorted, and the ghosts of the past will always return.[16]

The Japanese American incarceration is a disturbing tale. That people feel disconnected from it is somewhat understandable. This darker side of the country seemingly does not fit into the grand vision of the land of the free. There are more glorious World War II yarns to recount and relish. Hence, it is rarely told alongside "feel-good" American stories. Of course, the incarceration taps into the nation's deeply rooted unease about its racist history, especially slavery and the subjugation of Indigenous peoples. Many would like to avoid such topics or consider them simply bygone. Some even argue that the examination of racism in the classroom promotes nothing but division and resentment and, consequently, should be banned. The obscurity of the wartime Japanese American incarceration in the popular memory is thus regrettable but predictable.

The code of silence, however, befell the Japanese American families as well. Those who saw the penumbra of the war often grapple with what to pass on to the next generation; the sense of despair and humiliation about their plight as well as the anxiety and uncertainty of their predicament are probably what they would like to let die with them. After all, the war took place decades ago. Many believe it is time to move forward and not dwell on a miserable or misguided past.

Furthermore, there is a distance not only in time but also in space. Minnesota does not come naturally to one's mind when talking about wartime Japanese American experiences. There was no concentration camp in the state. The population of Japanese Americans was rather small then, as it is now. As important as the subject might be, it appears to bear little relevance for the North Star State. Do these Japanese American stories belong to Minnesotan history at all?[17]

The low recognition is justified to some degree, for the state is known as predominately inhabited by European settlers and immigrants. From the long-running radio show *A Prairie Home Companion* (1974–2016) to the Oscar-winning motion picture *Fargo* (1996), Minnesota has been portrayed in the popular imagination as a place of "whiteness," not least due to the snowy winters, and as a paragon of "white culture," including people with funny accents owing to their Norwegian and Swedish heritage. Minnesota is famous for its lakes and forests, or the legend of Paul Bunyan. Racial diversity might not easily rise to the top of the list. Nonetheless, first impressions do not always tell the whole truth.

One simply needs to look at the very name "Minnesota" (the Dakota tribe's word for the Minnesota River, meaning "sky-tinted" or "cloudy" water), or a random town on the state's map to know the place was not always "white." The erasure of Indigenous peoples and their legacies, mostly through violent means, by the European migrants to the United States was by and large complete by the mid-nineteenth century. A whiter Minnesota was then born. Apart from being the time-honored homeland to various native tribes, other communities of color, despite their relatively smaller sizes, did settle and take root in the North Star State. These stories from historically powerless groups are hardly ever told or heard. The Japanese Americans are no exception.

The twenty-first century marked a major turning point for the state. Intensifying racial tensions in recent years, highlighted by the murder of George Floyd in Minneapolis, sparked national protests and dialogues about racism, prejudice, and social justice. Calls for empathy—the ability to step into the shoes of another person, the willingness to comprehend other people's feelings and perspectives, and using that understanding to guide responsible actions—are eminent among all citizens. Beyond outrage and fury, the incident has forced a more critical reflection on the construction of whiteness and the state's overwhelmingly Eurocentric version of history. And the soul-searching process has only just begun.[18]

Maybe Minnesota's past was always splashed with "colorful" stories. Maybe Minnesotans do not need to look farther away but instead closer to home to find those "shoes" to step into and "lessons" to learn. Are the Japanese Americans' wartime experiences about only "them" and not "us"? Or, have the connections been here all along, merely hidden or forgotten with the passage of time? In fact, exploring the intersection between the wartime Japanese American saga and Minnesota offers a refreshing angle to examine the state's history, which brings us back to Yosh Murakami.

I first encountered Murakami's story when a group of my students and I worked on a summer research project about Asian Americans in Minnesota a decade ago. Being a person of Asian descent who moved to this state for professional reasons, I was eager to find out about anything Asian in this ostensibly "white" place. Who and where are the Asian faces? Why did they come here? What are their experiences like?

We interviewed ten different Asian Minnesotans from all walks of life that summer. The entrepreneur couple from Taiwan running a successful Chinese restaurant provided a familiar immigrant narrative. Meanwhile, members of

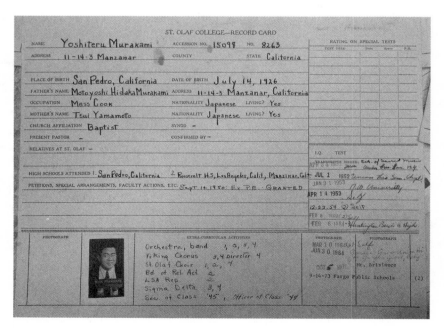

Yosh Murakami's transcript, St. Olaf College, 1944–1948. *Courtesy of St. Olaf College*

the Southeast Asian diaspora that began in the late 1970s—Hmong, Vietnamese, Laotian, Cambodian—told other poignant tales of war and displacement, as the refugees rebuilt lives torn apart by the Vietnam War.[19]

We also talked to a Japanese American alumna of St. Olaf College, a Northfield-born Minnesotan whose career in social services had taken her to different parts of the Midwest. Her name was Jane Murakami, and she was the daughter of Yosh Murakami. "My father was in Manzanar for three years," she recalled. "I believe he was the second student allowed into St. Olaf . . . [and one of] the first person[s] of color in the St. Olaf Choir."[20]

This project started with the desire to know more about Murakami, leading to the discovery of more stories about Nisei resettlers in Minnesota. In the following summer, my students and I decided to concentrate on wartime Japanese American experiences. Working with scholars, college archivists, the Twin Cities chapter of the Japanese American Citizens League (JACL), and many Japanese Minnesotans themselves, we unearthed unexpected yet exciting results on our research journey over the past several years. We were grateful for the opportunity to interview more than twenty individuals who were familiar with the Nisei's experiences—fifteen second-generation Japanese Americans in Minnesota who personally lived through the war, from removal to incarceration, and from attending college to serving in the military, along with a dozen of their family members and friends, like Jane Murakami.[21]

In addition, we talked with a number of experts on the matter, such as historians, biographers, and college administrators, to help us better grasp the intricacies surrounding the wartime events. We were fortunate to receive support from various organizations, making our investigation possible in not only different libraries and research centers throughout the state but also the Hoover Institution Library and Archives in California, which acquired important primary sources about the war. With the generous assistance of the archivists and librarians, we were able to locate valuable materials about Japanese Americans in Minnesota. We retrieved transcripts, yearbooks, school newspapers, letters, official and personal correspondence, and photographs, as well as documents from the NJASRC and the WRA. These artifacts, seldom discussed in the context of Minnesota, greatly informed and inspired this book.

Jane Murakami, 2014. *Courtesy of the author*

From Manzanar to Minnesota, the stories of Murakami and his fellow Nisei citizens tell of not only one of the bleakest episodes in modern American history, but also the underexplored links between Japanese Americans and the North Star State. As early as 1942, people in Minneapolis and St. Paul had already organized resettlement committees to help Japanese Americans leave camps and come to Minnesota. The Twin Cities were among the first in the nation to do so. The WRA opened an office in Minneapolis in March 1943, collaborating with existing civic groups to find housing and employment for Nisei.[22]

Similarly, a handful of private colleges and universities, such as Macalester, Carleton, and St. Olaf, immediately teamed up with the NJASRC to take in Japanese American students, while some other higher education institutions declined to participate. The backgrounds, politics, and people behind the acceptance or rejection of Nisei students were complicated. They revealed a glimpse of the state's educational record on the one hand, and on the other, its historical entanglements with race relations and civil liberties at a time when the country was engulfed in war hysteria and xenophobia.

This book spotlights the Japanese Americans in Minnesota during and immediately after World War II, and how Minnesota played a vital role in their lived experiences from three perspectives. Higher education, first and foremost, was an essential part of the narrative. The fact that Japanese American youths were able to leave camps and attend college owed as much to their own determination as the efforts by their allies, including those from Minnesota. The NJASRC was undoubtedly the most important and impactful.

The head of its East Coast office and later the chair of the council was John W. Nason, a St. Paul native and a Rhodes Scholar, who served as the president of Swarthmore College (1940–1953) and subsequently of Carleton College (1962–1970). Nason would later describe his successes in relocating Nisei students for higher education as among his proudest accomplishments. Likewise, under the leadership of Charles Turck, president of Macalester College (1939–1958), the school became the first in Minnesota to accept Japanese American students after the outbreak of the war. Besides the NJASRC, religious organizations were also crucial supporters of Japanese American students' relocations to Minnesota.

Moreover, the notion that the University of Minnesota rejected Japanese American students during the war was not quite correct. The issue was complex. Internal documents indicate that conflicting opinions were held by various administrators at different points in time. Actually, more than two hundred Nisei students did enroll in the University of Minnesota between 1941 and 1946 in a wide range of undergraduate and graduate programs. How Nason and his fellow educators in Minnesota overcame bureaucratic obstacles, wartime propaganda, and public hostility to bring Nisei students to this state deserves an in-depth examination.

Additionally, we learned that a larger number of Nisei students than previously estimated attended colleges and universities in Minnesota during the war years. Twenty-five higher learning institutions accepted Japanese Americans, with a total of 536 students. Minnesota ranked second in the nation for Japanese American college students during the war, behind only Illinois; it ranked third by the end of the war in 1945 and 1946, when students were allowed to return to California and Washington. Who were these young Nisei? Why did they choose to come to Minnesota? How did they get here? What were their lives like in the North Star State as Japanese Americans during the war? The answers to these questions are still elusive and hence became one of the aims of the inquiry.[23]

Also, Minnesota was home to the military intelligence language school at Camp Savage and then Fort Snelling. From its inauguration in 1942 to its closure in 1946, over six thousand students, roughly 85 percent of whom were Nisei, had graduated and been deployed to the Pacific, Southeast Asia, and, later, Occupied Japan (1945–1952). The MISLS was an excellent demonstration of the wartime contributions from both Minnesota and the Nisei soldiers. However, the operation was considered confidential and, therefore, sealed and shelved in a dusty corner of history. Not until the past few decades has the existence of the school been known to the public, and the declassification of military intelligence documents began only in the 1970s.[24]

Behind the secretive curtains stood the silent Nisei soldiers and their spectacular feats. "I wanted to show that I am ... just as American as anybody," MISLS veteran Bill Doi said; joining the military "was one way to prove it." The WRA perceived that the key for the Japanese Americans to "regain the status was the opportunity for service with the armed forces." In late 1942 Doi enlisted in the US Army and went from Tule Lake to the MISLS at Camp Savage. He settled in Minnesota after the war and became a leader in not only the local Japanese American community but also the national redress movement, as well as many other civil and human rights initiatives. We had the honor of interviewing him before he passed away at the age of 101.[25]

That the Japanese Americans served in the armed forces and sacrificed their lives for the country while their families were imprisoned behind

Bill Doi, 2015. *Courtesy of the author*

barbed wire was both ironic and tragic. In fact, not just Nisei male but also female recruits were trained at the MISLS. The military school is unknown to many, even Minnesotans themselves, however. Thankfully, the heroic exploits of the combat linguists, especially their gallantry in the Pacific Theater, have gradually received scholarly and popular attention. Also arriving in Minnesota were Japanese American women from another uniformed service program, the Cadet Nurse Corps, who received their training at hospitals mostly in Rochester. The northern experiences of these young Nisei are fascinating yet unfamiliar to many.[26]

Lastly, Minnesota became a safe harbor for many incarcerees to wait out and weather the wartime tempest. As those Nisei set for colleges and the MISLS came for their education, so did their parents, siblings, and other relatives. Many of them seized this connection to leave the camps. These family members certainly led their own lives that were different from typical students or soldiers. A number of adventurous mavericks, too, ventured into the state, where they knew no one, to seek job opportunities or restart their businesses during a time when the rest of the country had turned against them. Although most of these professional Nisei did not stay for long, some left noteworthy footprints from their sojourns. For a handful of them, their short-term refuge even converted into a lifelong residence. Their stories, more scattered and fragmented in nature, have scarcely been heard.

These three intertwined threads of Japanese American experiences, accordingly, form the central core of this book, and more importantly, the tapestry of a multidimensional Minnesotan history during the war. The subsequent chapters are devoted to these topics. Chapter Two, "Incarceration and Integration," provides an overview of Minnesota as the destination for the wartime Japanese American resettlement. Chapter Three, "Advocates and Agencies," illuminates the roles of individuals, higher education institutions, and civic organizations, especially the NJASRC, in helping Nisei students relocate to Minnesota.

The Japanese American stories are examined in the four following chapters. Chapters Four, Five, Six, and Seven weave their personal journeys into the larger historical fabric of Minnesota as well as the country at large. Whereas Chapter Four, "Ambassadors and Adversaries," looks at

Nisei students in the more conventional liberal arts colleges and universities, Chapter Five, "Courage and Combat," explores the lives of the Nisei soldiers at the MISLS. Chapter Six, "Compassion and Commitment," sheds light on the Cadet Nurse Corps and the intriguing tales from these Japanese American women. Chapter Seven, "Risks and Rewards," pays specific attention to the working Nisei who came to the state through business sponsorship, entrepreneurship, and vocational training.

All these newcomers constituted an integral component of not only Japanese American experiences in Minnesota but also the war effort in general. Bringing these Japanese Americans' past to the present, Chapter Eight, "Resettlement and Remembrance," revisits the major themes found throughout the book and reveals what these stories mean to the current and future generations of the North Star State. The final chapter, Chapter Nine, "Untold Histories and Unsung Heroes," is a brief conclusion.

How to talk about wartime Japanese American experiences can indeed be challenging. The most frequently used term to describe their incarceration has been "internment," referring to a legal process in which enemy aliens can be detained during times of war. Many scholars argue that this term, along with others like "evacuation" and "relocation," constitutes euphemistic language. Japanese Americans did not go through due process in any sense of the word. Hence, I use terms such as incarceration and forced removal in the book. However, I retain terms, including internment and evacuation, when they are used by interviewees and in original sources, respecting the historical contexts and personal choices from which they come. I acknowledge the sensitivity surrounding terminology and regret any failure to recognize the problematic nature of using certain terms.[27]

—

Minnesota history has always been multifaceted, multiracial, and multicultural. The arduous yet amazing saga of the Japanese Americans delivers a new lens to review the past in an exceptional present of local and national reckoning about race, diversity, and inclusion. "We may be different," Yosh Murakami stated, "but we are all people." And his story and legacy will continue to unfold in later chapters.[28]

I am, by all means, not a historian, neither by training nor by trade. This book is not a conventional history either. I consider myself merely a story collector and presenter. Although I deal with the bygone years of the last century, my approach is not solely historical but also interdisciplinary. The goal of this book is to share these seemingly different yet ultimately Minnesotan narratives with others and thereby enrich our understanding of the state's past through these voices of enmity and empathy. Above all, these are simply incredible, inspiring, and interesting stories.

2 | Incarceration and Integration

History and Relocation of Japanese Americans in Wartime Minnesota

"I guess for one thing a lot of people out here [in Minnesota] didn't know anything about it. You talk about internment camp, they don't know what you're talking about. Because maybe people on the West Coast do, but people out in this area, they didn't know anything about it, and I guess they [couldn't] care less."
—JIM KUSUNOKI

Born and raised in California, Kiyoshi "Jim" Kusunoki was a World War II veteran who served in Germany and later called the Twin Cities home. Like many other Japanese American families, the Kusunokis were forced to leave everything behind after the Executive Order 9066. They ran a successful tailoring business in San Francisco called "Oriental Embroidery Shop," which, along with their home, was abruptly sold in a couple of weeks.[1]

The teenage Kusunoki and his family were sent to the Topaz incarceration camp in Utah. "[The government] just put us all in a train, and the curtains were all closed," he recalled. The Nisei was soon drafted, however, while his parents were still in confinement. "There's not much you can do about it anyways. What can you do?" he told us in his Roseville home in the summer of 2015. "There's no sense in getting bitter about it, just make the best of it. Do whatever you can . . . *Shikata ga nai*, I don't know where I picked that up," he said with a faint smile.

That Japanese phrase came up again when we spoke with Stanley Kusunoki, Jim's eldest son, a poet, writer, and arts advocate who taught at Shakopee

Jim Kusunoki, 2015.
Courtesy of the author

Jim Kusunoki and son Stanley Kusunoki, ca. 1950s. *Courtesy of Jim Kusunoki*

public schools before his retirement in 2020. "*Shikata ga nai* means 'can't be helped; there's nothing we can do about it.' So, best to leave it alone," the younger Kusunoki explained, "and I think that was the approach to it." Regarding his parents' time in imprisonment, he remarked: "I'd have to really think hard and trace back, because they didn't like to talk about it."[2]

This sense of helplessness was shared by many of the incarcerees. "Like most parents, they wanted to forget about it," said Sally Ohno Sudo. The ninth of ten children in the Ohno family from Seattle, Washington, Sudo together with all her family members were confined in Minidoka. She was then six years old. "For my father, I think it affected him the most because he really was a depressed man by the time he got out of the camp. By then he was already sixty years old, and at an age when [he] should be thinking about retirement, he had lost everything," Sudo said. "It was like having to start his life all over again."[3]

Her family's reset began in Minnesota. Four of her siblings had come to the state during the war, including a brother who joined the military language school and a sister who worked as a stenographer at Fort Snelling. Decades have passed since Sudo entered her fourth-grade classroom in South Minneapolis in 1945. Now a mother, grandmother, and retired schoolteacher, she has made it her mission to raise awareness and urge vigilance by speaking to young people about her experiences. "I was surprised that there were students who would challenge me and say, 'That didn't happen in America' and 'I never heard about that,'" Sudo recalled from earlier days in the mid-1990s when she discussed the uprooting and incarceration with schoolchildren. Things have improved over the years. These days "people are more aware of it," Sudo believed.[4]

The memories of these Japanese Minnesotans are a part of the collective history of the state. There are surely many more untold "*shikata ga nai*" stories of the older generations—what they must have endured and wished to forget. Nevertheless, capturing them is a race against time. While many of the Issei (first-generation Japanese Americans) stories might already be lost, there are fortunately considerable numbers of records with which to interpret the experiences of the Nisei and Sansei (third-generation Japanese Americans). The extant literature has increasingly uncovered the dramatic removal and implementation of the incarceration as well as the dreadful mistreatment in the camps. The gradual availability of government documents related to the war also provides further insights into the good, the bad, and the ugly politics of the time.[5]

Listening to all these wartime stories, one cannot help but ask, what was the Japanese American imprisonment really about? Was it simply a matter of "military necessity" that was "in accordance with the best interests of the country"? Or, did the obvious rhetoric of "national security" obscure other motives? And how was all this related to Minnesota? Before taking a closer look at all these questions, it will be useful to first return to the most fundamental one of why such an unjust calamity happened to Japanese Americans.[6]

The short answer to the previous question was race. The "un-American" or "dangerous" attributes of the Japanese Americans used to justify their forced removal and incarceration exposed a time-honored racial problem in the country. To many, America meant "whiteness." Imperial Japan's attack on Pearl Harbor, as tragic as it was, easily became the excuse for imprisoning people of Japanese ancestry, who, noticeably, were not considered white.[7]

After the "threatening" Japanese Americans were confined in the desolate camps, how to deal with them became another predicament for the authorities. Race once again was the driving force behind both the incarceration and decisions concerning its operations. Despite the unthinkable violation of civil liberties and democratic values, the imprisonment presented an opportunity for the government to remold ethnic Japanese into so-called model Americans. The camps were, therefore, intended for cultural reformation as well as ethnic relocation. Americanization, or the "whitening" process, gave an overriding purpose and prescription for the imprisonment, as a longer-term response to those questions about "military necessity," "national security," and "best interests of the country."[8]

The irony was that many of the incarcerees were patriotic Americans. In a letter to President Roosevelt on May 22, 1942, the chapter secretary of the JACL at Florin, California, wrote: "We, who are Americans to the core, but in appearance betray our oriental ancestry, feel ashamed that the people of our own race are greatly responsible for the present conflict. . . . I am oriental in appearance, but O! my core is American!" Sadly, the politicians' concerns were only skin-deep. Two federal investigations also concluded that the vast majority of Japanese Americans were fiercely loyal to the United States and "pathetically eager to show this loyalty."[9]

Another official report by the Department of the Interior depicted the Nisei as fully Americanized. "These youngsters gave every appearance of being more American than their elders. They looked generally taller and straighter, and in some cases even seemed to have a less pronounced oriental cast of features. In all but a few cases, their language was distinctively American as were the clothes they wore, the games they played, the social customs they followed, and the entertainments they enjoyed—sometimes to the consternation of their parents." Though the issue of "Americanism" was not necessarily about any or all these things.[10]

The concern was ultimately over race. It might be hard to believe what President Roosevelt wrote in 1943, that "Americanism is not, and never was, a matter of race and ancestry," when over one hundred thousand Japanese Americans were still in confinement. Whereas the president disclaimed racist intentions, his executive action revealed otherwise. Indeed, lingering doubts about how truly American a non-white person could be remained in some of the leaders' minds. "How thoroughly have these young people with Japanese names and faces been imbued with American ideals, American traditions, and American modes of thought?" asked one of the government reports. "Is their Americanism merely a veneer or has our distinctive type of civilization become a deep and inherent part of their consciousness and their attitudes?" Evidently, these were only rhetorical questions, as the inquirers already knew the answers they wanted to hear.[11]

War created heroes and villains. Everything was painted in broad and bold brushstrokes, propagating a stark contrast of good versus evil, and us against them. Many people then believed that incarcerating these "dubious" elements was to a certain degree justified. In their minds, "white racism," as scholar Gary Okihiro described, "was caused by Japanese Americans" themselves—"they looked like the enemy, shared the religion, food, language, and behavior of the enemy, and lived in [enclaves like] Little Tokyos." That very visible difference "prompted an instinctual recoiling and hostility by Whites." It was the fault of the "others," and logically they needed to be corrected.[12]

While changing their "Japanese" ethnic origin was impossible, some type of "American" reconfiguration became important, especially for the future's sake. The concept of "Americanism" at that time was far from multicultural and rather unidimensional. It rested heavily on middle-class Anglo-Saxon Protestant notions of civility, conduct, and culture. In addition, government officials alleged that Buddhism and Shintoism were incompatible with American values, and intelligence agencies specifically targeted these religions' organizations as hindrances to Americanization and menaces to national security. Accordingly, Japanese language, heritage, spiritual practices, and even the basic family foundation were discouraged, if not disparaged. "The family unit was sort of destroyed," said Hannah Hayano Semba about her incarceration days. "It was community, you know, instead of family."[13]

The fifth of seven children of a Japanese potato farmer who had immigrated to the United States on a freighter, Semba was born and grew up in Seattle before being uprooted to Tule Lake and then Heart Mountain. Luckily, the teenage Semba was able to get out through the college route. She was accepted to Macalester College, then transferred to and graduated from the University of Minnesota in 1948 with a degree in food and nutrition. The North Star State has since been her home for more than eight decades. "In camp, we only lived in one big room, and everything else was community. Community laundry, community recreation, community mess hall . . . It wasn't family. So, the family unit sort of became very loose." Also loosened and lost was their sense of identity, what it meant or took to be a Japanese American, a topic that is set for further exploration in Chapter Eight.

Reeducation inside the camps was one thing. Reassurance of the result outside of confinement was another. Detention was never intended to be indefinite. Neither was that feasible. One of the objectives of the WRA was to break up the communities of the Japanese American population on the West Coast by dispersing them widely across the country. If the incarcerees could demonstrate their loyalty, they were eligible for release. But where they could and should go also had to be put into the calculation.[14]

Another of the WRA's objectives was to prevent the reestablishment of the large prewar Japanese enclaves. WRA Director Myer, before the US Senate in January 1943, testified: "I am frankly hoping that quite a number of

Sisters Judy (Hayano) Tabata and Hannah (Hayano) Semba at the Heart Mountain Relocation Center in Wyoming in 1943. They were transferred from the Tule Lake incarceration camp to Heart Mountain in 1942. *Courtesy of Hannah Semba*

those people will get established in positions in different parts of the country other than on the Pacific coast . . . where they can gradually be absorbed as American citizens, and thus dispose of a racial problem that has been a pretty tough one for the coast people and for the United States." The ideal locations would be places where the incarcerees would have no choice but to identify and associate with the white middle class. President Roosevelt and his advisers believed that concentration of urban-based minority groups would breed poverty and intergroup tensions, as historian Greg Robinson pointed out. A geographic fanning out of the Japanese Americans to places that were unfamiliar to them sounded like a great idea. Consequently, primarily white Minnesota came into the picture.[15]

Minnesota and Japanese Americans might seem an odd match at first glance. Historically, Japanese constituted a very small share of the state's total population, from only two persons of Japanese descent (Nikkei) in the 1890 census to fifty-one (more than half of whom were American-born Nisei) in 1940. The cold winters and the lack of suitable job opportunities were likely among the reasons. Rather, Japanese Americans were clustered heavily on the Pacific coast in California, Oregon, and Washington, where almost nine out of ten Nikkei lived. The 1940 census counted over 125,000 persons of Japanese birth or ancestry on the mainland United States. The families of Kusunoki, Semba, and Sudo were cases in point. Another 150,000 resided in the Territory of Hawai'i.[16]

Before zooming in to the wartime experiences of Nisei students, soldiers, nurses, and workers in Minnesota, it is imperative to step back and take a look at Japanese American history in context. The majority of Issei immigrants originally came from rural areas of Japan during the late nineteenth century. Most voyaged to the United States in search of economic opportunities, starting at the lower end of the social spectrum and slowly working their way to a better life over the years. Some even became wealthy, while most enjoyed steady and stable prosperity as farmers, fishermen, domestic workers, and entrepreneurs.[17]

Success, however, was a double-edged sword, especially when racism was lurking behind the scenes. Throughout the history of the United States, politicians and pundits have manipulated the meaning of "America" amid moral panics and national conflicts. People from Asia have been ostracized as the "Other" at best and demonized as "Yellow Peril" for worse. Like their Chinese counterparts, Japanese immigrants were subjected to many forms of discrimination from the very beginning. The Gentlemen's Agreement of 1907–1908 by the American and Japanese governments and the Immigration Act of 1924 barred further Japanese immigration by stating that aliens ineligible to become citizens could not be admitted to the United States as immigrants. California's Alien Land Law of 1913 then forbade those who were ineligible for citizenship, literally Asians, from land purchases, and allowed them to lease land for only three years.[18]

Immigration restrictions, particularly national-origin and numerical quotas, were concocted to remap America not only by emphasizing the nation's contiguous land borders but also by creating new categories of racial differences. As there were almost no new settlers from Japan since the mid-1920s, the Japanese communities on the eve of Pearl Harbor were composed of as many American-born Nisei and Sansei as Issei, who had been in the country for nearly two decades but were not allowed to naturalize. All of them were no less "American" than any other ethnic group of immigrants. The only problem was their skin color.[19]

The discriminatory laws notwithstanding, animosity continued to brew and build against Japanese Americans. James Phelan, a senator from California, warned as early as the 1910s that the Pacific coast "would be an easy prey in case of attack" because Japanese immigrants in California were not peaceful settlers, but rather the "enemy within our gates." Analyzing interracial contacts, the sociologist Jesse Frederick Steiner at the University of Chicago wrote in 1917 that an "immigrant invasion" from Japan would only add to the United States' extant racial problems, referring to African Americans.[20]

The resentments were economically motivated as well. The *San Francisco Examiner* on January 21, 1924, for example, bemoaned the spectacle of "thousands of acres of our richest and most productive farmlands" being under the control of "an unassimilated race." Many were seeking excuses to drive the Japanese Americans away and take their lands. Governor Chase Clark of Idaho, in a speech reported by a local newspaper in 1942, claimed a "good solution to the Jap problem in Idaho—and the Nation—would be send them all back to Japan, and then sink the island. . . . We don't want them buying land and becoming permanently located in our state."[21]

These xenophobic sentiments were then channeled for political ends. DeWitt, the lieutenant general of the Army whose name appeared frequently and prominently in the history of the incarceration, was a fervent enabler and endorser of "baseless" rumors that were used to justify the removal and imprisonment of Japanese Americans. "Racial affinities are not severed by migration," he opined. "The Japanese race is an enemy race," and "it makes no difference whether he is an American citizen, he is still a Japanese."[22]

However, not everyone in the military bought the conspiracy theory. Major General Joseph W. Stilwell recorded in his diary that under the war

Sally (Ohno) Sudo, age three, with her father, Yosaji Ohno, ca. 1930s. *Courtesy of Sally Sudo*

frenzy led by DeWitt, "common sense is thrown to the winds and any absurdity is believed." Nevertheless, the more rational voices were in the minority and often kept private. Their resistance, even when made in public, was drowned out by the loud noises of fearmongering and gaslighting. Looking back, the incarceration of Japanese Americans might have seemed shocking at the outset but not a complete surprise for those who paid close attention.[23]

Having been isolated since the late nineteenth century, the Japanese Americans had to form a tightly knit community, a necessary survival tactic for marginalized ethnic groups. By the 1940s, few were integrated into the larger population, even though the Nisei were fairly well adapted to mainstream American life. "My father Yosaji Ohno came to the States at the age of eighteen in 1899," Sudo recounted. "In Seattle we had lived in *Nihonmachi* (Japantown), which was a segregated Japanese neighborhood. My parents . . . really didn't have to learn English that well, because all the neighbors conversed in Japanese. They could do all their business [and] their banking in Japanese."[24]

The war changed everything, not only the life of Sudo's parents but also Minnesota. Coming to the Twin Cities, Sudo's family was part of a major influx of Japanese Americans into the state. Their numbers rose from double digits to several thousands in the mid-1940s. That Minnesota became a magnet for Japanese American resettlers during the war was not by chance. The colleges, universities, and MISLS provided a robust force of attraction. Of course, the reasons why the military selected the Twin Cities for the language school are worthy of further investigation. The "resettlement" itself as a concept and a program, too, deserves a closer examination.

The wartime resettlement was part of an ambitious government project. The WRA, the federal agency created in 1942 to care for the incarcerees, was bestowed the task of not only refashioning ethnic Japanese to become more "American" inside the camps, but also arranging their new lives out of incarceration. This massive dispersal of a minority group, according to many historians, became a perfect test case for the country's race problems. The *Pacific Citizen*, a newspaper organized by the JACL, provided some hints of its reception among Japanese American leaders. The columnist Bill Hosokawa described it plainly in late 1942: "Our only salvation lies in abolishing racial clannishness and going out to fight for acceptance in and integration with the America that has grown from people of the many European national origins."[25]

The Nisei author went on to applaud those who had relocated to the metropolises of the Midwest and East Coast as well as the towns of the Intermountain West. Hosokawa praised their "foresight, courage, luck or cussedness, as it may be, to have torn up their roots" and lived "as full-fledged citizens of those communities." Another journalist, Larry Tajiri, also endorsed the "permanent resettlement." His hope was that "a large degree of social assimilation of the nation's population of Japanese origin may be accomplished within the lifetime of the Nisei generation."[26]

He continued to highlight its promise. The end goal was total assimilation. "If the program is successful, we have seen the last of the 'Little Tokyos,' save those monoracial communities created by fiat and wartime exigencies in the deserts of western states and on the second-growth pineland of the Mississippi bottoms." As the Nisei were allowed to leave the trying but familiar camps for college, military service, or employment, they were instructed to "assimilate," "blend in," and not "make waves." Most, if not all, of them performed their part dutifully.[27]

Likewise, there was a precise and prescribed role for the host destinations to play. The Committee on Resettlement of Japanese Americans, in cooperation with religious and civic organizations, deliberately put out specific guidelines for the various states that planned to accommodate Japanese American resettlers. "Special attention should be given to the development of a sound program to prevent the formation of a 'Little Tokyo' or segregated district in your community," the government instruction announced. "Do not plan large functions for the benefit exclusively of the Japanese Americans," "urge them to participate in the group life of the community," and "[disperse them] throughout the interior of the country, only a few families to any one community" were just some of the key reminders given to accepting locations. "The Japanese Americans themselves are willing to be assimilated," a resettlement committee report claimed, "but there has been no real opportunity offered to them."[28]

A Midwestern state like Minnesota, with hardly any history involving Japanese Americans or even Asian Americans, turned out to be one of the few available prospects. The final locations for resettlement were also the outcome of a gradual elimination process. The military zone on the West Coast was completely off the list. Chances in the interior states under the jurisdiction of DeWitt's Western Defense Command—Arizona, Idaho, Montana, Nevada, and Utah—were also slim. The Southern region, with its own "Jim Crow" segregation policy, was not interested in being a host. Neither was it a paragon of racial integration and assimilation. While the Atlantic Seaboard, in the grip of a deepening labor shortage, offered a viable possibility, Lieutenant General Hugh A. Drum, head of the Eastern Defense Command, made it clear that he would prefer not to have people of Japanese descent relocated to the eastern coastline. The choices were hence quite limited.[29]

Meanwhile, a number of major cities in the northern central states rose to the occasion. Through negotiations with employers, community leaders, and local officials, the WRA Employment Office found, somewhat unexpectedly, "that there was a considerable fund of good will toward the evacuated people in this region and remarkably little of the deep-seated public apprehension which had prevailed on the West Coast and in the Intermountain states." The employment chief reported in 1943 that his first field trip through the Midwest convinced him "that a considerable number of evacuees, especially the Nisei, could find new homes" there. The reason was not due to a "widespread enthusiasm for a relocation program" but rather because "there was someone or a number of people who were deeply interested in the problems growing out of the evacuation and were willing to give their support to doing something practical to solve them." Empathy mattered and made a difference.[30]

The support from local communities and civic groups was vital. The initial release authorizations by the WRA "would be granted only for resettlement east of the Western Defense Command area, and that preference would be given for applications to the Middle West." Nisei students were the first group to whom leave permissions were awarded, followed by a small number of laborers. In general, the WRA's plan to disperse the Issei and Nisei incarcerees in the Midwest appeared to be effective. Small groups of Japanese Americans were successfully scattered, from bigger urban areas to smaller towns, a few families to one place at a time.[31]

Minnesota's location, demographics, and culture certainly fit the profile
that the government envisioned for the resettlement program. Minneapolis, being an industrial urban center known for flour and wheat markets, a
railway hub that connected Chicago with the rest of the region, and a "nice"
place with tolerant Scandinavian immigrants, active churches, and liberal
arts colleges, surged swiftly to the top of the WRA's list.

Another advantage was its very small prewar Asian American population. The most significant group was the several hundred Chinese in
St. Paul. Many of them were descendants of families that had moved there
when the railroads to the Pacific coast were being built. The Japanese American community was even more insignificant. Prior to 1940 there were just
a dozen people of Japanese ancestry living in St. Paul, with a total of fifty-
one living in Minnesota. Most of them were Issei bachelors working on the
Great Northern Railway. Families were few and far between.[32]

Gradually, the resettlement program and the MISLS altered the ethnic
landscape of Minnesota. By the 1950s, with several thousand Japanese Americans staying after the war, the Japanese had surpassed the Chinese as the
largest Asian American population in the state. They remained on top until
the mid-1970s, when Hmong and Vietnamese immigrants arrived due to the
Vietnam War. Another destructive war indeed brought another diasporic
group from Asia to the North Star State.

Released from three different camps, three Nisei—Kusunoki from Topaz,
Semba from Heart Mountain, and Sudo from Minidoka—all ended up in
the Twin Cities for different reasons and through different pathways. One
would likely wonder how they were able to leave the camps, and what the
process was like. The background of their journeys and the role that Minnesota played in their resettlement seemingly warrant further explanation.

—

Minnesota was a wartime destination where many Japanese Americans
either temporarily stopped or permanently settled. As early as July 1942,
the WRA made it possible for those considered loyal and assimilable by
administrators to receive indefinite release. It also set forth resettlement as
the main agenda for the rest of that year. The decision to let the Japanese
American citizens and their families out of confinement was complex and
not without opposition. It was a product of several forces in combination—

an increasingly severe wartime shortage of labor nationwide, growing worries that the camps would devolve into "something akin to Indian reservations," and accumulating apprehensions of many liberal-minded officials about the propriety and legality of keeping innocent people in the unnatural environments of the camps, to name a few.[33]

Progress was slow, however. Throughout the fall of 1942, the resettlement program moved forward, in the words of the chief of the Employment Division, on a case-by-case "retail" basis. The first releases were granted in October. By the end of 1942, only about seven hundred Japanese Americans had been cleared for departure. The actual movement of people out of incarceration to resume residence in "normal communities" did not take on significant momentum until the spring of 1943.[34]

To expedite the operation, the WRA established dozens of field offices in Intermountain, Midwestern, and Eastern states. The inaugural field office was established in Chicago on January 4, 1943. Initially it was designed to supervise relocation activities throughout a large part of the Midwest. Within a few weeks, additional branches were set up in Cleveland, Denver, Kansas City, Salt Lake City, and many other locations, including one in Minneapolis, which opened its doors in March 1943.[35]

For many incarcerees, the road to Minnesota was a demanding and winding one. Although the WRA had established the right of any Japanese American to apply for indefinite leave at any time, it made the granting of such release contingent on the satisfaction of four specific requirements: (1) a personal record which indicated no potential danger to national security; (2) a reasonable degree of public acceptance for people of Japanese ancestry in the community of proposed destination; (3) some prospect of personal economic security outside the center; and (4) assurances to keep the agency informed of changes of job or address. Of these requirements, the first requirement was by far the most important to the WRA. The concerns of the military and the FBI, as much about political performativity as national security, needed to be addressed. Even though it was probably the simplest step in the relocation procedure—checking an incarceree's name and record against the FBI files—it often took the longest amount of time.[36]

Moreover, the thorough clearance had to do with public perception. The incarceration itself had vilified Japanese Americans in the eyes of a large segment of the population, and this very stigma was magnified through wide-spread misinformation, rumors, and "fake news" at the time. Some degree of assurance that incarcerees were being carefully vetted and that those with a hint of suspicion were not being allowed to get out was surely in the interest of the WRA relocation program. The communities to which the resettlers went would feel more confident and comfortable accepting them, too. The Reverend Daisuke Kitagawa, an Issei Episcopalian minister who directed the Minneapolis Council of Churches in 1944, wrote, "Like those who have been released from mental institutions with a doctor's certificate of cure, the Japanese Americans were to be trusted because they have certificates of loyalty issue by the WRA."[37]

The problem was that such an official certificate in itself called attention to Japanese Americans being suspect for wrongdoing or disloyalty to begin with, rather than emphasizing their innocence and patriotism. As a result, the incarcerees faced even more scrutiny. They had to jump through many bureaucratic hoops and complete tedious paperwork in order to fulfill those requirements.

With respected leaders like Kitagawa on the ground, Minnesota scored highly on the second requirement as an inviting place for the Japanese Americans. Even before the opening of the WRA's own office in Minneapolis in March 1943, the International Institute of St. Paul (now the International Institute of Minnesota), founded in 1919 as a branch of St. Paul's YWCA, had received letters from incarcerees who wanted to relocate to Minnesota as early as the summer of 1942. However, their road to the north was not without obstacles or obstructions.[38]

Following the news that Japanese Americans were forcibly removed from the West Coast in early 1942, the St. Paul police chief, Clinton A. Hackert, proposed to bar any of them from entering the city. In spite of his first failed attempt, he tried to initiate a system whereby no people of Japanese ancestry could enter the city without a permit issued by him. Civil groups reasonably protested such actions and realized that strong and organized efforts were necessary to aid the new arrivals.[39]

In September, a citywide St. Paul Resettlement Committee was set up by the WRA and the International Institute, including members representing social service agencies, college faculty, interfaith churches, and other local community leaders in the Twin Cities. Comprised of "prominent men and women," the committee was tasked with helping relocated Japanese Americans find job opportunities and accommodations in the cities, fulfilling the third and fourth criteria; it also served "as a local clearing house for accurate information" to combat racist mendacity. Their goal was modest at first, helping Japanese Americans to find jobs "on a case-by-case basis without any publicity except by word of mouth to carefully chosen small groups."[40]

Amid an unpredictable wartime milieu, the committee members, even knowing the social scene of the Twin Cities thoroughly, still had to test the water before introducing Japanese Americans into the workforce. Employment deals were made in advance, initially through personal connections. In the first six months of the committee's establishment, two dozen Nisei landed clerical, household, and menial jobs as stenographers, nurses' aides, mechanics, janitors, nursery workers, and domestic attendants, among others. Shortly after, a WRA directory listed more than eighty Minnesotan groups and individuals who had offered opportunities to resettlers. The committee was staffed by passionate volunteers. All of them devoted countless hours to the efforts, assisting over a thousand Japanese Americans to secure work by the end of the war.[41]

On the other hand, housing was a pressing issue. The dormitories of the YMCA and YWCA, the Catholic Guild Hall, and the Methodist Girls Club were open to Japanese Americans on arrival before they could find themselves a place to stay. In addition, the Board of American Missions of the United Lutheran Churches of America in December 1943 started a hostel on Clifton Avenue in Minneapolis, which accommodated more than a thousand Japanese Americans in its two years of operation. The St. Paul Resettlement Committee later also responded to the postwar needs of the Japanese Americans as the camps approached closure. It leased an old hotel on West Kellogg Boulevard, renovated it, and then opened it for resettlers from October 1945 until 1948.[42]

All in all, the Twin Cities provided a relatively friendly and safe location for the influx of newcomers. The executive secretary of the International Institute of St. Paul, Alice Lilliequist Sickels, wrote in her 1943 report that

"Japanese Americans now found a welcome in St. Paul because they had something to contribute and were willing to do their part."[43]

Ruth Nomura Tanbara and her husband Earl Kazumi Tanbara were the first Japanese Americans to resettle in Minnesota. They arrived in St. Paul on August 9, 1942. The Tanbaras' experience was exceptional, or some might say lucky, in many ways. Born in Portland, where her father Frank Jiro Nomura owned a Japanese grocery store, Ruth grew up on the "sunny side of town" and attended the Japanese Methodist Mission. Fluent in Japanese, she attended Oregon State Agricultural College (now renamed Oregon State University) in Corvallis in 1926. She was the first Nisei woman to enroll at the college and graduated with a degree in home economics in 1930.[44]

Ruth then worked for the Portland YWCA for a few years before meeting her husband, Earl Tanbara. Born to Issei parents from Okayama, Japan, Earl graduated from Los Gatos High School in 1923 and went on to receive his bachelor's degree from the University of California, Berkeley. He worked for the Dollar Steamship Company, which, at its height in the 1920s, was the largest United States shipping firm, and he later became its director of marketing stationed in San Francisco. Ruth married Earl in September 1935, moved to Berkeley, and took up a position at the International Institute of San Francisco, serving as a social worker for the Japanese community there.

The dawn of the Pacific War changed everything. As the Tanbaras were undergoing the registration process for their transfer to the camp in Poston, Arizona, the provost marshal of the US Army gave the couple the option of moving to the Eastern or Midwestern states to help build community acceptance and aid in resettling incarcerees from the camps on a volunteer basis. "We were in our early 30's, married and had been employed, so we chose to move to the Midwest," Ruth Tanbara recalled. "We were willing to work even as a cook or gardener to make ends meet, avoiding going on welfare." Fortunately, they did not have to do that. The couple came to Minnesota in the summer of 1942 and called it home from then on.[45]

With Ruth's brother Paul Nomura already at the MISLS at Camp Savage, letters of recommendation from former employers at the Portland YWCA and the International Institute of San Francisco, and an offer of a place to stay by a family friend, the Nisei couple was permitted to go to Minnesota and start working right away. Ruth was first hired to be a part-time stenographer at the St. Paul YWCA. Since there was so much wartime turnover, she was promoted to the head of the clerical staff in just six months. Earl was appointed as the representative from the St. Paul Resettlement Committee to the JACL to coordinate the logistics for the relocation with other federal and local programs.[46]

Before long, the Tanbaras brought their family to the Twin Cities. Earl's parents, his sister Grace Tomiko Tanbara, and her son, Tom Kurihara, joined the couple in August 1945 after they were released from Poston. Kurihara was a ten-year-old fifth grader when he arrived in Minnesota. Throughout high school and until he left for Stanford University in 1953, the Tanbaras' residence on South Avon Street in St. Paul was his home. "There were eight people living together," he laughed. "My grandparents, my aunt and uncle, my aunt's parents, my mother and I were all in a small two-bedroom, one-bath house. For a month or two, my aunt's sister, her husband and their baby moved into the pantry. So, there were eleven people. But we got along pretty well." Kurihara remembered his uncle Earl was a "jokester," whereas his aunt Ruth was rather serious. Both were generous and genuinely caring, he recalled. "There were lots of people in and out of the house," Kurihara said. "YWCA associates, family friends, and a number of the Japanese Americans in the community. My grandparents would always cook Japanese food for them."[47]

Beyond their own family members, the Tanbaras were determined to assist other fellow Japanese Americans the best that they could. Both Ruth and Earl were active members of the St. Paul Resettlement Committee. Having already gone through the ordeal, they knew how difficult the journey could be. Their first task was to support the Japanese American students as they continued their education in Minnesota. The Nisei students needed to find employment, oftentimes odd jobs like housekeeping and landscaping, to defray the school and living expenses that otherwise they could not afford. The strained finances of many Japanese American families because of the forced removal, exacerbated by the government's freezing of "alien enemy" funds, created extraordinary roadblocks for them.[48]

Meanwhile, local leadership provided by civic groups and churches was an important component of the WRA program. In many cities where a

significant number of Japanese Americans went, there was sponsorship on
the part of "resettlement committees" on which "citizens of respected opinion" in the areas served. These gave substance to the efforts of the federal
government and enhanced the degree of community approval. The Tanbaras were, consequently, not only faces of but also part of the forces behind
such endeavors. Alice Sickels from the International Institute praised the
couple, whose promise to be an asset to Minnesota was more than fulfilled.
"They have been the best possible ambassadors of goodwill," she said.[49]

Together with the WRA office in Minneapolis and other organizations,
the St. Paul committee supported two to four thousand Japanese Americans as they resettled during the war, although half of them in the end did
not choose to come or stay. The Twin Cities received about four hundred
Japanese Americans by the end of 1943; the number had risen threefold to
1,369 a year later. They continued to arrive as the camps were closing.[50]

It might not be a surprise to learn that the several thousand Issei and Nisei
overwhelmingly concentrated in Minneapolis and St. Paul; the other non-
Twin Cities destinations received at most a handful of resettlers. Rochester
stood out as a distant third, with about sixty Japanese American residents,
owing to the Nisei nurses working in its hospitals and those in the medical
profession who were transferred to the Mayo Clinic for various programs.
Coming in fourth was Duluth, which welcomed roughly three dozen Japanese Americans by the end of the war.[51]

Between the Twin Cities, more Japanese Americans settled and sought
assistance in Minneapolis than St. Paul, approximately two-thirds more. It
was mostly because all the gates through which Japanese Americans first
entered Minnesota were in Minneapolis, such as the WRA office, the Lutheran
hostel, and the United States Employment Service; once they had secured
their lodging, it was troublesome for them to move. The distance and double fare on streetcars also deterred their willingness to commute to St. Paul.
The negative attitude toward Japanese Americans of its police chief did not
help either. Most importantly, Minneapolis had better access to the military
language school, where many spouses, relatives, and friends of the resettlers
were based.[52]

Sally Sudo's family, once again, can illustrate this part of the story. Four
of her older siblings had already been in the Twin Cities before the war

concluded. In order to leave Minidoka, two of her brothers had volunteered to serve in the military when the recruitment started. According to Sudo, "my oldest brother Fred [Ohno] was the first one . . . but he didn't pass his physical. He didn't want to go back to camp, so what he did was he found a job in Salt Lake City as a bellhop at one of the hotels."

Her second brother, Joe E. Ohno, because of his Japanese language skills, "qualified for the MISLS." He went to Camp Savage for training and began to bring his family members, one by one, to Minnesota. "He contacted my brother Fred and said, 'You know, I think you might enjoy living here, and there's a school called the Dunwoody Institute. Why don't I see what we can do about getting you into that school so that you can learn a trade and do something else with your life instead of being a bellhop all your life?'" Fred quickly packed his bags.

Her other siblings followed suit. The next was her sister, Amy Ohno Shimada, who came to work for the military at Fort Snelling. Then it was her brother Tom T. Ohno's turn. "He was still in high school, but Tom refused to go to school while we were in Minidoka. Fred said: 'If you're not going to go to school, come on out here and we'll get you into school here.' So, they sent for Tom, who worked as a houseboy for a family around Lake Calhoun [now Bde Maka Ska]," before returning to attend West High School in Minneapolis.

The end of the war saw the reunion of the entire family in the North Star State. "My father did not want to go back to Seattle, because of all the discrimination we had faced before the war, and we had nothing to go back to," Sudo lamented. "My brother Joe said: 'Why don't you consider Minnesota? It seems like a really friendly place.'" To rightfully make it their new home, her brother even borrowed money from his employer to put a down payment on a house in South Minneapolis to convince his parents. "It was three days after Japan surrendered, August 18th, that we boarded the trains to come out here to Minneapolis," Sudo remembered vividly. "Even my oldest sister Marian [Ohno Kikuchi] who was married and had a child in the camp came with us, and we all lived in this big house."

Minnesota was not for everyone, however. After one winter, her eldest sister found the snowy weather simply not her cup of tea. "'This is too cold,' my sister said, so they moved back to Seattle," Sudo chuckled. "The rest of us stayed on until we either got married or went off to school or for some other reasons left the city, but a good many of us grew up here." It was a drastic change for them though. "When we first moved into this house in South Minneapolis," Sudo noted, "we were the only Japanese family for several miles around." Especially for her Issei parents, the transition was not easy at all. "They were really at a loss for not being able to speak the language well, making it very difficult for my father to find work," Sudo remarked.

The family survived, and the Twin Cities became Sudo's new home. She credited her oldest brother, Fred, who took over as the head of the household. "He worked a regular daytime job, then a night job and a weekend job, just to support the family. He even put off getting married until he was in his late 30s." Sudo was then only nine years old. "I was here from fourth grade and all the way through the University of Minnesota." There Sudo met her husband, Toshio Sudo, an exchange student from Japan. Because of a job opportunity, they lived in Tokyo for seventeen years with their three children.

The unfortunate and untimely death of her husband brought Sudo back to Minnesota in 1984. From Seattle to California to New Orleans, she scouted out other places before she moved back. "I decided that Minnesota would be the best place because I had, at that time . . . three or four siblings living here, and . . . I knew I was going to need family support." She has since devoted her career to education, teaching for the Minneapolis Public Schools and at Ramsey International Fine Arts Center, a K–8 school. Sudo had also been one of the leading members of the Twin Cities chapter of the JACL and before her retirement served as the chair of the education committee that grants scholarships to minority students.

Her three brothers also chose to settle, and they now rest in peace in Minnesota. Fred ran a successful dry-cleaning business in Highland Park. Joe, after his military service, graduated from the University of Minnesota with a degree in computer science and worked as an analyst at the New Orleans Police Department. He later returned to the north and retired in Richfield. Residing in Bloomington, Tom was a beloved mathematics teacher and baseball coach, with a career that spanned three decades, including positions at Cretin–Derham Hall High School in St. Paul as well as Lincoln Junior High School and Roosevelt High School in Minneapolis.

As in the case of Sudo's family, the establishment of the MISLS attracted numerous Nisei and their loved ones to the state. "Many Nisei girls came to the Twin Cities because their boyfriends or brothers were stationed at Fort Snelling," Ruth Tanbara explained. Since Minnesota was an unfamiliar place for them, re-creating some form of social and cultural life for the Japanese Americans was vital. Along with help from the International Institute, the Tanbaras organized gatherings, parties, and dances for the young resettlers. "Many weddings of Nisei brides and enlisted grooms were held in the chapel at Fort Snelling," she added. "Earl and I were often invited to substitute for their parents who were not able to attend." Considering the families of many MISLS Nisei were still in confinement, the small Japanese American community in town became their new home away from home.

Ruth Tanbara worked for the YWCA in St. Paul for thirty years until her retirement in 1972, devoting her time and energy to making the Twin Cities more conducive to racial diversity. In 1947, she led the first Japanese group to participate in the "Festival of Nations," a program created by the International Institute in 1936, and carried on such work for decades. She was also a founding member of the St. Paul–Nagasaki Sister City Committee in 1955. In 2000, Tanbara received the Japan–Minnesota Partnership Award from former Vice President Walter Mondale for her outstanding contributions to the building of cooperation and respect between the people of Japan and the United States. She was recognized by the former mayor of St. Paul, Randy Kelly, with a "Ruth Tanbara Day" on August 20, 2005, for her work. Tanbara passed away in January 2008, at the age of one hundred.[53]

Advocates such as the Tanbaras and many other volunteers from different organizations made the Twin Cities less "white" and more welcoming for the Japanese Americans. "It was very enlightening to see all these Nisei when we came to Minneapolis," Mikio "Micky" Kirihara said. Born in Oakland, California, he was incarcerated at the age of thirteen with the rest of his family at Topaz. They moved to Minnesota right after the war since three of the older Kirihara children were already studying and working there. "A lot of our friends in camp who volunteered for the service came through Fort Snelling," Kirihara recalled. "We had many people on weekends . . . like thirty of them. They would come over. My mother would make dinner, and they would come and talk." Even though only a tenth grader then, Kirihara remembered how much his parents enjoyed those moments and treasured their special connection.[54]

The Kirihara family, like the Tanbaras and Sudos, was a new phenomenon. By March of 1945, there were approximately one thousand people of Japanese descent residing in the state, besides the thousands of Nisei soldiers training at Fort Snelling. The expanding MISLS during the war continued to be the catalyst behind the boost.[55]

While the story of MISLS will be examined in Chapter Five, a brief overview of the school's background would be helpful for our understanding of the Twin Cities at the time. Following the exclusion order, the Fourth Army Intelligence School, which was established in the Presidio, San Francisco, had to be "relocated." To where it could move was a tricky matter. Similar to the dilemma of the WRA's resettlement program, the choices were few. The government's own action in confining Japanese Americans from the West Coast, combined with sensational newspaper coverage, left most of the country convinced that Japanese Americans were treacherous. Several states rejected the school's request bluntly, not least because of the potential risks regarding the "dangerous" presence of Japanese Americans within their borders.[56]

Minnesota, on the contrary, embraced the risk as an opportunity. Governor Harold E. Stassen supported the proposal to house the school. He claimed that not only did the state have adequate facilities, but more importantly, its residents were also accepting of people of color. Above all, Minnesota had no history of anti-Asian prejudice. Such a track record was probably due to the very small non-white, let alone Asian American, population, rather than actual interracial relations. Reality was not all that rosy. In fact, Minneapolis had quite a reputation for hostility toward the Jewish community and was a hotbed of militant antisemitism.[57]

Combating discrimination did weigh on the governor's mind. Therefore, Stassen formed the Minnesota State Committee on Tolerance, Unity, and Loyalty. The main objective was to "prevent misunderstanding and animosity," according to its promotional brochure "An Appeal to the Citizens of Minnesota." The committee also defined the meaning of "citizens" of the state. They were the "fine men and women [who] came from France,

Ireland, Norway, Sweden, Germany, and other European countries" who never "looked down upon the other" but "all joined hands and made Minnesota the great commonwealth it is today." Ironically, the rousing words mentioned no citizens of non-European ancestry, whose existence was either ignored or considered inconsequential.[58]

Yet it was enough to convince Captain (later Colonel) Kai E. Rasmussen. The North Star State, he believed, was ideal for the new school. He had been searching for "a suitable location where a community would accept Oriental-faced Americans for their true worth—American soldiers fighting with their brains for their native America," and eventually picked "the Twin Cities because the area selected not only had to have room physically, but room in the people's hearts." State officials were "extremely cooperative in arranging for this camp," Rasmussen told local journalists, "and we hope the public will show the men every courtesy due to American soldiers." According to the later report *The Oriental in Minnesota* (1949) by the Interracial Commission of Governor Luther W. Youngdahl, "Minnesota was chosen because the European background of its people stemming from many nations had resulted in the most favorable climate in the United States."[59]

The newly renamed "Military Intelligence Service Language School" hence began its first lessons on June 1, 1942, with a class of two hundred students. It was located in a cluster of rundown wooden buildings in the former Civilian Conservation Corps facility in Scott County, aptly called Camp Savage. The school gained popularity among the Nisei very quickly. It soon outgrew the post and moved to Fort Snelling in August 1944 before returning to California after the war. The twenty-first and final commencement in June 1946 included 307 students, bringing the total number of MISLS graduates to more than six thousand.[60]

Minnesota might have been a nicer, or at least less racist, state than others, but the military, the WRA officials, and the St. Paul Resettlement Committee, among other civic groups, took nothing for granted. They joined forces and initiated proactive steps in educating the public about Japanese Americans and their contributions to both the national war effort and the local Twin Cities. Indeed, many people had thought that Camp Savage was one of the "concentration" camps for Japanese enemies or dangerous traitors about which they had vaguely heard; others, ostensibly failing to recognize the uniform of the United States Army, even called the police or the FBI to report that they had seen Japanese soldiers roaming freely in the cities. As unobservant or even comical as such stories might sound in retrospect, the MISLS knew something needed to be done.[61]

The school was in cooperation with the news media from the beginning to bolster the Japanese Americans' resettlement in the Twin Cities. Rasmussen and his staff had a deliberate public relations plan. The major local newspapers all "adopted a very fair and friendly attitude," running cheerful pieces such as "Japs Loyal Soldiers—at Snelling" (*Minneapolis Star Journal,* March 24, 1942), "'Model' Soldiers Pose at Fort" (*Minneapolis Morning Tribune,* May 7, 1942), or "Snelling's Jap Language School Proves Army Opposition Wrong" (*Minneapolis Morning Tribune,* October 23, 1945) to stress the point. The *Tribune* editor William P. Steven explained: "We realize that any new minority group is going to have hard sledding, and we felt it our duty to ease the situation for them as much as possible while still being consistent with good reporting and good newspaper operation." Headlines and stories about Japanese Americans were cleaned up or at least emphasized only the bright side. This overtly positive portrayal of Japanese Americans, as many scholars have pointed out, also helped usher in the rise of the "model minority" stereotype.[62]

Evidently, the media campaign worked. Reverend Kitagawa, for example, wrote to the Interracial Commission of Minnesota and stated that the MISLS "laid the foundation for friendly relations between Nisei soldiers and the local citizenry." In charge of not only ministering to the Nisei soldiers but also organizing the church's response to the Japanese American resettlement in the area, Kitagawa praised the Nisei soldiers as "men of mature age and judgement" whose "behavior was really outstanding, and they quickly won the good will of the people of Minnesota. An excellent atmosphere was thus created in the Twin Cities for Japanese Americans to resettle from the relocation centers."[63]

There was another, less lofty reason for their trouble-free existence. Based on comments from an executive from the International Institute, it was "because one often could not tell the Chinese and the Japanese apart." It certainly held truth then and probably still does now. Since "few of the Nisei fit the old stereotyped notion of a 'Japanese type,' they pass largely unnoticed in a city where there has always been a few Chinese," the staff observed; "and at first glance the curly-haired Nisei girls seem not unlike the local Mexican Americans." As long as the Japanese Americans did not make a scene, they would not draw any unwanted attention to themselves, at least in the urban area where people were more accustomed to seeing Asian faces. They could go on with their rather safe and peaceful lives.[64]

By and large the Nisei soldiers were well received in the Twin Cities. "There were no [or just] very little instances," Doi said. There might have been some confusion or misunderstanding about why there were groups of Asian men around, such as when the "boys go into stores," but those minor "problems" did not trouble him. Minnesota is a "comfortable place for all," he asserted. In a July 1942 letter to the *Minneapolis Sunday Tribune and Star Journal*, Japanese American Army Private James Tsurutani also lauded his reception: "I am very happy that I am here in Minnesota. There is more kindness, congeniality, and fair play towards Americans of [Asian] ancestry than I have seen elsewhere."[65]

Other MISLS soldiers shared similar appreciation. "Many of us made warm, lasting friendships with the understanding people of Minnesota, especially in the Twin Cities area. None of us can forget the kindness, friendship and the helping hand accorded the Nisei," Private Edwin M. "Bud" Nakasone wrote in the *Minneapolis Star Journal* on September 3, 1946. Drafted in August 1945, the Hawai'i born Nakasone came to the military school for training in December that year. "At Fort Snelling . . . it was a very good experience

Edwin "Bud" Nakasone, 2015.
Courtesy of the author

because the old saying 'Minnesota Nice' worked out really nicely here for us," he mentioned. "We had good news, good vibes, good background stories of how the Minnesotans would invite the Nisei soldiers to come get dinner with them, and they were very kind to us. They didn't have any bad feelings against the Nisei soldiers." It was this openness and optimism that brought Nakasone back to Minnesota for good after his service in Occupied Japan. He went to the University of Minnesota in 1950 and became a lifelong educator in the state.[66]

———

Despite all the pleasant testimonials, to presume or pretend that Minnesota was untouched by racism would be naive. How hospitable the state was for Japanese Americans during the hostile war years remains questionable. Since the prewar community of Japanese ancestry was quite small, it was difficult to judge the acceptance or rejection of them as an individual case or a systemic issue. However, they were reportedly denied membership in private organizations such as the Minneapolis Athletic Club and Automobile Club of Minneapolis, which at least demonstrated that some unpleasant encounters did exist. The war ultimately escalated the tension, no matter how subtle it might have been, to a new, alarming level.[67]

The winter of 1941 felt particularly cold and cruel to the Japanese Americans in Minnesota. Within hours of the attack on Pearl Harbor, federal agents had already begun taking action against ethnic Japanese residents in the Twin Cities. On December 8, 1941, Federal Reserve officials aided by Minneapolis police shut down the sandwich shop of Edward Yamazaki under a Treasury Department directive to freeze businesses owned by Japanese nationals. Immigrating to the United States at the turn of the century, Yamazaki served as a steward's mate in the racially segregated Navy from 1906 to 1908, and eventually landed in Minneapolis in 1914. The Issei married Anna Hansen, a daughter of Norwegian immigrants, and started his own family in the state. By the 1940s, Yamazaki was running a modest sandwich shop on West Broadway Avenue in North Minneapolis. "My family and I have no ties in Japan," he said after the forced closure. "We are sorry to see the war come, but what can we do?"[68]

Yamazaki was not the sole target of the government. Jiro William Akamatsu was ordered to close his gift shop on East Sixth Street in St. Paul on the same day. Like other Issei immigrants, Akamatsu set out for the United States in the early twentieth century and finally found himself in the Twin Cities for better job opportunities during the Great Depression. He, his wife Yoshiko Ruth Akamatsu, and their two children had already been in St. Paul since the 1930s. In the winter of 1941, the family of four was "caught in a world situation which they hardly understand," the *St. Paul Dispatch* reported on December 9 that year. "The [federal agents] took our camera . . . thinking we might be spies," the then not yet six-year-old Minnesota-born daughter Hideko Akamatsu Tachibana remembered.[69]

Meanwhile, all Japanese aliens in the state, presumed to be potential enemy agents until the evidence proved otherwise, had to stay in their homes while treasury officials examined their financial records. For example, the government put on hold the medical practice of Kano Ikeda, a renowned expert on pathology at the Charles T. Miller Hospital (which merged with St. Luke's Hospital to become United Hospital in 1972). In addition, the attempts by St. Paul's police chief and public safety commissioner to bar Japanese people from entering the city added a further layer of hostility.[70]

Being powerless against the sudden shutdowns and severe restrictions, the Twin Cities residents of Japanese descent nonetheless aroused their neighbors, colleagues, and friends to the dangers of war hysteria. Many came to defend and support these Issei and their families. Both Yamazaki's sandwich café and Akamatsu's gift shop were authorized to reopen under a special Treasury Department license four days later, as merchants on the North side and members of the Central Park Methodist Episcopal Church, respectively, interceded on the businessmen's behalf. However, the two stores had to deposit all their receipts in supervised bank accounts, and the owners were allowed to withdraw only two hundred dollars a month each for living expenses.[71]

Many Minnesotans, especially those with Jewish, German, or Italian heritage, strongly related to the difficulty faced by the Japanese community and repudiated such scapegoating by the government. The St. Paul Resettlement Committee later noted: "The fact that unjust restraint could come to Japanese Americans who had won the trust and esteem of their fellow townspeople . . . swiftly won sympathy for the tragic plight of citizens whose birth placed them at the mercy of officialdom."[72]

Regarding the case of the Japanese doctor, two hundred local physicians signed a petition demanding that Ikeda be released from house detention. He was freed in a week. Interestingly, not until a decade later, at the age of sixty-seven, was Ikeda able to naturalize and become a United States citizen, the first Japanese national in Minnesota to do so.[73]

It was a divided country then, and the war was a divisive issue. Few Minnesotans had ever met a person of Japanese extraction. Whereas some were appalled at the racially biased actions against the Japanese Americans based on moral and constitutional principles, others were antagonistic owing to hideous and dangerous stereotyping. Alice Sickels from the International Institute had heard her fair share of misinformation. Groundless rumors like "Could one be sure they wouldn't put poison in the soup? They hate all white people" or "How would you know they weren't harboring a spy?" easily came to her mind. Among all the problems in resettling Japanese Americans in the cities, the most frustrating one for Sickels, both professionally and personally, was housing.[74]

Finding accommodation was extremely difficult for the Japanese Americans and their families. Furnished apartments, for certain, were scarce and hard to come by for anyone at the time. The resettlement committee was also "careful not to allow the Nisei to take rooms in undesirable districts or to congregate in one neighborhood." Still, racial discrimination was often the central obstacle to their endeavors. Sickels and her social worker colleagues often called repeatedly and even drove to the places for rent to explain the situation in person; however, the responses were negative without exception. "Invariably I could get agreement that the Americans of Japanese ancestry were no more responsible for what Japan was doing than our citizens of German background were for Hitler," she said, "but my efforts did not result in an apartment."[75]

The landlords might assure Sickels that they were not in the least prejudiced themselves; their refusal was because of objections from their other tenants and not their own unwillingness. Concocting such excuses was probably the sign of a guilty conscience, or at least shame, which did nothing to change their minds or help the Nisei resettlers. "Perhaps our conversation set some of them to thinking about what it meant to be an American," Sickels concluded. "Perhaps not. People are rarely saved through their intellects."[76]

Nearly all Nisei experienced discrimination when they looked for accommodation. Japanese American participants in a panel discussion in January 1946 cited housing as the biggest problem. "Fifty percent of us have encountered some sort of discrimination when looking for housing," panel member Grace Shimizu told the *Minneapolis Morning Tribune*. A cloud also seemed to be over the Tanbaras and Sudo. When the Tanbaras made a bona fide offer to buy their first house, the real estate agent told them that the owner, a physician, was afraid to sell to people of Japanese heritage; the neighbors might not like it, and their resentment would hurt his practice. The Nisei found out that there was actually one objecting family, who were patients of the doctor. The deal fell through. A year later the house that they wanted was still on the market.[77]

Whereas some Minnesotans simply refused to rent or sell to Japanese Americans, others were more aggressive. "It was just a matter of days when we started getting hate mail saying, 'We don't want any Japs in the neighborhood. Get out or else' kind of threatening letters," Sudo said. "They were kind of frightening to me. You never knew how serious these people were. So, we weren't exactly welcomed with open arms."[78]

Other occurrences of prejudice came up in less expected places. Ruth Tanbara remembered that Nisei male students at MISLS could not get a haircut because the barbers turned away Japanese Americans. She had to ask the church for help finding members in the congregation who would be willing to open their shops for these basic services.[79]

Suspicion of Japanese activities in the cities also appeared in a rather peculiar news item. In April 1942, a St. Paul federal grand jury recommended "internment" for jujitsu instructor Seizo Takahashi of Minneapolis. The fifty-two-year-old man had once taught "his rough-and-tumble" art to the Twin Cities police department but was dismissed in recent months. Being an "enemy alien," Takahashi was arrested twice. The first time was in February for "hanging around the Great Northern Railroad Depot"; he was later released after questioning by naval intelligence officers. The second case took place in April due to his "appearing in a store" and "being in a company" of a US Marine private, who was cleared of any wrongdoing. According to the report, Takahashi was "picked up for investigation when his relationship with the marine drew attention." One does not need to read too much between the lines to speculate that his detention had little to do with espionage, and the real reason, besides racism, was something that dared not speak its name.[80]

Everything was relative. Compared to friends who resettled in other states, Tanbara decided that "Minnesota was outstanding in accepting Japanese Americans." Even "though the weather was truly cold . . . in general, the hearts of the people were warm and gracious."[81]

A sociology class report from the University of Minnesota that surveyed 137 Japanese Americans at the Minneapolis Lutheran Hostel between 1943 and 1944 affirmed that general evaluation. "When I came to Minneapolis, I was one of the first Nisei to arrive here. People did not know just what to think of us, but most of them were very kind," interviewee Mrs. K. commented. Another MISLS trainee concurred. "[My wife and I] have found Minneapolis a refreshing experience as compared with what other Nisei have found in the communities they have chosen to enter. Here the atmosphere is so much freer. The people express no feelings of animosity." What amazed the couple was the local radio programs, which were very different from those in California. "Here, there are many religious and musical programs!"[82]

While they personally experienced "no anti-Japanese feeling" in the Twin Cities, their friend and his Caucasian wife had "met with a great deal of animosity." The Nisei soldier rationalized: "Intermarriage of races is another problem, and it hasn't had its foundation in the present war situation. They would have had the same difficulty in the most cosmopolitan cities on the West Coast."[83]

Ignorance bred racism. Education and communication were key. The Interracial Commission of Minnesota explicitly put the onus on the "majority" Minnesotans to get to know the minority "Orientals" to eradicate "existing prejudices." To illustrate this point, Tanbara recounted one more story, this time about her brother Paul Nomura, who was at the MISLS.[84]

On Sundays, the Tanbaras would often invite him and his friends in training for a home-cooked dinner. "One of the neighbors complained to the FBI that we were entertaining Japanese soldiers. The FBI came to visit us," Tanbara said. As a result, Colonel Rasmussen had to personally call on the homes in their neighborhood and explain to the residents that those were American soldiers receiving training in the military language school. "He suggested that I place a service flag in our window to show that we had a relative [who is] serving in the U.S. Army," she recalled. The proof of Americanism seemed to always fall on the shoulders of the marginalized group. It was very likely that the neighbors would not have complained if the Tanbaras were white.[85]

The misfortunes that the Japanese Americans experienced in the Twin Cities were not out of the ordinary. Neither were they out of the blue. It was, after all, during a brutal and bloody war. The bombing of Pearl Harbor and the "death march" of American prisoners of war (including a company of the Minnesota National Guard) on the Bataan Peninsula in the Philippines in April 1942 were still fresh in the public's mind. A national survey in 1945 revealed that 61 percent of Americans opposed giving Japanese Americans equal job opportunities after the war, and 48 percent of African Americans agreed with this sentiment.[86]

The *Minneapolis Morning Tribune* editorial in January 1945 assumed that this "special resentment held against Americans of Japanese descent" was merely "temporary" as "a part of the wartime psychology." Nonetheless, the remedy would "require educational efforts." The piece titled "White Supremacy" concluded: "The day is surely coming when the white man will cease to lord it over peoples with different complexions. A modernized Asia will see to that."[87]

Many decades have passed since that news column was written. Has that day come? It is not easy to say whether enough progress has been made or enormous problems remain. Perhaps the answer is both. Especially in cross-racial relationships, only through listening to and learning from one another can a clearer understanding be reached. Even back in the days of wartime panic, one can find stories about how human connections changed the hearts of hard-liners and the lives of those in hardship for the better. "Understanding will have to come through seeing, feeling, experiencing—and then believing," a Nisei student wrote in a letter to the National Japanese American Student Relocation Council in 1943. The reflection of this young Nisei is poignantly apt and wise. Empathy seldom comes from abstraction.[88]

With this in mind and to put a period on this historical episode of Japanese Americans and Minnesota, let's conclude with a house-hunting tale

Mikio "Micky" Kirihara, 2015.
Courtesy of the author

from Lucy Torii Kirihara, the wife of Micky Kirihara, who appeared earlier. The search for a place to live in the Twin Cities proved to be a challenge for this new Japanese American family. Kirihara's two older sisters, Esther Torii Suzuki and Eunice Torii Okuma, both came to Minnesota for college during the war. They were determined to bring their parents and little sister out of the camp, too.

The two Macalester students walked door to door, day after day, looking for housing, yet with no success. "My sister Esther sometimes exaggerated a little bit. But she said they went to ninety-nine places for rent, and every one of them said it was full," Kirihara noted. "My sister would call when she got home, and those places would still be available."[89]

Finally, they came across a barber shop with living quarters above. "Do you have a place to rent?" the sisters asked. "Are you Japanese?" the Caucasian owner replied with a question. "One sister was going to lie, and say no," Kirihara noted. However, the sisters decided against it and instead answered: "Yes, we are." Another failed attempt, they thought.

Just when the two young women started to step out of the door, they heard the owner call out, "Wait!" The sisters turned around, and the man began to speak: "My son was in the service, and this Nisei girl helped, nursing him back to health. This is one way I could pay you back. You may rent the place." It turned out that the son of the owner, Mr. Munson, had been badly injured in the Philippines; under the loving care of a Japanese American nurse from Hawai'i, the young soldier was able to live and return home.

Experience changed perception. This was unbelievable to the two sisters. "The upstairs had five rooms, bedrooms, a living room, a dining room, and a kitchen," said Kirihara. "That's another thing, that our family was together. While we were in camp, our sisters were gone, so we missed her. I just remember it was a happy time, getting together and living together in this apartment. That was good!" War tore people apart, but it could also bring people together. Like the barber shop owner, many Minnesotans lent their helping hands and lifted their fellow citizens up despite their differences, or even because of them.

3

Advocates and Agencies

The National Japanese American Student Relocation Council (NJASRC) and College Education for Nisei Americans

"I look upon what I did for the Japanese American students as one of the, perhaps the most significant, single thing that I've done in my life [that] I look back on with satisfaction and pleasure.... And I look upon it as one of the constructive things that I've been able to participate in and will present it to Saint Peter when I present my credentials."—JOHN NASON

While Nason joked about his efforts for Nisei students, what he achieved was no laughing matter. "Here's a man, as an educator, concerned about what young Japanese American students were not getting at the time amidst the [problems of the] country, and these are bracketed by college presidency and a philosopher," said Bardwell Smith, professor emeritus of Carleton, who served as the dean of college under Nason. He further cited their conversation, when Nason revealed: "I became really disturbed at FDR's decision to put Japanese American citizens in these detention camps, and I was particularly disturbed about young men and women who were deprived of their college education because of this." Between 1942 and 1945, Nason chaired the NJASRC, which eventually helped liberate more than four thousand incarcerated Nisei students from the camps and enroll them into over six hundred colleges and universities outside of the restricted zone on the West Coast.[1]

While the Nisei students themselves are the protagonists of their own stories, they would have been unable to leave the camps without the support of others. Allies are important, especially in the face of war and racism. To present a richer and better-informed Japanese American history in wartime Minnesota, and that of the nation, requires a focus on race without just playing the blame game or ignoring the contributions of one's fellow citizens. Certainly, the actions or indifference of numerous white folks, some of whom might not have even harbored ill intentions, were part of the forced removal, imprisonment, and dispersal.

A handful of them, despite their privilege, fought alongside their ostracized compatriots during the maelstrom of war hysteria. Nason and his colleagues at the NJASRC permanently altered the lives of many young Nisei. However, it was never a white savior tale. Japanese Americans were not simply victims in distress who did nothing but wait to be rescued. The experience of wartime Japanese American college students was a far more complex narrative with an ensemble of different actors, agents, and adversaries.

Nason was among those Minnesotans who stepped up and stood by the Nisei students in a difficult time. Born in St. Paul at the turn of the century, Nason grew up in a rather comfortable household as his father had made a small fortune in the coal business in Chicago. Since "everybody in the Nason family" went to Carleton College, including both of his parents, who were good friends with its President Donald J. Cowling, Nason attended the Northfield school for his baccalaureate education as expected. Unfortunately, halfway through college, his father lost everything due to bankruptcy. Nason went from being privileged to poor and had to work to support himself. He tutored students, waited on tables, "did all sorts of things and ended college with considerable debt," which Nason later claimed "was probably the best thing that ever happened" to him.[2]

Both economic hardship and a liberal arts education widened young Nason's horizon. His father's struggle in his business venture made Nason reconsider his own career: "There must be a better way of living one's life than this." Being intellectually curious and interested in helping others, he decided to become a teacher. He changed his major from chemistry to philosophy, put himself through college, and graduated *summa cum laude* in 1926. Under a fellowship from the Council on Religion in Higher Education, he studied at the Yale Divinity School for one year (1926–1927). He then pursued a master's degree in philosophy from Harvard University in

1928. In addition, he was named a Rhodes Scholar and spent the next three years at Oriel College in Oxford University (1928–1931). Upon returning to the United States, he became an instructor of philosophy at Swarthmore College in Pennsylvania and served as an assistant to President Frank Aydelotte.

Higher education was Nason's vocation. His illustrious résumé included the stewardship of the two aforementioned liberal arts colleges. He was appointed the president of Swarthmore (1940–1953) at the age of thirty-five and guided the school during the challenging years of World War II as well as the rapid expansion of higher education and integration of the student body in the subsequent decade. Serving as the fifth president of his alma mater Carleton (1962–1970), Nason steered the college through the tumultuous 1960s—the civil rights movement, the sexual revolution, and the Vietnam War. Before joining Carleton, Nason presided over the Foreign Policy Association, a nonprofit organization founded in 1918 to promote public discussion about global affairs. Through the association, he established "World Affairs Councils" in many major American cities and led resistance to the "red scare" of McCarthyism in the 1950s, which suspected any internationalist body of being sympathetic to communism.[3]

Nason was articulate, charming, and reflective. "He always did his job in the context of other people," Smith noted. The task for Nason and the NJASRC was not easy, considering the wartime politics, bureaucratic red tape, and fearmongering propaganda. The feats of Nason and the NJASRC, therefore, set the stage for the amazing stories of the Japanese American students who relocated to Minnesota and regained their freedom during the war.

—

Not long after the incarceration began, the US government realized that imprisoning young, college-aged Nisei was a waste of human resources. It also meant that the country would be seriously deprived of potential leaders of the Japanese American community and thus of able citizens in the future. However, the Western Defense Command and the Fourth Army, led by DeWitt, adamantly refused to allow these students to stay and continue their studies on the Pacific coast. Providing an alternative path elsewhere for the American-born Nisei—those considered loyal and competent anyway—became a pressing issue.[4]

The imprisonment also weighed heavily on the conscience of many college faculty and administrators, civil right activists, religious leaders, friends of the Japanese American community, and even federal officials. Besides advocating for the rights of the Nisei, educators were defending their own positions in the moral order of American society as keepers of enduring values, sorters of intellect, and facilitators of assimilation. Those who could pursue college, they argued, would prove that the country was still a land of the free, and education was the best route to a successful future. Moreover, sending them to universities would cost no more than maintaining them inside the incarceration wards. The total number of students was a few thousand at most, an undertaking that seemed manageable. All hence agreed that something needed to be done.[5]

About three months after President Roosevelt signed Executive Order 9066, the NJASRC was formed on May 29, 1942. The council was a privately organized and funded agency, led predominately by the Quakers of the American Friends Service Committee (AFSC). Its purpose was to relocate Nisei students to inland colleges and universities so that they could continue their academic careers. These young people were the "next generation of Japanese American citizens," Nason asserted; "if they did not feel themselves as American citizens, but as aliens, we had an ethnic and difficult problem on our hands." To Nason the educational dilemma was also an ethical one. "As a country, we had no reason to believe that they would be disloyal. There were no episodes of sabotage of any sort. It was wartime panic, and it was disgraceful." Nason determined to right the wrong and tried his best to support these Japanese American students. The Swarthmore president then accepted to chair the NJASRC.[6]

During his three years tenure leading the council, about four thousand Nisei men and women were able to go to colleges instead of remaining in confinement. About half of them were students who had already started higher education on the West Coast, and the other two thousand graduated from high schools in the camps during the war years. More than five hundred of them came to Minnesota. While not all these students stayed or completed their education in the state, many chose Minnesota as their permanent home, including Yosh Murakami from St. Olaf, who went on to become a music teacher in Northfield, and Esther Torii Suzuki from Macalester, who rented the apartment above the barber shop. They were both among the first Japanese American students on their respective campuses and eventually became prominent members of the local community.

The accomplishments of the NJASRC were impressive; however, its establishment was a challenging quest. Numerous negotiations, from funding to logistics to execution, took place among the various founding members. The council's relationships with government agencies, military authorities, college administrators, civic groups, and Nisei students themselves were also complicated. Nason recalled that the Navy told him at one point that they could put the Japanese American students at "any colleges and universities" as long as the places were not within thirty miles of a railway or power plant. That sounded feasible at first, but then how many schools actually qualified under such a condition? "There was one we found in Idaho; that was about all," Nason noted.

—

While the inner workings of the council offer fascinating details on the politics of the time, the genesis of the student resettlement was intricately connected to Minnesota in unexpected ways. Commencing almost immediately after Pearl Harbor and going into the spring of 1942, higher education administrators had already discussed the possibility of helping Nisei students transfer to inland institutions. The Army at times did allow individual students to move eastward on a case-by-case basis, but a more concentrated and collective response was required.[7]

Significant efforts were made even before the exclusion orders went into effect. "If wisely handled," Clarence Pickett, the executive secretary of the American Friends, wrote in a letter to the president of Occidental College in 1942, "this gesture may well become the 'Boxer Indemnity' experience of our generation." Some 630 students were then able to locate sponsors, mostly due to personal and professional connections of faculty, to transfer outside the prohibited zone, and thereby avoided imprisonment.[8]

Education was a priority for the Nisei students. They preferred going to school, wherever that might be, over staying with their families in the camps. Most of them were attending large state schools on the West Coast, such as the University of California and University of Washington. In March 1942, the University of California sent out a questionnaire to all the Japanese American college students in the San Francisco Bay District who faced forced removal. A total of 257 of them responded. The overwhelming majority (88 percent) wanted to continue their studies, yet less than 20 percent of them had adequate funds to do so.[9]

Regarding their choice of location, about one-third (79 students) answered "no preference." For those who named a school, the University of Minnesota came out on top with eighteen votes, Iowa State College was next with thirteen, and the University of Wisconsin placed third with eleven mentions. Knowing that their prospects were more promising in the Midwest, they seemingly picked large state institutions in that region, which offered programs similar to the ones in which they were already enrolled on the West Coast. Still, the Department of War and the Navy had problems with Japanese Americans in large state universities. The odds of attending any of them were not at all favorable.[10]

Under the banner of national security, the Army objected as anticipated. DeWitt and his like-minded associates had pushed strongly for the mass eviction and incarceration of peoples of Japanese ancestry from the start; they even opposed the enlistment of Japanese American soldiers. The close ties between the military and large research universities, therefore, provided a pretext for exclusion.[11]

Since the Pacific Theater of operations began, federal agencies had actively approached higher education institutions to generate new research projects or establish Navy and Army Reserve Officers' Training Corps (ROTC) units on their campuses. Research contracts on sensitive matters such as aviation technology, poison gas, and infectious medicine were initiated with major universities across the country. These commissions and collaborations were lucrative in nature. They could be vital to the university's financial well-being. School budgets were already in a tailspin because many students had left college for service in the armed forces or simply dropped out during the war. The higher education sector needed to survive the formidable years ahead as well as contribute to the war effort. Engaging with the military seemed to be a winning formula to do both.[12]

The University of Minnesota was one such institution that faced the quandary of resettling or rejecting Nisei students. Its president, Walter C. Coffey, who headed the institution during the war years between 1941 and

1945, was among the first leaders to start the discussion about letting incarcerated Japanese American students attend Midwestern colleges. Since the University of Minnesota was a desirable destination, Coffey had received inquiries from his West Coast colleagues in March 1942 about the university's willingness to accept Nisei students. He immediately wrote to seventeen of his fellow presidents, including those from the Big Ten conference, for advice. In his March 18 letter, he asked whether the issue had been brought up in their constituencies and hoped that "there were some ways we could reach a policy in these matters to which we could all agree."[13]

The replies indicated both confusion and caution. The greatest worry was that a large influx of Japanese American students would inundate their campuses. For example, Arthur C. Willard, president of the University of Illinois, believed the board of trustees would not "look with favor upon the admission of either Japanese aliens or Americans of Japanese ancestry." He wrote to Coffey on March 20, 1942: "We have had some problems of our own along this line and naturally are reluctant to take on any more such responsibilities." It was unfortunate that American citizens had to suffer "because of the aggression of the country of their ancestors," Willard continued, but "it would be a mistake to place them in a position wherein the public would feel . . . that they were being given special privileges and protection."[14]

The University of Wisconsin's Clarence A. Dykstra faced a similar situation. In his reply on April 2, he suggested that Coffey contact the director of WRA, Milton S. Eisenhower. After all, resettling Nisei students should follow a national plan. If it were under federal guidelines and the Japanese American students were distributed widely, Dykstra opined, most individuals and institutions in the Midwest would find that acceptable. However, others were blunter and more negative, like the leadership of Indiana University and Purdue University, as they flatly denied admission to Japanese American students.[15]

Coffey's concern was not hypothetical but real and imminent. By April 1942, the University of Minnesota had received thirty-two formal applications from Nisei students; nine even showed up on campus without official admittances. The number of inquiries was growing at a high rate. Coffey's persistent support for segregated housing of African American students that year did not sound like an auspicious sign for the Japanese American students. He seemed uncomfortable with the informal manner in which the relocation situation had been playing out thus far. At the same time, he felt uneasy about potential scores of Nisei students rushing to the Twin Cities if the university opened its doors.[16]

Consequently, Coffey relayed his doubts in a message to Eisenhower at the WRA about the need for a systematic plan and a national policy on Nisei student resettlement. "Urge that Army give immediate attention to problem of Japanese American students of West Coast areas who are seeking to migrate to inland universities," Coffey wrote; "numbers have arrived Minnesota University in last three days without any assurance of admittance." He then reiterated the fear of a mass migration of students to a single institution. Coffey suspected that smaller colleges would be more likely to admit Nisei students. He also expected a government agency to coordinate the relocation effort, working with "large numbers of institutions each willing to accept one or two thus spreading the students," and that the federal mandate would shield them from public criticism.[17]

Until then, Coffey decided that the University of Minnesota would stay on the sidelines. "Pending formulation of a plan by a responsible federal agency, we would hold up the matter of transfers," he explained. The University of Minnesota was not alone in taking a defensive stance. The University of Chicago, to which Coffey looked as an example, reacted similarly. Like other major research universities, the University of Chicago was flooded with letters from Nisei students seeking admittance. Faculty members received numerous requests from their colleagues on the West Coast asking them to accept Japanese American students as well.[18]

Finally, an internal memorandum from the dean of students announced the university's formal position in the summer of 1942. Considering the extensive naval and military research being conducted under government contracts and in the absence of federal authorization, the University of Chicago argued that it was inadvisable to enroll incarcerated students. The school would continue to seek insights from official agencies, the memo stated, and when the government permitted it, the university would accept applications from Japanese Americans in the camps.[19]

Many university leaders were in the same boat, waiting for the storm to clear rather than heading into uncharted waters. The response from the University of Chicago was strikingly comparable to what Coffey had proposed. In an April 1942 meeting, the University of Minnesota's Board of Regents agreed with the president's decision. On June 2, local newspapers— both the *Minneapolis Morning Tribune* and the *Minneapolis Star Journal*— reported that the university would take in Japanese American students only after a federal management plan was in place. Picked up by national wires, the story somehow became that the University of Minnesota regents had voted to exclude Japanese Americans. Hence, the university received the negative reputation of rejecting Nisei students when the school might not have deserved it. Still, the university did not accept Japanese American students in the 1942–1943 academic year. Going against the grain were some Minnesotan liberal arts colleges. Macalester College in St. Paul had already admitted five students, whom the FBI cleared, for the fall 1942 semester.[20]

Bringing Nisei college students to Minnesota during the war years was an intricate dance with the government, military authorities, higher education administrators, activists, and allies. Nason and Coffey were two of the leading men. Each faced their own unique challenges, and thus, marched to the beat of their own drum. From Coffey's call for a national response to Nason's chairing of the student relocation council, the two Minnesotan educators bookended the chronicle of the NJASRC. Regardless of its "wait and see" strategy, the University of Minnesota did set up an urgent case for a mutual collaboration among all parties to develop an organized approach to address the predicament of the Japanese American students. The timing was ready for the NJASRC to make its debut.

Fighting for the wartime cause of Nisei students, the NJASRC was a voluntary agency, staffed mostly by Quakers from the AFSC. The Quakers were a logical choice to manage the nongovernmental organization, for many of their members, including Nason, had been involved in student resettlement from the beginning. First Lady Eleanor Roosevelt promptly endorsed the idea. "As far as we know, they are loyal Americans," she said. "We are not asking colleges to take aliens . . . but refugees from our own coast to the interior." On May 29, 1942, Nason joined forty-four representatives from various religious and civic groups, together with one Japanese American, Mike Masaru Masaoka from the JACL, for a meeting in Chicago. The NJASRC was formed as a result.[21]

Funding was not a part of the deal. Neither the White House nor the War Department was interested in financing the student relocation. On the contrary, WRA officials realized such a program could not be supported by public funds due to the widespread hostility toward Japan and Japanese Americans, owing much to the propaganda campaign; to do so would incite massive protests and "sink the program."[22]

Instead, the council had to rely on private fundraising for scholarships in order to cover the Nisei's college expenses and moving costs. "The church, missionary, and charitable student organizations" would be the key sponsors for the relocation program, stated John H. Provinse, head of the WRA's Community Management Division. Money was always a problem. The task inevitably fell on the AFSC and other philanthropic groups and remained a major challenge for the NJASRC.[23]

On a brighter note, resettling the Nisei students was seen as a test case for releasing other Japanese Americans from the camps. "When the story of relocation is written and the War Relocation Authority's objective of emptying the relocation centers is achieved," Dillon Myer, the second WRA director, claimed, "we will be able to state that the first impetus to resettlement . . . was provided by student relocation." However, the success of the program ultimately depended on how "good" the students were. Arriving in locales where Japanese Americans were rare, the students were under extreme scrutiny and needed to prove themselves as truly "American" as they could. At the inaugural meeting in Chicago, NJASRC's founding members decided that Japanese American students would be chosen on several criteria, all components of "the ambassador of goodwill persona."[24]

In short, the students had to be a "model minority." Loyalty was the first and foremost qualification. Academic achievement and the ability to be an "outstanding representative of the Japanese people" were next, for both features were "equally important in disseminating better attitudes toward the Japanese race." To avoid public uproar, student resettlers were initially limited to Nisei, US citizens who had never traveled to Japan, a rule that was dropped later. The chosen ones would then go through various clearances and be matched with appropriate colleges or universities. It was a long and complex process. Helping students navigate it became the mission of the NJASRC.[25]

The wartime climate made the council's job a daunting ordeal. The military authorities and government bureaucrats were notoriously difficult to work with, and the NJASRC was merely a voluntary organization with no institutional status or political clout. The council members believed early on that progress could only be made if the NJASRC played its cards right. Although the Army had the preponderance of power, it could be dealt with, "even if tediously, if it is gentled." Too much pressure applied too hastily might trigger the military to call off the student resettlement altogether, an unwise confrontation that the council would be destined to lose.[26]

Nason demonstrated patience and composure in such a chaotic time. The official policies for resettlement were inconsistent, confusing, and constantly changing. He often served as a moderating influence in the council and offered practical advice to keep up with the ever-shifting conditions in and out of the camps. "We had first to get permission from the Army and the Navy in Washington to do this—and that was difficult. We then had to get colleges and universities to agree to accept them . . . on complete scholarships, because most of them had lost all their money," as Nason summarized the workflow of the council. "We had to raise enough money to provide for the personal perquisites of students—they had to have toothpaste and clothes, and a few things like that. And we had to set up committees of welcome in these colleges and universities, so that they wouldn't be badly treated when they got there—which some of them were. It was a very complicated business."[27]

Dealing with the government and other agencies presented only one of the numerous obstacles with which Nason and the NJASRC had to contend. They might have been tedious and irritating, but they were probably easier to solve than other, more deep-seated problems, namely racism. Among the groups that mobilized to oppose the Nisei resettlement were the American Legion, the Native Sons of the Golden West, the Eagles, the Americanism Educational League, the House Special Committee on

Un-American Activities, and the congressional delegation from California. Many of these opponents claimed it was hard to fathom why, at a time of national crisis, people whom the government did not "see fit to trust with rifles" were allowed "to pursue uninterruptedly their college and professional" education.[28]

These antagonistic voices created a butterfly effect. The alarmist messengers meant to scare and sway the public. Selling fear and hatred was as popular a business then as perhaps it is now. Colleges that contemplated accepting the Nisei students were confronted with fusillades of local protest; many universities refused the relocation out of timidity—fear of undermining the prestige of their institution among conventionally minded citizens, worry about losing the support of conservative trustees, or dread of the onerous procedures required to bring in Nisei students. There were even college administrators who went out of their way to hinder Japanese American students' transfers by refusing to release the transcripts of their Nisei students.[29]

The trepidation was not one-sided but mutual. Weary of the bigotry beyond the barbed fences, many Issei parents would rather their children stay by their sides than let them go out alone to unknown places for college. There were also reports that many Caucasian teachers in the camps, despite the progressive veneer of their profession, discouraged Nisei students from pursuing college. "Some of this hostility," observed one of the field directors, was "born of race prejudice" but masked in the guise of "realism." According to these camp instructors, it was a mistake for Japanese Americans to think in terms of a college education since the fields for which they trained were likely closed to them.[30]

Morale in the camps sagged as the war dragged on another year. Nason acknowledged the growing apathy and apprehension among the incarcerees. He realized that the number of resettlers would dwindle significantly unless steps were "taken to encourage more of the potential students to apply for relocation."[31]

Running the NJASRC was a delicate balancing act. Nason knew the limitations of the council and the rules of the game. As chairman, he had to handle demands, questions, and complaints, sometimes unreasonable, from all directions while producing the fastest results possible to reverse the injustice. In many private letters that Nason wrote to his colleagues and

NATIONAL JAPANESE AMERICAN
STUDENT RELOCATION COUNCIL

1201 CHESTNUT ST., PHILADELPHIA, PA.

RITtenhouse 9372

JOHN W. NASON, *National Chairman*
ROBERT W. O'BRIEN, *National Director*

November 26, 1942

TO THE PRESIDENTS OF COLLEGES, UNIVERSITIES AND PROFESSIONAL
SCHOOLS

Dear Friends:

    May we of the National Japanese American Student Reloc-
ation Council submit a progress report at this time? We were able
to place approximately 330 students in 93 colleges and universities
for the first term -- in spite of difficulties and obstructions
which were not cleared away until the first of August. A reasonably
good start under the circumstances, but only a start.

    We are bending every effort at this time to place
students for the second semester or the winter term. Could you
accommodate some or, if you have already welcomed a certain number,
could you increase the number for the second term? The majority of
these students have lost their sources of financial support. Could
you give scholarship help to those whom you are prepared to accept?
If you have recently given this information, please ignore this
request. For your convenience we enclose a copy of the Procedure
Program under which we operate.

    The reports which come to us from the colleges and
universities which have already received Japanese American students
tell a happy story of easy and successful adjustment. The response
of many institutions to the challenge of the Japanese American
situation is an episode in the history of higher education in this
country, of which we may all be proud.

                    Yours sincerely,

                    John W. Nason

                    CHAIRMAN

P.S. Would you be kind enough to have a copy of your institution's
      catalogue sent to each of the ten war relocation centers?
      Their names and addresses are given on a separate sheet.

A letter from John Nason, chair of the National Japanese American Student
Relocation Council (NJASRC), to presidents of colleges, universities, and
professional schools, dated November 26, 1942. *Courtesy of St. Olaf College*

students, he strongly expressed his aversion to the imprisonment and the racism that caused it. Nonetheless, he refrained from direct and public criticism
of the government's actions. "This Council is a privately financed agency. It
determines its own policies freely, but . . . operates within a framework of the
regulations of the military and civil authorities," he elaborated in a February
1944 letter. Compromise was just one of the ways in which Nason worked.
He could "put up as strong a fight as possible" when he felt warranted.[32]

The NJASRC, though imperfect, was successful. By May 1943 the council had placed more than a thousand Nisei students into 175 institutions of
higher learning in thirty-seven states; the number exceeded 1,500 by August.
Some attributed its achievements to the "Friendly Way" of the Quakers,
as the AFSC assumed a central role in operating and managing the council. These pacifist "friends" offered unequivocal support to Japanese Americans at a time when even many liberals were rationalizing the incarceration
as a regrettable yet "necessary evil."[33]

All good things must come to an end. Confident that the NJASRC had
"fulfilled" its "original purpose" and facing difficulties in raising additional
funds, Nason believed that it would be best "to look toward a conclusion of
our affairs instead of toward a lingering death by financial inanition." In an
open letter to the press on February 28, 1944, Nason summarized the achievements of the council for the past two years: "There are now about 2,500
students of Japanese ancestry enrolled in 450 colleges, universities, and
other institutions of higher education located in 46 different states. . . . Since
the Council's inception in 1942, more than $10,000 has been allocated . . . to
students who would have been able to meet their college expenses." Nason
was content with the outcomes and envisioned that the curtain would come
down by the year's end.[34]

Not everyone agreed, of course. The council would postpone its cessa-
tion until June 30, 1946, to further support resettled students or refer them
to other agencies as the camps closed. The extended year and a half brought
the total number of Japanese American resettlers to more than four thousand in over six hundred institutions of higher education.[35]

In retrospect, Nason was proud of his work at the NJASRC while serving
as a full-time college president at the same time. "If I had not done that,"

Nason once said, "it might not have been done." As World War II became a closed chapter in history books and the incarceration a minor footnote, not many people knew about the council and Nason's pivotal leadership in it. "He was truly a modest person," biographer Bruce Colwell commented. Nason "was not a man to boast, but as he looked around to see what happened in the country, how difficult the challenges were, and what he accomplished through the council," Smith noted, "he's probably right, that nobody else would have done it."

One might be curious what inspired an advocate like Nason. His experience in Europe seemingly had a significant impact on his steadfast conviction. Studying as a Rhodes Scholar offered Nason the opportunity to better attune to global affairs and clearly witness the sinister nature of war. "He was concerned during the 1930s over the rise of Hitler and thought the United States ought to be involved in stopping Nazis," Smith recalled. Lived experience, once again, was a key to empathy.

War brought out the best and the worst in people. In a 1944 letter to Ida I. Mai, the sister of a prospective Nisei student of Swarthmore, Nason expressed his personal feelings about the situation. "The war has necessitated actions which I am confident the majority of the people of the United States deplore and dislike," Nason wrote. "There are citizens of the country who express race prejudice and bias toward anyone of Japanese ancestry. They are a minority although a vocal one, and I feel that the rest of us must see to it that their un-Christian and unwise point of view does not prevail."[36]

To Nason, the most effective way to combat racism was education. "One of the things he always believed was that education would not only give you a broader world view," Colwell said, "but it also made you at least aware of whatever prejudices you might have, or just really more open to different people [and] different cultures." Leading the NJASRC became a concrete way for Nason to help his fellow citizens and rectify injustices. Certainly, the wartime resettlement of Nisei students to campuses across the country was a tricky and trying exertion. Even within higher education, attempts to place them were met with all kinds of obstruction, which brings us back to the other lead actor in Minnesota.

Coffey at the University of Minnesota was among the first educators to raise questions about Japanese American students' resettlement back in March 1942. He worried the campus could become a magnet for more Nisei students than the school could handle and about what the wartime public reaction would be. Those appeared to be his top concerns. Coffey did not mention the military-related research and the ROTC program in the archival documents; the federal contracts with the campus evidently did not factor into Coffey's consideration then. Until a national policy was set, Coffey and the Board of Regents rationalized, the university would not make a move.[37]

In the summer of 1942, a new development in Minnesota took place, which complicated the university's dilemma. The MISLS began its classes officially at Camp Savage on June 1 with two hundred students, the majority being Japanese Americans. Minnesota, perhaps by association, gained popularity among the Nisei. As the fall semester began, the university received over a hundred applications. Due to the lack of any federal instruction, the school had no choice but to reject them all.[38]

To seek some clarity, Coffey contacted the Secretary of War Henry L. Stimson on September 30, 1942, inquiring about the government's view on the Nisei issue. His letter was passed on to the WRA, which oversaw the student relocation program. What Coffey heard back in early October was not helpful. The directives from the government were perplexing. On the one hand, the WRA stated that the university had not yet been cleared to accept Nisei from the camps, but those who were not incarcerated or were allowed to leave confinement could be admitted as "any other students of American citizenship." On the other hand, the Navy, disagreeing with the WRA, objected to the enrollment of Japanese American students at the university, because Minnesota hosted "confidential training and research for the Navy Department."[39]

Undersecretary of the Navy (later Secretary of Defense after the war) James Forrestal confirmed that the University of Minnesota was on the proscribed list that included fifty-three colleges and universities as well as twenty-four vocational schools. Accordingly, the university was prohibited from taking in Nisei students, since they "might reveal information of the Navy activity" or other sensitive information "to the enemy or enemy agents." Forrestal claimed that such caution was necessary in order to ensure the "security of our war effort." Irrespective of the establishment of the military language school, it seemed nothing had changed. "[We] are back to just where we started!" Malcolm Willey, the assistant to Coffey, lamented.[40]

The situation became even more puzzling on October 31, 1942. The Agricultural College at the University of Minnesota, known as the "Farm campus," showed up on the newest War Department list of "cleared" colleges. The university, therefore, engaged with the WRA and NJASRC in a series of exchanges in the hope of illuminating the prospect of accepting Japanese American students. Ultimately, the ban persisted. Observing the Navy's orders, the university simply could not admit Nisei students. The council naturally expressed their disappointment with the decision. It argued that the Agricultural College housed no military research project, and the location was far from the Twin Cities campus that did. The rejection seemed to be an overreaction.[41]

True E. Pettengill, director of admissions, later explained that even though permission was granted to the Farm campus, it still made no difference because the main campus had not yet been approved. The two campuses were not considered independently. "If clearance cannot be given for admittance of Japanese Americans on the main campus, the reasons that govern that decision are equally effective with respect to the Farm campus," Willey explained to the council.[42]

Learning about the incident in November, the Friends Student Association at the university denounced the school's refusal as unfair: "We have had previous experience with discrimination on our campus and feel that probably this is another stall." The general consensus implied that the University of Minnesota's administration was amicable and agreeable, but the truth was probably that some officials were, and some were not.[43]

The stalemate condition lasted through the entire 1942–1943 academic year. In June 1943, Coffey reached out to Forrestal at the Navy again about any changes regarding the prohibition of Nisei students on his campus. "The University of Minnesota still receives applications from Japanese American students who wish to enter here, and there are many in our local community who do not understand why we have refused to admit them, especially since some other institutions in the immediate vicinity have done so," the president wrote.[44]

Predictably, the Navy was unmoved. Forrestal replied that the policy was still justified and necessary so as "to prevent information of value . . . from falling into possession of those who are or may be inimical to the interests of the United States." Moreover, the undersecretary stressed: "I am sure you also recognize the importance of this problem and that while our nation is fighting for the maintenance and preservation of principles and doctrine that have made it great, any doubts arising must be resolved in favor of the United States, regardless of apparent injustice and hardship."[45]

Rather than opening up campuses for Nisei students, the Navy announced a new list of ninety-one proscribed schools in June, bringing the total number of such institutions to 150. Despite the fact that more than one-third of these colleges had been previously cleared, they were then excluded because they had recently obtained classified research contracts with or provided training programs for the Navy, the Marine Corps, or the Coast Guard. The director of NJASRC, Carlisle V. Hibbard, who was also a YMCA executive, decried the Navy's latest list as a "power jolt."[46]

Even the typically calm and collected Nason responded in vexation. "Our student relocation work is being increasingly hampered by the restrictions of the Navy. We now have a list of nearly 150 proscribed institutions. This is all the more serious because the American students of Japanese ancestry who were interested in going to the liberal arts institutions have to a [great] extent been placed," Nason wrote to the WRA in July. "At present [a] very considerable number of candidates wants technical training and most of the large universities where the technical training is available have not been approved by the Navy." That was the time when Nason felt the need to put up a strong fight. Like Nason and Hibbard in the council, Coffey must have felt exasperated, too. He sent a brief memo to his dean and assistant Willey, noting that this extended list "really [made] our situation relative to the admittance of Japanese American students worse rather than better."[47]

Worse, even absurd, the situation in Minnesota had become indeed. The frustration of the higher education administrators was caused not so much by the strictness of the military policy but its arbitrariness. Many Nisei who applied to the university as well as to other research and employment opportunities had been cleared by the FBI to leave the camps. One would be hard pressed to claim these people were dangerous and hence refute the FBI's assessment without presenting any evidence. Moreover, Japanese Americans had been attending the MISLS in Minneapolis for a year by then. There was no security issue at all, and excellent responses from the local community. The basis of the policy seemed neither valid nor convincing.

Adding to the contradiction was a concurring development that involved Japanese language teachers in higher education institutions. The MISLS was set up to support the war effort on the Pacific front, as the military lacked officers fluent in the Japanese language. However, having only one school was deemed insufficient. To accelerate progress, the military sought help from universities and colleges, urging many schools, such as the University of Chicago, to offer Japanese language studies in their curriculum. The next logical and logistical question would be who could teach these courses. If recruiting students with some linguistic background to join the MISLS was difficult, finding instructors with the desirable proficiency and cultural knowledge was even harder. Once again, the military turned to the confined Japanese Americans.[48]

The new recruitment further exposed the hypocrisy of the official policy. To fill all these vacant positions, the target was not limited to Nisei in general, but expanded to Kibei, American-born Nisei who received part of their education in Japan and so were usually barred from release owing to their history in or connection to the "enemy state." The military eventually allowed these Nisei and Kibei to leave camps for teaching jobs on the campuses with Japanese programs. Furthermore, release exemptions were given to those Japanese Americans who had expertise in science, technology, and engineering to work as researchers or teaching assistants. Hence, they could serve as instructors and researchers at various universities but were not allowed to enroll in classes as students. This arrangement baffled many institutions and the council. It made no sense, besides the rationale of exploiting the Japanese Americans when they were useful and excluding them when they were not.[49]

The University of Minnesota was one of these schools with an added Japanese language program. Willey raised this confounding issue with the Army in the late fall of 1943. Five Nisei instructors taught Japanese at the university "without causing the slightest difficulty," but Japanese American students and employees were barred from campus under the Navy's ruling.

Even as the military continued to enforce the security provisions, another federal policy took effect. Japanese Americans, both as students and university employees, could now be admitted and hired on a case-by-case basis. The exact reason for the modification was unknown, although it might have had to do with the lackluster recruiting effort. Wartime demands overrode baseless concerns. The university could then request and obtain clearance from the military for each of its Nisei students and staff members, as long as the individual complied with specific terms.[50]

It was a game changer for the University of Minnesota. For example, the Army approved a Nisei language instructor on the University of Minnesota's campus only on the condition that the person be "placed under surveillance" and "not be allowed access to classified information, documents and similar matters"; otherwise, "it will be necessary to terminate" employment. As a result, on November 20, 1943, the university's Board of Regents officially adopted the policy of accepting Nisei students and hiring Japanese Americans subject to military clearance. In December 1943, the council sent its first cohort of recommended students to the University of Minnesota. The military clearance and application process was bundled with bureaucratic red tape as expected. Still, the gate of the University of Minnesota was finally open, which was a hard-fought and well-deserved triumph of both the Japanese Americans and their allies.[51]

Contrary to popular belief, the University of Minnesota not only accepted Nisei students during the war, albeit belatedly, but also was the top institution for accommodating the highest number of Japanese Americans in the state. It accounted for nearly half of the total number of 536 students who came for college in Minnesota. Between the fall of 1943 and the end of the war in 1945, 228 Nisei students attended the University of Minnesota according to the NJASRC files and the university archive. The actual number could be larger, as documentation might have been lost or not kept, especially during the war.

Additionally, the school employed at least two Japanese American teachers (five were mentioned in Willey's letter). In fact, the NJASRC tried to gather information and reach all the Nisei students at the university that the council had been in correspondence with before its closure in the summer of 1946. The staff wrote to the university to inquire whether there was a list of Nisei students there; however, the school did not maintain such a record, replying that they did "not classify students by nationality" and that the only way to do that would be by going through the university's address book.[52]

Overall, the NJASRC was pleased with the outcome. In a letter to the director of admissions on December 6, 1944, the council thanked the university, for it "has been receiving many letters from the students who are attending the University of Minnesota telling us of their happiness and splendid adjustments on the campus. They all especially note the cordial attitude of the administration and the friendliness of the students."[53]

There were also other welcoming gestures by the university. In June 1945, Director of Student Loans and Scholarships George B. Risty approved Japanese Americans for "resident fee privileges" rather than out-of-state fees "until such time as the parents are permitted by the armed forces to return to their original place of residence or until they acquire domicile elsewhere." In June 7, 1946, one of the Japanese American students, Cherry Tanaka, requested information on the financial assistance that was provided to Nisei students while writing her piece for the newsletter. Verifying the numbers, the administration was surprised "to learn the amount of scholarship aid which Nisei students have obtained through the generosity of [the NJASRC] and through several church groups." According to this report, there were twenty-seven Japanese Americans who received scholarships, with an average of $157.13 (approximately $2,853 today) for each student, and the total was $4,242.50 (about $77,043 today). A few of them were granted awards from different sources, sometimes multiple times.[54]

The mass removal and confinement of Japanese Americans during World War II was "an outrage, unnecessary, and illegal," Nason asserted. "I was asked to be the chairman of a group that would try to get these students out of the camps and back into colleges and universities across the country." The St. Paul native accepted the challenge. The NJASRC became the chief advocate and central agency through which incarcerated Japanese American students could reclaim their rights, regain freedom, and resettle for college. "They are full citizens of this country," Nason remarked. "Most of them are happy citizens of this country. Most of them are very grateful for their chance to get out and are singularly free of anger over the way in which they were treated."[55]

Powerless yet not hopeless, more than five hundred young Nisei braved the snow and weathered the storms to start their new college lives in Minnesota. Were they really not indignant about the injustice? How did Minnesotans treat them? What about assimilation and alienation in this predominately "white" place, and their playing the role of "model minority"? What were their experiences like? What were their stories? The next chapter will attempt to answer these questions.

4 | Ambassadors and Adversaries

Japanese American College Students in Wartime Minnesota

"For my first assignment in freshman speech class,
I began by declaring, 'The happiest day of my life was
the day I left for college.'"—ESTHER TORII SUZUKI

I t was September 8, 1942, four months after Esther Suzuki's family was forced to leave their home in Portland, sell everything for nothing, and move to a temporary detention center along with nearly four thousand other Japanese Americans where they lived in hastily converted horse stalls with extreme heat, fly infestations, and foul odors. They were set to transfer to the Minidoka camp in Idaho on that very day. "Just two hours and fifteen minutes before the appointed time, a telegram arrived from Washington D.C. releasing me to attend Macalester," Suzuki recalled. "I was the first person to be freed from detention in Portland. We hurriedly repacked my belongings separately, and my family gave me the only suitcase we owned."[1]

The sixteen-year-old Suzuki's dream of going to college had finally come true. She was able to escape from the imprisonment, too. However, the happiest day suddenly did not feel joyful anymore. "I remember my father, mother, and two sisters standing on the other side of the barbed-wire fence in Oregon, waving goodbye, smiling bravely through their tears. I broke down and couldn't continue."

Suzuki was the first Japanese American student accepted by Macalester College. She was joined in St. Paul by four other Nisei in the fall of 1942. Eventually Macalester took in twenty Japanese Americans by the end of the war. "Suzuki has become one of our real touchstones," said the sixteenth Macalester president, Brian Rosenberg. "Every college has its key historical figures. And for us, Esther Suzuki has become one of those." The college established the Lealtad-Suzuki Center in 2002, which "focuses on diversity on campus" and is named after two women alumnae of color: Catharine Deaver Lealtad (class of 1915), the first African American graduate and a distinguished physician, and Suzuki (class of 1946), the first Nisei student, a tireless social worker and activist in Minnesota.[2]

The experience of Suzuki tells a unique tale of how a Japanese American woman triumphed over hostility to lead a distinguished life in the North Star State. "Somewhere way back I learned the importance of taking pride in one's heritage and of knowing that one's course should be true rather than expedient," Suzuki remarked. "It hasn't been easy to maintain a feeling of self-worth at all times, but the gift of life expects lifelong learning, adventuring, giving, resilience and affirmation. My parents, children, and grandchildren have experienced the good life in Minnesota and express their appreciation continuously, for Minnesota is home."[3]

More than grace and gratitude, Suzuki's story reveals the universal history of what the young Japanese Americans had to endure during the war to reclaim their right to an education, and the important lessons which we all need to learn from, reflect on, and remember. This chapter is dedicated to these stories in the North Star State. The Nisei students were not alone. Many Minnesotans, from college administrators to teachers to fellow classmates, along with the NJASRC and others mentioned in the previous chapter, played critical roles in the narratives.

—

There are many aspects to the Nisei wartime saga in Minnesota. More than five hundred Japanese American pioneers pursued higher education in twenty-five institutions in the state during the war. These Nisei students were pioneers on several fronts. They were the first group of Asian Americans who systematically migrated to Minnesota, thus marking a defining moment in Minnesotan educational and racial history. However, these young people did not come to merely study and perform academic excellence, which, of course, was expected. They also had to be goodwill ambassadors, loyal patriots, and model citizens, proving themselves as worthy of their basic human rights as any other Americans.

Esther Suzuki was a typical Nisei student at that time. Her background resembled numerous other Japanese Americans. Both her parents were Issei immigrants from Japan. Her father Tokichi Torii came to the United States in 1903 during the Russo-Japanese War. He started as a houseboy and gardener, working his way up to become the executive secretary of the Oregon Growers Association and one of three founders of the Japanese Methodist Episcopal Church in Portland. Torii was able to bring his bride from Japan, Tomae Tamaki, "a godsend" sewer and embroiderer, just before the Johnson-Reed Act of 1924 that barred further immigration from Asia.

Suzuki was the eldest of the three Torii daughters—Esther, Eunice, and Lucy. Their carefree childhood in Portland was abruptly thrown into fear and uncertainty after Pearl Harbor. It began with a curfew, surveillance, and shortly thereafter forcible removal. Within a week's time, the life that Suzuki had known crumbled into pieces and was stuffed into a few duffel bags. The family was herded into a temporary detention center on May 5, 1942, awaiting their transfer to Minidoka.

Although "days dragged endlessly" in detention, Suzuki was neither aimless nor hopeless. Being incarcerated, Suzuki was not allowed to attend her high school graduation that June. College was always on her mind though. She was busy sending out her applications to schools all over the country. "Then the pieces of a great cosmic puzzle began to miraculously fit together," she said; "the Quakers set up a scholarship called the Nisei Student Relocation Fund that awarded me $100" (equivalent to about $2,000 today). She was supposed to attend Willamette University of Salem in Oregon, but institutions on the West Coast were off-limits to the Japanese Americans.

Missing that opportunity led her to another in Minnesota. "My high school English teacher, who was a Quaker, suggested Macalester," Suzuki noted, "because she had read a book by Glenn Clark," a literature professor there. The talented Japanese American girl, perhaps with a little bit of luck, was accepted. The letter from Macalester President Charles J. Turck was the first step in securing her release. "I had to send President Turck's letter to the War Department and obtain its approval. I also needed letters of recommendation from three Caucasians attesting to my loyalty and honesty," Suzuki said, "and letters from the St. Paul police and fire chiefs acknowledging my residence in their city."[4]

Pursuing college was one of the few available routes for Nisei to escape imprisonment and rejoin the world of normal communities during the early days of the war. Since the NJASRC was established in May 1942, Nason and other advocates had been contacting institutions of higher education outside of the restricted zone and requesting them to accept Nisei students. Fighting for their right to freedom, Japanese Americans wrote hundreds of letters to the few Caucasians whom they felt were genuinely interested in assisting them, and those letters piled up at the offices of the American Friends Service Committee and the NJASRC. Nason emphasized that Nisei students did not have to work with the council; they were "free to apply to colleges independently of it, but experience shows that it is usually more effective to make use of the council's services."[5]

Higher education was imperative and meaningful for the Japanese American community, especially the Issei generation who saw it not only as a respected path to a better life but also a practical way out of confinement for their American-born children. "Education has been the single most important factor stressed by our parents," Suzuki remembered. "From the day that my father escorted me to the front of the kindergarten class and entrusted me to the teacher with these words, 'Please, you teach her English,' I have been on a one-track course."[6]

Yet higher education in the United States was also about money. Banding together, the Japanese American incarcerees supported such aspirations in spite of adversity, as they raised more than $3,000 (approximately $60,000 today) from the camp at Topaz alone to give college scholarships to Nisei students. After a series of negotiations, the WRA informed the NJASRC on June 16, 1942, that the government agreed to pay for the students' transportation expenses to inland schools and to allow the regional office to issue travel authorizations. In mid-October 1942, Nason and his colleagues felt cautiously optimistic that the relocation of larger numbers of students was possible and thus began sustained efforts to raise funds beyond the Quakers; a $10,000 grant from the Carnegie Corporation provided the council with early outside funding, for example.[7]

Applying to college was not easy under normal circumstances. How could the young Nisei do that in such an unusual and unpleasant situation? What a Nisei student like Suzuki had to go through to obtain permission to leave the camp for college was a lengthy, laborious, and labyrinthine process. A brief overview here would be helpful to grasp the challenges faced by the students, institutions, and the NJASRC.

Not surprisingly, the procedure entailed layers of paperwork both inside and outside of the camps. Students first had to fill out a council questionnaire and apply for resettlement. Most of the applications in 1942 were completed with council representatives who visited the temporary detention centers and the camps during the summer. Application information included the typical documents: the individual's and their family's ability to finance the year(s) of college, along with the student's records, such as high school and college transcripts, as well as letters of reference. Both the students and the council contacted the previous schools about transcripts and former teachers, professors, or guidance counselors for recommendations.[8]

The West Coast office of the NJASRC was the clearinghouse for these records. Apart from all the educational information, students needed to complete various WRA and Wartime Civil Control Administration (WCCA) forms. Once these government papers were in order, they were placed in a student's file for evaluation. In the summer of 1942, a volunteer group of West Coast registrars, college deans, and personnel advisers formed a committee to assess students' qualifications. They then recommended the candidates to colleges and universities. The raters were experienced college admissions staff, and two of them reviewed each applicant independently; if their evaluations differed, a third person was brought in and made a final decision on the case.[9]

What was the yardstick or rubric that the rating committee used to rank Nisei students like Suzuki? Through interviews, school records, and recommendations, the committee gathered information and provided assessments of the students. The members scored students in two areas: scholarship, which by and large "was reduced to grade-point average," and "'personal factors" that were defined as "the sum-total of [their] personality, adaptability, and general promise where not related to scholastic ability." In addition, "reliability, diligence, special interests, leadership, evidence of successful

Caucasian contacts and contribution to the Japanese community" were taken into consideration as well.[10]

The rating system stressed the Nisei as "goodwill ambassadors" who ought to represent the exemplary character of Japanese Americans to the mainstream. An editorial in the *Santa Anita Pacemaker*, the longest-running newspaper published in the temporary detention centers and incarceration camps, explained the anticipated role for these young men and women: "Upon their scholarship, their conduct, their thoughts, their sense of humor, and their adaptability will rest the verdict of the rest of the country as to whether Japanese Americans are true Americans. So, upon the students will be the onus of proving to people to whom they are strangers that the first word in 'Japanese American' is merely an adjective describing the color of our skin—not the color of our beliefs. There is no place for cry-babies or weaklings in this program. The burden must be borne."[11]

More than the Nisei's academic futures were at stake here. The success of the student relocation program would ease the NJASRC's relationship with government officials, notably with the WRA, because highlighting the goodwill of the individuals helped promote the agency's wider "assimilation" and resettlement agenda that also included employment. The council affirmed, from the very beginning, that the Japanese American students themselves should be careful, and they "should fit into the community in as natural a way as possible." When a student's dossier received endorsement from the committee, their file was then forwarded to the council's East Coast office to get clearance from federal agencies, such as the Office of the Provost Marshal General (PMG), military intelligence, and the FBI. This was where the real bottleneck for the process lay.[12]

While individual cases passing through the "security" checkpoints took a long time, finding appropriate and accepting schools for the students was equally difficult. The initial approval list distributed by the military on August 5, 1942, included only fifty-seven colleges and universities nationwide. The council continued to submit institutions to the Army and Navy for clearance, but the process lagged painfully behind. During the summer of 1942, there were many more qualified students, and colleges willing to take them, than there were schools greenlit by the military. By October 1, the West Coast office had received 2,321 Nisei applications, and of that total,

800 had completed dossiers, and 500 of them were already accepted by colleges but awaited their release documents. Eventually, only a very small number of Japanese Americans, 152 students to be exact, received permission to leave the camps that fall.[13]

The Army and Navy apparently did not deem granting Nisei students their right to higher education a priority. Expectedly, the military cleared mostly liberal arts colleges and some smaller universities. Larger institutions that were strong in sciences, engineering, and medicine were inaccessible to Japanese Americans, including the University of Minnesota, as discussed in the preceding chapter. Writing to West Coast colleagues, the national director of NJASRC Robbins W. Barstow lamented: "We must resign ourselves to a very slow and cumbersome process."[14]

It was not a lack of will from the WRA, especially from its first director, Eisenhower; their hands were tied just as much as those of the council were. Barstow concluded: "Now it is quite as heart-breaking for me to have to write this way as it must be for you to get this discouraging word, but we simply have to [be] realistic and face the fact . . . that the situation is beyond our control." The NJASRC had to settle for "trial and error methods," as they would get "turned down again and again, from this or that institution," by the military. There was a gender imbalance issue, too. About two-thirds of the acceptances were for women, whereas two-thirds of the applicants were men.[15]

Other hindrances to the Nisei college path and the council's workflow involved the schools. One came from "the ignorance of prospective students concerning available colleges." Most knew nothing about institutions away from the Pacific coast. A letter to Nason on February 12, 1943, from Poston in Arizona put forward the predicament clearly. "We have here a nearly complete collection of catalogues of approved institutions and are trying to inform students about places which they have never heard of," the Adult Education Department in the camp wrote. The council's October 1942 progress report admitted that "many of the remaining vacancies are in small denominational schools," and there were "openings waiting to be filled and students who may be persuaded to fill them."[16]

The task for the NJASRC was thus twofold. Not only did the council have to sell students to colleges, they also needed to sell colleges to students. The report continued: "Colleges like Haverford, Swarthmore, Kenyon, Rochester are sometimes as unfamiliar and unattractive as Shreiner, Simpson, Stephens, or Sterling." Suzuki was fortunate to learn about Macalester from her high school teacher in Portland. Likewise, many Japanese American students counted on the camp counselors and the NJASRC for advice on which Midwestern or Eastern schools to apply to. To some, however, it was just a gamble.[17]

Another school-related problem had to do with the local communities where the Nisei college students resettled. The council needed to validate the local acceptance of Japanese American students. Pertaining to the approval process for those Nisei in the temporary detention centers, which were run by the Army, "a statement from some public official such as a public welfare agency, Mayor, Chief of Police, District Attorney, or other responsible town or county Peace Officer" was required, testifying that they saw "no reason why Japanese American students should not be relocated in that community." The double-negative wording from the procedural guideline did not convey a sense of confidence about the situation. However, for those in the camps overseen by the WRA, "no statement from the mayor or public official is required." Instead, "a statement from some official from the receiving college or university is sufficient." The two different rules for two detention locations were seemingly arbitrary and confusing.[18]

Concerns about local reception were sensible, for there were reports that the destinations to which students were relocated "had turned sour." The council pointed out Oberlin College in Ohio as an example. "There have been so many unfavorable reactions by narrow-minded community folk reflected or quoted by public officials," an NJASRC letter to the college president wrote, "that we cannot now proceed to relocate students at Oberlin despite the college's favorable attitude." Even though the college leaders, faculty members, and extant students welcomed the Japanese American newcomers, some local residents, especially in the more rural areas, did not.[19]

Once again, stars were aligned for Suzuki. Minnesota was a friendly place for Japanese Americans, with the establishment of the military language school at Camp Savage over the summer and support of agencies like the YMCA and International Institute of St. Paul. Suzuki and the NJASRC were able to quickly gather those community acceptance letters for clearance.

Taking in Suzuki and her four other fellow Nisei, Macalester was among the first three Minnesotan colleges to enroll Japanese American students by September 1942. The other two were St. Mary's School of Nursing in Rochester and Hamline University in St. Paul. Granted, many colleges, like St. Olaf, did accept Nisei students for the fall. However, the delayed permission from the military and FBI prevented their admission on time. Larger institutions would soon follow suit and open their doors, including the University of Minnesota a year later. Maintaining a good reputation and a collegial relationship with the council, the North Star State ultimately became one of the top choices for Nisei students during the war.

That Nason, the chairman of the NJASRC, came from St. Paul might have had something to do with its more favorable impression among NJASRC staff and counselors. Trudy King, a field officer on the West Coast, told a student who had just relocated to Minnesota: "St. Paul seems to be an educated city, as we also know of Hamline [in addition to Macalester], the College of St. Catherine, and the College of St. Thomas. My geography of the country, in fact, is known purely by colleges which will accept Nisei, and, therefore, there are some states about which I know nothing, but Minnesota is not one of them." So, what was the Nisei wartime experience in Minnesotan colleges? How did the schools and the communities cope with the challenges? The next section will look at stories from Macalester, with Suzuki continuing as our guide.[20]

⁓

Suzuki's journey from confinement to college is representative of a familiar story of wartime Nisei students who voyaged to unfamiliar places. "I was born in Portland and had only visited Seattle, so traveling to Minnesota was a great adventure," Suzuki said. "When the conductor announced we were crossing the Mississippi—a big thrill since I had read Mark Twain's books—I became excited and raised the curtain. He loudly ordered me to lower it and asked if I knew there was a blackout. I felt everyone was looking at me as though I were a spy." Upon arriving in St. Paul, she was instructed to complete, as truthfully as she possibly could, the Minnesota Multiphasic Personality Inventory with five hundred questions. She recalled questions like "Do you feel people are out to get you?" and "Do you feel at times that someone is following you?" Her answer to them all was an honest "Yes."[21]

The warmth of college faculty and friends soon melted her anxiety. Suzuki believed her years at Macalester taught her about "human kindness and concern for others." Dr. Milton McLean, a professor of religious studies, was the academic adviser to the five Japanese Americans, including Suzuki. "On Sunday evenings he held open house, and all students were welcome to join his family in a light supper and fellowship." Suzuki was also able to support herself by securing employment through her teachers. She worked at the Macalester Park Publishing Company and typed scripts for drama professor Mary Gwen Owen, whom Suzuki particularly remembered.

Suzuki was the first Nisei to arrive at Macalester in the fall of 1942, but family was always on her mind. One day her youngest sister, Lucy, told her in a letter that the entire family was ill with food poisoning. The sobbing Suzuki caught the attention of Owen, who went out of her office and bought an ice cream cone. "One can't cry and eat ice cream at the same time," said Owen. When Suzuki graduated in June 1946, the drama professor threw a party at her Wisconsin farm for Suzuki and invited her whole family, who had followed her to Minnesota after the camps closed, to the celebration.

Suzuki thrived on campus. She had fond memories of Margaret Doty, the dean of women, who gave the Nisei "free tickets to the symphony, and for graduation, a year's membership in the St. Paul chapter of the American Association of University Women." The Christmas section in the December 1943 issue of the student newspaper *Mac Weekly* featured the happy second-year student. "Dear Santa: Small vivacious Esther Torii, sophomore, loves those cuddly stuffed animals. Says she, 'I'd rather have a stuffed animal than a stuffed shirt.'" As for playing the part of a goodwill ambassador, Suzuki graduated *cum laude* with a major in sociology and minors in Latin and home economics. "I was inducted into Pi Phi Epsilon (National Honor Society), Pi Gamma Mu (National Social Sciences Honor Society) as president, and the Classical Club (for Greek and Latin students) as president," she proudly wrote in her memoir.[22]

Macalester was in the vanguard among Minnesotan higher education institutions that accepted Japanese Americans. The vision of its president, Charles Turck, especially his "internationalist view," contributed to the openness of the college. The atmosphere that Turck "created was more welcoming

Esther Torii Suzuki graduation
photo, Macalester College, 1946.
Courtesy of Macalester College

Esther Torii Suzuki (left) with two friends, *The Mac Yearbook*, 1944. *Courtesy of Macalester College*

of diversity than lots of other places in the country," noted former Macalester president Rosenberg. Certainly, diversity was defined rather differently than how it is understood today. "If we contextualize it for that moment," Rosenberg underscored, "I think he created that climate and those institutional priorities" that were helpful to the Japanese American students on campus.

In the summer of 1942, Macalester was noted as one of the main references for Gustavus Adolphus College in deciding whether to allow Japanese Americans or not. Letters exchanged between Turck and his counterparts, like Coffey at the University of Minnesota, revealed that the action by the school was greatly admired, albeit not necessarily imitated, by others. A total of twenty Nisei students came to Macalester during the war. Not all of them successfully graduated, including Suzuki's husband, George Suzuki, who was drafted shortly after arriving. Her second sister, Eunice Torii, was also accepted to and attended Macalester in 1944 but later transferred to the University of Minnesota when it lifted its restriction.[23]

Acceptance and advocacy had to come not merely down from the top but also up from the ground. Following the leadership of Turck and other progressive faculty, the majority-white students at Macalester took an active part in addressing the plight of the "minorities" on campus. They organized a discussion group in 1943 called the Mac-Intercultural Forum, and for the first meeting invited Harold Mann, head of the state relocation office in Minnesota, to discuss "Is there a future for Japanese Americans in the United States?" Students also contributed more per individual to the World Student Service Fund (WSSF), which offered scholarships for Nisei student resettlement, than students of any other college or university in the nation in 1943. Ethel Ikeda, a Japanese American student, was one of the ten captains in charge of collecting the WSSF funds in 1944.[24]

Peer support, after all, was vital for a positive Japanese American college experience. Judging from the student newspaper and the yearbooks, Nisei students seemed to enjoy rather ordinary college lives even though it was such an extraordinary time. One could find, for instance, Tadashi David Imagawa, student manager of the basketball team, receiving a letter of honor; Ellen Yoshi Okagaki, the house chair of the girl's hall, playing coed football for homecoming because men were away at war; or Suzuki dining in the home of her professor, Dr. Edwin Kagin, who had been a missionary to Korea. When the dormitory was closed for the holidays, Suzuki knew that someone would always invite her to their house. She would not have to be alone.[25]

There was a catch for the Nisei students. As long as the invitation was from people in Minnesota, there was no problem. However, Japanese Americans, as "free" as citizens as they should have been, were not supposed to cross state lines. "The first Thanksgiving I was invited to Eau Claire, Wisconsin, which meant I had to get permission from the U.S. Attorney's office," Suzuki said. A mother of her friend, who felt so badly about the Suzuki family's incarceration, even offered to wash clothes for her. "She did my laundry in a gas operated washing machine with homemade soap, so I smelled clean in all my classes," Suzuki noted. However, the "large oatmeal cookies" that the lovely mother "baked and packed in the laundry box" also smelled like the homemade soap. "But I ate them with relish," she remarked.[26]

Ellen Okagaki (left) plays football with Lois Baldwin (blocker), as Natalee Carlander carries the ball, *The Mac Yearbook*, 1944. *Courtesy of Macalester College*

Similarly, her roommate Jean Oliver cherished their wonderful times together, when diversity was still a novelty at Macalester. Suzuki "came here when she was sixteen," Oliver said, and the college "allowed only five Japanese American students on campus." There were few African Americans at the time. "There couldn't have been more than two or three," she continued. "It was ridiculous. But Esther and I just hit it off." While the campus inside was friendly toward Japanese Americans, the community outside could prove otherwise. Whenever the two friends went to a restaurant in the city, people would come up and ask whether Suzuki was a Chinese. "My dad was about six feet three and he worked in downtown St. Paul," Oliver said; "he'd take us out, and he always walked first so we followed him. Nobody dared say anything."[27]

Still, racism could appear anywhere. Oliver remembered when Suzuki came home with her for Thanksgiving and went to church. "Two people got up and left because she was Japanese. I don't think she ever knew about it." Suzuki noticed no major racist incidents throughout her college years, except for people occasionally praising her: "My, you speak good English." Of course, one might remember the apartment hunting story, in which two Suzuki sisters, Esther and Eunice, finally found one after nearly a hundred calls.[28]

As determined and independent as she was, Suzuki reckoned that "survival would not have been possible without many thoughtful friends." There were new ones in Minnesota and those who were far away in her old hometown. In her first semester at Macalester, Suzuki received a letter with ten dollars enclosed from long-term substitute teacher Margaret Rodman, a Quaker from her high school back in Portland. Having started a full-time job in a small town in Oregon where there was no Friends meeting, the teacher decided to send her tithe for that school year to Suzuki. Her salary was a hundred dollars a month then. "I immediately wrote her a thank you note which she answered immediately," Suzuki recalled, but "she asked that I not put my name on the return address. She expressed concern that she might lose her job if the community discovered her friendship with a Japanese American." Racism was rampant, wreaking havoc on not only people of color but also their allies who dared to help.[29]

Reminiscences of Suzuki's college years were full of bittersweet stories of friends and teachers. Romance was also in the air. Macalester was where she met her future husband. George Suzuki was first released from Minidoka to work at a Mormon beet farm in Idaho, and from there he was accepted by Macalester. While his parents and siblings were still in the camp, he arrived in St. Paul in April 1943.

George Suzuki adapted quickly to Midwestern college life. He was an avid and adroit basketball player, joining the Macalester team in its several victories in the 1943–1944 season. According to Suzuki, her husband "earned his tuition by scrubbing floors for a small restaurant in exchange for meals, cleaning oil drums, chauffeuring, and washing glasses at the University Club, from which he was summarily fired when a Filipino who had seniority objected to a Japanese American working there." The tension was allegedly caused by Imperial Japan's invasion of the Philippines in 1941 and the subsequent occupation until late in the war.[30]

The Suzukis were one of the families that stayed in Minnesota after the war. "George was drafted in 1944 and was accepted into the Military Intelligence Service Language School at Fort Snelling," Suzuki explained. Of all places, he was shipped to the Philippines and then Occupied Japan. The two married in 1946 upon his discharge. He later returned to school and graduated with a business degree from the University of Minnesota in March 1949. The Suzukis decided to call Minnesota home. The couple raised two children and became pillars of the Japanese American community in the state.

Macalester and Minnesota, in many ways, changed Suzuki's life. The Macalester alumna, in turn, also transformed the lives of many others in Minnesota. For twenty-five years, Suzuki devoted her career to helping others, educating the country about the injustice of the incarceration and advocating for human rights. After her children were grown, Suzuki put her passion to use as a social worker, the only one of Asian descent in Ramsey County at the time.

The year was 1975 when the first wave of Southeast Asian immigrants arrived in Minnesota. Besides working with state and federal agencies, Suzuki collaborated with organizations such as the JACL to provide materials, resources, and scholarships for those whose lives had been disrupted by war, including Vietnamese, Hmong, Laotians, and Cambodians. "I was glad that for once I was in the right place at the right time," she said.[31]

Along with Minnesota's acceptance of Southeast Asian immigrants surfaced "racial hatred among a certain segment of society," Suzuki recounted of the days in the 1970s. "Since I was easily mistaken for a Southeast Asian, one co-worker jokingly said that he would be my bodyguard, but later suggested I wear a T-shirt saying, 'I am a Japanese American.'" The only problem then was not "going near the Ford plant in that outfit." Perhaps every joke has some truth to it. Her friend's funny remarks, unfortunately, turned into a sad racist story a few years later—the murder of Vincent Chin by two white Michigander autoworkers in 1982.

Suzuki knew very well that America needed to face its own past demons in order to find peace in the future. History must be understood critically, considering different voices and angles. She learned over the years that "storytelling" was important, but it had to be done the right way. "People don't like to hear a sob sister," Suzuki explained in her last interview in 1999. Ever since she first came to Macalester, she had been asked to give talks about her experience. "I would go to these churches and say, 'This internment is unconstitutional,' and I would tell the truth about it. Everyone in the audience, especially older church women, would tell me, 'My dear, you must realize this is wartime.' They would either justify it, or they would get defensive. I used to cry on the way home after I gave these talks."[32]

Tears alone would not transform apathy to empathy. The older Suzuki was wiser. "Obliquely" was how she learned to get her message across. "I decided that I must let people know what happened, but I cannot try to guilt anybody because no one will accept that, so I made it more palatable. I'll tell these little stories. There is a point to every story, but I don't come right out and say it."[33]

Even in difficult situations, Suzuki never lost her sense of humor and her belief in social justice. "One person can make a difference, and whenever someone is trampling on another's rights, I speak up." And she did, for the rights of women, refugees, gays and lesbians, and ethnic minority groups. When the Ordway Theater in St. Paul decided to stage *Miss Saigon* in 1994, Suzuki was on the front lines of the protests, along with other Asian Americans who believed the show perpetuates harmful stereotypes—"a demeaning portrayal of Asian women as light-brained, sub-servient inferiors."[34]

"Macalester was a haven in a world of madness," Suzuki concluded. "It will take the rest of my life to pay back into the vast well of human kindness that I found at Macalester." Many would agree that she did more than her fair share. Suzuki conjures loving memories of a gentle talent and a self-evidently genuine woman in the minds of many Minnesotans. She passed away in 1999, from complications of heart problems.[35]

Suzuki was a unique individual, yet her experiences were far from uncommon. Being an outspoken and outgoing person, Suzuki was only more open to sharing her stories. Others chose to bear their pain and bury the past in silence, although the injustice they suffered should never be forgotten. The play *Internment Voices*, which debuted in the summer of 1998 at Theater Mu in South Minneapolis, illustrated the dilemma. Based on Suzuki's autobiography and cowritten by her and David Mura, it told of the emotional struggle of coping with the legacy of the incarceration through two elderly Japanese American sisters, as one forces the other to face up to the true damage of the trauma.[36]

There were many *"shikata ga nai"*—cannot be helped—stories that took place on the various campuses across Minnesota. Macalester was just one of the twenty-five higher education institutions that accepted Japanese American students amid the wartime frenzy. The remainder of the chapter will look at the broader situation of young Nisei in Minnesota, and the individuals who were sympathetic to and supportive of them. Let's start with representatives from three Lutheran colleges—Augsburg, Gustavus Adolphus, and St. Olaf.

Joseph Tobey Seto was one of the first two Nisei students to attend Augsburg College (now Augsburg University) in Minneapolis. "I have found the people of Minnesota very friendly," the first-year student told his school newspaper in March 1944. "Some people have been afraid to ask questions, thinking they would hurt our feelings. However, I would rather have the students know about evacuation and the Nisei problems."[37]

Augsburg actually received inquiries about accepting Japanese American students back in the fall of 1942, although approval from the Army and Navy came only in July 1943. Reverend Fredrik A. Schiotz of the American Lutheran Conference had contacted the school about three non-incarcerees—Jeanne Namba, Shizue Murashige, and Nora Maehara, who were not from the restricted zone—regarding Augsburg's ability to accommodate them in September 1942. The college was not yet cleared by the military then. Those students ended up attending the University of Nebraska–Lincoln.[38]

Responding to the NJASRC, Augsburg sent its catalogue to the council in November for potential resettlement. Seto was one of the Nisei whose dossier the council reviewed and recommended to Augsburg. Seto's "grades are not high, but his letters of reference make us feel that we ought to help him go on to college," the interim director of the council wrote on May 11, 1943. "Since he is already in Minneapolis, he will be able to enter your college at any time without going through the usual governmental procedures, which he has already fulfilled."[39]

Born in Tacoma, Washington, Seto shared a similar background with Suzuki and many other Japanese American college students at the time. Shortly after graduating from Lincoln High School in the spring of 1942, Seto and his family were removed to Fresno and later transferred to Tule Lake. Like George Suzuki, Seto was released from the camp to work in beet fields; his assignment was in Montana. In January 1943, he arrived in Minneapolis, joining his two older brothers, Paul and Hugh, who were already working in the city. "Paul went to the University of Michigan, but then he couldn't enroll. So, he went to Minneapolis hoping to get into the University of Minnesota, but he encountered the same problem," Seto recalled. "He got a job as a busboy at a restaurant, together with my brother Hugh."[40]

The young Seto had dreams larger than clearing tables and filling glasses. "Here I was an eighteen-year-old, never been away from home, but I had to support myself completely with low-paying jobs," he remarked. "I realized I wasn't accomplishing much, so while working as a busboy, I attended Central High School as a special student. I took academic courses which I should have taken when I was in high school, [but] I was so involved in athletics. I enrolled at Augsburg College, a Lutheran college, because the University [of Minnesota] would not allow me to enroll. And the church colleges were very receptive and helpful."

Seto was an active student during his one-year career at Augsburg. He was a chemistry major and a math minor. His focus, however, was on the basketball court rather than the classroom. He played basketball for the college from February of 1944 through the end of the season in 1945. He also coached the off-campus team in the girls' tournament. In the summer of

1945, the sophomore was drafted. Seto first went to Texas for training, and in August when the war ended, he was transferred back to Minnesota to attend the MISLS at Fort Snelling. "My Japanese was not proficient enough, so I was relegated to an administrative job," Seto said. "Then we moved to Monterey, California, which is wonderful."[41]

During the war, Augsburg accepted three but hosted two Japanese American students. The other was John Satoshi Oshida, who was "a favorite coach among coed basketeers and an outstanding player on the varsity." Oshida had already attended one semester at the University of California, Berkeley, when the war broke out. His college life was short-lived due to the forced removal order. From May to September 1942, Oshida's home was a horse stable at the Tanforan Assembly Center at San Bruno, and then he was sent to Topaz.[42]

Like Seto, Oshida's two older siblings were released for employment in Minnesota—his brother Akira at Camp Savage and his sister Mireko working for a family in Hopkins. He was permitted to leave Topaz in October 1943 and started at Augsburg in February 1944. When asked about his future plans by the school newspaper, Seto teasingly replied on his friend's behalf: "He'll probably end up in a psychopathic ward!" Oshida was a pre-med student and wanted to specialize in psychiatry. Shortly after, he transferred to the University of Minnesota. Although neither Seto nor Oshida graduated from Augsburg, they recognized the friendliness of the campus and felt that "as a small school it offers something which a larger college could not give."[43]

Augsburg was one of the five schools from which Gustavus Adolphus College in St. Peter sought advice on accepting Japanese American students. The other four were Carleton, Hamline, Macalester, and St. Olaf. Being the oldest Lutheran college in Minnesota, Gustavus provided an interesting case to examine the Nisei resettlement. In particular, there was a gap in enthusiasm or confidence between the students and leadership concerning the issue; the driving force behind the wartime Nisei enrollment appeared to come from below rather than above.

The students were quite excited about the arrival of their Japanese American fellows, and the Student Missionary Society was designated in the early summer of 1942 as the campus organization to coordinate the sponsorship.

Donald Wilson of the Society, a senior who was due to work at the Lutheran Theological Seminary in Pennsylvania, even wrote to the NJASRC directly in August 1942. "As a former classmate of the Nisei in Sacramento both in public and Japanese language schools for seven years," Wilson declared, "[and] certainly as Christians and as fellow Americans, we cannot let them down!" He continued to ask the council the likelihood of immediately having Japanese American students, if the school board decided in favor of doing so in their September meeting.[44]

Another student advocate for the Nisei, George Lindbeck, who later became an eminent Lutheran theologian, also reached out to the NJASRC over that summer. He wrote to the council that the college president Walter A. Lunden had spoken with alumni and students about how the administration would admit Japanese American students if a "sufficient number of sister colleges pursue a similar course of action." He iterated: "In short, the administration, although well-meaning, is excessively timid and needs a great deal of 'bandwagon' support. This can be supplied by showing the responsible individuals in black and white that such action is not as unprecedented as they imagine. At present they are not convinced that any college in this general area are admitting Nisei evacuees." The sister colleges that Lunden referred to were the four aforesaid schools, which the president would go on to contact. Lindbeck also mentioned that "a minimum of a two-hundred dollars scholarship, funded by the Lutheran Student Association of America, could be awarded to an incoming student who intended to enter Christian service."[45]

The council replied to both Wilson and Lindbeck with similar encouraging notes. The national director of the NJASRC claimed that nearly all institutions on the list demonstrated willingness to accept Japanese Americans, and that three Minnesotan colleges—Hamline, Macalester, and St. Mary's School of Nursing in Rochester—had already initiated admission. Surely, financial assistance was much appreciated. Given that it was already September, Barstow cautioned that it might be too late to send a student for fall semester but he believed with the right procedure the relocation should go through.[46]

The leadership of Gustavus reacted positively, with a condition notwithstanding. The Board of Directors met in early September and passed a

677 University Avenue
St. Paul, Minnesota
August 24, 1942

President
St. Olaf College
Northfield, Minn.

Dear Sir:

Contacts with young Americans of Japanese ancestry have
aroused the interest of a group of Lutheran Twin City students (of
whom I am one) in their plight, and that of their fellows. As you
know, most universities have pursued the policy of the University
of Minnesota in denying admission to Japanese-Americans. It would
therefore seem that the responsibility of enabling these fellow
citizens to continue their education devolves upon smaller institutions. Feeling this to be the case, we would like to know what
colleges in the North West are opening their doors to them. Information on your college's policy in this matter would be greatly
appreciated. Do you admit loyal Japanese-Americans, and, if you do,
on what basis?

Some evacuee students are capable of financing their own
education, but there are many, of course, who will require considerable aid. Is your college making any provision for part-time work,
or any other form of assistance for these students? Will they be a
accorded the same treatment as other students, or do you anticipate
special difficulties in finding employment for them in the college
and community?

Your answers to these questions will be considered confidential. Our purpose is not to publicize the information we receive, but simply to use it for the benefit of loyal Japanese-
Americans.

The opening of school is rapidly approaching, so we would
greatly appreciate an immediate answer.

Yours truly,

George Lindbeck

George Lindbeck

Letter from George Lindbeck, member of the Lutheran Twin Cities student
group, to St. Olaf College inquiring about its stand on accepting Nisei, dated
August 24, 1942. *Courtesy of St. Olaf College*

resolution permitting Nisei students to enroll, provided that there were at least four. They believed that "one or two Japanese American students might feel somewhat isolated." Four sounded like a good number. While scholarship assistance from the college would not be available, the campus, faculty, and community were still favorable toward receiving Japanese American students. As soon as the necessary arrangements were completed, Gustavus was ready to welcome Nisei students.[47]

The minimum requirement of four ended up hampering NJASRC's recruitment. At that moment, the council could identify only three students interested in attending a liberal arts institution: Helen Haruyo Ogata, Larry Keiso Orida, and Arthur Akitaru Noma. Lacking one student, the council called on the United Lutheran Church for assistance. The hope was that these three students could be admitted to Gustavus for the second term. The school did accept them, but no one arrived in time for the spring 1943 semester due to the logjam in security clearances.[48]

In the meantime, a different Nisei question was presented to Gustavus. Two Japanese Americans, Masako Pat Kato and Akiko Penny Kato, sisters from Denver, Colorado, applied to the college, which caused some confusion. Since the Katos came from a non–military restricted zone, they did not fall under the jurisdiction of the WRA and its resettlement program. Gustavus, therefore, sent a letter to the NJASRC asking whether there was a difference in desirability between "non-evacuees and evacuees." The council responded that no systemic check was performed on those who were out of the "evacuation" area. "In general, it is assumed that these are all loyal fully accredited Americans," the letter stated. There was also a third student, Mariko Kitagawa from Manzanar, who sent in her application on her own, independent of the NJASRC. Gustavus eventually accepted all three young women.[49]

More complications were on the way, however. In January 1944, the NJASRC informed Gustavus that it had been taken off the list of approved institutions and was now categorized as a "proscribed" college. Apart from military and FBI approvals, it now needed an additional clearance from the provost marshal general before letting Nisei attend. The reason behind the change of status was unclear; it might have had to do with a unit from the Navy taking an academic refresher course on campus. Some members of the military might be on campus, but how it was related to national security was anybody's guess. What became clear was its impeding effect on the college's ability to take in Japanese American students. More bureaucratic procedures entailed lengthier waits and increased the risk of rejection.[50]

By the end of the year, five Nisei showed up on the St. Peter campus of Gustavus. There were the two Kato sisters and Kitagawa, Arthur Noma from the initial group of three, and another student named Toshiko Nishioki. Unfortunately, the Kato sisters experienced some setbacks. They were deemed ineligible for the financial aid under the United Lutheran Church's grant because they were not "evacuees." The sisters forged onward nonetheless. They were seen singing "Jesus Loves You" in both English and Japanese for the Christmas party in December 1943 and giving a "talk on prayer, relating to the rude awakening of the reality" in June of 1944. Noma joined the Army after one semester on July 27, 1944, and shifted to Fort Snelling, and one of the original three students who were interested in the college, Helen Ogata, did not go to Gustavus but went to St. Olaf instead.[51]

Also affiliated with the Evangelical Lutheran Church, St. Olaf was another college that Gustavus considered as a reference in the Nisei students' matter. Like other inland colleges and universities, the NJASRC had solicited St. Olaf's commitment to accommodating Japanese American students in the summer of 1942. Not only the council but also the American Lutheran Conference had beaten the drum quite passionately in support of the Nisei resettlement, as in the previous case with Augsburg. Perhaps because its leader Schiotz was a St. Olaf alumnus himself, or perhaps due to his Norwegian Lutheran heritage, the church's advocacy was strongly felt at his alma mater.

Writing to the Acting President J. Jörgen Thompson in August 1942, Schiotz confirmed the "acceptances from several of the church colleges in the American Lutheran Conference," but thus far no affirmative replies had come from Norwegian Lutheran Church of America (NLCA) institutions. He was eager to see one of his own Lutheran colleges helping with this cause. "At Gustavus Adolphus," he said, "the students took the matter up last spring and voluntarily raised enough money to help one student through college. It is almost assured that this effort will be extended to make it possible for two students to be taken care of during this coming year." Amplifying his plea, Schiotz concluded, "the possibility of placing Nisei students on church college campuses in the United States appears to offer not only an exceptional missionary opportunity, but also the possibility of avoiding real afterwar complications for these unfortunate American citizens."[52]

The verdict did not take long at St. Olaf. Thompson announced in late August that the administration had decided unanimously to permit American citizens of Japanese ancestry to attend on the same conditions as all other students, providing their registration was sanctioned by the War Department and the NJASRC. However, the college was in a position neither to make any provision for special part-time work nor to allow any cancellation of fees or tuition payments; otherwise applications from the Nisei would be treated in the regular manner. Accordingly, St. Olaf became "the first of the NLCA institutions of higher learning to offer the privilege of matriculation to Nisei students." On November 9, 1942, the approval from the Army and Navy came through for the college. The process of admitting Japanese American students commenced.[53]

There was one individual in Tule Lake the Lutheran Church already had in mind to recommend to St. Olaf. Her name was Mary Harue Hayano. Before the military clearance even came through, Schiotz had written to the school in October to introduce the candidate. "Hayano is a Nisei girl who is known by Rev. O.E. Hemdahl of Mt. Vernon, Washington, one of our pastors. As I understand it, she virtually counts herself as a girl of the Norwegian Lutheran Church. She has now been cleared by the National Student Relocation Council . . . and the Board of American Missions of the United Lutheran Church . . . has recommended that Miss Hayano be assigned to St. Olaf."[54]

In order to speed up the course of action, Schiotz urged the college administrator to seek a statement from several Northfield residents and civic officials giving assurance that there would be community acceptance for Hayano. Thompson's reply to his Lutheran colleagues showed optimism. "In sounding out representative students I do not sense any tendency towards criticism or a negative feeling developing towards this girl if she decides to come," he answered.[55]

That was how Hayano became the first Japanese American student at St. Olaf. Knowing more about the upbringing of the Hayanos could surely help elucidate why the Nisei student practically considered herself "a girl of the Norwegian Lutheran Church," and was thus quickly accepted. Born in Mount Vernon, Washington, Hayano was eighteen years old when she came to Minnesota. Her family story resembled many of those from other Nisei students, like Suzuki and Seto earlier. The Hayanos ran a potato farm in rural Mount Vernon and sold their crops mainly to the US Army mess hall. They had seven children, four sons and three daughters. The youngest one was Hannah Semba, who already appeared in previous chapters. Mary Hayano was two years older than Semba.

The family could claim to be a successful case of assimilation. They spoke English at home and socialized with mostly white neighbors and friends. "We were the only Japanese in town," Semba said of her childhood; "I knew I had never played with any other Japanese." The Hayano sisters were also baptized and went through confirmation as Lutherans. Both of them were attending Mount Vernon High School when the Pacific War erupted. Recalling the day of her forced removal, Semba remarked: "We got on the train, and here are all the dark-haired people that I'd never seen, never knew existed. And then the fellows who were watching [or guarding] us were all Caucasians."

Incarceration might have deferred Hayano's college plans, but it never deterred Hayano's resolve to attend. "I don't know how," Semba remembered, "but she got the results from our high school and then applied to go to St. Olaf. And she was accepted." Like Suzuki, Hayano was able to graduate from high school but was forbidden to attend the graduation ceremony. In Tule Lake, Hayano reached out to the Lutheran Church and NJASRC for assistance to put her dossier together. She was admitted to St. Olaf on September 28, 1942, although her FBI clearance did not come through until four months later.[56]

Hayano began her life as an "Ole" on January 31, 1943. It was a Sunday. The next morning, she officially registered, planning to major in home economics. There was one other Japanese American student, Mayme Shizuyo Kishi from Camp Amache at Granada, who started with Hayano at the same time. Already a graduate from San Jose State College, Kishi knew that St. Olaf did not offer a master's program but still wanted to study choral work there, with the hope of attending Juilliard. She was classified as a special student taking courses in the field of music and then moved to Boston a year later. The registrar of St. Olaf told NJASRC that the school would be happy to accept more Nisei students, granted that they could obtain clearance. "We had two Japanese American girls here during the second semester of the school year, and we found that they were excellent students and good citizens in every way."[57]

Three more female incarcerees joined Hayano and Kishi in the subsequent academic year. They were Helen Yukiko Kinoshita from Minidoka, Yoshino Elaine Uyemura from Gila River, and Yuki Takei from Heart Mountain. The dean of women, Gertrude Hilleboe, in writing about Takei, said: "We are very fond of Yuki as we are of all the Japanese American girls who are with us. They are working hard and trying to make good academically. All of them are finding that their academic duties keep them very busy."[58]

More Nisei students were coming, but a quandary comparable to that of Gustavus's took place in 1944. The US Naval Flight Preparatory School held classes at St. Olaf at least through the opening month or two of that school year. Even though the college was previously not "deemed important for the war effort," additional "PMG clearance of students" was needed. One more layer of red tape in Washington delayed five newly admitted Nisei. Three of them finally cleared the hurdles and arrived in time for the 1944 fall semester, including Esther Nagao, Paul Seigo Sugino, and the one who appeared at the very beginning of this book, Yoshiteru "Yosh" Murakami. The *History of St. Olaf College* recorded that two "revered traditions" were broken in the year of 1944 "when the price of a coke went up to eight cents and when jovial Yosh Murakami, of Japanese ancestry, became a member of the St. Olaf choir." Murakami's unprecedented participation in the choir as a Nisei seemed like a more welcome sign of change than the rising cost of a soft drink. He would spend two years at the college before enlistment.[59]

The wartime college life of these Japanese Americans, at least in the relatively secluded, hilly campus, was not that different from more peaceful eras. As this first group of Nisei were carefully picked and screened to serve as "goodwill ambassadors," delinquency was probably not in their character and definitely not in their interest. The war did make its presence felt, however. Since almost all young men were drafted in those war years, including Murakami, Joseph Seto, Arthur Noma, and George Suzuki, there were far

Yosh Murakami (second left) with classmates Louise Ekstam (left), John Colberg (middle), and Milton Christensen (right), Viking Yearbook, 1946. *Courtesy of St. Olaf College*

more female students, and they were often perceived to be more docile and obedient than the young men. Covering life on campus, Hayano wrote in one of her letters in the fall of 1943 that the enrollment of colleges overall in the country "must be rather small with the men going into service. In St. Olaf, we have 570 some girls to 96 boys; we feel fortunate in having as many . . . at this time."[60]

Faculty and staff were impacted, too. "Today [September 13, 1943] was registration day for most of us," Hayano stated, "and it was a difficult task arranging for the desired courses with preference to certain professors. It seems that St. Olaf has lost a number of its most competent instructors, either through death or deployment." St. Olaf was only one of the many higher education institutions that encountered such problems. It had been hectic for all American colleges and universities since Pearl Harbor. For example, the University of Pennsylvania saw the departure of more than one hundred faculty members and administrative officers for government service, and enrollment declined at least one-fifth in the 1942–1943 academic year.[61]

Mary Hayano (left, second row from front) was the only Nisei student in this group of first-year students, Viking Yearbook, 1944. *Courtesy of St. Olaf College*

The show had to go on, even if times were tough. As far as can be told from school newspapers, yearbooks, and personal letters, the Nisei all shared youthful and cheerful spirits. They played sports, hung out with friends, sang in the choir, and studied for exams. The Lutheran campus was evidently hospitable and inclusive to this first group of Japanese American students.

Still, it was in no way completely free of bigotry. One of the chapel sermons in March 1944 revealed something truthful, though not quite beautiful, about the time. "Race prejudice and hatred, class distrust and strife are rampant in our land, which is supposed to be a haven for the oppressed," the speaker contended. "Even on our own campus, students echo the intolerance against such groups as the Japanese, the [African Americans], and the Jewish people. Closer to home than that, among ourselves, the moment someone is different, ill-dressed, or lonely, we say he is 'queer' or 'corny.' Plenty of room for the leaven of Christ here." The message was aimed at a hysterical world at war then, yet it remains uncannily relevant today.[62]

While the Japanese Americans' experiences at St. Olaf resonated with their counterparts at Augsburg, Gustavus, and Macalester, Hayano and her Nisei classmates were able to illuminate a lesser-discussed part of wartime student life. How did the students living outside the Twin Cities support themselves financially? Scholarships eased some of the burden but could not cover all expenses. The average cost of college in the 1940s, including room and board, was several hundred dollars annually. Whereas the United Lutheran Church in America offered the newly admitted Helen Kinoshita a scholarship for $260, the WSSF could send only $67.50 for Esther Nagao. Furthermore, most of these checks arrived quite late due to bureaucracies. The college thus needed to allow for the students to postpone payment while attending school. The NJASRC recognized the efforts by St. Olaf, which had "always been most kind to these young Americans of Japanese ancestry."[63]

Many Nisei students struggled with financial uncertainties. How they could make ends meet, considering they came from camps with at best minimal support from their families, was a concern. Hilleboe, the dean of women, told the council that "the average amount earned by students is about $100 per year. A very few who are skilled stenographers, especially strong students, and who can put in more hours, do earn up to $150 or even $200, but those cases are very rare." Besides on-campus employment, it would be reasonable to imagine a student working off campus in an office job, like Esther Suzuki in the publishing house, or cleaning floors and washing dishes at a restaurant like her husband. Yet such opportunities were easier to find in the Twin Cities and scarcer in rural areas. Even fewer positions considered appropriate for women were available.[64]

One option was performing domestic help, which occasionally included room and board. In the case of St. Olaf, a good number of students lived in private homes, because there was not enough residence space to accommodate nearly six hundred female students. About half of them lived in the dormitory on campus and the rest stayed in houses nearby. Since Northfield was a small town, most people did their own household chores. Four places allowed working for room and board, although it was difficult to do so while adjusting and carrying a full course load. Hayano was one of the students in that situation.[65]

Most of the students could afford to work full time only during school breaks without sacrificing their good academic standing. In the summer of 1943, Hayano was hired as "help" in the home of Mrs. L. D. Stiefel, a volunteer at the Minneapolis WRA office with whom she had established a collegial relationship. In later personal exchanges, Hayano would share her family updates with her former employer—such as the relocation of her family from Tule Lake to Heart Mountain and an accident involving her brother in an incarceration farm that led to the amputation of his right leg.[66]

Equipped with a wonderful working record and recommendation, Hayano secured another room-and-board arrangement in the fall of 1943, this time with the Fossum family in Northfield. It must not have been an easy job. "A girl who is a very strong student academically and who is willing to forgo participation in extracurricular activities, except on a very limited scale, is able to meet her academic demands and also do the amount of work that is necessary for both room and board," the dean of women explained.[67]

In a letter to her old boss Mrs. Stiefel in Minneapolis, Hayano described her new home: "Mrs. Fossum appears to be a fine woman, and I'm inclined to think my work will not be too heavy. There are three boys, [. . . and] the two younger children are so lively that I'll undoubtedly have a handful trying to keep them out of mischief." Hayano continued: "My work, as I understand it now, includes preparing the noon dinner [Monday through Friday] and whatever is necessary two afternoons a week. I presume this will be dusting and occasional ironing. With my program of sixteen hours plus this part-time work, my days will be quite full."[68]

Another student, Yuki Takei, was less fortunate at first. She was unable to earn room and board right away like Hayano. Takei had worked at a defense plant in the fall of 1943 to save up for college expenses, but she still owed the school fifty-one dollars. Takei was already employed for five days a week in the campus administration office, receiving forty cents per hour, or two dollars each week. Devoting entire weekend afternoons to work off campus was all Takei could do, which at most added up to about thirty dollars. She felt that she could not depend on her family for financial help as they were already in a dire economic situation. The dean estimated an aid of fifty dollars would take care of her needs and advised Takei not to work more than the current amount.[69]

Seeking funds for the Nisei student, Hilleboe wrote to many agencies in hope of assistance. "Yuki is working hard. It is not easy to make an adjustment to college in the middle of the year," the dean asserted; "by the end of the semester she will be able to do a stronger type of work than was possible in the very beginning. She is a lovely girl, and we enjoy having her here very much." Luckily, her efforts were successful. The NJASRC granted Takei a $100 scholarship from the Hattie M. Strong Foundation, and $275 for the coming academic year through the WSSF. As a result, Takei could carry on with her college career, smiling for pictures in both the 1945 and 1946 Viking Yearbooks.[70]

In total, eleven Nisei enrolled in St. Olaf during the war years. Before the NJASRC closed in 1946, St. Olaf sent a letter to the council and affirmed its support for the Nisei: "We welcome Japanese American students. We have had several of them here [in] the past three or four years and they have established a good record both in scholarship and in relation to students and faculty"[71]

Not all of the wartime students stayed, and only a handful graduated. Those who quit departed for a variety of reasons. Mie Helen Oshima was a twenty-five-year-old nursing student who came to Northfield for the 1944 spring term. She left after just one week. "She had been out of school for some two years," the dean of women said. "[Oshima] believed and felt herself quite lost when she tried to take up her academic work again. I think if she had stuck it out a little longer she would have found that she could make the adjustment." Hilleboe later received "a very lovely letter" from Oshima, stating that she "is in Minneapolis, has a job, and is also doing some studying." Although Oshima said her goal was to return to St. Olaf in the fall, she did not. Maybe her priorities had changed. In late summer 1944, Oshima married a Japanese American soldier attending the military language school at Camp Savage.[72]

Obviously, conscription interrupted the studies of many male college students. Murakami was a sophomore when he was called for duty in 1946. After two years as a military interpreter in Occupied Japan, where he met his future wife, Mikiko Anzai, he returned to St. Olaf in 1948. During his junior year, he broke another tradition as the first non-white director of the Viking Male Chorus.

The year 1951 was celebratory for Murakami thanks to two occasions: The veteran graduated from college with a bachelor's degree in music. He also brought his fiancée to America through a special bill introduced in Congress by Minnesota Senator Edward John Thye and signed by President Harry S. Truman, which made the young couple quite famous. After their wedding in Denver, the Murakamis settled down in Northfield, where their four children were born. "We were all given very American names, Paul, Stephen, Jane and Jonathan," his daughter Jane Murakami said. "We grew up pretty much not having any Japanese culture, because of the timing and everything." There were even jokes about them being more Norwegian than Japanese.[73]

Murakami accepted the music faculty position at Northfield High School upon his graduation and soon made a name for himself as an excellent music instructor and choral conductor. "At the time he was hired, it was still close enough to the end of the war that there was considerable resistance to anything Japanese," the high school music director Paul Stoughton remembered. None of this dampened the enthusiasm for the Nisei teacher. "Students very quickly learned to value him as a human being and not as a member of a particular race." Murakami later served as the vice president of the Minnesota Music Educators Association in the 1950s and led the Northfield High School Choir to win top rating at the Minnesota Centennial State Fair in September 1958. In 1968, he was invited to join Concordia College at Moorhead and also to be the music director at Trinity Lutheran Church there. He then worked for the Fargo public schools from 1971 until his untimely death four years later.[74]

Still, Northfield remained special in the family history. Murakami's farewell performance in May 1968, the annual high school pop concert in Northfield, attracted broad public coverage. It was aired by WCAL local radio, and the concert also contained a heartfelt surprise gift from all 240 members of his various school choirs. Conspiring secretly with his wife, every student had chipped in a few dollars to fly in Murakami's parents from California to see their son, whom they had not seen for six years. There was not a dry eye in the hall when the magical reunion happened on stage. The columnist Oliver Towne, the pseudonym used by the newspaperman Gareth D. Hiebert, even picked up the touching story for the *St. Paul Pioneer Press and Dispatch*.[75]

Northfield remembered the wartime Nisei student turned educator with much affection and admiration, but he was not the only Japanese American student to become a beloved local figure. The town is home to two liberal arts colleges: across the river from St. Olaf is Carleton. It should be noted that

Carleton was also on the list of schools to which the Gustavus administers looked for guidance in August 1942 on whether to open their campus to Japanese Americans. There were, altogether, nineteen Nisei students enrolled in Carleton during the war years, making it one of the most accommodative liberal arts institutions for Japanese Americans in Minnesota. Many of their stories are poignant and powerful. It will thus be appropriate to conclude this chapter on Nisei college students on this side of Northfield, before shifting to the narratives of the young soldiers, nurses, workers, and other adventurers in subsequent chapters.

The story of Carleton's most famous Nisei student during the war is one of heartbreak, honor, and hope. His name was Frank Masao Shigemura. He was the first Japanese American enrolled in the Northfield college. The background story of Shigemura, not surprisingly, is a familiar one. Born in Seattle, he was the only son of Takejuro Shigemura, an Issei who immigrated to the United States in 1906 in search of a better life. His mother, Kay Kono Shigemura, was an American from Bainbridge Island in Washington. He had one older sister, Shigeno, who died at age sixteen in 1931. Shigemura graduated from Broadway High School in 1941 and immediately started at the University of Washington that fall, majoring in economics and business administration.

The first-year student's narrative then followed the common arc after Pearl Harbor. The family of three was sent to Minidoka. The young Shigemura, however, did not lose sight of college. With the help of the NJASRC, he applied to and was accepted by Carleton. The council highly recommended the Nisei student, affirming that he ranked "in the highest ten percent on basis of scholastic performance and personal qualities." In October 1942, he bid farewell to his parents behind the barbed fences and set off for Minnesota, a state where he had never been, to continue his college dream.[76]

Carleton was ready to embrace Shigemura and other Nisei students from the start. President Donald J. Cowling, a family friend of Nason, quickly took in Shigemura, who resumed his career there as a sophomore in the fall of 1942. Even though the Seattle native was the sole Japanese American on campus at that time, five other Nisei men would join him by the end of the academic year. Earlier in the summer, Cowling responded to the NJASRC and indicated his plan to take in around six students, with at least half of them being male, for the upcoming fall term. Scholarships of $150 for each student were available, since there had been six Chinese students who all received comparable financial support the previous year. The arrangement would be considered fair to everyone, although neither reduced tuition nor part-time work was an option. Cowling further wrote to the council, confirming that Northfield was gauged to have no local prejudice and that the campus opinion toward Japanese Americans was "favorable for the most part."[77]

The NJASRC took note of the college's preference for male students as the council launched its outreach. At the end of July, Carleton revised their request to wanting only men, because all the women's dormitories had been filled due to high enrollment of female students. The school simply could not accommodate more women. The NJASRC promised that as soon as the military ratified Carleton's status, six Nisei men would be ready to leave for Northfield. The military's approval was based on filed cases. For Carleton to be cleared by the government, it had to accept a student first. On August 26, 1942, Shigemura was promptly admitted to Carleton.[78]

Frank Shigemura, Carleton College, 1944. *Courtesy of Carleton College*

Once again, the authorization process was slow. Carleton finally received the green light on September 30, after the fall semester had commenced. The NJASRC, therefore, advised the six students to hold out until the next term. Yet the council had already contacted Shigemura with a leave permit, and the enthusiastic young man started his journey to the North Star State right away. He reached Carleton on October 12, 1942, despite it being fairly late in the semester. The other five Japanese American men were set to arrive for the second semester beginning February 1, 1943. They were Aiji Esaki from Poston, Hiroshi Eguchi and John Takao Yoshida from Minidoka, and Roy Shinichi Hamaji and Woodrow Odanaka from Granada.[79]

Most of these Nisei students fulfilled the roles of goodwill ambassadors effortlessly. They were exemplary scholars with excellent academic achievements as well as exceptional members of sports like basketball, baseball, and track and field. "Each of [them] is proving himself a good citizen and a satisfactory student. We are more than pleased with the group that has been sent to us," the assistant to the president, Robert E. Allen, wrote to the NJASRC in early April 1943; "and as a result President Cowling and I have decided to admit six more Japanese American students next year."[80]

Hamaji, for example, was said to be "making a splendid record at Carleton, and it would be unfortunate if he were not able to complete his work here." Allen later told the council in July 1943: "Last semester he made a straight 'A' record with us, which is indeed unusual. He seems to be doing the same caliber of work in the summer session." Hence, Carleton offered him a scholarship which amounted to $180, or half of the tuition, and would also give him a part-time job for board.[81]

However, there was one "outlier" in the group. Aiji Esaki, who came to Carleton in February 1943, appeared to be a problematic individual and had a rather poor academic record. Specifically, he drew the ire of a history instructor, Mildred D. Babcock, by "reading a newspaper through the entire lecture" and not taking notes in class; his reason was being "too sleepy to study." The instructor concluded that Esaki "is getting nothing out of college, and he very definitely is making no contribution" to the school. Moreover, Esaki was accused of stealing money from a classmate, a charge that he denied. Regardless of all these unfortunate incidents, Dean of College Lindsey Blayney never framed Esaki's plight in relation to other Nisei students. He even gave Esaki second chances contingent upon his apologizing and repaying the aggrieved victims.[82]

His fellow Japanese American classmates were less forgiving of the black sheep of the family. They worried about the potential harm Esaki might bring to them as a group. According to Blayney, other Nisei students had come to him and "deplored the impression that this young man was making in this region." Esaki eventually withdrew in October 1944. Blayney was conscious of how other institutions would view Esaki as well as the larger Japanese American community. Blayney thus went out of his way to send the School of Business Administration at the University of Minnesota a series of letters urging their denial of Esaki's admission based on his past indiscretions, namely his "dishonesty" and lack of "fundamental ideals of integrity." Perhaps Esaki was a troubled soul to begin with, or he was not meant for college, which perhaps would not have been too unusual given the demands of higher education and the tension of the war.[83]

The first cohort of Nisei men at Carleton, with the exception of Esaki, upheld the positive image of Japanese Americans in general, paving the way for their fellow citizens in camps to leave imprisonment. More students arrived in Northfield before the war ended, such as Hiroshi Henry Goto, Minoru Corky Matsumoto, and Saylo Seiro Munemitsu from Poston in 1943, and even female students like Jean Hanako Akita and Louise Hana Yamazaki from Tule Lake in 1944. In correspondence between the Council for Social Action and the administrations of five Congregational colleges in August of 1944, Carleton proclaimed: "For the past two years we have averaged twelve or thirteen Japanese students on the campus each year and have found them loyal, good students, and good citizens of the community. The local chapter of the American Legion joins with [us] each year in the Community Dinner in which all foreign students including the Japanese, are honored."[84]

One unique fact about Carleton was that it also welcomed an international student from Japan to its campus. Kiyoaki Murata was studying in San Francisco when the war set the mass incarceration in motion. He was imprisoned in Poston with the Japanese Americans for about six months before he could attend Carleton in the fall of 1944. He graduated two years later in 1946. After receiving his master's degree from the University of Chicago,

Murata returned to Japan in 1948. He later became the managing editor of *The Japan Times*. Nearly four decades later, he revisited Carleton to speak at the 1984 commencement.[85]

Whether they were Japanese nationals or American citizens, the northern campus might have sheltered them from the chaos of the outside world for a while but not for long. The war would ultimately catch up with them. For a year and a half, Shigemura spent his time like any other student. Along with his friends, the first Nisei in Carleton took classes in economics, mathematics, Spanish, and English, making good grades and living the life of a twenty-year-old college student. But it was also a time of war. Shigemura joined the Army's Enlisted Reserve Corps at Carleton on November 18, 1942, only a month after he arrived. In the spring of 1944, all sixty members of the reserve corps were shipped to Winona for officers' training. Three days later, Shigemura returned to campus. He alone had been rejected. The personnel in the training program explained: "You see, people might misunderstand" that the Nisei was the enemy. Apparently, simply being of Japanese ancestry had disqualified him from becoming an officer.[86]

Disappointed yet not disheartened, Shigemura gathered himself and went back to class. "This is just something else that happens," Shigemura told Blayney, the dean of college. "Let me go ahead and study here." The dean, however, did not take it as calmly as the student. He wrote letter after letter to selected military and service officials throughout the coming month. Blayney was in a protest mood. One of his letters to the adjutant general of the Army argued: "The sincere efforts being made by this young man to do his part on behalf of his country merits, in my judgement, the earnest consideration of the proper authority. The fact that he is now in the Enlisted Reserve instead of being in a Relocation Center has . . . worked to his disadvantage rather than the contrary."

Blayney urged an appeal on behalf of this "Japanese American student of fine character now at Carleton College." He concluded: "There is no question about his patriotism. We hope very much that you will direct the proper authority to investigate this case in the interest of full justice being done to him." Just after the end of the semester in June, the dean called Shigemura into his office. "You've just been called up," he told the student. "Your notification's coming." Shigemura was speechless. He shook the dean's hand.

Almost immediately Shigemura was in his uniform and on his way to join the Army.[87]

Pieces of Shigemura's news in the military drifted back to Northfield. In the summer of 1944, he received his basic training first at Twin Falls, Idaho, and then at Camp Shelby, Mississippi. He became Private First Class (Pfc.) Shigemura and subsequently was sent to Europe with the all–Japanese American 442nd Regimental Combat Team. He fought in Italy with the 34th Division. The 442nd was then deployed to France and spearheaded the secret attack which brought about the liberation of the "Lost Battalion." On October 20, 1944, Shigemura made his last effort helping his wounded comrades to safety. The twenty-two-year-old soldier was killed in the mission.[88]

Shigemura lost his life in action while serving his country. Yet his connection to Minnesota did not end with his demise. On December 2, 1944, Blayney wrote to his parents, who were still in the incarceration camp, to express the college's condolences. "Frank made a most favorable impression upon all who knew him and enjoyed the respect of both faculty and students. It is a great source of regret to all his friends to hear of his death upon the battlefield."

The dean continued on a more personal note: "I am particularly proud of our Japanese American soldiers. I am sure their courageous conduct is going to have a deep influence in changing the narrow-minded attitude of some of the most ignorant Americans. . . . I think you should know of the earnest efforts that Frank made to be accepted by the Army at a time when the Army was hesitant about admitting Japanese Americans." The dean was the one who went the distance to help Shigemura enlist. "It is pleasant for me to recall that I even wrote to the Army on his behalf, explaining how anxious he was to be accepted as a soldier," he noted. "This makes my regret all the deeper that, after showing such patriotism, Frank was not able to return again to the United States."

The closing of the letter mentioned the school was planning a war memorial fund, supported by students, alumni, and friends of the college, to pay tribute to all the Carleton students who had fallen in World War II. It perhaps was some consolation to the Shigemuras to "know that Frank's name will appear among those of others who have given their all upon the altar of our country." The project would come to fruition two years later, in 1946, as a booklet celebrating those brave yet brief lives of young patriots, of whom Shigemura was one.

It is impossible to understand what the parents must have gone through after losing their only son. Responding to the dean in a handwritten letter in beautiful cursive script, Mrs. Shigemura wrote: "It is hard to realize that Frank will never return. I can only say that I am thankful that he was able to serve his country, Dad and us all. I shall always be proud to be the mother of a true American." Mrs. Shigemura told the dean that her late son often wrote in his letters about the fair treatment and kindness he received, from both professors and students of Carleton. "I cannot find words adequate enough to fully express our thanks. We are ever so grateful to you all." These were the words from the Shigemuras, merely two months after the passing of their child.

In grief the Shigemuras found grace. The letter was only the beginning of their engagement with the college. Replying to the request for information about the gold star men featured in the commemorative booklet, the Shigemuras sent a picture, a few lines about their son, and a $100 check in March 1946. Next year came another letter from Seattle. "I am very happy to learn of your proposed student-union building that will be dedicated to those who served and died. As parents of the late Pfc. Frank M. Shigemura we feel greatly honored. Enclosed find check for $500. Please accept this small contribution." Two more checks from them for the new student union arrived over the next two years, totaling $1,200 (approximately $20,000 today).

In the spring of 1950, the fourth president of Carleton, Laurence McKinley Gould, traveled with Alumni Director Warren Breckenridge to the Pacific coast on their alumni tour, and thanking the Shigemuras, who lived in Seattle, for such a hugely generous gift was on his mind. They wanted to invite the important donors to an alumni banquet.

Hence, Breckenridge hailed a taxi, which took him to the middle of *Nihonmachi*, or Japantown, to an apartment building that had seen better days. On the lobby board he found the name Shigemura, went upstairs, and knocked on the door. No one answered. Across the hall, another door opened. "Mrs. Shigemura is ill," said a Japanese American lady. "I don't think she can see you. Anything I can tell her?" The man from Carleton told the neighbor that they wanted to invite the Shigemuras to a dinner given by alumni from their late son's college back in Minnesota. The woman then offered a solution. "Why not go down to Mr. Shigemura's place of business. You'll find him down at Union Station. Just ask for him. Everybody knows him." The station was only two blocks away.

Meeting Shigemura was an inspirational and emotional moment. At the Seattle station, Breckenridge finally found the generous benefactor. However, he was nothing like the alumni director had expected. Wearing a red cap, Shigemura had been working in the train station as a porter for thirty-nine years. All those donations came from the tips he earned carrying bags and luggage across the railroad station. The Shigemuras were not the wealthy philanthropists or powerful politicians to which Carleton was accustomed. The Japanese American couple literally gave, and continued to give, everything they had, including their son, to the college and to this country.

The story was so unusual and touching that the *Minneapolis Sunday Tribune* published a column by George Grim about the Carleton Nisei student and his parents on May 7, 1950. *Reader's Digest*, the most popular family magazine at the time, picked it up and reprinted this "Newspaper Human-Interest Award of the Month" story in September that year.[89]

The sacrifice of Frank Shigemura and the gifts from his parents were meaningful to Carleton in many ways. With gratitude, Gould wrote: "Because of the story which appeared in the *Reader's Digest*, I know that Frank is probably more widely known than any other student who ever attended Carleton College. Somehow, this fact pleases us very much. It is completely in line with the tradition and aspirations of this place that a Japanese American should have this record."

Meanwhile, he also showed his growing concern for the Shigemuras, since he knew the two of them lived very modestly on Shigemura's income as a porter. "I have some idea what gifts of this sort mean to you," Gould wrote in 1951. "When I realize the goodwill that goes with them, I know that the gift itself is multiplied many times in its usefulness to Carleton College and its students. My best thanks to you and my deep request that you do not have any sense of obligation to Carleton College."[90]

The kindness of the Shigemuras did not wane over the years to come. In 1951 there came a letter from them to the alumni director, saying: "We would like to establish a scholarship, a small one, in Frank's name this fall when the college year begins." A check for $1,000 fluttered from the envelope. "Please accept this in memory of our son, Frank Masao Shigemura," the mother wrote. The first scholarship recipient was senior Annie Kaneshiro Yamada, a daughter of a Japanese farmer from Oahu, Hawai'i.

The couple actually met Yamada in person, when they were invited to visit the Minnesota campus during Thanksgiving in 1951. "This is all we will ever want to see," Mrs. Shigemura said, looking at the dormitory where her son lived and the buildings where he had his classes with teary eyes. "This college that meant so much to our son, and to us. It is just as we hoped it would be. And please, let us know if we can do more to help. We think we can do a little more."[91]

The young Shigemura was every inch a war hero under the Star-Spangled Banner; his parents, however tired, poor, and unassuming in the "huddled masses," were equally heroic. Many Carleton students benefited from their generosity as a result. Altogether, the couple's gifts to the college amounted to more than $5,000 (about $85,000 today).

Although Shigemura's life was cut short, his legacy has lived on at Carleton. A small plaque designates Classroom 204 in Willis Hall as the "Shigemura Room," where pictures of fifty-four Carleton students who died in World War II are hung. However, the Shigemura story is more than just a typical American tale about the courage of a young man and the sacrifice of a fallen solider. Memorials are meant as much to commemorate the dead as to inspire the living. The name engraved therein carries the weight of resilience, remembrance, and sacrifice—not only from the young soldiers who braved the front lines but also of those who stood silently, steadfast, and unwavering, behind them. It speaks to a tragedy that redefines the familiar image of heroism, which does not end in death but lives on in the afterlife of love.

The Shigemura story seems to have faded from memory with the passage of time though. The plaque in the "modest classroom" and the Frank Shigemura Scholarship are "the only acknowledgement of this chapter in Carleton's history." Shigemura and the incarceration were the subject of an artist's book titled *Deeply Honored* by Professor Fred Hagstrom of Carleton, who handmade fifty copies. He dedicated the book to the Nisei's parents, Kay and Takejuro Shigemura, and to John Nason.[92]

Looking back at Shigemura's life, one might wonder, if it were not for the impassioned and persistent pleas from the dean, would the young man still have enlisted, or would he have instead escaped the ill-fated turn of events? Perhaps the Japanese American would have stayed on campus and moved on to a long, rewarding life. Or, perhaps fighting, and even dying, for his country was all he ever wanted, and he would have ended up on the front lines one way or another. It might not have made any difference.

Hindsight could be perfect, but it could never change the outcome. There was nothing left behind to indicate what Shigemura would have thought. However, one may make a conjecture, referring to a fellow Japanese American for insight. Yosh Murakami, who attended college at the same time in Northfield, across the river from Shigemura, and also answered the military's call, once remarked: "In spite of all the shame this is the best country I know. This is where I want to live, this is where I want to die, this is where I want to raise my children. And, if this country is attacked, I will serve to defend it." Young men sacrificing their lives for their country is, after all, an essential theme in the myth of a nation. Shigemura was a heroic figure in its making. It is the stuff of which patriotic American dreams are made.[93]

5 Courage and Combat

Japanese American Soldiers and the Military Intelligence Service Language School (MISLS)

"Going through school . . . nobody even knew about Camp Savage being here. A lot of people did not know Camp Savage was a military intelligence service camp. . . . It was just a secret. When I got to high school, the librarian actually was a Caucasian civilian [who] worked at Camp Savage. And she knew Dad. She would give me all these books to read. . . . It's incredibly important for people to know what happened in the country in hopes that it will never happen again . . . but I'm not so sure."
—PEGGY DOI

Born and raised in Minneapolis, Peggy Doi is the eldest daughter among five children of Bill Doi, a Military Intelligence Service (MIS) veteran, who appeared earlier in Chapter One. However, her parents did not talk much about their wartime experiences when she was growing up, including her father's service at Camp Savage, and later Fort Snelling. Just like many other Sansei, third-generation Japanese Americans, Doi discovered the hidden past only bit by bit, year after year.

The history of the MISLS, albeit faded or forgotten, can be found around the corner in Bloomington. There, on a two-acre plot next to Normandale Community College, stands a beautiful Japanese garden that is uniquely Minnesotan. A plaque by the hexagonal shrine (*bentendo*) next to the koi pond reads: "We, the Japanese American veterans of the U.S. Army Military Intelligence Service Language School, dedicate this *bentendo* and bridge to the people of the Twin Cities and all of Minnesota for the kind treatment we received while we were stationed here during World War II[,] 1942 through 1946." Not many people know about the Japanese garden these days. Even fewer have heard of those who helped to build it.[1]

During the war, young Nisei did not go to Minnesota just for college. They also traveled far and near, from the incarceration camps and different parts of the country, to join the MISLS. The military school trained and graduated more than six thousand linguists—the majority of whom were Japanese Americans. Their knowledge of the enemy's complex and difficult language, which very few Allied forces besides them could understand, struck an unexpected and devastating blow to their foe. These resolute and resourceful soldiers served in all campaigns and on all fronts of the far-flung war throughout the Pacific—in China, India, Myanmar (known as Burma then)—and some even in Europe. They performed a critical role in the victory over Imperial Japan. Many served in the Allied Translator and Interpreter Service (ATIS), the Joint Intelligence Center Pacific Ocean Area (JICPOA), and the Southeast Asia Translation and Intelligence Center (SATIC).[2]

The impact of these MISLS graduates on the war was invaluable and immense. "Had it not been for the loyalty, fidelity, patriotism, and ability of these American Nisei," Colonel Sidney F. Mashbir, Commander of the ATIS, says in his memoir, "that part of the war in the Pacific which was dependent upon intelligence gleaned from captured documents and prisoners of war would have been a far more hazardous, long-drawn-out-affair." According to General Douglas MacArthur and other military leaders, these Nisei warriors "shortened the Pacific War by two years" and "saved a million lives." In addition, they were among the first Americans to set foot in Japan after its surrender and worked in important positions during the occupation, such as the Repatriation Program, the Civil Censorship Detachment (CCD), and the Counter Intelligence Corps (CIC), as well as during the war crimes trials held in Japan, China, and Southeast Asia.[3]

Regrettably, Peggy Doi could not possibly learn any of this when she was growing up, even from her father. The shroud of silence was not just personal but also official. While the unrivaled records of the Nisei combat units, the 100th Infantry Battalion and later 442nd Regimental Combat Team, were widely and rightfully recognized, the exploits of their military intelligence counterparts remained untold for more than a quarter century. The MISLS and its military linguists were considered a part of "classified military affairs," and any discussion of their activities was prohibited after the war. The ban was lifted only after the passage of the Privacy Act amendment of the Freedom of Information Act in 1974. As time went by, the story of the MIS and the school should no longer have been a mystery. That was not necessarily the case, unfortunately.

The saga of the "Yankee Samurai," as these brave Nisei soldiers are nicknamed, has been told mostly in the margins thus far. Many in the public, including Minnesotans, are unaware of the contribution of these Nisei veterans and their connection to the North Star State. Little is left of Camp Savage today except for a historical marker erected in 1993 and the last standing building now used by the Minnesota Department of Transportation; the adjacent land has been turned into a public dog park. Fort Snelling has transformed into a historical park that honors the diverse past of not just European pioneers but also Dakota, Ojibwe, and other Native Americans, African Americans, and Japanese Americans, although the "former military

Military Intelligence Service Language School plaque at the site of the camp in Savage, Minnesota. *Courtesy of the author*

reservation resembles only a fragment of what it was." If the once-celebrated sacrifice of Frank Shigemura of the 442nd and his family can wither away over time, the underappreciation of the MISLS does not come as such a surprise.[4]

—

The military linguists' story is a challenging one to tell. A variety of complications lie in the way of rewarding it with the attention that it deserves. The long prohibition against discussing it is just the first hurdle. The Army believed that the Nisei soldiers were America's superb "human secret weapon" in World War II. Revealing their existence would have meant disclosing the sensitive operations, techniques, and capabilities of US military intelligence to both actual and potential adversaries. Unlike the feats of the 442nd combat team that had been well covered in contemporary news and government releases during the war years, there was no official descriptive information about the MISLS and its students or their roles and deeds on the battlegrounds.[5]

The hush-hush policy extended after the war, because of the continued military intelligence operations in Occupied Japan and subsequently in the Korean War and the Cold War. The Nisei, hence, served in total anonymity. All was in the name of their beloved country, which, sadly and ironically, also incarcerated their families behind barbed wire. Of course, the Nisei linguists were not the only ethnic minority group whose wartime contribution was suppressed for the sake of national security. The instrumental and incredible work of hundreds of Navajo "code talkers," whose use of their traditional tribal language for communications in battle led to Allied success, was also kept a military secret for many years. The code talkers' program was eventually declassified in 1968, several years earlier than the Nisei military linguists. By then the ink in the World War II history books had long dried.[6]

Secondly, there are barriers to presenting the language specialists' narrative even once it became permissible. While the all-Nisei 442nd Regimental Combat Team represents a conventional and cohesive war tale of gallantry, the story of the MISLS students is different and dispersed. Linguistic military intelligence work entails strength and skills unlike those of typical action figures, even though many of the linguists were also in the line of fire. Their heroism manifested in subtler ways. Their main duty was information procurement through captured documents, intercepted messages, and interrogations of prisoners of war, which was apparently not as "glamorous" as one veteran stated, since their work did not directly result in an easily visible military outcome for untrained eyes.[7]

More problematically, the Nisei linguists' stories were spread all across the vast Pacific Theater and beyond. There was no single Japanese American military intelligence team, and there was no straightforward way to describe their accomplishments. The MISLS graduates formed numerous small detachments that operated secretly with a wide range of combat divisions, army corps, military campaigns, and intelligence offices. Not only did their assignments shift frequently, from one unit to another, to wherever their expertise was in demand, but they were also loaned out to aid foreign militaries, such as those of England, Australia, New Zealand, and China. What was salvaged decades later in governmental files about them was often scant and scattered.[8]

In many instances, the hard work by the Nisei linguists was unacknowledged or even deliberately erased. The soldiers were not listed in the official roster of the combat units, as they were detachments, and therefore served literally without a trace. Even though some individuals were identified and decorated for valor, citations for the awards earned were brief, general, and in some cases nonexistent. Further obscuring the Japanese Americans' accomplishments was that white officers who signed the intelligence reports often took credit for what the combat linguists had done. The books were closed, the merits were claimed, and the Nisei names were nowhere to be found. Although critical historians and military officials have unearthed some of the actual Japanese American heroes behind the scenes in recent years, most of those involved had long since passed away.[9]

Lastly, another difficulty came from the Nisei themselves. The military intelligence officers were, by training and profession, discreet and cautious about publicly discussing their confidential endeavors. These Nisei patriots, according to an MISLS alumnus, were often reticent and modest by nature, and were contented in their own minds regarding what they had done to prove their loyalty to the United States. Nothing more remained for them to fight for or prove. Nor was it their duty, desire, or disposition to announce to the world what they had done. Many carried the pledge of secrecy to their final resting places. Their stories were inevitably lost forever.[10]

Even if a complete picture of the wartime Nisei soldiers can never be put together, some veterans feel that their experiences should be shared before it is too late. Since the 1970s, activists like the Dois, along with other MISLS soldiers, scholars, and organizations, have been preserving and promoting this significant part of American history. Owing to their tireless advocacy, the secrets of the MIS and the MISLS have come to light through books, articles, documentaries, exhibitions, websites, and various media.[11]

In 2010, President Barack Obama granted the Congressional Gold Medal to Nisei veterans, collectively to those who served in the 100th Infantry Battalion, the 442nd Regimental Combat Team, and the Military Intelligence Service. The belated, and for many posthumous, acknowledgment cannot turn back the clock or undo the time of exclusion, yet it helps to forge a new path for a more inclusive future. It is not about reimagining history but rather recognizing what really happened. Historical literature needs to remember, reflect, and reevaluate the true American past, whose anthem can never be sung by one dominant voice or in just one language but only with a colorful chorus ensemble in all its diversity.[12]

Every hero has an origin story. The Nisei combat linguists were no exception. Although the union of the MISLS with Minnesota was relatively short, from May 25, 1942, to June 6, 1946, those four years had a long-lasting impact on the military, the state, and the nation. The school operated in full swing during the tempestuous war years, producing America's "superb secret weapons" that contributed to the Allied victory. The need for Japanese language specialists in the military, and the concept of a school to train intelligence linguists, went back to way before the Pearl Harbor attack. Before the First World War, the US embassy in Tokyo had already started a joint language attaché training program for the Army, Navy, and State Department.

The possibility of war with Japan was mounting rapidly by the summer of 1941. Intelligence work became more imminent and urgent. A language training school was founded at Fourth Army Headquarters, the Presidio of San Francisco, which was also the US Army's area command on the West

Coast. The school was headed by Brigadier General (then Major) John Weckerling, Colonel (then Captain) Kai Rasmussen, and Colonel (then Captain) Joseph K. Dickey, a Minnesota native who had graduated from West Point. All three officers went through the attaché program and served in the US embassy in Tokyo. From approximately 1,200 servicemen on the West Coast, they picked fifty-eight "loyal" Nisei students for the inaugural program. The Fourth Army Intelligence School, as it was initially called, opened on November 1, 1941. Two Caucasian soldiers with some colloquial Japanese skills were added to the Japanese American group, but neither was proficient enough to graduate with the first class.[13]

How this school became the MISLS in the north deserves more elaboration. After Pearl Harbor and President Roosevelt's Executive Order 9066, the West Coast descended into unprecedented wartime hysteria. On March 31, 1942, the War Department notified Selective Service that it no longer accepted "Japanese or persons of Japanese extraction, regardless of citizenship status or other factors" for service with the armed forces. All Nisei registrants were reclassified into the category IV-C, "enemy aliens." The War Department then issued another directive that no Japanese American soldiers were to be sent overseas.[14]

Although the ban was lifted on April 7, 1942, the Military Intelligence Division insisted that a Caucasian officer had to lead each team of Nisei in the field. By mid-June, DeWitt announced that all American-born Japanese in the US Army had been removed from the Western Defense Command and transferred to noncombat interior posts. It was only a year later, on March 23, 1943, that the War Department allowed the organization of the segregated 442nd Infantry Regimental Combat Team.[15]

Complying with the forced removal of all people of Japanese ancestry, the Army school, with its Nisei instructors and students, could no longer stay in the Presidio. The school needed a new site with a calmer and friendlier atmosphere as well as "better and larger facilities." Still, Minnesota must have seemed like an odd choice not least because of its climate, geography, and communities, which were far different from those of California and, more to the point, the Pacific Theater where most of the students would go.[16]

Racial factors appeared to weigh heavily on the Army's decision. That Japanese American soldiers and their families would be accepted with relatively little hostility was a main concern. Rasmussen was tasked with finding such a suitable place. The Danish-born Rasmussen served three years in the Philippines and spent four years with the US Army in Japan in the 1930s. His experience as both an underprivileged immigrant who had suffered many rejections in his previous career and a firsthand observer of Asian affairs helped him to set the racial priority high on the list.

With the support of Minnesota Governor Harold Stassen, Rasmussen chose Camp Savage to be the place for a restart. The North Star State was said to have the most favorable social climate in the country. Rasmussen believed the Twin Cities area "not only had room physically, but room in the people's hearts" to welcome the Nisei fighters "for their true worth." The school's new address was located in the Minnesota River Valley near the Fort Snelling army post. The 132-acre camp with rustic wooden buildings, originally used by the Civilian Conservation Corps in the 1930s, was at the time a home for elderly indigent men. The state of Minnesota promised to remove the residents and leased it to the Army for a nominal sum. On June 1, 1942, the first classes began with 160 Nisei and 30 Caucasian students. Later that month on June 26, the school was officially put under the jurisdiction of the War Department and renamed the "Military Intelligence Service Language School."[17]

The chief instructor for the Fourth Army Intelligence School and then the MISLS was a thirty-one-year-old private from Los Angeles, John Fujio Aiso. Considered the most capable and mature among all Nisei enlistees, the Brown- and Harvard-educated Aiso successfully led his team to create the intensive curriculum for Japanese combat linguists that defined the school's training program at Camp Savage and Fort Snelling. No matter where or when the MISLS narrative is told, there is always John Aiso. "At some point in time his story merges to become the [Nisei linguists'] story," said Tadao Ichinokuchi, an MISLS veteran and the editor of a volume about their exploits. "We Nisei, who were raised in this period to become the first American born of Japanese descent, can almost write a parallel to his biography," he continued.[18]

To better understand the lives of Japanese American soldiers in Minnesota, one needs to first explore the reasons why these young men, and later women, willingly joined the MISLS when their family members were still imprisoned in the camps. While each Nisei's experience was unique, Aiso was deemed the most representative of them all. He was the "hope" of every Issei and an "icon" for every Nisei in his time. His accomplishments might have been greater in many aspects, yet the aspirations and hardships of other young Japanese Americans during this period were similar.[19]

Appointed the director of academic training of the MISLS, and subsequently the first Japanese American judge in California, Aiso would pass away in 1987 due to an injury sustained in an attempted mugging, demonstrating the best and worst of what lay ahead in a Nisei's pursuit of the American life. Born in 1909 in Hollywood, California, where his immigrant father worked as a gardener, Aiso grew up in a household where pictures of Washington, Lincoln, and Jesus hung on the walls. When racial slurs were thrown at him in streetcars or on schoolgrounds, he responded by solemnly studying harder. Two widely publicized incidents during his teenage years underscored both his character and the Japanese American dilemma.[20]

The first happened at Le Conte Junior High School during the academic year of 1922 and 1923. Aiso ran for student president and won by a large margin. However, angry Caucasian parents held mass meetings and refused to have their children under a Nisei boy. The petition to remove Aiso as the president-elect read, in part: "We stand for America and want no other than an American as our student body president . . . based upon those principles of freedom for which American patriots sacrificed their lives and fortunes."[21]

Of course, Aiso was a true "American" born in the United States, albeit with different skin pigmentation and facial conformations than his white compatriots. The school principal, trying to appease the "vocal" pressure group and avoid the call for his resignation, decided to suspend the student government until after Aiso graduated rather than allow the Japanese American boy to take office.

The second incident took place in 1926, his last year at Hollywood High School. Aiso received double honors as a graduating senior: He was selected as the class valedictorian, having achieved the highest academic ranking. He also won first place in a debate competition, earning a spot in the national oratorical contest. Once again, the Nisei's successes irked the white parents and students. The principal cautioned Aiso that an unfavorable feeling would arise in the school if he were to monopolize the two accolades. In the end, Aiso had to choose just one, and he reluctantly handed over the debate opportunity.[22]

The local Japanese newspaper *Rafu Shimpo* reported how "sad" that Aiso was "cursed by detestable racial discrimination" and forced to give up his participation "because of jealousy." Sympathizing with Aiso's quandary, the president of the *Los Angeles Times*, Harry Chandler, decided to sponsor the young Nisei to accompany his high school delegate to the contest in Washington, DC. As a result, Aiso enjoyed a lifelong friendship with Chandler and came to be a well-known exemplar in the Japanese American community.

Unsurprisingly, the overachiever did not disappoint as an adult. Graduating from high school at the age of sixteen, Aiso went to Japan to study the Japanese language for ten months before beginning his Ivy League education in the fall of 1927. He received his *cum laude* bachelor's degree in economics from Brown University, followed by a degree from Harvard Law School in 1934. It was the time of the Great Depression. Seeking better opportunities overseas, Aiso left America and accepted a position in Mukden in Manchukuo (Japanese Manchuria) in 1936 as head of the legal department of the British-American Tobacco Company's subsidiary for three and a half years. He returned to California in 1939 as the situation in the East worsened. After he passed the bar exam, he set out to practice law in Los Angeles and tie the knot with his fiancée.

However, his legal career and wedding plans were interrupted when he was drafted in April 1941. The Army made him a buck private and assigned the overqualified Nisei to a truck repair outfit as a parts clerk in the Quartermaster Battalion, at Camp Haan, Riverside. There Aiso came across Rasmussen, who was in search of instructors and students for the fledgling Japanese intelligence language school. Before long, Aiso was asked to report to the Presidio, San Francisco.

Although Aiso had no intention of staying in uniform, one line from Weckerling supposedly changed his mind. Aiso's primary goal at the time was getting out of the Army. Already over thirty, he was waiting to be discharged so he could resume his law practice and start his own family in Los Angeles. When offered the post of chief instructor at the brand-new school in the Fourth Army Headquarters, his initial answer was to decline. The turning point, as the story was recounted, came when Weckerling walked out from behind his desk, put his hand on Aiso's shoulder, and said, "John, your country needs you."[23]

Those simple words surprised and overwhelmed the Nisei. "No American person had ever told me that America was my country," Aiso later recalled. "Yes, sir, I will take the job" was his instantaneous response. And just like that, the MISLS found its academic director. Since it would be unseemly for a buck private to be running a school in which full colonels might be among the students, and Aiso was too old for a direct commission, Weckerling furloughed the Nisei to the enlisted reserve and hired him as a War Department civilian employee.[24]

Aiso's "your country needs you" scene was among the most celebrated MISLS anecdotes. According to Shigeya Kihara, one of the four original instructors, hearing those four words uttered by an authoritative figure was "a cultural shock, an American cultural shock to an American." He thought that the "symbolism" of the exchange between Aiso and Weckerling was momentous. "This event established a personal, special and unique relationship between the United States Army and Japanese Americans," he claimed; "respect, confidence and trust on the part of the Army, and loyalty and service to America on the part of the Nisei soldier." Weckerling was not only talking to Aiso but also "saying this to all Japanese Americans," Kihara stated.[25]

In the dark and bitter period of World War II, Japanese Americans naturally felt anger, humiliation, and shame, especially during the ensuing forced removal and incarceration of innocent citizens. Nisei like Aiso and Kihara believed the Army enabled them "to maintain a semblance of human dignity and individual worth and faith in America," granting them the opportunity to show their patriotism, fight for their country, and contribute to its victory. A more somber tone hid behind such sentiment though. Karl Gozo Yoneda, another MISLS student who later became an eminent union organizer and activist, asserted: "The immediate objective was to destroy Fascism, and thus there was no choice for us but to 'accept' the U.S. racist dictum at that time over Hitler's ovens and Japan's military rapists of Nanking."[26]

Facing anti–Japanese American prejudice, Aiso took action in his own way and at his own pace. In the fall of 1942, he wrote a letter to California Attorney

General Earl Warren, who was running for governor and later became argu-ably the most influential US Supreme Court Chief Justice of the twentieth century. Warren was a firm proponent of the forced removal and declared he did not want the Japanese Americans to return after the war. "I thought, at heart, he was a very religious man," Aiso said. "I wanted him to know that some of us so-called 'Japs' were in the United States Army. I felt that after the war was over, he would change his mind and let us come back."[27]

The story of Aiso and Warren continued after the war. Japanese Ameri-cans were eventually allowed to return to the West Coast, and Warren even appointed Aiso to the municipal court of Los Angeles in 1953 as the first Nisei to serve in the state judiciary on the mainland. Yet Warren did not publicly admit during his lifetime any regret or wrongdoing regarding his support of the incarceration. Aiso, once again playing the role of model minority, urged the Japanese American community "to respect [Warren's] reluctance and display a little magnanimity," because "it would serve no pur-pose to press him further." War unleashed suffering and required sacrifices. It seemed the Nisei were the ones who had to bear them all silently, hoping things would get better.[28]

To many Nisei, the MISLS was their hope for that "better." Situated along a railroad line and state highway, Camp Savage was an isolated and quiet location, where the Japanese American soldiers could concentrate on their studies and remain inconspicuous. The camp was also close to Fort Snelling, an established Army installation with a capacity of several thousand men, as well as Minneapolis and St. Paul, the convivial Twin Cities, for off-duty activities and recreation.[29]

Nonetheless, the camp was not "like going to the West Point" or "the rosy picture" that many recruits anticipated. Nobuo Yamashita, a volunteer from Manzanar, recalled: "Camp Savage used to [house] elderly people. . . . The first group that went there spent an awful lot of time cleaning the place up; there was urine smell, all that [unpleasant odor] in there. So, they spent most of their free time making the place livable." The Nisei pri-vates lived on what they jokingly dubbed "the pig farm." Some thought the barracks were "reminiscent of the historic settlement of the Pilgrims way back in the 1600s." Whereas instructor staff stayed a few miles down the road from Savage, the white officer candidates were allowed to reside at Fort Snelling.[30]

Although the overall situation was deemed "fairly decent," the camp was not conceived with permanence in mind. In the beginning, its handful of extant structures could facilitate a few hundred students. By July 1944, the school had become the host for eleven hundred students and close to one hundred instructors. The increasing student body size was caused not only by the rising number of Nisei recruits. Besides the MISLS, there were additional military intelligence Japanese programs, with predominately Caucasian students, such as the Army's program at the University of Michigan and the Navy's counterpart at the University of Colorado in Boulder. All these military branches sent their graduates or enlisted men to Minnesota for advanced training.[31]

The student body soon outgrew the space at Camp Savage. Some of the classes and service units had to function in makeshift barns. Buildings that could be used for recreational events were especially missing. A theater and gymnasium were added, but barely caught up with the expansion of the population. The classrooms were crowded, facilities were overtaxed, and venues for social events left much to be desired. Since the MISLS administrative functions were partially handled through Fort Snelling, shifting the whole operation to the more established military installation seemed expedient and logical. The MISLS was thus moved there in August 1944.[32]

Fort Snelling was a significant improvement. Classrooms, for instance, were in "a tasteful line of light-colored brick buildings set amidst tall elm trees and expansive lawns along Taylor Avenue." The school structures were "the very blueprints for convenience" as well as "bulwarks against Minnesota's climatic ferocity." Edwin Nakasone was pleased that "Snelling had some very commodious classrooms, and very well accoutered as far as lights went . . . [and] most importantly, radiated heating and so on." He also found "big, long desks" that fellow students could sit around and study. "We were able to use our dictionaries, open it up and learn how to write *kanji*, and we were able to get into . . . conversational Japanese, and classes of that nature, in a circular form."[33]

Less than appealing, however, were the substandard huts in what was nicknamed the "Turkey Farm" in a remote part of the fort that housed

Military Intelligence Service Language School students in class, Fort Snelling, ca. 1945. *Courtesy of Bill Doi*

incoming yet unassigned individuals and outgoing graduates. "They were tarpapered—almost tarpaper—shacks or sheds," Nakasone explained with a chuckle; there was literally nothing in the "Turkey Farm" huts but "a small potbellied stove."[34]

More positive changes also came in terms of the length of courses and diversity of languages offered. At Snelling the average course time grew from six to nine months, beginning with the February 1944 class. "The Snelling days were easier on studying," the school's album staff proclaimed, "than the compressed training days at Savage." Although each class lasted longer, new classes launched more frequently, and therefore, the number of students also soared. From August 1944 to July 1945, 2,400 recruits started classes, nearly double the combined student input of the previous three years.[35]

The first graduation at Snelling and the ninth of the MISLS was held in November 1944 with 382 Nisei and 11 Chinese Americans receiving their diplomas. The Chinese Division, which trained Chinese intelligence linguists, was initiated in December 1944. A Korean language class was added in October 1945. Similarly, the first Women's Army Corps (WAC) class began on May 28, 1945, with 48 Nisei women. The spring of 1946 saw the MISLS reach its peak with 160 instructors (all Japanese Americans) and 3,000 students. Fort Snelling graduated its last class of 307 students on June 6, 1946, representing its eleventh commencement and the twenty-first overall in the school's history, for a total of 6,000 graduates. The school then moved to the Presidio of Monterey in California and changed its name to the US Army Language School. In 1963, it became the Defense Language Institute, which continues its operations to this day.[36]

While the student population of the MISLS was overwhelmingly composed of Nisei, they were not a homogeneous and harmonious group from the outset. It was the first time that Nisei from the mainland mixed and worked with Nisei from Hawai'i. Their lived experiences and political situations were very different. On the Hawaiian islands, Japanese Americans constituted a majority of the population. They were considered boisterous and rowdy, yet more culturally Asian, even speaking their own regional language, a pidgin English. They were mostly trainees from the 100th Infantry Battalion and 442nd Regimental Combat Team who had already been bonding at Camp McCoy in Wisconsin. Their famous motto, "Go for Broke," indeed came from Hawaiian pidgin, meaning the soldiers had given and gambled everything—that they would be bankrupt if they lost. On the contrary, the continental Nisei were a minority of the Asian minority in largely white communities. They were quieter and more reserved and, sadly, had gone through the traumatic removal and incarceration.[37]

A certain degree of antipathy inevitably sprung up between them, partly due to long-held Hawaiian biases against outsiders, and partly to perceived snobbish attitudes on the part of the better educated mainlanders. They quickly tagged each other "Buddha Heads" and "*Kotonks*." There were many explanations behind these two nicknames. The former appellation might come from island elders calling Nisei children *Bobura*-head (Pumpkin head) when they goofed off, and the latter was perhaps a variation of a practice from Schofield Barracks in Honolulu of referring to one's juniors as "donkeys."[38]

It took a while before the two groups reconciled. Both Buddha Heads and Kotonks decided that they had to get along to survive the training, and even more so, the ruthless battlefields to which they would soon head. They needed each other. Above all, making friends was easier when facing common foes—the undesirable living conditions and the unforgiving school program.

How "bad" were the conditions and programs at Savage and Snelling that they could swiftly unite the Nisei? To better comprehend the life of the MISLS soldiers in Minnesota, let's take a closer look at some of their experiences on and off camp, from curricular activities to city escapades to cold winters.

—

More than a secret military program, the MISLS, first and foremost, was a serious academic institution. Examining the curriculum would be a good starting point before exploring what lay outside of the classrooms. Overseen by Aiso, the school's intensive program was its unique signature. Top students from each class were kept on for a year or so after graduating to serve as instructors. Eventually, Aiso developed a staff of over 160 supervisors, curriculum developers, and teachers.[39]

Although the educational content was continuously modified during the war, it consistently emphasized both oral language usages and military specific purposes. Courses included reading, writing, listening, and speaking Japanese; translation, interpretation, and interrogation; captured document analysis; radio monitoring; Japanese military and technical terms (*heigo*); cursive "grass" scripts (*sōsho*) that were used in handwritten notes; Japanese geography and map reading; the social, political, economic, and cultural background of Japan; and information about the organization of the Japanese army. Furthermore, the school introduced students to Japanese films, large quantities of which the US government had confiscated since the war began.[40]

Japanese linguists were as vital in peace and governance as in war and battle, if not more so. Sensibly, the instruction stressed the military side during the conflict, and then favored more general communicative skills as well as subjects on civil affairs and government administration subsequent to the victory. Nakasone recalled: "From August 1945, we no longer had *heigo*, no longer had to go through *sōsho*, no longer did we have to learn all the battle, weaponry, [and] military items. Now we concentrated on civilian things, especially conversational Japanese and learning the simple *kanji* and so on." To meet new demands, the oral language course on conversational Japanese was highlighted, which departed from the earlier emphasis on written forms that only incidentally touched on the spoken tongue. The Snelling course was also shortened back to six months; some even hurried through in three months, to meet the demand of the occupation of Japan.[41]

Toshio Tsukahira, one of the eight original civilian teachers whose story will be featured shortly, believed the MISLS training made major contributions to not just the war and peace efforts but the field of second language pedagogy. Pioneered by the Nisei instructors first in the Presidio and then fully applied in Savage and Snelling, the "total immersion" method was tested, utilized, and proved to be very successful. The faculty developed this approach to teach Japanese, and thereafter other difficult languages as well, for native English speakers. The practice essentially consisted of dawn-to-dusk intensive and concentrated immersion in the study of a second language, which in modified form is still used today.[42]

The "immersion" language training started on day one. Upon arriving at the school, the students were assigned to one of the ten companies, which made up the "School Regiment" for housing, messing, administration, and basic military training. They were then given a four-hour placement test to determine their Japanese proficiency to group them into level-appropriate sections. The classes were divided into three levels—upper, middle, and lower—based on students' capabilities. "Depending on how good you were," Nakasone explained. "[T]hose that were extremely good, the Kibei . . . were placed in [the upper] 1–5 sections. I wasn't that good, so I was placed in [the middle] section 14. There were 22 sections" at that time in 1945.

All MISLS students could testify to how rigorous their academic experiences were. A typical day began at 6:00 a.m. with the school call at 7:30 a.m. Classes met at 8:00 a.m. and lasted for roughly four hours. Apart from a lunch break from 11:45 a.m. to 1:30 p.m., students were engaged in language instruction until 4:30 p.m. There was a period for exercise and dinner, after which students marched back for supervised evening review from 7:00 p.m. to 9:00 p.m. Most of the students had to prepare fast and furiously for the quizzes of the next day. However, voluntary study was allowed only until 10:30 p.m. At 11:00 p.m., all the lights were out. That was the weekly life of the MISLS students. The only exception was Wednesday afternoon. Instead of language courses, they were given "military training"—quite often a "long stiff cross-country march from five to ten miles," recalled Nakasone.[43]

Like many other students, Bill Doi remembered vividly his MISLS days of rapid tempo, heavy workload, and exhausting training. "It was a six-month course. Accelerated, and I mean accelerated." Admitting "his Japanese was not very good," Doi was placed in the second to the bottom level section. "After a whole day of studying, that still wasn't enough time," he said, "so a lot of students would go to the latrines after lights out and [study] by flash-light." Saturday mornings were devoted to examinations. An observation from Tad Ichinokuchi on the montage of scenes from Snelling read: "Students cramming for the exams at night on the rest room stools looking like the 'Thinker' from Michelangelo's statue." Freedom came between Saturday afternoon and Monday morning, before another week of drilling began.[44]

In addition to the expected fatigue from the grueling routine, many Nisei students had to soldier on with unusual distress and disquietude. Learning the language of their parents to fight against enemies from their ancestral land was incredibly fraught, and for some posed complex questions about identity and heritage. Aiso was steadfast in calming and steering his students. He knew fully well how the Nisei were mistreated and misunderstood, and that the forced removal had robbed two generations of Japanese Americans of the fruits of their labor. His solution was to bear down harder to prove their worth and loyalty.[45]

Infusing the school with his ethics of diligence, self-discipline, and patri-otism in the face of prejudice, Aiso was a harsh and unbending taskmaster to many students. Doi noted: "Whether you like him or not, he was really smart.... I don't know anybody [who] could have done any better in a posi-tion than he did." The personal secretary of Aiso, Mitsue Kono Matsui, tes-tified to that claim. "He was a great Nisei leader," she asserted, "and to me a mentor, a role model and a professional in every sense of the word."[46]

The curricular, pedagogical, and logistical difficulties were rather easy for Aiso to handle; the harder ones were those involving family or personal issues. Matsui gave as an example when a student requested a leave of absence to be with his wife, who was expecting. Aiso turned him down because it was not considered an emergency. "I felt really sorry for this student, because it's probably his first baby," she sighed. "He was quite strict about that. He had to be that way." Matsui knew Aiso, "a real nice person" at heart, simply could not let his more "human side" show. Only years after the war did Aiso admit to having been a "martinet" who had overlooked the "personal comfort and welfare" of the students.[47]

Tight schedule, tough leader, and tense milieu aside, MISLS life was interspersed with delightful moments, too. Aiso and Rasmussen were not oblivious to the morale of their recruits. They recognized the need to alleviate some of the pressure and boost the school's spirit. The extracurricular elements of the school, therefore, were very important for the trainees. Doi was assigned to the "Special Services Office," whose main task was to organize "beneficial activities to take care of" the young soldiers. Being misdiagnosed

Bill Doi at the Special Services Office with colleagues, Military Intelligence Service Language School, Fort Snelling, 1944. *Courtesy of Bill Doi*

Military Intelligence Service Language School soldiers learning to ski, ca. 1944.
Courtesy of Bill Doi

with tuberculosis and quarantined for two months, Doi had some time to spare as he was deferred to the next class. He soon became the chief clerk of that office, which would later expand from two staff to ten. The construction of the theater and gymnasium at Savage was an early achievement.[48]

Doi and his colleagues put together recreational and athletic programs, such as baseball, softball, football, basketball, skiing, and boxing—the Minnesotan boxing team even went to the Golden Gloves tournament at the Seventh Service Command meet, where it took third place. Sports brought people together and helped manage stress. Doi was impressed by a hidden side of Aiso exposed on the volleyball court. "He was a good player," Doi mentioned. "That was a surprise to a lot of people because he was so strict and businesslike, [but] he could let himself go and enjoyed himself."[49]

Banking was also a part of Doi's responsibility. The students regularly received "checks from home, and there was no way to cash them. . . . They were tied up in camp," Doi said; but "people got to have money." Therefore, the Special Services would send an armed guard to the First National Bank and pick up a representative or two, who then processed 2,500 or even 3,000 checks on-site in a day. "For a while I was the only one who dealt with traveler's checks," Doi further stated; "up to June of 1944, I had written $139,000 worth of travelers checks, and there was not one incident."[50]

Speaking of money, poker games were a favorite pastime for the soldiers. However, Harry Tsutomu Umeda, a draftee from California who later made his home in Richfield, Minnesota, lamented that they often ran out of money. "We were getting only eighteen dollars and seventy-five cents a month. It didn't last very long." Coming up with a creative solution, Umeda and his friend "used to put their boots on and went into the town of Savage" with hamburgers taken from the mess at camp. "We [sold] them to the kids, and made some money to play poker," he chuckled. "You got to make some fun."[51]

Adding to the fun side of the school were touches of art and the sound of music. Doi was an artist himself, and he would later build a successful design and advertising career in the Twin Cities after the war. There were art contests, events, and publications that involved many talented Nisei students. In 1943, Chris K. Ishii, a former Disney Studio animator for films like

Military Intelligence Service Language School soldiers at Camp Savage, Minnesota, ca. 1943. *Courtesy of the Tanaka Family and the University of California, Santa Barbara Library*

Fantasia (1940) and *Dumbo* (1941), designed a humorous "emblem" for the school in honor of Minnesota's state animal that was meant to be as iconic as the MGM lion or the Army mule. The image was a snarling gopher with buckteeth wearing a Native American war bonnet and ready to fight.[52]

While the inspiration from the mascot of the University of Minnesota was evident, the satirical reference to the caricature of Japanese ethnic features was, too, noticeable. The gopher image might seem offensive these days. It was a different time with different sensibility then, and the students wore it as an MISLS shoulder patch with pride nonetheless. Working together with Ishii was his fellow colleague at Disney, Sadayuki Thomas Okamoto, who was another illustrator for the camp. He took on the art editor role for the *MISLS Album* (1946). Comic strips and cartoon drawings by both Ishii and Okamoto decorated many pages in the newsletters, as well as posters and leaflets of the school.[53]

Meanwhile, the Fort Snelling Nisei Choir was both a local and a global sensation. The choir was organized by Peter Tamio Yamazaki with thirty singers in October 1944 and within a few months grew to 125 members, all Japanese American, with both Nisei soldiers and WACs. The director was Corporal Joseph Martin Running. A Minnesota native from Zumbrota, Running graduated from St. Olaf College, where he was part of the famous choir, served three years in the Army during the war, and later had a musical career as a pianist, organist, and choir master.

On December 21, 1944, the *Minneapolis Morning Tribune* printed the headline "Fort Snelling Nisei Choir to Have Share in Worldwide Yule Program," accompanied by three large photographs. On Christmas Eve, the singing group was heard on the radio for the first time during the "Army Hour" (2:30–3:30 p.m.) through the National Broadcasting Company (NBC), reaching American troops in all corners of the globe, from the Philippines to Panama, France to Alaska. The Nisei voices were also featured in an evening program on KSTP (a station based in the Twin Cities) and the Northwest network, which was rebroadcast on West Coast radio stations. Ironically, their performance was introduced with a speech by Governor Earl Warren of California, who had played a major role in the forced removal and incarceration of Japanese Americans in the Golden State as noted earlier. The Nisei Choir's holiday presentation finished with a Christmas Festival service the next day in the field house at Fort Snelling that had been converted into a chapel, to which the public was invited.

Of all the special events at Savage and Snelling, the ones that interested the Nisei the most were the dances. Those were times when they had the chance to meet and mingle with new friends outside of school. "The Saturday night dances at the Fort were quite a morale booster," Ichinokuchi proclaimed. The gymnasium was a much-celebrated venue for the Battalion and Company dances, avoiding the discomfort of an earlier event that had been held in a barn after a farmer had milked his cows and sent them out to pasture. Doi marveled at the cooperation from volunteer organizations in Minneapolis and St. Paul, like the YWCA, United Service Organizations (USO), and the Red Cross, that made the events possible. "When we wanted to plan a dance, all we had to do was just called someone, made sure how many partners we would like, and arranged the bus to pick them up," Doi said. There were live bands and refreshments. "The guys loved to, if not dance, just socialize, and the [ladies] were very well chaperoned. There was no funny stuff going on. If a woman came out on a bus, they had to go back on the bus. . . . We never get any problems."[54]

Similarly, dances and other social events happened off the school site. The Minneapolis YWCA–USO was known as "the place to go for all the lonely" MISLS bachelors during the war. Since the first open house on June 5, 1943, the door count of the dances averaged over five hundred on any given Saturday night. More grandiose and popular were the special occasions, such as Christmas and Valentine formals, Easter and Halloween balls, and birthday parties, which attracted almost a thousand attendees. In addition, the young soldiers and their companions enjoyed having seasonal fairs, bus tours, buffet suppers, and many more fun activities.[55]

"We had weekly dances, picnics, swimming parties; we had those up at the lakes. It made me very happy to be in Minnesota," Nakasone reminisced. "I was most surprised to be able to dance with our *haole* [Hawaiian term primarily for people of European ancestry] compatriots. They were so nice to us." At that time racial segregation was still practiced, and interracial

Military Intelligence Service Language School soldiers dancing with members from the Minneapolis YWCA–USO during a weekend event, ca. 1944. *Courtesy of Bill Doi*

interaction remained taboo, in many parts of the country. Nakasone was even invited by a Caucasian nurse he had met through the dances to her home in Fairmont for an Easter dinner. "This is Minnesota. This is how they treated us even though we're of Asian descent." He added: "Thanks to Fort Snelling, I've become Minnesotan all the way through."[56]

Unlike the hostility of the West Coast, the Nisei were relieved to find the hospitality of Minnesotans who viewed them as patriotic American soldiers and not pernicious enemies of the state. Reasonably, transition to life in the north, even temporarily for several months or a couple of years, required some adjustments. It would be interesting to learn more about the Japanese Americans' adventures outside of the training camp and, of course, how they balanced their professional and private lives as well as physical and spiritual well-being.

Being a respectable Midwestern metropolitan area, Minneapolis and St. Paul were able to offer all their attractions and distractions for the young soldiers. Hundreds of them, with their weekend passes in their pockets, descended on the Twin Cities to enjoy parties, movies, restaurants, and bars in their leisure time between Saturday afternoon and Monday morning. "Over the weekend we used to go into town and eat—there was a chop suey joint; we used to eat there, eat the rice, you know," James Shimpei Oda said. A Kibei from California who became Aiso's assistant and a teacher in the school, Oda believed the cities provided a break from the grinding routine. "I used to stay at the hotel. That was the only recreation I had." Although Oda was given his own room and a cot as an instructor, it was no "fancy" accommodation. He remarked: "It's so nice to sleep in a bed in the hotel" once in a while.[57]

Bar hopping on weekends was "one of the vices" that the Nisei picked up during their tenure at Snelling, George Shigeru Hara confessed. "It didn't take long to learn how to drink beer and enjoy yourself. That was a good form of relaxation," he said; but "we never got to the point [of] laying out on the streets. Sometimes close but somehow, we got back in time to meet the Monday call." Likewise, Umeda, the poker player, claimed that he never forgot the first time he and his fellow soldiers, after thirty days confined in the camp, took the bus and went to downtown Minneapolis. They ended up at Nicollet and Washington Avenue and a bar caught their eyes. "We stepped into the bar. We wanted to have a cold drink. But the bartender said, 'No Indians. We can't serve Indians.'" Umeda explained who they were, and beer started flowing. The bartender even congratulated them for serving the US Army. "That's the kind of reception we received, where we understand each other," he added. "We found many, many people here in Minneapolis; they were friendly."[58]

Affability also arose from various organizations that furnished entertainment to lighten the Nisei's burden at school and brighten their days far from home. The expanding Japanese American community in the Twin Cities, guided by Earl and Ruth Tanbara, Reverend Daisuke Kitagawa, and many others, played an important role in assuring a more comfortable stay in Minnesota for the MISLS students. The Bar Association of Hennepin and Ramsey Counties, for example, donated prizes to honor outstanding students at commencement exercises, as did the local newspapers. The speech by Gideon Seymour, the editor of the *Minneapolis Star Journal and Sunday Tribune*, at the MISLS graduation on January 15, 1944, stated: "I know that your good manners and behavior in the community, your intelligent interests, and your concept of the basic American and Christian spirit of individual human dignity, have won for you as individual citizens and as a group the respect and admiration of thoughtful Minneapolis people. We are proud of Camp Savage and its men." Many churches and numerous citizens also took the Nisei into their homes as guests on weekends and on holidays.[59]

Generosity and gracefulness did not come automatically. No matter how "nice" Minnesota could be, good relationships required cultivation. Among those actively aiding the MISLS cause was Spark M. Matsunaga, a decorated 442nd veteran and later a US congressman and senator from Hawai'i. He stayed in Minnesota between June 1943 and March 1944 on a mission. "I was assigned, after returning from Italy, to Fort Snelling . . . primarily for the purpose of orienting the community, the business as well as the social community, to accept incarcerees from the camps in the hopes that they would fill jobs which were crying for workers," Matsunaga clarified. The school had taken a survey of the Twin Cities area and found that, of the seven hundred firms responding, not a single one would hire a Nisei. The public needed to be disentangled from the web of misconceptions and misinformation about Japanese Americans. Consequently, a six-month intensive campaign got underway.[60]

Matsunaga was a leader of the task force. He went all over town to speak with various businesses, the chamber of commerce, the American Legion, Veterans of Foreign Wars, Disabled American Veterans, and many social organizations, with crowds ranging in size from thirty-five to even three thousand at one time. "[People] could not distinguish the difference between Japanese of Japan and Japanese Americans. In their eyes . . . we all looked alike, and they looked upon us as enemies," Matsunaga said.

It was not until after he talked about his experiences on the battlefront with the men of the 100th Battalion and the 442nd that their minds changed. He pointed out that those "younger brothers were fighting in the European Theater, sacrificing their lives for their country, to prove their loyalty [and] to help in the preservation of American heritage." He then told his audience about the mortally wounded Nisei comrade who died in his arms. The soldier's last words were: "I know I'm going to die, but I have no regrets. Because I know that as a result of my dying, those who will go back, and our folks back home, will be finally recognized as pure Americans and have a better life."

The follow-up survey in early 1944 brought much-needed positive news. Every one of the seven hundred firms had hired or indicated a willingness to hire Japanese Americans. "It was indeed a very successful campaign," he concluded, "and I look upon that period of my life as one of the most useful [times] I spent in service."[61]

The MISLS students had to be the living proof of loyal compatriots and excellent citizens. During their Minnesota days, the Nisei shouldered their civic responsibilities with pride and perseverance. The school always ranked near the top of the units in the Seventh Service Command for war bond drives. Harris L. Romerein, field director of the Red Cross War Fund Drive, wrote in 1944 that "on a per capita basis, the voluntary contributions of the men and officers at Camp Savage exceeded that of all other stations in our jurisdiction." In terms of the Red Cross blood donations, the MISLS also set an enviable record, surpassing every requested quota.[62]

When Mayor John J. McDonough of St. Paul appealed to Colonel Harry J. Keeley, post commander of Fort Snelling, for assistance to the Twin Cities Coal and Coke Companies that was struggling to make adequate home deliveries due to a severe cold wave and lack of labor, the Japanese American soldiers went to work right away, driving trucks and delivering coal in subzero temperatures.[63]

Not surprisingly, Minnesota's winter was one indelible memory that many Nisei shared with a mixture of fondness and frustration. One might rightfully expect that the Japanese American newcomers, who grew up in the balmy climates of California and Hawai'i, would have a word or two to say about the snowy season. Toshio "Bill" Abe from San Diego, who was drafted in 1941, remembered his first winter at Camp Savage in 1942. "I looked at an outside thermometer. It said thirty-six degrees below," Abe remarked. "We didn't even know how to dress. The idea in cold climates [was] that you put on layers of clothing . . . to keep warm. Not knowing that, many of us suffered frostbite on our feet, hands and ears."[64]

The barracks, with only three old-fashioned potbellied stoves, did not seem propitious either. The drafty camp structures in Savage were no match for Minnesota winters. In each building one individual was given the "coal detail," to keep and stoke up the fires throughout the night. Aiso actually turned the circumstance to his advantage, letting it be known that those who failed the course would get assigned to the job until orders came through for duty elsewhere.[65]

Abe swore that his first would be his "last winter" in Minnesota. It did not turn out that way. Abe decided to settle in Bloomington and brought his incarcerated family from Poston with him after the war. He recalled his Savage days when he and his fellows went into the Twin Cities. "The civilians don't look at you like you're some kind of subhuman animal like they did on the West Coast. People were pleasant and friendly." There was nothing left for them in the West, he reckoned, and the freezing winters were not too bad when the people were warm and kind.[66]

Indeed, lovelier recollections also abounded. Many of the Nisei experienced snow for the first time. They were excited to learn to ski and ice skate, with disastrous results for one member who broke his leg yet still managed to graduate. They sang Japanese tea-house songs or Aloha melodies when they marched around the countryside for miles in the snow.[67]

Walking more than a mile against five-below-zero bitterness on Hennepin Avenue, Nakasone claimed that he was "nearly froze to death" on his first Christmas Day in Minnesota. "We knew that there were some Chinese restaurants there, and that's where the Hawai'i boys would go," he said. Frequented by the Nisei were a number of Chinese eateries in the area, such as Nankin Café, Yuen Faung Low (better known as "John's Place"), and Kin Chu Café, the one for which Nakasone was searching. "I still remember to this day, even though it was cold, I walked into the restaurant, and I saw a bunch of Hawai'i boys in there and was greeted warmly by them."[68]

Another food adventure took some of the Hawaiian Nisei to a Minneapolis restaurant where they asked for *sashimi*, a Japanese delicacy of thinly sliced raw fish. Although the chef had never heard of such a dish before, he complied the best that he could. The following Monday, school officials ordered the Nisei to stop ordering uncooked freshwater fish, since it might harbor parasites.[69]

Sometimes a little comfort food was all the Nisei needed to keep them going. Hardly any Japanese restaurants existed in the Twin Cities at the time. There was reportedly one between 1945 and 1946 opened by Saburo Sugita, a Japanese American from Hawai'i whose family briefly relocated to St. Paul after their release from Heart Mountain. The restaurant generated quite a following among Hawaiian Nisei soldiers, but the Sugitas returned to the islands after about a year. Hence, chop suey and fried rice were the closest dishes the Japanese Americans could find. Once a week or so was never enough though. Craving home cooking, the Nisei taught the small eating houses in the Savage-Shakopee neighborhood how to steam and serve rice to their liking.[70]

Bennie Kiyoshi Ouchida, an Oregonian who stayed in Minnesota until 1954, confirmed that "John's Place was a good one." He also recalled Rasmussen telling them about the food at the MISLS: "I'm going to treat these boys good. I'm going to turn all the beans back and ask for rice at the Chicago Commissary." And the rice came to Savage and Snelling. The Nisei were happy.[71]

Ouchida and his friends contended that rice went better with *tsukemono*, Japanese pickles. Therefore, the school asked farmers in the area if they could raise *daikon* (white turnips), even though the region had only ever produced the shorter and rounder type of radish. They were close enough, the soldiers thought. They then got a barrel and started to make *tsukemono* in the basement of one of the companies. Fermented food is often culturally specific and an acquired taste. Ouchida said the non-Japanese comrades complained about the "rotten" smell and had no idea what it was. Hiding *tsukemono* in a footlocker had also caused an inspector to order the soldiers to rewash their socks to eliminate the pungent odor in the barracks.[72]

Condiments were needed as well. When Captain (later Colonel) J. Alfred Burden, the "only *haole* from Hawai'i" at the Presidio and leader of the first combat intelligence team in the Pacific battles, returned to the United States in 1943, he had a gift for the Nisei. Burden was invited to give lectures at the school that fall, and besides "three sacks of documents, diaries, and one bundle of maps" from Asia, he brought back a barrel of captured Japanese *shoyu* (soy sauce), a rarity in wartime Minnesota, for which Rasmussen was grateful.[73]

All these Nisei soldiers mentioned in this chapter thus far were only a handful of the many outstanding individuals who spent their war years in Minnesota and subsequently left their unique marks on Asian American history. The MISLS at Savage and Snelling produced skilled intelligence linguists who helped not merely to bring about victory in World War II but also to maintain the peaceful occupation of Japan. The "Merrill's Marauders" in Southeast Asia and the "Dixie Mission" in China are cases in point. Over the past few decades, their heroic feats, in the steamy jungles of New Guinea, on the bloody beaches of Iwo Jima, or in the sweltering mountains of Myanmar, have been gradually revealed and recognized. MISLS alumni also include prominent politicians, entrepreneurs, academics, and artists. Their contributions are numerous, far exceeding the scope of these pages, and deserve a telling of their own. Going beyond the more traditional narrative, the next section will focus on the lesser-known aspects of the school through its more "atypical" members, whose stories intersect with class and gender in interesting ways.[74]

Besides the Nisei soldiers, there were also Nisei civilian teachers. How was life for them? Did they see things differently? The first storyteller who provided a more detailed depiction of a Californian Nisei's life at the MISLS, while also disclosing an unseen side of Minnesota, was Toshio Tsukahira. His background was characteristic of most young Japanese Americans at the time. He was born in Los Angeles in 1915 to immigrant parents, who owned a dry goods and menswear store in Little Tokyo. The young Tsuka-hira went abroad after high school to Meiji University in Tokyo from 1933 to 1936 for an associate of arts degree. He then attended UCLA, where he received a master's degree in history and political science in 1941.

Like many other Japanese Americans, Pearl Harbor changed his life dra-matically. His family, including his older brother who was already in the Army, were taken to Santa Anita and then to Heart Mountain. "There was no choice," he recalled. "This is inevitable, what can you do about it? We didn't know." What the Nisei did know was a way to avoid incarceration and make himself useful for his country. Tsukahira, studying for his doctoral degree and working as a teaching assistant at the time, applied to and was hired as a civilian instructor in the Fourth Army Intelligence School at the Presidio. It was February 1942. "[G]iven the war, and the fact that . . . all bets are off now; the one thing that I could contribute was some knowledge of Japanese, and with that I got my first real job."

Shortly after the school's relocation to Camp Savage, Tsukahira quickly made plans with his fiancée, Lilly Yuriko Fujioka, to wed, as she would other-wise have to follow her parents and siblings to Heart Mountain. "She came to San Francisco, and we got married practically the next day at [an] Episco-pal church." The town, he remembered, was deserted, as people were forced to leave.

The couple's honeymoon was "the trip from California to Minnesota." Tsukahira affirmed: "It was kind of fun; we were just like vagabonds. A little caravan of three cars and a dozen people, moving along the highways up through to Minnesota." They drove cross-country, from San Francisco to Reno to Idaho to Yellowstone, and then through the Black Hills and South Dakota to Minnesota. "[We] ended up in a hotel, the Radisson Hotel in Minneapolis. And we stayed there for two or three weeks, while we com-mitted to this new campus, [which] was really an old man's camp . . . a clus-ter of log cabins."

The newlyweds started their new life in rustic Camp Savage. They did not live in the main campus but another facility about a half mile down the road that had been turned into faculty living quarters. Those were "much solidly built" cabins, about the size of an Army barracks, which had been used by charitable organizations in the area to take care of seniors. The bachelors had their own space, whereas the married couples had what was called an apartment, with a kitchen, a living room, and two bedrooms, heated by a potbellied stove in the middle of the room.

The young couple found the environment "sort of rough," but did not consider it a "hardship" at all. Tsukahira said: "Considering what our folks [had] been subjected to, we felt we weren't that bad off. . . . Things look different as you look back, but at the time you're part of the climate of the period, and you can't stand off and look at the situation from any theoretical ground. You just lived it as it came along."

Apart from the "unbelievably" cold winter, Tsukahira had no qualms about his MISLS experience. "Minnesota was very pleasant, even in the middle of the war, because . . . the Midwest is pretty much an isolationist place, and the people were friendly," he maintained. "In fact, Savage was a very friendly town," including "the tradesmen and the local garage men. All of a sudden you have a thousand Japanese young people plunk down in your neighborhood, and there was no trouble, no incident."

The daily lives of the instructors seemed not to vary much from those of the students. Both worked hard from dawn until dusk. "We lived in a community down the road, [so] we got in our cars in the morning and commuted to the school," Tsukahira noted. "It was like a regular school schedule, the only difference was [that] we taught Japanese grammar, reading, writing, and *kanji*. . . . Then you'd give an exam every day."

Because of his academic background, Tsukahira was interested in Japanese grammar, which many of the instructors believed was "nonsense" or at least "not important." The standard practice was that all the students had to do was repeat and memorize what the teachers said. Yet there was a demand for more, especially from those intellectually curious students. "We can't just follow you by example. We want to know why this verb comes out this way, and that verb comes out that way," Tsukahira remembered his students telling him. Consequently, he and another faculty member, Richard Nichols McKinnon, a Hokkaido-born American whose father was white and mother was Japanese, compiled an instructional text of Japanese grammar specifically for the school.[75]

Since Tsukahira was one of the original instructors from Presidio, he also took on the supervisory role of the "Chairman of the Special Section." It was designed as a block of classes that focused on applied linguistic skills that "were necessary in the field." The teachers would come up with "dramatized" exercises of real-life scenarios, like dressing up in Japanese military uniforms and acting like prisoners of war. The students were then told to interrogate or "handle" them in Japanese. These were the critical skills that these military intelligence soldiers needed. The whole curriculum became more and more comprehensive as time went on, Tsukahira observed, as more and more "feedback from the graduates" in the Pacific reached the Minnesotan campus.

Inspired by the news from the front lines, Tsukahira believed he could better utilize his talent and contribute more to the war effort. Teaching the same materials, one class after another, four or five times a day, became repetitive and "boring" for him. In June 1944, he enlisted in the Army, "giving up a GS12 civilian job to be a buck private." Tsukahira said: "I felt that I had to do it, and I did, even though people thought I was crazy." Leading a successful military career during and after the war, Tsukahira would later become the highest-ranking Japanese American foreign service officer in his time. After his retirement in 1975, Tsukahira continued to teach at several major universities and undertook translating, writing, and consulting assignments. He passed away in his hometown of Los Angeles in 2011.

While the accomplishments of Tsukahira might not seem too unusual for an MISLS instructor or Nisei soldier, there was something special during his time at Camp Savage that few, if any, others experienced. He met and mingled with the "upper crust" of the Twin Cities and saw an extraordinary facet of the wartime North Star State. And it came about because of one of the Caucasian students. "Toward the second year, we had a lot of Caucasian officer candidates," Tsukahira said.

Compared to the Nisei students, the white students in general had more "interesting backgrounds" and, in the cases of some, even very "attractive personalities." The stories of the Japanese American soldiers were rather uniform, and in Tsukahira's words "pretty drab, to be honest." They were typical youngsters, second-generation children of working-class immigrants, be they mainland Kotonks or Hawaiian Buddha Heads. On the other hand, many of the Caucasian students were more mature and worldly, often having already graduated from universities, and a handful of them had lived and worked in Japan as missionaries, merchants, or academics.

Moreover, there were those who came from theater and the arts. Tsukahira remembered these refined students put together a musical, a series of very polished skits called *Nips in the Bud*. Many creators and performers were actually experienced professionals on the New York stage. One particular student also knew his way into Minneapolis high society. Hence, on Friday afternoons, Tsukahira and his companions, including the Presidio student-turned-faculty Thomas Sakamoto, who would later become a colonel, would take the bus or drive their own car to escape the camp and enjoy the lively city.

Tsukahira felt fortunate that he had the opportunity to glimpse the sophisticated flair of the Twin Cities. Certainly, it was common for soldiers to spend their breaks in town after five days of stringent training. They visited families and friends, had dinners with their fellows, joined a dance party, or simply went to bars and got drunk. The weekend evenings of Tsukahira were slightly more exclusive. "The editor of the leading local newspaper had a beautiful home in the heart of Minneapolis, and she loved music," he stated; "somehow we got to be frequent guests at this woman's house and her parties." There, Tsukahira was able to hobnob with not merely writers, journalists, artists, and intelligentsia from the Twin Cities but also "rebellious" bohemians from Greenwich Village, New York, as well as expatriates from Europe.

Among these "prominent people" was one whom Tsukahira could not believe—Minnesota's own Nobel Prize laureate Sinclair Lewis. "One night, Tom [Sakamoto], my wife, and I were invited to the home of Sinclair Lewis," the Nisei teacher said. "We had a dinner that I still remember. It was pheasant, which is a native game bird in Minnesota, and wild rice, which is also harvested by the [Indigenous peoples] in northern Minnesota. And that was aside from meeting this famous character." The star-struck Tsukahira found Lewis "not a very attractive man" at first, but a "fascinating" person when their conversation began in front of the fireplace.

Sakamoto concurred that the famed author of *Main Street* was "kind of a skinny man [with] very rough skin complexion." Lewis had lectured one of the literature classes at the University of Minnesota, which Sakamoto attended then; he even autographed a book for the Nisei solider. "Lewis was what we call a true old-fashioned liberal," Tsukahira asserted, "a part of a generation of Minnesota people, [and his] novels were critical of the American life."[76]

Another detail that Tsukahira did not forget was their discussion about the incarceration. He recalled Lewis asking him: "Why do you people put up with this outrage?" It was the first time that he had heard someone say that out loud. Tsukahira knew that to raise such questions required not only courage and conscience but also privilege and power, something that the Japanese Americans did not possess at the time. "There was nothing we could do or say," he lamented, unless one wanted to end up in jail or be expelled to Japan. The celebrated novelist "left a real impression" on Tsukahira; that he, a Midwestern figure, who probably had no contact with Japan or Japanese before their encounter, would look at the matter that way. That night was November 10, 1942. In fact, Lewis wrote about the house dinner with "Tsukahira and [his] lovely wife [Lilly]" in his diary.[77]

Tsukahira concluded that the language school was interesting "professionally" because there were all kinds of challenges there. Socially, however, the couple's stay in Minnesota would not have been as enjoyable and exciting without his student friend, the "host" of their city adventures. His name was Faubion Bowers, the second storyteller. He would become Supreme Commander General Douglas MacArthur's aide-de-camp and interpreter during the occupation of Japan, also later known as "the man who saved Kabuki."[78]

—

Bowers was already a seasoned musician and traveler by the time he reported to Camp Savage. He was only two years younger than his teacher friend Tsukahira. The Nisei instructor claimed that the Army would let in anybody who could remotely utter something that sounded like Japanese, but Bowers was a genuinely promising linguist. "We had a lot of duds, but we also had some of these . . . brilliant people [like] Faubion Bowers," Tsukahira said. Born in Miami, Oklahoma, in 1917, Bowers grew up in Tulsa and attended the University of Oklahoma. The bright-eyed young man soon found his way to New York City, transferred to Columbia University in 1935, and consequently studied at France's Université de Poitiers and at the École Normale de Musique. Upon his return to the Big Apple, he entered the Juilliard School to become a concert pianist. His interests then shifted to Javanese gamelan music, and he set out on a mail boat for Java (then a part of the Dutch East Indies and now Indonesia) in 1940. During a layover in Tokyo, Japan, he changed his mind to stay there instead, studying at the Japanese Language and Culture School (*Nichigo Bunka Gakkō*) while working an English teaching job at Hosei University.[79]

The reason why he remained in Japan was simple. Bowers was enthralled by the theater of Kabuki, literally meaning the "skillful performance of song and dance." A popular art form developed in seventeenth-century Edo Japan, Kabuki was renowned for its stylized acting, spectacular costumes, and glamorous makeup, with traditional tales of loyalty, love, honor, and revenge that were often intended to mirror current events. "It was really out of this world," Bowers said. "I was finally able to understand art." He added, "then I fell in love with Japan."[80]

As the tide of militarism washed over the empire and war tension intensified, Bowers realized it was increasingly difficult for a white person to stay there. He eventually had to leave under the suspicion of espionage. Bowers returned to the United States in September 1941. Two weeks later, he was drafted and sent to Fort Bragg, North Carolina, to train in the artillery as a private.

Immersing himself in Japanese theater circles for a year had converted Bowers into not only a Kabuki aficionado but also a fluent speaker of the language. Caucasian soldiers who knew Japanese well were few and far between yet in enormous demand. It still took the Army a few months to discover his linguistic talents. Bowers was tapped for the Presidio, and then off to Minnesota. Bowers's Army life instantly turned a more "pleasant" new leaf. "Rather homesick for the language, the people, and the country [he] had come to love," Bowers was now "surrounded by Nisei and Kibei," including his lifelong friend Tsukahira, whom he called by the nickname "Tusky," and apparently the glamorous parties in the Twin Cities.[81]

Bowers's move to the MISLS would prove to be beneficial for not only Bowers himself but also the Nisei soldiers. "I suddenly became a valuable property," he said. Like the Nisei students, Bowers joined the Army as a private. As a result, he was unable to receive a promotion similar to the Caucasian officer candidates, notably those who transferred from the University of Michigan or University of Colorado, despite having a comparable academic background and military training. The same situation applied to the Nisei soldiers. None of them were "qualified" for promotion.[82]

Predictably, tension developed between the Nisei soldiers and those Caucasian officer candidates when they met at the MISLS. Race was a factor, obviously, though the problem was more complex. Koji Ariyoshi, a Nisei labor activist from Hawai'i, summarized the dilemma aptly. The supply of white MISLS students was limited, and basically came in two types. First were the repatriates from Japan. They were immediately invited to Camp Savage and made captains or even majors. "Their aptitude for Japanese was far from impressive to deplorable, considering they had lived in Japan for ten to fifteen years," Ariyoshi later wrote in a newspaper. The second cohort was composed of Caucasian students from other military language programs, like those from the University of Michigan. "They were called 'cadets' and after the short period of training at the camp, they were to become officers," Ariyoshi continued.[83]

In retrospect, the white students probably did not need to be brilliant Japanese linguists. They were meant to be leaders; the dirty and dreary groundwork would have been done not by them but the Nisei. A Kibei instructor commented on these students' language facility: "Generally speaking, they're poor linguists, I'm afraid. If all the Caucasians work for me and I'm a commanding officer, I'll be scared stiff." Among the few exceptional Caucasian students was Major Sheldon M. Covell, who started in the first Savage class. "We were told," he remarked, "that our principal mission was to learn sufficient Japanese so that we could be sure the Nisei were translating, interrogating and reporting accurately, and not deceiving our intelligence people with false information." Covell hastened to point out that he never noticed such activity, "but that is what we were trained to detect."[84]

Resentment inevitably began to brew among the students because of the different treatment. "Here were the Nisei, brilliant in Japanese far beyond the ken of the *hakujin* [Caucasian] officers. They were drafted privates or PFCs at best," Bowers attested. "Their parents were confined in concentration camps, their worldly goods and homesteads sold at fractions of their value. And here they were, serving their country in the most invaluable way possible." Ariyoshi confirmed: "Nisei who studied with the [white cadets], in the same classrooms, under the same instructors, and who covered the same subjects, were to be assigned under [them] and were not made officers the same as them upon graduation." Many Nisei, like Ariyoshi, had attended or completed college. Their exclusion from commissions was never about education, competency, or language ability. The disparity, if not discrimination, bothered the Nisei and worried the school leaders.[85]

Alarmed at the diminishing morale and growing dissonance, Rasmussen and Dickey knew prompt action was needed. It was imperative that some of the outstanding Nisei be promoted. Since the Army moved on precedent, and "never in its history had anyone ever been commissioned on the basis of language," the colonels decided to make Bowers "a test case." The chosen one contended: "I was the best of the *Hakujin* linguists, and [Rasmussen] reasoned with the authorities in Washington, that to keep this poor private a private was a grave injustice."[86]

With Rasmussen's special intercession, Bowers was elevated to second lieutenant with "the little gold bars," as he would call it. "Once I was an officer on the basis of language, it became possible for the first time in the U.S. Army for all the more deserving, far better than I, Nisei and Kibei to be commissioned," he said. If it had not been for his case, Bowers believed that the Nisei would have remained privates, or at best, corporals, throughout the war. From Camp Savage, Bowers's military career took off to the Pacific, and he gradually rose in rank. At the war's end, he became the interpreter and secretary of General MacArthur in Japan. Not yet thirty then, Bowers began his "privileged existence" in the country with which he had fallen in love.[87]

On a different note, Bowers's highly placed position also granted him substantial clout in reviving Kabuki, which the Supreme Commander deemed feudalistic and therefore to be banished. After his demobilization in late 1946, he worked for the Theater Censorship Section of the Civil Censorship Detachment (CCD) at the GHQ and succeeded Earle S. Ernst, another Fort Snelling alumnus as well as a scholar of Asian performing arts, as its chief. Bowers was determined to keep the traditional theater alive, prevent it from censorship measures, and support his struggling artist friends during the postwar devastation. Be it by fate or coincidence, the MISLS connected both Bowers and Ernst to the postwar world of Kabuki, which, without them, would not have survived unscathed and become known to the West.[88]

What remains unknown yet potentially noteworthy about the Savage and Snelling alumni, like the two Kabuki champions, is how sexuality played a role in their military life and afterward. Although once married and the father of a son, Bowers and lifelong bachelor Ernst are two of the few military men known to be more embracing of gender and sexual fluidity— though not openly gay by today's standards—who received training at the MISLS and subsequently served in Japan during the occupation. If racism had been plaguing the nation, especially during wartime hysteria, homophobia was similarly rampant and severe. World War II was a turning point for gay men and lesbians in the military. Nevertheless, its history is difficult to trace. The case is probably even harder in the Asian American community. Were there any Nisei gay, lesbian, and queer military linguists who, too, fought the war with their lives but were forced to live in the shadows? This is a fair question with no clear answer until those minority voices, if they ever existed and can be discovered, find a place in the dominant historical narrative that equitably honors their service, suffering, and sacrifice.[89]

When talking about Japanese American linguists at the MISLS, one must realize that it was not a men-only club. Nisei women also played a role. Eventually, forty-eight Japanese American women, about half of them from Hawai'i, came to Fort Snelling and were trained as translators for the Army. How did they end up in the military, and hence, contributing a vital yet less visible chapter to the wartime MISLS story in Minnesota? A brief review of the backdrop behind these Nisei alumnae could be helpful.

Despite the obstacles, marginalized groups, including African Americans and women, made historic advances in the United States military during the war. Throughout World War II, the country had to rally all available resources, and as in conflicts past, the Army realized the potential of women to contribute to the cause. The WAC (Women's Army Corps) started as WAAC (Women's Army Auxiliary Corps) on May 14, 1942. About a year later on July 1, 1943, "Auxiliary" was dropped, and the WAC became an official part of the Army. There were altogether over 140,000 women whose services went beyond simply civilian volunteers in the war years.[90]

Like their male counterparts, female Japanese Americans were denied entry to the military after Pearl Harbor. When the War Department lifted

Bill Doi (left) and Aubrey Funai (right) working at the Special Services Office at Fort Snelling, 1944. *Courtesy of Bill Doi*

the ban on Nisei men joining the language school and the 442nd Regimental Combat Team, Nisei women also became eligible for enrollment. In March 1943, the WAC director, Colonel Oveta Culp Hobby, sent recruiters to the incarceration camps, but the response, similar to what Rasmussen encountered, was disappointing. If the Japanese American parents were hesitant about sending off their sons, they were even more reluctant to let go of their daughters. This problem was exacerbated by a slander campaign in the spring of 1943 against WAC members—accusing them of low moral character and sexual promiscuity. According to an FBI investigation, the rumors originated from military men who held negative views toward servicewomen. The news was fake, but the damage was real.[91]

Despite the unwarranted bad press and the Japanese Americans' own unjust imprisonment, some determined Nisei women were still eager to prove their loyalty and join the war effort. When Eleanor Roosevelt visited the Gila River camp in April 1943, several Japanese American women were said to have approached the First Lady about participating in the military. In the late spring of 1943, the Army Map Service in Cleveland, Ohio, accepted twenty Nisei women as civilian translators and sent them to Camp Savage for a two-week orientation. Concurrently, the Army turned to Hawai'i for potential contenders. In November 1943, the War Department officially started taking in Nisei women, yet "only thirteen could be obtained in the first six months of enlistment, and only negligible numbers thereafter."[92]

Throughout the war years, a total of 142 Japanese American women volunteered for the WAC. Showing their loyalty to the United States was the main impetus behind their enlistment. Furthermore, the opportunities for Nisei women were limited at the time; some believed that the military would provide them with not just travel and adventure but also education and job skills that would be useful after the war. Because their number was modest, not enough to form a Japanese American women's corps, they were integrated into teams with other ethnic groups, unlike the Nisei men as well as African Americans and Puerto Rican women, who all served in segregated units. The inducted women usually went through five weeks of basic training at one of five centers. Most of the Nisei women were sent to Fort Des Moines, Iowa, and Fort Oglethorpe, Georgia.[93]

The four-dozen strong Nisei WAC group began to arrive at Fort Snelling in November 1944, receiving classes separated from the men and noncombat assignments upon graduation. Three outstanding Nisei female students even broke the glass ceiling and joined the previously all-male teaching staff at the MISLS after the war's end, as the school retained them as enlisted instructors. Eleven of the Nisei, along with one Chinese American and one Caucasian American, were sent to Occupied Japan, and the rest to the Pacific Military Intelligence Research Section (PACMIRS) at Camp Ritchie, Maryland, which was later moved to the Central Document Center in Washington, DC. Only one Nisei WAC member, Ruth Yuriko Fujii, from Kauai, Hawai'i, was sent to the Pacific Theater in the Philippines and China during the war. Luckily, a few stories from this group of Nisei women at Snelling have been passed down and preserved.[94]

—

Sue Suzuko Ogata Kato was among the original five Japanese American women in the WAC, inducted on December 13, 1943, in the office of Colorado Governor John F. Vivian. Born in North Platte, Nebraska, Kato grew up in a farming area which included about twenty-five Japanese families. Kato's father was an "adventurous" and "assimilated" Issei from Fukuoka; "I talked to my dad in English. He was very Americanized," she remembered; "his dream was to be naturalized as an American citizen." It was an impossible dream at the time. Kato also kept in mind what her father told her. "Because of our physical looks, we would never be fully Americanized. . . . And that's why it was important to remember our Japanese heritage."[95]

After she graduated from high school in 1938, Kato's father chose to settle in Greeley, Colorado, where, unlike California and Nebraska, Japanese immigrants were allowed to own land. Although her family in Colorado did not go through the forced removal and incarceration, the small town in the Centennial State was not immune to war hysteria and racism. Her father's funds were frozen after the war broke out due to his Japanese descent. The young Kato was also "shocked" to experience "three or four young boys" who "threw pebbles" at her while walking on the street. When the twenty-two-year-old Kato saw the WAAC's recruiting announcement in the newspaper, she immediately wrote a letter to volunteer in May 1943, but months went by without any response.

As soon as the WAAC became WAC and began to accept Nisei women, Kato received her notice after the FBI had cleared her. At first Kato's father was "horrified" by her decision. Then Kato explained her reasons. "I joined the WAC . . . to prove my Americanism," she declared, "to release the boys who were tied down from the desk jobs but would want to go to combat." Finally her father gave his blessing. Kato continued: "I know my father and the rest of my family were proud of my joining the military service. . . . My two brothers were not old enough." One of them, Kenneth Ogata, eventually went to war at nineteen with the 442nd Regiment. Her brother came back from the war safely, but they never talked about it.[96]

Kato received her travel orders to report to Minnesota in the winter of 1944 after the six-week basic training at Fort Des Moines and about a year of clerical duty at Fort Devens, Massachusetts. "There were ten of us who were sent there initially, [and] later they recruited about twenty or twenty-five from Hawai'i," she said. "That's how our WAC detachment was formed at Fort Snelling." Since Kato "didn't have that much of a background," she was placed in the middle class. For "nine months, every day, we had compulsory study time [even] on Saturdays," she said. Upon graduation, she was transferred to Camp Ritchie, then to Washington DC, working mostly on document translations.

Apart from learning about military life and the Japanese language, Kato had another reason to find her time at the MISLS to be special. There she met her future husband—Minori Kato, who was stationed at Snelling at the same time. Kato's memories of the MISLS and the WAC were lively, and live on in some ways today. "I have this huge scrapbook while I was in the

Military Intelligence Service Language School job and liaison section, ca. 1945. *Courtesy of Bill Doi*

service, and I was getting . . . to the boys before they went overseas to autograph it." Her scrapbook is now digitalized and available at the California
State University Dominguez Hills Photograph Collection.[97]

There was one person whom Kato claimed had it "for the longest time,"
but he returned the book without signing or writing any message. The soldier was Thomas Okamoto. "After I got discharged and years later when I
got all these things to put in my book . . . then I run across this." Kato found
"a caricature of Minnie Mouse" of her. "He was working for Walt Disney
Studios before the war . . . [and] I felt so sheepish after thinking all those
bad thoughts about him." Kato smiled: "I often wanted to thank him for the
best autograph out of the whole scrapbook. . . . My friend Miwa borrowed
this some years ago. She's the one who mentioned it."

The friend "Miwa" of whom Kato spoke fondly was Miwako Yanamoto,
a fellow MISLS alumna and a WAC veteran. Born in Los Angeles and raised
in Boyle Heights and Little Tokyo, Yanamoto was a student at Los Angeles
Community College when she and her family were removed and incarcerated at Poston. While working as a secretary in the law department at
the camp, she received permission in September 1943 to join a WRA office
in New York, first in the city and then upstate in Rochester. Yanamoto then
decided to "take a more active part in the war effort"; she applied to the
WAC and was accepted in April 1945. After completing her training at Snelling, Yanamoto was sent to Japan in September 1945 as one of the eleven
Nisei WACs.[98]

Serving as Japanese American WACs, Yanamoto summed up their role as
"unofficial ambassadors" and "mannequins of democracy." By and large, the
WACs' assignments "did not transcend the domestic sphere," and hence,
were mostly composed of clerical work. More specifically, the Nisei corps
members were expected to accentuate their "femininity" through their physical appearances, meaning short skirts and makeup as a part of their uniform.
They had to act as "American women" yet retain their Japanese linguistic
heritage to set an example of modern womanhood for all Japanese women
to observe and follow. Indeed, Yanamoto learned that MacArthur did not
approve of enlisted women serving overseas. The general ordered them to
either return to the United States as WACs or serve one-year contracts as
civilians in Tokyo with the Civil Intelligence Service.[99]

Yanamoto chose the civil servant option and stayed in Japan. The war was over by then, which made her tenure easier. After serving in Tokyo for a year, Yanamoto returned to Los Angeles and carried on her civil service career throughout her life. In addition, she was an active member in the local Japanese American community and a keeper of the Nisei WAC history. She passed away in 2006.

While the Nisei WACs had various experiences before, during, and after the war, they all recapped their time at the MISLS as "intense." The school seemingly did not treat the female students more leniently. The only difference was that the WACs were exempted from learning about interrogation of prisoners, which was the responsibility of the men. The women soldiers also did not have to handle firearms. "We can't carry guns, but we had parades and gas masks," Alice Tetsuko Kono, a Nisei from Hawai'i, recalled about her basic training in Georgia, before coming to Minnesota.

Kono belonged to the group of fifty-nine WACs from Hawai'i, including not just Nisei women but also Chinese, Filipina, Korean, and mixed-race Americans, who reported for duty in November 1944. Kono described her six months in Minnesota as "fun" regardless of the "rough" language classes. Like many other MISLS students, she took the bus to the Twin Cities on weekends and used the furloughs to travel to Chicago, Salt Lake City, and even down south to Alabama to see old friends from Honolulu.

In addition, "the food was generally good," she noted, "because we put on a lot of weight." One particular menu did not earn much praise from her though. "I remember every Friday at the mess hall they gave us fish." Kono thought the shoyu-style fish was tasty at the beginning. After getting the same dish that was cooked in the same way every week, she had second thoughts. "I don't know about others, but I was tired of that fish," she laughed. "I don't want to eat fish anymore."[100]

One of Kono's Snelling classmates was Haruko Sugi Hurt from Gardena, California. Like her fellow Nisei WACs from Hawai'i, the "all day" routine at MISLS was among her most unforgettable memories in Minnesota. "Each of us had a desk with dictionaries, big ones [and] little ones . . . all lined up, English, Japanese dictionaries," she noted. "We had lessons in history, geography, and military terminology . . . about five subjects." At the end, it was the rigorous curriculum, not the language itself, that made a lasting impression on Hurt. "The minute I got discharged, I didn't want to think one thing about Japanese language," Hurt laughed. "I managed to forget everything except the very simple things."[101]

The reason why Hurt joined the WAC was simple as well. She wanted to pursue a more "inspiring" career. Her backstory indeed echoed many of the other Nisei on the West Coast. Coming from a "poor" but caring lease farming family of Issei immigrant parents, Hurt was sent to Rohwer, Arkansas, with her family as the removal began. Understandably, she sought ways to avoid incarceration and found sponsored employment in Chicago, first as a domestic helper for a Jewish American family and then a couple of clerical jobs. Her sister, who rode the train with her upon leaving the camp, went to Minnesota to join her fiancé at the MISLS. "Towards the end of 1944, I heard about the Japanese language school run by the military in Snelling [from] my brother-in-law," Hurt said. "I contacted them. . . . I got correspondence back saying [they] were . . . forming a WAC unit."

Hurt was the sole Japanese American in her WAC class and the only one who went to Minnesota after the six-week basic training at Fort Des Moines. She arrived at Fort Snelling in the spring of 1945. "The WAC group had not come together yet. They were waiting for the Hawaiian WACs . . . [who] were training at Fort Oglethorpe." In the meantime, Hurt served as a clerk at the headquarters for Aiso, the director of academic training. "He had his little private office there, and right outside the door, I had my little typewriter."

Looking back at those dramatic decades of the twentieth century, from World War II to McCarthyism, the civil rights movement to the Civil Liberties Act of redress and reparation, Hurt counted her WAC experience as the most valuable and satisfying. She knew that she did her share of serving the country. After finishing the language program in Minnesota in the fall of 1945, she was sent to Camp Ritchie and then the Central Document Center in Washington, DC. Japan had surrendered by then.[102]

At the intelligence offices, most fellow servicemen and women with whom she associated were Americans, but she also worked together with linguists from other nations. "The women counterparts, especially, the British were less than friendly. They tended to never speak to us Nisei or even acknowledge our presence," she opined; "but, this was a minor matter."

Through the GI Bill after her discharge, Hurt was able to attend college and graduate school at the University of Southern California School of Social Work, a field to which she dedicated her post-military career. Before she passed away in 2012, Hurt had these words for the next Japanese American generation: "Politically, they should become more active . . . rather than just sitting back and complaining if things don't go right."[103]

Peggy Doi, the daughter of Bill Doi whose words began this chapter, is one of those active Sansei. Even in her retirement, she has continued to share the story of her father and the MISLS through various public presentations, notably collaborating with the Twin Cities chapter of the JACL as well as other organizations. "Going through school, it seemed like almost every year I would have to give a talk about internment because no one knew about it," Doi said. "Nobody even knew about Camp Savage being here. A lot of people did not know [it] was a Military Intelligence Service Language School."[104]

Even fewer people know about the Nisei women who sojourned and studied at the MISLS, or the gay white alumni among its graduates. Since the wartime connection between Japanese Americans and Minnesota is no longer a military secret but instead a critical lesson, hopefully more efforts will be devoted to uncovering the missing pieces of that history and to keeping the memories of the school and its diversity of teachers, students, and staff alive.

Vestiges of the yesteryears are often closer than one expects. The MISLS veterans were, for example, key benefactors of the Normandale Japanese Garden in Bloomington. Plans for the garden began in 1967 when the Normandale Community College campus was still being developed and the college donated two acres of land for the project. "From the groundbreaking ceremony in 1972 to the dedication ceremony in 1976, many individuals and companies donated money, time, and materials to construct the garden."[105]

Led by Frank Yanari, a Nisei alumnus from Colorado who settled in Minnesota after the war, the fundraising campaign of the local MISLS group came up with an impressive $25,000 to start making the dream of the garden a reality. In November 1971, a national organization representing the six thousand MISLS veterans threw its support behind the cause and pledged to match the funds to a total of $50,000. The construction was hence able to begin the next year in 1972. In particular, the school alumni's donation made the hexagonal shrine and its adjacent drum bridge possible. The project was overseen by famed garden architect Takao Watanabe, who chose plants, shrubs, and trees that could not only meet the authentic Japanese aesthetics but also withstand the cold of Minnesota winters.[106]

The garden is more than a heartfelt gift to the place that treated the MISLS veterans with empathy and dignity. The "hidden gem" also symbolizes the long historical link between Minnesota and Japanese Americans, which, as time goes by, might have waned yet should not be allowed to waste away. Yanari, along with his fellow graduates, sensed an opportunity for them to connect the past to the present. The MISLS file was declassified in 1974. The dedication day on July 18, 1976, attracted seventy-two MISLS alumni, many of whom traveled across the country, to witness this memento of their time at Savage and Snelling. In 1981, the garden held its first "sukiyaki dinner," a successful fundraising event that quickly established itself as an annual affair for the Twin Cities Japanese American community that continued until the first decade of the next century.[107]

One of the founding members of the garden and a prominent organizer behind the dinner was Kimi Taguchi Hara, who represents a different group of Nisei in Minnesota during the war as a nurse who served at St. Mary's Hospital in Rochester, now a part of the Mayo Clinic Hospital. The next chapter will focus on her story along with the Japanese American women in the US Cadet Nurse Corps in the wartime North Star State.

6 | Compassion and Commitment

Japanese American Nurses and the US Cadet Nurse Corps

> "One of the highlights of coming here [was] being young and inexperienced, and you're an overnight supervisor. How am I going to handle students when they come up in the middle of the war, and they come by not one or two? ... I came to Rochester in March 1942, and I've never left Minnesota."—KIMI TAGUCHI HARA

imi Hara was among the initial group of Japanese American professionals who moved to the North Star State during the war. She started at St. Mary's Hospital, where she worked as a night supervisor in the obstetrics department. Born in Green Lake near Seattle in 1916, Hara was the eldest daughter of an Issei truck-farming family. She began working at the age of fourteen after her father passed away. Yet Hara managed to attend the University of Washington and then the Swedish Hospital School of Nursing, while supporting her four younger siblings in school. She graduated and became a full-time nurse in 1940, a year before the attack on Pearl Harbor, "when all hell broke loose," as she described. The familiar story of losing their home, surveillance by the government, and forced eviction soon followed.

That was a time of crisis and chaos when no one really knew what might happen to them. "Because I had my mother who was a widow with five children," she realized, "if I could find a job in the middle or east of the Rockies, but away from the Pacific coast, we would not have to go to the camp." The chief of staff at the Swedish Hospital then was a retired doctor from the

Mayo Clinic who had discussed Hara's dilemma with Sister Domitila, the superintendent at St. Mary's Hospital. "She was very understanding and helpful because she agreed to take many people," Hara noted; "and others would take care of the workers, skilled farmers or whatever of all kinds. It wasn't only nursing." What Hara referred to was the third route, besides going to college and joining the military, that Japanese Americans could take to avoid the fate of incarceration—securing sponsored employment. Those Nisei who came to Minnesota for work and vocational training are the focus of this and the subsequent chapter. They are smaller in number, approximately a few hundred, with scant or scattered records at best. The majority did not stay for long. As a result, their wartime stories are seldom talked about, even if they are just as interesting.

Their ability to restart their lives in a place they barely knew certainly shows their audacity, resilience, and perhaps luck. However, their relocation became possible only when people and communities were willing to stand with their fellow Japanese American citizens against the backdrop of war hysteria and political hypocrisy. Minnesota was one of these friendly places. "I didn't know Sister Domitila or anybody. I was hanging onto [my doctor's] good recommendation," Hara said. "That's all I needed. He told me if they don't pay you enough, you can go beg a roll or two. He didn't know how much I'd like to eat a roll or two."[1]

For those who knew and met her, Hara was a person full of life, wisdom, and optimism. According to her granddaughter, Elizabeth "Liz" Hara, "grandma was always so busy, so social, and so generous. She could not sit still, always having somebody visiting or cooking." The cookie jar was never empty when she was around.[2]

Being a trailblazer in many ways, Hara was the first Nisei nurse serving in a Minnesota hospital and rose to be a prominent figure in both the profession as well as the Japanese American community in the state. Starting at St. Mary's in 1942, she immediately brought her mother and siblings, including her younger sister Reiko Taguchi Sumada, from Minidoka to Rochester. "I was fortunate because I had established a residence here; so, they were one of the early ones to leave the camp," Hara said. The family stayed in Minnesota and did not look back.[3]

During the war, she worked at a station hospital at Fort Snelling, where she met her husband, Sam Satoshi Hara. He was a member of the famed 442nd Regimental Combat Team. The wounded fighter had just returned from France after a knee surgery in England. The nurse and the hero married in 1945. Knowing the challenges of the Nisei soldiers, Hara tried her best to make them feel welcome and have a taste of home. "We gave them rice and Japanese food. . . . My mother raised vegetables, and she fed the boys," Hara remarked. "They did really well, and I think we all had a pretty good time."[4]

Hara's nursing career took off after the war. She attended the University of Minnesota and received a bachelor's degree in nursing education in 1953 and a master's degree in nursing administration in 1957. Her impressive résumé included the Ripley Memorial Hospital (closed in 1957), the Fairview hospitals, and the Minnesota Health Department. She was one of the founding faculty of the nursing program at St. Olaf College. Her son Thomas Hara recalled his mother being the instructor to all these young nurses, and she would have each class come to their house for a Japanese dinner. "My mother said there was a notice posted on the bulletin board of the hospital,

Kimi Hara graduation photo,
University of Minnesota, 1953.
Courtesy of the Hara Family

advising the nursing students to go to Riverside Park to pick up some twigs and practice using chopsticks, because Nurse Hara had no silverware," he said. "She thought that was hilarious."[5]

Hara's embrace of nursing in the North Star State lasted a lifetime. Between 1955 and 1973, she taught emergency childbirth procedures at the Minnesota Bureau of Criminal Apprehension and the State Patrol Division. "That job got her out of a couple speeding tickets," her son chuckled. From 1963 until her retirement in 1980, Hara was the associate executive director at the Minnesota Board of Nursing, overseeing its licensure examinations, education, financial aid, and scholarship programs, and handling all disciplinary cases filed with the board. In addition, she was a leader of the Minnesota Nurses Association and a school inspector for the World Health Organization in Okinawa before the island's sovereignty was returned to Japan in 1972.[6]

Also, invaluable and indispensable was Hara's contribution to the local Japanese American community. She was instrumental in founding the Twin Cities chapter of the JACL in 1949, directing the scholarship program to raise funds for college-bound Japanese American high school graduates. On weekends, Hara was a Sunday school teacher at Gethsemane Episcopal Church in Minneapolis. She, too, helped to establish the Normandale Japanese Garden Committee and the Japan America Society of Minnesota, where she served as chair and president, respectively. Besides being a cultural and linguistic bridge for the Issei, particularly on medical issues, Hara fought for fair treatment of Japanese Americans in town and lobbied against discriminative housing developers. In 2003, she received the Japan–Minnesota Partnership Award, named after and presented by former Vice President Walter Mondale himself, for her dedication and service. "She just knew everybody," Liz Hara added; "you couldn't go anywhere without her running into someone she knew."[7]

Hara's popular "sukiyaki" fundraising dinner for the Normandale Japanese Garden, a painstakingly prepared traditional Japanese hot pot with simmering beef and vegetables, was legendary. Beginning in the 1980s, the annual gathering was the social and cultural event for the community, lasting for more than two decades. "It was easy to buy two hundred and fifty pounds of rice and get three hundred pounds of rib steak, but getting the butcher to slice the beef into one-eighth of an inch, and arrange them up in a one-pound package, that's more difficult," Thomas Hara noted. "But she found such a butcher, and he soldiered on for twenty years." Liz Hara also had warm memories of the day before the sukiyaki dinner. "I would be part of the old lady crew, helping chop vegetables," the Yonsei (fourth-generation Japanese American) explained. "My grandma was very particular about how the vegetables got chopped, always on the diagonal." The last dinner was held in 2007, the year that Hara passed away.[8]

Certainly, Hara was most remembered and revered as a role model for the young Nisei nurses, many of whom came to Minnesota, to live on their own for the first time. Few, if any, hospitals in the state had seen a nurse of Japanese or Asian ancestry then. "We were accepted so easily by St. Mary's simply because Kimi Taguchi Hara was already working there," Sumiko Ito Dahlman attested; "I've always wanted to be a nurse. . . . Kimi has been a real

Kimi Hara (right) met with President John F. Kennedy (left) along with the US Army Corps nurses at the White House, ca. 1962. *Original photo taken by Cecil W. Stoughton; courtesy of the Hara Family*

inspiration to me all my life. She was a wonderful nurse, and her reputation went [beyond St. Mary's]."[9]

Dahlman was a University of Washington nursing student whose life was abruptly interrupted in 1942. Wartime circumstances drove her and her family of five out of their home to Minidoka in Idaho, where she worked as a nurse's aide. Camp life took a heavy toll on her family, and Dahlman desperately wanted to leave and take them with her. After countless yet fruitless applications to nursing schools, she received the acceptance letter from St. Mary's a year later. Delighted and determined, Dahlman came to Minnesota and answered the call from the US Cadet Nurse Corps.[10]

Like their soldier brothers and sisters, the Cadet Nurse Corps, which operated between 1943 and 1948, opened the door for more than 350 Nisei women who wanted to reclaim their freedom, prove their loyalty, and serve their country in uniform. During the war, these nurses worked in more than sixty hospitals and communities throughout the country. Minnesota should be proud that St. Mary's in Rochester, affiliated with the Mayo Clinic, took in forty-five Japanese American students, more than any other school of nursing in the nation. The nearby Kahler Hospital School of Nursing (now a part of the Mayo Clinic College of Medicine and Science) also participated in the program and admitted fifteen Nisei students.[11]

—

The path through which Nisei women could join the Cadet Nurse Corps resembled the twisting trails of their fellow Japanese Americans in higher education and the military. Forced to leave their homes on the West Coast, these women were confined to remote incarceration camps, denied the right to enroll in nursing schools, or not permitted to complete their courses after the war started. Echoing the hardships of other aspiring students, they had to navigate the tedious application process and secure clearance from the authorities—including the War Department, the Navy, and the FBI, oftentimes with the help of the NJASRC, the student relocation council. Unlike "ordinary" university students, however, the cadet nurses received a tuition-free education together with a monthly stipend of fifteen dollars (approximately two hundred today). In return they pledged to put their professional training at the federal government's disposal for the duration of the war.

Comparable to the Nisei soldiers in the armed forces, the cadet nurses also served in uniform, providing critical support to the war effort, protecting the health care of the home front and preventing the collapse of the country's medical system. Nevertheless, these women were not considered veterans, despite a recent congressional attempt to grant honorary veterans' status to surviving members of the corps. Their experiences were hence similarly difficult but slightly different from the other two trajectories. Before turning the spotlight to the Japanese American cadet nurses, a succinct overview of this special program will offer useful context to their stories.[12]

That Nisei women were able to become nurses was a feat in itself. The dawn of the twentieth century saw nursing, as both a civilian career and military role, redefined as "a white, female, and middle-class occupation." When the Nurse Corps was established in 1901 and later redesignated as the Army Nurse Corps (ANC) in 1918, men were no longer accepted as nurses. However, the competition for womanpower at the time was very acute. With more and better paid jobs available for Caucasian women in industries, as well as the high demand for nursing services and the high nursing student dropout rate, new ways to augment the country's nursing force had been a concern long before the war. Gender and racial politics, in this case, gave an entry point for a minority group like Japanese American women to pursue nursing as a vocation, which faced one of its gravest shortages in history after the surprise attack on Pearl Harbor.[13]

The Cadet Nurse Corps emerged as an answer to the problem. In fact, the Army ran its own school of nursing in World War I, with 21,480 women serving with the Army Nurse Corps in 1918. At the onset of World War II, the Army estimated that at least twice that many nurses would be necessary, and it had neither the facilities nor the personnel to support their training. The burden of supplying nurses for both military and civilian needs then rested with the public health authorities in conjunction with nursing organizations and major hospitals. In the spring of 1943, they worked together and drafted a nurse training bill that aimed to alleviate the problem. House Representative Frances Payne Bolton from Ohio sponsored the legislation, first introduced as the "Victory Nurse Corps" in March of 1943. Under the supervision of the United States Public Health Service (USPHS), the corps would provide accelerated training of nurses (twenty-four to thirty months) for the armed forces, governmental and civilian hospitals, and health agencies through existing accredited nursing schools.[14]

Congress swiftly passed this Nurse Training Act, commonly known as the Bolton Act, and authorized the Cadet Nurse Corps on June 15, 1943; President Roosevelt signed it into law on July 1. The act did not standardize nursing schools or their curricula throughout the country, but rather helped them to attract students and continue with their own programs of education with federal funds. From its creation in 1943 to its closure at the end of 1948, a total of 179,294 student nurses enrolled in the program at 1,250 schools of nursing; 124,065 women graduated, almost four hundred of which were Nisei. It was the largest and youngest group of uniformed women to serve the nation during the war and the early postwar years.[15]

Although the corps was open to all women between the ages of seventeen and thirty-five with good health and a high school diploma, Japanese Americans had to weather the storm of racism to claim their rightful place. Before one could enter the corps, the cadet needed to first enroll in a nursing program. Expectedly, it was not simple or easy. As soon as the exclusion orders began in February 1942, concerned educators, like the director of the University of California School of Nursing, Margaret Anthony Tracy, had already started inquiring about the possibility of transferring their Japanese American students to other institutions away from the West Coast to carry on their studies. She had twenty-two Nisei women who were all academically at the top of their class at the time.[16]

Sadly, the response from a meeting of the National League for Nursing Education was far from encouraging. They doubted if any school in the country would accept Japanese American students. Tracy persisted nonetheless. She pulled some strings of her own and contacted Henrietta Adams Loughran, director (and later dean) of the University of Colorado College of Nursing, for assistance.

The Centennial State was among the earliest states to accept Nisei nursing students. Supported by Governor Ralph Carr, Loughran devised a plan to bring Japanese Americans from schools of nursing at universities in California and Washington to Colorado. Many believed that Carr's morally upright yet politically unpopular choice to fight alongside Japanese Americans against bigotry and oppose incarceration might have doomed his career; he lost the

US Senate election in 1942. Still, he helped to change the lives of more than five hundred young Japanese Americans, who were able to avert imprisonment and continue their education in Colorado. Many nursing students among them were grateful and deemed themselves lucky.[17]

Likewise, some of the fortunate Nisei students found their way to Minnesota. In the fall of 1942, the NJASRC had already reached out to St. Mary's School of Nursing about relocating students to their program, after it appeared on the approval list of the Army and Navy. Aware of the plight of the Japanese American women, Sister Antonia Rostomily, the school director, believed that St. Mary's, with its experience in serving international patients and especially its partnership with the Mayo Clinic, would be a suitable place for these young nurses. She shared the idea with the student council and presented it at an all-school meeting. The students were reportedly in favor and saw no reason why their fellow citizens could not be part of their school.[18]

St. Mary's was among the earliest institutions to open their doors to Japanese Americans. Peggy Tokuyama Fukushima of the Santa Clara School of Nursing in California was the first Nisei transfer student to continue her studies in Rochester on October 16, 1942. Besides nursing students, St. Mary's employed other Japanese Americans for a variety of positions as well, including nursing instructor, night supervisor, dietitian, head nurse, and secretary for the school of nursing. Leading the way, notably, was Kimi Hara.[19]

St. Mary's also participated in the Cadet Nurse Corps program immediately following the implementation of the Bolton Act in the summer of 1943. However, this chance for Nisei women to join a uniformed service and pursue a nursing education was not guaranteed. Rumors circulated that the program excluded non-white applicants. The NJASRC thus had to explicitly ask Surgeon General Thomas Parran of the Department of Public Health Service to clarify whether Japanese and African Americans were qualified for such scholarships.[20]

At last, the issue was settled by the director of the Cadet Nurse Corps, Lucile Petry Leone, who had been a faculty member and assistant dean at the University of Minnesota School of Nursing for more than a decade before assuming the federal position in 1941. Leone cited Public Law 74 of the 78th Congress in her written response that read: "There shall be no discrimination in the administration of the benefits and appropriations." Nisei women ought to have the equal and legal right to join the cadets. She concluded: "In a war which we are fighting for democracy, we believe it behooves all of us to weigh any action which might be interpreted as discriminatory."[21]

Not surprisingly, eligibility did not necessarily translate into admission. In 1943 there were only about twenty nursing schools in the country that would enroll American women of Japanese ancestry. Some programs admitted one or two students at the most. Dahlman, for example, had filled out many applications with disappointing replies such as "We are sorry, but our quota is full." The pretexts for refusal sounded like a broken record. They usually blamed the unwillingness of the hospital board or the university administration, the lack of necessary clearances from the federal departments, and the potential challenges of Japanese Americans working directly with a mistrusting public in the hospital wards or health facilities.[22]

The outlook was so gloomy that *The American Journal of Nursing* felt the urgency to address the problem of prejudice against Nisei women, who were excited to take this opportunity to join the corps. "It is not the function of this magazine to urge upon schools of nursing the course they are to take in this matter," the editorial in October 1943 stated. "It is the function of this magazine to place the facts before its readers and to urge careful, unbiased, and imaginative study of the situation by faculties of schools of nursing, members of hospital boards, and representative citizens, to the end that a solution may be found for loyal American girls whose ancestors happen to have been Japanese." The editors went on to stress that the Student Relocation Council handled the entire process of placement with extreme scrutiny, and the FBI checked each individual with due diligence. The Japanese American women were cleared to go, ready to work, and eager to serve.[23]

Acting against the grain, the sisters and students at St. Mary's greeted Nisei nurses with grace. "My first impressions of Rochester and St. Mary's were of a beautiful city," Dahlman recalled. "I could hardly wait to start studying and working." She was one of the initial fifteen Japanese American women admitted to the school in 1943. "I was very happy to be able to be accepted—my classmates, instructors, and hospital staff helped us immensely," Dahlman added. The congeniality and respect were mutual. "We have found them all to be loyal, ambitious, outstanding in their scholastic accomplishments as well as skillful in their care of patients," Sister Antonia said of the Japanese American women. "Many tributes of praise have been paid them by patients, students and instructors. They should certainly be commended for their splendid adjustment during their trying period of war."[24]

How well these Nisei nurses adapted to their new careers at St. Mary's and their new lives in the state is worthy of a closer examination. Obviously, the Cadet Nurse Corps was conceived as a short-term expedient to cope with a crisis, and the graduates were meant to serve in various parts of the country after their training. Therefore, nearly all of them left the state within a few years. However brief and fleeting, their sojourns lend a unique angle of ethnicity and gender to draw out a richer and more nuanced picture of a wartime Minnesota. Continuing with Dahlman, the next segment introduces three more Nisei women, whose stories provide different views of the peoples and places of the state in that special era.

The St. Mary's alumnae, at least those who were willing to talk about their experiences, all had fond memories of their time in Rochester. "My three years of nurses training at St. Mary's were wonderful years," Dahlman proclaimed; "being a part of the Cadet Nurse Corps helped us to become better citizens. We were proud of our insignia, and we did our best to uphold the Corps." Performing her patriotic and professional duty was important, but that fortunately was not the whole life of the twenty-one-year-old Nisei cadet. "I worked hard as a student. I also went out with friends, when possible," she said. "We truly enjoyed the teas and parties!"[25]

After one such party in her early student days, an incident occurred that Dahlman vividly remembered for decades. She was compelled to send a letter to the nursing school's alumni office fifty years later to share her story. "It was with a thankful heart and a fierce determination to succeed that I entered my probationary period," she wrote in 1994. "Toward the end of my probation, a bunch of us were invited to a get-together at a friend's house. Time got away from us." Fear of missing the curfew turned into reality even though they "ran all the way back to the nurses' home."[26]

The next morning, she and her friends found a note on the bulletin board summoning the offenders to the office of Sister Antonia. They anticipated the worst, as the Franciscan sisters appeared to be very strict and serious. "With great trepidation, I entered her door," Dahlman stated. "To my vast astonishment, Sister Antonia did not admonish or discipline us." Rather, the sister simply wanted to start a conversation with the Japanese American students. "Knowing we were undergoing many adjustments and were subject to racial intolerance, she asked how we were doing and if everyone was treating us well. She used this episode just to talk to us. I have never forgotten her kindness and concern."[27]

Dahlman stayed in Minnesota longer than most of her classmates. One year after her arrival at St. Mary's, she found a job for her father and moved her parents to be with her. As a senior cadet nurse, she was assigned to serve in the Schick General Army Hospital in Clinton, Iowa, for six months. She soon returned to the Twin Cities upon graduation. Dahlman then worked at the Northwestern Hospital (now Abbott Northwestern Hospital), received her bachelor of science degree from the University of Minnesota in 1950, and started her own family with Clark Emil Dahlman, a native of Minneapolis. "My husband was an engineer, so we had to make a lot of moves," she said. The Dahlmans later relocated to Texas. She passed away in December 2010. Looking back at her time in Rochester, Dahlman concluded: "St. Mary's guided me greatly. I will always remember the sisters and the instructors." The friendships she made during the war were also unforgettable and unbroken for more than half a century.[28]

Fumiye Yoshida Lee was one of Dahlman's lifelong friends, a Japanese American nurse at St. Mary's who later also joined the corps. She was slightly more mature than her peers, at the age of twenty-five when she boarded the train from the Minidoka camp to the Rochester campus. "A day in January was the silver lining for me—acceptance from St. Mary's to commence February 2, 1943," Lee said. Born in Tacoma, she came from a typical farming family in Washington with her Issei parents and five Nisei siblings. Then the all-too-familiar forced removal and incarceration followed.[29]

The letter from Sister Antonia made her two wishes come true—to regain her freedom and to rekindle her passion. "I had aspirations of being a nurse, but my parents definitely did not want me to become one," she explained.

"Because in Japan, that's one of the lowest and most demeaning professions at that time, even below a maid, for [it] had to deal with death and bedpans and everything in between." Still, that did not stop her from pursuing her goal. Lee was rather shocked to receive the good news from St. Mary's, to which she did not apply. "I had sent an application to the University of Minnesota, but it was unable to enroll students of Japanese ancestry," she later discovered. "They, thank goodness, transferred my case to St. Mary's. . . . I was thrilled to be accepted by one of the best nursing schools in the nation."[30]

On January 21, 1943, the barbed-wired gates clanged behind her. Only this time, she finally stood on the outside. "I left with mixed feelings— elated on one hand to be rid of the morbid situation, disheartened at leaving my family behind on the other, and then apprehensive, after all the negative propaganda, about what kind of reception awaited me," Lee recalled. "I had to excel for my folks, for myself, and for all Americans of Japanese ancestry."

Whatever excitement she had was short-lived. When Lee stepped on the train at Jerome station, she saw that only standing room remained. "[Being] a free woman on my way to fulfill my early dreams of becoming a nurse, I had visualized a comfortable trip, enjoying passing through the states I had studied in geography," Lee said. Instead, all she could think about was how she might be able to "stand" all the way to Minnesota. Shortly after the steam-engine whistled, an African American porter picked up her bag and beckoned her to the last empty seat on the train. "How he saved it without someone complaining I don't know, but I was truly grateful," she said. "His kindness and thoughtfulness will never be forgotten." And there, with the goodwill of a stranger, began her adventure at St. Mary's.

To the new Nisei nurse, the training program was both rigorous and rewarding. "Concentrating was a challenge after being out of school for seven years," Lee admitted, "except for four months of business college I had started in September 1941, which was curtailed by the war, curfew, and evacuation. This was totally different—so much to learn, absorb, and remember." After three months of intense studying, she was introduced to the floor for four hours a day under strict supervision. Classes lasted for three years, and students had only three weeks of annual vacation. Lee's student surgical nurse training was in orthopedics. Five months prior to graduation, Sister Antonia assigned her to General Surgery, Operating Room VII, as the head nurse.

Intimidated at first, Lee saw it as a blessing in hindsight. "Sister Antonia knew better—it rounded out my surgical experience—a million-dollar experience, assisting for a year the world-renowned Mayo Clinic surgeons." She even stayed for seven more months afterward. Before Lee could be a "registered nurse graduating from one of the best training schools in the nation," she had to take the state board exam, which, according to her, was a nightmare. "Two days of exams—two in the morning and two in the afternoon. We'd run across the street for lunch and cram for the next two tests," she said. "After the last test, I felt like a limp rag, totally drained. There were many anxious moments until we saw our names posted."

The four years of student life in Rochester were filled with seemingly mundane but specifically memorable events for Lee. "I'll never forget the rustle of the nun's habit as she came through the halls to bed check—the door would creak, and a blade of light would flash on the beds," she recalled. "One night I couldn't drop my book—[it was] too interesting; I tucked a pillow in bed and crept to the closet with a flashlight to finish the book. Fortunately, I was not caught."

She was less fortunate on a different occasion. The winters were bitter cold, but the nursing students were told not to walk through the hospital in slacks. "If we walked outside to the bus stop, we would have had to walk three full city blocks on treacherous icy sidewalks," Lee said. The Nisei women thought of wearing pants under the uniform skirts with the legs rolled up, so they could take short cuts inside the hospital. "As I ran into one of the nuns, one of my pants legs dropped," she chuckled. "I was near the exit, and I beat a fast retreat." She was not reprimanded for the violation. Underneath their stern facades, the sisters were all caring and compassionate, Lee gathered; "under the circumstances—road condition and subzero weather—it was too much to ask to follow the rules." She would forever remember Sister Antonia and Sister Mary Brigh, who were influential in the nurses' everyday activities and classes.

A Japanese American woman working and living in a southern Minnesotan city was rather uncommon during the war. Racial diversity might have been a concept in the making but not yet a scene in reality. "Whenever we are out somewhere, [my friend] would say someone is staring at you," Lee observed. "I would turn slowly and flash a smile and taken by surprise [the person always] smiles back. People are curious most of the time. A smile goes a long way and is magnetic. At St. Mary's or Kahler Hospitals, they would have seen us scurrying along the halls, tending to our duties." Lee fathomed that many people had never been acquainted with Asian individuals in their lives, let alone a Japanese or Japanese American. The bewilderment was unavoidable.

She shared a "funny" anecdote of a time she was on her way to Minneapolis to visit a friend at Camp Savage. Lee sat next to a young gentleman who asked her, "Is the Chinese consul seeing you off?" He motioned toward a distinguished Chinese couple by the bus. After a slight pause, he added, "Of course, you're Chinese." When she told him she was a Japanese American, the man "recoiled as if he was facing a menacing creature." She asked: "Am I any different than a few minutes ago?" The awkwardness continued throughout the ride to the Twin Cities. Embarrassed by his faux pas, the man repeatedly and apologetically invited her to have dinner with him before they reached their destination. "After I refused politely, he said to please call him at the Hotel Nicollet if I should change my plans." She did not.

Lee had quite a few hospital tales up her sleeves as well. Smiling to a passerby on the street from a distance was an easy gesture. Receiving medical care or working with a perceived "outsider" in a ward that required closer interactions and trust was another matter. There was "one little old lady from the Dakotas" who had her newspaper scattered all over her bed. Picking one up and scanning it, the Nisei nurse was just about to clean it up. "My dear, can you read?" the lady asked Lee astonishingly. Her reply: "If I couldn't, I most certainly would not be here."

People might understand more about microaggressions these days, but that was a different era. The old lady was not to blame, Lee knew. Without lived experience or adequate information, one processed the world mostly through stereotypes and misrepresentations. Recounting a darker instance, she once was accused of being "a traitor" in surgery by a doctor in orthopedics with whom she had worked. Lee brushed it off right away, backed by Sister Antonia. However, she could never tell whether his grievance referred to her transfer out of his department or the larger national context.

In the absence of positive images of Japanese Americans, Lee had to win people over with extra patience and excellent care. One day, she felt that a new patient's eyes had been keenly following her all around the room as soon as she entered. Was it curiosity or animosity, Lee wondered. "I let the patient get accustomed to me being in the room. I can imagine what was whirling through her thoughts. What is she? Not Japanese—she's too tall, no horn-rimmed glasses, no buck teeth . . ." Lee tried to debunk the myth and break the ice, little by little, by being professional and attentive as she normally would. When the woman was discharged from the hospital after two weeks, she invited Lee to be her houseguest in Iowa. "All you need is train fare," the patient said. "This to me was a victory," the Nisei recalled. "She'll go home and tell her family and friends about this young Japanese nurse she had, and it will have a snowball effect. A small wonder she might start."

When the opportunity for joining the Cadet Nurse Corps came along in the summer of 1943, Lee envisioned how it could allow her to not only support her career but also serve her country, albeit with some reservations at first. "Being disillusioned by my government, I was skeptical that we [had to] stay in essential nursing for the duration of the war," she said. The forced removal and incarceration, where many Japanese Americans were still imprisoned, weighed heavily on the Nisei's mind. After lengthy discussions with her friends and thorough consideration, she surmised that her participation would "offset the prejudice aroused by the anti-Japanese propaganda." She needed to move forward with resolve and not look back with regrets. "Thus, I donned my gray and red cadet uniform and marched with 269 other Rochester student nurses to the Mayo Clinic Auditorium," she said; "an impressive induction ceremony witnessed by a delegation from the Netherlands, England, U.S. Dental Corps, U.S. Medical Corps, Naval Service, and clinic and local dignitaries. It was quite a show." She was among the first group of cadet nurses to be admitted to the corps at St. Mary's.

From then on, Lee wore her white cap with pride and gratitude. Continuing her nursing career, she returned to Tacoma in 1946 and went to Seattle the next year. "My nursing helped in raising my family and assisting friends." Throughout the 1950s and '60s, she moved around Tokyo, Honolulu, and Maryland after having married a Korean War veteran. The Lees retired in Las Vegas in 1979, and she passed away in 2017.

When evaluating her wartime experiences, Lee did not mince words. "Members of the Associated Farmers from California were active in demanding the evacuation, so they could take over the productive farmlands the Japanese farmers had created through hard work—which is what my father had done," she stated. "The evacuation resulted in a tremendous loss emotionally and financially to all of us Japanese Americans. This was not a military emergency, as stated, but concealed greed." In a world of wartime hostility, her tenure in Rochester stood out as one of the exceptions. "St. Mary's had opened the doors to us when we were facing discrimination," she said, "and we lived up to their very high expectations."

The same sentiment was shared by her fellow cadet nurse and Washingtonian Sharon Setsuko Tanagi Aburano, who arrived in Rochester on February 7, 1944. "The motto of St. Mary's Hospital School of Nursing was 'Enter in to learn, Go forth to serve.' Nursing with love paved my way," she emphasized. Born in Seattle and growing up in the International District, where her father ran a successful grocery store, Aburano was the youngest of three siblings. She was a junior at Broadway High School when the war dissolved and dispersed her happy family. She finished high school in the Minidoka incarceration camp, where she worked as a nurse's aide. Her brother Frank Shigeo Tanagi was drafted into the Army and sent to the MISLS in Minnesota. Even though the incarceration was supposedly a war emergency, no one could tell how long that would last or what would come next. Aburano knew she had to leave. The only question was how.[31]

Nursing emerged as a viable option. "I knew I could never be a housekeeper. I'm just not good at cleaning and doing those things," Aburano laughed. "I wanted to go in art, but that was an impossibility. I knew one thing—I had to develop a skill of some sort that was practical. And though I wasn't crazy about nursing, I just went along with it." Her decision turned out to be "the best thing," she realized; "that was the right thing at the right time."[32]

The idea of the Cadet Nurse Corps was proposed by Father Leopold H. Tibesar, a Catholic priest who had followed his flock to Minidoka. "He was instrumental in bringing me the information and aiding me to obtain papers for leaving the camp," Aburano said. "He knew we had no funds and hated to see us languishing in camp. He gave me hope. . . . I still have the letter of acceptance from Sister Antonia dated November 2, 1943."

The recommendation from Father Tibesar helped her secure a spot at St. Mary's. Also carried with her to Rochester were his parting words. "He told me no matter if you get vilified, you must not retaliate; turn the other cheek, or we won't be able to send anybody else out if you don't make good," she recalled. The eighteen-year-old Nisei suddenly felt she had to grow up and be a "model student." The fate and freedom of others fell on her shoulders. "But that was great for me, as it kept me on track."

Putting her best foot forward, Aburano embarked on her journey to Minnesota and began her "tremendous education" at St. Mary's. "For all of us as student nurses, we had galleries like you see in *Grey's Anatomy*." She talked about their times at the hospital as if they were in the television show. They resided in the spacious four-storied dormitory that was connected to the hospital by a tunnel and housed three hundred students, who were always busy coming and going. It had "lovely lounge parlors" as well.

Their nursing education was both theoretical and practical. Aburano remembered her science lessons like chemistry, which were hard, and the guest lectures that included prominent visiting medical experts as well as the Mayo Clinic doctors. She watched as new medicines were developed and tested; for example, she saw sodium pentothal used for the first time, along with some anesthesia drugs and penicillin. She saw the polio epidemic and the operation of the "iron lungs," something that is no longer employed. She was taught more advanced early rehabilitation of patients and care of the wounded. She also learned to follow through all the daily procedures, from making a bed to giving a bath for a bedridden patient. "You don't grade on a curve like you do in normal schools," Aburano said; "it's on what they observe you were doing."

For these Japanese American women, time at St. Mary's was not about just training and studying. Extracurricular activities included swimming, tennis, and, sometimes, a hike or a picnic. Fellow student Martha Masako Morooka stated that one popular pastime was the school choral club. "We all enjoyed the camaraderie and performing as a group," Morooka recalled. They also had brief sessions of marching drills with the Cadet Nurse Corps representatives from Washington, DC. No reward felt more satisfying than a good meal after a hard day of work. "On occasion, we used to run over to the '19th Hole' restaurant which specialized in hickory barbecued ribs," Morooka added. "That was a treat! It was only a couple of blocks from the hospital." Mary Izumi Tamura, also a member of the corps, found "the people in Rochester quite sympathetic towards the Nisei girls." She said: "They would invite us to churches, and we felt very comfortable. . . . The atmosphere was just good."[33]

There were myriads of reasons that these Nisei nurses' lives in Minnesota were remarkable and enjoyable. "Kimi Taguchi [Hara] was supervising in the obstetrics department when we got there. She was already a registered nurse, so that helped us, too," Aburano noted. "Her family lived on the outskirts, and her mother was cooking Japanese foods as much as she could. That's where we loved to go because we could get something that we're used to. Otherwise, we used kosher pickles for the *tsukemono* and substitutes like that."

Another highlight of her time at St. Mary's came from taking a glimpse at Helen Keller, the famed deaf-blind author and disability rights advocate, when she came to Mayo Clinic for her physicals. "I was on night duty, and her specialist asked me if I wanted to see her. Nobody was allowed then, but I got to step into her room," Aburano chuckled. "For sure, you can't talk to her, but I felt so lucky to be able to even see her."

As a cadet nurse, she was "thrilled with the white starched uniform" and the "blue wool capes with 'St. M. H.' emblazoned on the collar." The beret insignia was pinned on the left front, and matching handbags were swung from the left shoulder; the silver Maltese cross was centered on each red epaulet for a junior cadet, and then a second cross was added to designate senior status. "Receiving our caps which folded into 'sailing caps' made us 'real' nurses," Aburano said, "and we thought our caps are nicer than the Kahler nurses." She was proud of the decision she had made and recognized that nursing was her vocation. Even though the war had ended in her second year, the government decided to let all the students in the corps finish their programs, with the obligation to go into the armed forces after graduation suspended.[34]

The war still had its own way of continuing to interfere with the education of the young Nisei. After peace was declared and the incarceration camps began to close in late 1945, Aburano needed to assist her parents to resettle in Seattle. The second-year nursing student knew that she might not be able to return to Minnesota, for many things could go wrong. A highly possible scenario would have her stay behind, find a job, and take care of her family that had been left with nothing. She asked permission to take a leave from Sister Antonia, who graciously agreed and allowed her to complete the courses later, even if she lagged behind.

At the same time, her classmates extended their kindness to her. "I didn't have enough money," she said. "We got fifteen dollars for allowance a month, but we had to buy clothes, cosmetics, personal necessities, and especially white stockings that wore out fast. If we went out on a date, we used to dye them beige, and then we'd come back and bleach them out white and wear it. It was that bad." Certainly, her fellow students understood and chipped in to help; she finally got thirty-six dollars for the trip.

Counting every penny she had, Aburano planned to skip the meals in her two-day Greyhound ride from Minnesota to Washington. She did share her story with some of the fellow passengers at the back, who wondered about this lone woman on the bus. "I don't know if they realized the enormity of what I was saying," she said. "I don't think so. They just knew that I was young, I was going back home, and I didn't have any money." When they stopped at the lunch counter, one of the older men noticed Aburano only sat at the corner but did not eat. He told her to order hot water, then picked up the ketchup bottle, poured some in the cup, and stirred it around. She remembered vividly what happened next—"'There's your tomato soup,' he said, and they all gave me their crackers. So that's what I had the entire trip." Blessedly, all went well for Aburano and her family. She soon went back to Rochester and continued her study.

Her senior year was eventful and exciting, sprinkled with unexpected twists. Aburano signed up for the "rural nursing" program and thus had the chance to encounter northern Minnesota up close and personal. Together with three Caucasian cadets, two from the Minneapolis General Hospital and one from St. Paul's, Aburano left for Grand Rapids, a logging and mining town in Itasca County that was about 190 miles away from the Twin Cities and known as the gateway to the Chippewa National Forest. The four young women got along well from the start and imagined a fun adventure ahead of them. Greeting the nurses at the bus stop was Ilo Meyers, the coordinator for the field experience, who took them to the sole available apartment in the forty-family village.

They arrived rather late in the evening, and it was dark and cold. When Aburano was about to retrieve her bags and follow her three colleagues inside, Myers told her to remain in the car. She was perplexed. Back in the car, Myers explained that although the war was over and the veterans were returning, some people had lost their children in the Pacific Theater. The anti-Japanese sentiment was still high, and they would not understand the differences between the foes and their fellow citizens. To put it bluntly, the landlord did not want a "Jap" living there, since his soldier son was stationed on Guadalcanal.

Instead, Aburano was on the road again and driven to a small house. She learned that the Stokes family of four was willing to accommodate her. There was a surprise when she arrived at the door though. The Swedish American couple, Bob and Sigrid Stokes, were both deaf and communicated via sign language. "I didn't like the idea that I was isolated from the rest of the girls," she recalled. "I was really upset." Aburano was also nervous about how to behave properly, as she had never lived with people with disabilities.

The unease was mutual. It was the first time, too, that the Stokes rented out a room. They had no choice, due to the family's increasingly tough financial situation; they needed the income. Consequently, all of them had no idea what to expect from each other. "When I went in, the first thing they did was to sit me down at a table and they had this paper," Aburano said. The couple then wrote down questions and spelled out their rules. Obviously, "answer the door" and "answer the telephone" were on top of the job description list, which they put down in parentheses, among other common chores. The night went by uneventfully, as did those that followed. However, the topic of separate lodgings never came up among the cadet nurses as they worked together.

Living with a frugal family with physical challenges turned out to be an enriching experience for the Nisei girl. "The house was cold all the time because they wouldn't put up the heat," she noted. "They were wearing sweaters, but I'm not used to that." Aburano was amazed by the elder son, at the age of five, who already knew sign language and normally did all the daily tasks that required communication for his parents. "He was my best helper," she exclaimed. The nurse and the child gradually formed a lasting friendship. They kept in touch for more than four decades. The second son, Darrell Stokes, later a professor emeritus of biology from Emory University, would become a Fulbright scholar and study in Japan for six years. He told Aburano that his fondness of Japanese culture might have to do with knowing her as a young boy.

Having a stranger around would have been unusual for such a small rural place, much less someone who looked like Aburano in this primarily Nordic and Slavic American community. "They didn't know I was a Japanese American. The owner of the apartment had heard that a 'Jap' was coming. That was all they knew," she said. "It's so funny. They invited me to all the functions and tea parties in the village, but they thought I was a French-Canadian Indian girl." The Stokes family certainly knew she was a Japanese American. "But people hardly visited their place . . . his mother came, then the pastor, and one friend who was also deaf. I don't remember anybody else," she remarked. Their disability, Aburano assumed, had created social distance. "It was great because I didn't have much to do with the towns-people unless they were sick and in the hospital."

After a few months, Aburano had to spend a significant amount of time doing outreach nursing to even more remote areas. The four cadet nurses were assigned to the Itasca County Community Hospital, a fifty-five-bed establishment governed by the "Poor and Hospital Commission." The commission also ran the county home and the welfare board. Moreover, the Japanese American was paired with a social worker to conduct health checks, home birth deliveries, and other medical services all over the north, from the twelve-bed hospital in International Falls to the secluded families around Hibbing to the Indigenous communities near Duluth. Aburano loved driving through the tranquil backwoods and meeting folks whom she would not have known otherwise. Her host family did have concerns about her safety. "Bob and Sigrid, they were worried about me, which I really appreciated," she said. Overall, Aburano felt "accepted" and "no overt prejudice of any type," except for one incident.[35]

The story sounded like it could easily be a scene in a teenage drama. The twenty-year-old Nisei was then going out with a local man, a Finnish

American and a returned solider. There were not many places to go for entertainment in Grand Rapids at the time. The High Hat Tavern was one of the spots. One night, on a double date with a Caucasian couple, she noticed the men had been missing for quite a while. She wondered what had happened. "They're out in the back fighting," her female friend replied. Aburano was confused and could not figure out why the altercation had occurred. She would never have guessed that the reason was her.

Their interracial relationship, probably having little to do with her being a Japanese American specifically but non-white in general, must have raised some eyebrows. It seemed a few customers started laughing and talking about them. One made some comments and put on the song "Night and Day" on the jukebox. "I guess, that was to say, I'm the night, and he's the day," the Nisei thought; "because he's tall, blond and blue-eyed and I'm petite and dark, and that touched off something." Whether the fight was triggered by the mockery of racial differences or simply a display of misguided machoism, Aburano was still amused by it after all these years. "That was the only incident I know of openly," she said, smiling. "I don't know what else they went through." The "romance" did not carry on for much longer, and neither did Aburano's northern residence.

Her time in Grand Rapids came to a hasty end on Christmas Eve in 1946. She was badly injured in a car crash, caused by an inebriated motorist without a license driving on the wrong side of the road. She was transferred back to St. Mary's in two days, having the Mayo Clinic doctors in charge of her treatment and recuperation. "I survived. And it doesn't take long to heal when you're young," Aburano said. As soon as she could walk, the nurse cadet was sent to work. "In the morning, I would get a codeine shot to take care of the pain, and then I started my shift," she laughed. "Amazing, those nuns get the most out of you. But it was good. It took my mind off my pain."

Riding both the high and low tides with a positive attitude, Aburano completed her courses and graduated in 1947. The "open-and-shut" accident case earned her a settlement of five thousand dollars from the insurance company. "At that time, it was quite a bit of money," she stated. The fund came at a perfect moment for her to support her parents and prepare for her final return to Seattle. "I left as a fifteen-year-old going on sixteen, but I went back with a skill in nursing, which enabled me to make a life," she said. "And with the Bolton Act, my nursing was free. I was educated enough to be considered a professional."

The postwar beginning for Aburano included receiving a degree in public health nursing and later a master's degree in library science from the University of Washington, forming her family with Paul Fusajiro Aburano, a World War II veteran and a Boeing electronics engineer, and their two sons, and working as an educator for safety and drug awareness in elementary schools until her retirement. "St. Mary's wall painting has stayed with me; that plus I still repeat the prayer of St. Francis," she said. "It has given us the means to have an 'abundant' life."[36]

—

No one seemed to know Aburano's growing pain and pleasure in Rochester better than her roommate Ida Chiyoko Sakohira Kawaguchi. Both were born in the same year in 1925, attended St. Mary's at the same time in February 1944, and graduated from the Cadet Nurse Corps in the same class of 1947. Kawaguchi also volunteered for "rural nursing" at Itasca County Community Hospital in Grand Rapids for three months, replacing Aburano after her car accident. Similarly, she also underwent a major surgery during her training, with the sisters and her classmates assisting in her care after the operation. Of course, both shared the dread of forced removal and imprisonment that was all too common for Japanese Americans from the West Coast, although their backgrounds varied slightly as Kawaguchi was a Californian.[37]

Going to Minnesota for nursing school was a monumental yet easy decision for Kawaguchi. She was the youngest of six children, born in 1925 about ten miles south of Fresno in Fowler, where her Issei father from Hiroshima rented a grape vineyard. Her father's first wife died of labor complications after their fourth child. He thus went to Japan, remarried, and brought back his second bride, Mitsuye Ouye Sakohira, the mother of Kawaguchi and her older brother Todd Sakohira. Worn down by the trying times and failing health, her father passed away when Kawaguchi was in the sixth grade. "Death was a sad event that I experienced early in life," she said. Prior to her father's passing, a half brother was killed in an automobile accident. "My ambition to become a nurse has been a long-standing desire," she continued. "As my father was in pain, I felt so helpless, and wished I could make him feel better."

The war, which was declared in the final months of her senior year in high school, altered Kawaguchi's life. It also made her dream of becoming a nurse come true. Since the family lived in the countryside outside the prohibited area, they were not initially required to move to a temporary detention center. Only night curfews were imposed. Therefore, she was able to attend her graduation in June 1942, before signs were posted about the removal of all residents and citizens of Japanese ancestry from the Western states. She recalled the long, hot, and uncomfortable train ride that took them to a barren land and the prison, surrounded by barbed-wire fences with watchtowers and armed sentries.

The future seemed bleak, yet Kawaguchi did not lose hope. "I always admired and looked up to the nurses. . . . When I heard that nurses' aide classes were being offered, I jumped at the chance to enroll," she said. The Nisei soon found herself walking the wards and working alongside the doctors in the camp hospital, which was furnished with the barest minimum of equipment. "We had many learning experiences," Kawaguchi stated. For example, "nurses' aides and the orderlies were given the opportunity to observe childbirth and surgical procedures." The recruitment drive for the Cadet Nurse Corps reached the incarceree about one year later. She filled out her applications straightaway.[38]

The new year of 1944 ushered in a new chapter for Kawaguchi. She was elated to receive two letters of acceptance, one from St. Mary's in Rochester and the other from a nursing school in Kansas City. She chose Minnesota over Missouri. She was among the seven Japanese American women, including Aburano, who were admitted to St. Mary's cadet nurse program that spring.

Excitement came with fear and sorrow for the young Japanese American woman. One by one, her siblings answered the call to serve and left the family. Her eldest brother, Harry Torao Sakohira, had already enlisted in the Army before the removal. Another brother Frank Sakohira, who did not pass the physical exam, was sent to Harvard and Columbia to teach Japanese language for the Navy officer programs. Todd Sakohira had just departed for Camp Shelby in Mississippi to join the 442nd Regimental Combat Team in Europe. It was then the little sister's turn. "The day I left camp was a sad one for me," Kawaguchi said. "I was in tears as I waved goodbye to my family.

I was happy that there were some familiar faces on the bus to keep me company. I was scared as this was the first time I was to be on my own and live outside of California."

Minnesota offered a novel experience for Kawaguchi. Rochester in February was nothing like the Arizona desert or semiarid Fowler. "Snow was entirely new to me, so I had to learn how to bundle up for protection against the cold, inclement weather," she said. She also picked up other shortcuts quickly. The underground passageways that connected the nurse's dormitory to the hospital allayed her worries about those freezing and stormy days. To the Nisei Californian, the four seasons of the north were captivating and beautiful. Winter soon gave way to spring, along with warmer and cheerier events. "We were happy to have made it through our probationary period, which was the first three months of training," she recalled. "We were honored to wear our school uniforms and participate in an impressive candle lighting ceremony to receive our caps."

Kawaguchi was touched and thankful for the generosity showered on her by the people she met in Minnesota. More than a school and a workplace, St. Mary's was her home away from home. Comfort came from not only being supported by the sisters but also bonding with other Japanese American women who faced comparable adversities and went through the challenging time together. She knew she was not alone. Holidays were when she especially missed her loved ones—those left behind in the incarceration camp as well as those on the front lines in distant lands. "I shall never forget a couple who befriended the Nisei nurses," Kawaguchi said. "Every Christmas they invited us over for dinner and had a small gift for us under the tree."

Her expedition to Grand Rapids, without the romantic interlude and car accident like her friend, was calmer but still compelling. The occasionally served "lutefisk" dish was a sensation not easy to forget, and she found the Swedish and Finnish names quite difficult to pronounce. In the quaint and quiet town, Kawaguchi was able to regain a sense of normalcy, spending her free time socializing with other cadet nurses and attempting to ice skate on a frozen pond. The war had been over for a year. People were apparently in a better mood. She noticed that most families were living in modest and simple cottages in the backwoods country. A colleague from the hospital once invited her to his house for a home-cooked meal. "His wife prepared a most delicious dinner on a wood stove. I was impressed with the cleanliness of the small cabin," she noted. "I feel kindly towards the hard working and friendly people of Minnesota."

The terrific episodes on her memory lane were marred by one terrifying afternoon. "The most traumatic event was the day that Sister Antonia called me into her office," Kawaguchi recalled. It happened several months after the Nisei student came to Rochester. Sister Antonia inquired if there was an illness in her family, because she had just received "a telegram marked with a death notice." Kawaguchi knew of no sick member of her family but had a brother who was serving with the 442nd Regimental Combat Team in Europe. "What a shock when I learned that Todd had been killed in action on July 4, 1944, in Italy," she lamented.

Her brother and all of the officers in Company G, except the commander, had become casualties in a fierce firefight near Castellina known as the "Battle of Hill 140" or "Little Casino." Todd Sakohira was twenty-two years old. The news was particularly devastating for Kawaguchi. She had not seen her brother before his overseas assignment, and she would never see him again. It was all too late, she reckoned, as Sister Antonia told her that there was nothing she could do at that moment.

Three weeks later, on July 29, 1944, Kawaguchi received permission to attend a memorial service for her brother; the solider was interred in the US Military Cemetery in Follonica, Italy. Her other brother in the Army, Harry Sakohira, had also been granted a brief military furlough to join his family in the camp. Whether it was a pure coincidence or a planned arrangement, Harry Sakohiro was shipped across the Atlantic to Company G of the 442nd Regimental Combat Team, the same one in which his deceased younger brother had been, upon his return to duty.[39]

Wearing her cadet nurse uniform, Kawaguchi stepped back inside Gila River one more time. She must have carried herself well and made an impression. "I was asked to speak to the high school class," she remembered. "I gave my talk and answered questions on how to become a cadet nurse and hopefully steered them into a nursing career." Of course, she saw her sorrowful yet stoic mother holding the Purple Heart Medal posthumously awarded to Todd Sakohira, as had many other Issei parents before her. Her bereaved mother coped with her loss by repeating "*shikata ga nai* [it can't

Ida (Sakohira) Kawaguchi in 1944 with older brother Private First Class Harry Sakohira, who was the replacement for his younger brother Todd of the 442nd Infantry, at Gila River. *Courtesy of St. Mary's School of Nursing Alumni Association*

be helped]," a phrase uttered again and again by Japanese Americans just like her.[40]

The medal was the only trace left of her brother, along with a letter from Dillon Myer, director of the War Relocation Authority. Admitting that neither patriotism nor condolences could fully assuage the grief of a mourning mother, Myer wrote that he was proud to see Sakohira as "an American who had the strength and courage to fight for his country in her great crisis; proud that he was willing to give his blood as a last great measure of devotion." Myer acknowledged that the Nisei had "fought to win the war against two foes"—the Axis powers on the global battlegrounds as well as "the enemies of democracy at home who use[d] race and ancestry to confuse and defeat the real meaning of America." Like many other Japanese American soldiers, Sakohira "could not have lived to see his bravery, his sacrifice and his suffering bear fruit in a better world for all peoples."

Harry Sakohira, the "replacement" of his younger brother, was one of the few "who made it out alive," although the Silver Star recipient never talked much about the war. "One experience he related was about the rescue of the 'Lost Battalion,' a Texas unit that was trapped in the path of enemy lines," Kawaguchi said. "There were unspeakable casualties of this mission. There were more rescued than what remained of the rescuers." The 442nd Regimental Combat Team sustained more than eight hundred fatalities to save two hundred and eleven men. "Harry attributed his safe return from the war to a special binder that mother had sown for him," she noted, "with a thousand stitches by hand which he wore under his uniform."[41]

Kawaguchi resumed her studies in Rochester after the memorial service, trying her best to move forward and bring meaning to her own life. Nursing, above all, was her calling. Three years flew by smoothly. She and her classmates had then completed all the requirements, and commencement day arrived in the summer of 1947. "How proud we were when we received our diploma and school pin," she said.

While some of the cadet nurses stayed on to accept positions at the hospital, Kawaguchi decided to go back to Fowler, where her family had returned after the war. She began her career at the Fowler Municipal Hospital and later transferred to the Veterans Hospitals in Santa Monica and Oakland. Subsequently, she attended San Francisco State University for an undergraduate degree in nursing and worked as an instructor at St. Francis Hospital. It was at a YMCA dance in the city that she met her husband Masaru "Mas" Kawaguchi, a native of San Francisco, Army veteran, and civil engineer. The couple married in 1954. Kawaguchi continued to be active in nursing, especially in the fields of psychiatry, gerontology, and community mental health, after she had raised her family of three children. She named her eldest son Todd.

The loss of her brother, and the lack of closure, lingered for decades and left crevices in Kawaguchi's broken heart. When she was asked to reflect on her times at St. Mary's for a reunion half a century later, she found herself suddenly overwhelmed with emotions. "It was a difficult task for me to overcome my mental block and begin to write," Kawaguchi revealed. "Once I started, the ideas, memories, and the feelings flooded, [especially] my despair centered around the death of my brother, Todd." The more she read

Budget Bureau No. 68–R145
Approval expires August 31, 1945

Form 300A
FEDERAL SECURITY AGENCY
U. S. PUBLIC HEALTH SERVICE
DIVISION OF NURSE EDUCATION

SERIAL No. 50778

NAME OF CADET NURSE Sakohira, Ida
(PRINT OR TYPE)

SIGNATURE OF CADET NURSE Ida Sakohira

NAME OF SCHOOL St. Mary's S. of N.

CITY Rochester

STATE Minnesota

DATE OF ADMISSION TO SCHOOL Feb. 7, 1944

DATE OF ADMISSION TO CORPS Feb. 7, 1944

DATE OF ISSUANCE OF THIS CARD March 15, 1944

SIGNATURE OF DIRECTOR OF SCHOOL OF NURSING Sister M. Antonia

DO NOT WRITE BELOW THIS LINE

THIS SPACE FOR CENTRAL OFFICE USE	TERMINATION DATES		
	BY GRADUATION	WITH DEFAULT	WITHOUT DEFAULT
👉	5/24/47		

(4409)   16—38249-1

Ida (Sakohira) Kawaguchi cadet nurse identification badge, February 1944.
Courtesy of St. Mary's School of Nursing Alumni Association

about the wartime history of Japanese Americans, the more baffled she became. "I have heard that during combat when there are so many casualties in a unit, the units are normally removed from the battle fronts. The soldiers in the 442nd Infantry were not given this alternative," Kawaguchi wrote. "For this, I was very bitter."

Putting her indignation down in words unexpectedly turned out to be the therapeutic solution she needed. "I came to the realization that this life review and reminiscence involved has helped me release the anger and negative feelings from the past. I feel that I can now work towards future goals with energy and a more positive attitude. I will be forever grateful to the U.S. Cadet Nurse Corps who gave me the opportunity to fulfill my lifelong ambition and the opportunity to contribute to the war effort."

Finding solace after all these years was a formidable task. Kawaguchi at last was able to come to terms with the tragedies in her life. Her fellow cadet nurses Dahlman, Lee, Aburano, among others, had also risen above their miseries and misfortunes. Evidently, Minnesota had something to do with their successes. St. Mary's was the safe harbor during the war that not merely provided them shelter from the storm but also prepared them to set sail for the distant shore. "That was a happy time—working hard, making friends, and realizing that together we were getting an education in a school of nursing regarded as one of the best," another cadet nurse, Teruko "Teddy" Wada Tanaka, attested. Aburano could not agree more. "The values I learned at St. Mary's and the nursing skills they taught me have affected all parts of my life," she concluded. "We all went out into uncomfortable places, but they matured us."[42]

These female voices, often unheard or unheeded outside their communities, give a fuller profile of the war and the state. It is by no means complete, of course. St. Mary's had taken in two groups of Japanese Americans who found refuge in Minnesota during the war—the nursing students as well as regular staff. Information about the latter was notoriously difficult to find or verify. Different from college students, Army recruits, and cadet nurses, with the support of the NJASRC as well as alumni and veteran organizations, there was no systematic effort to keep records of those who went to Minnesota simply for work. Available employment opportunities for them at the time were mainly manual laborer or domestic helper, which often did not last long or lend themselves to documentation. Kimi Hara was an exception, both for her nursing profession and community activism. Fortunately, a handful of Nisei like her saw the North Star State not as a momentary stopover but as their final destination. A few social service agencies preserved related paper trails, too. Some Japanese Americans, despite their temporary stay, also brought their Minnesota memories with them when they moved onward after the war. The next chapter will present their stories.

7 | Risks and Rewards

Japanese American Mavericks, Entrepreneurs, and Workers in Wartime Minnesota

"All I can say is that Minneapolis–St. Paul to me has been just a wonderful place. There was prejudice from way back, but I didn't let it bother me too much on things like that because I was able to mingle with everyone."
—WILLIAM "BILL" YOSHITADA HIRABAYASHI

innesota welcomed Bill Hirabayashi right after the war, and it was his home for the rest of his life. "As far as I'm concerned, I am the happiest guy." When most people talk about wartime Japanese American stories, or perhaps any history as a matter of fact, few think of the ordinary working people. Often these quotidian tales are completely overlooked. Unremarkable as they might be at first glance—factory mechanic, dental technician, or car dealer—a closer inspection shows that there are invaluable details about remarkable day-to-day lives in the North Star State, along with the problems of the Japanese Americans.

His lack of military decorations or diplomas from universities notwithstanding, Hirabayashi uncovered a part of Japanese American history in Minnesota that is as honorable and spirited as the more well-known stories yet is hardly ever told or heard. Admittedly, experiences like his can be seen as more mundane, without overt dramatic twists and radical turns. Hirabayashi was a son, a husband, and a father. He had faith, good friends, and a successful business. What he had learned from his employer as the war was set in motion always stayed with him: the country needed "corn and beef just as much as armor and bullets." He joyfully and quietly contributed to the cause. The always optimistic Hirabayashi eventually started his own automobile business in the Twin Cities. Alongside his fellow Japanese American resettlers, the Nisei entrepreneur made difficult adjustments and got down to the task of earning a living, raising a family, and living with his neighbors—and, in the process, helped defend, protect, and support the nation.

While the tales of these working folks may be more fragmented and nuanced, signifying only a small slice of the resettled lives of Japanese Americans during the war, their portraits are telling and touching nonetheless. Hirabayashi represented the group of Nisei who relocated to the state because of familial connections, with children, siblings, or relatives pursuing higher education or training at the military language school. Some of them stopped by momentarily and then moved on to other places. Some stayed permanently. Hirabayashi was one of the latter. There was a myriad of colorful characters indeed, from intrepid mavericks who sought opportunities in St. Paul to the diverse alumni of a trade school in Minneapolis, from an extraordinary Issei religious leader in the Twin Cities to an exceptional Nisei family that founded a chicken-sexing business in Mankato.

Bringing the stories of these everyday heroes to the spotlight ultimately teased out the risks, rewards, and reminiscences of a different side of wartime

Bill Hirabayashi, 2015.
Courtesy of the author

Minnesota. Before diving into the various characters and their personal accounts, let's step back and take an overview of the working environment and labor market in the state, which is important to put their experiences in context.

———

As soon as the release program in the incarceration camps began, the Twin Cities rose to become one of the most popular destinations for Japanese American resettlers. The metropolitan area was better at accommodating Issei and Nisei job seekers than many other urban centers in the country. Throughout the war, there were an estimated two to four thousand who inquired about or sought assistance from the International Institute, St. Paul Resettlement Committee, and the WRA district office in Minneapolis, helped by Nisei leaders like Ruth and Earl Tanbara on relocation matters.[1]

Those were not the easiest times. Doing without resources as a way of life continued after the Great Depression, although strong wartime demand also created plenty of work opportunities. The Midwest was deemed the most productive and important region in the world during the war, as it poured forth meat, grains, vegetables, eggs, dairy products, and scores of manufactured goods that supported not only the United States but also its Allied partners. Certainly, Minnesota was a valuable player, with companies such as Cargill, General Mills, Hormel, Pillsbury, and 3M bearing their share of war duties. Furthermore, large munitions factories were founded, offering thousands of additional positions. The Twin Cities Ordnance Plant (TCOP) in Arden Hills (now the Twin Cities Army Ammunition Plant) that opened in the spring of 1941 was one of them.[2]

The new prospects brought new possibilities. As the Minnesotan workforce, predominately composed of Caucasian men, dwindled due to increasing military conscription, visible labor shortages began to occur in 1943. Some doors were opened for ethnic minorities and women to participate in the job market as a result. Yet many of the opportunities were not the high-paying and desirable ones, which often had white-male-only policies. That created a social and economic justice problem.[3]

Racial bigotry was so detrimental to the nation, or at least severe enough to be alarming, that President Roosevelt issued Executive Order 8802 as a response on June 25, 1941. It prohibited discrimination against workers on the basis of "race, creed, color, or national origin" by the federal government, together with all unions and companies engaged in war-related industries. While many defense plants still resisted or refused to enforce this policy, the TCOP, for example, was fully integrated and committed to providing equal opportunities for Black employees as well as women at all levels.[4]

Compared to the Western and Southern states, Minnesota led the way in combating workplace prejudice. The *Summary of Twin Cities Labor Market Area Survey*, conducted by the Minnesota Division of Employment and Security in September 1941, proclaimed that there were "no minority group problems of any significance." The assertion was perhaps an overstatement; however, people of color in the North Star State overall, at least on record, did not suffer from overt racism as in other parts of the country. Governor Harold Stassen did pay attention to the national pulse and formed the Minnesota State Committee on Tolerance, Unity, and Loyalty in 1943 to address some of the racial concerns.[5]

Discrimination existed but was exhibited in subtler ways. The unity banner of patriotism and integration obscured the reality that, for people of color, freedom and fairness inside insulated workplaces, like the TCOP, did not extend to the outside world. Stories about Nisei workers, for better or for worse, were few and far between. One anecdote talked about a Japanese American who stood for hours in long lines at thirteen employment offices, only to learn that all the positions he sought had supposedly been filled; another told how labor leaders publicly dissuaded a Nisei nursing student from applying to St. John's Hospital, because "Indians and [Black people] were not favorably received in Red Wing . . . Japanese would fare no better."[6]

The concerted efforts by the federal government, state agencies, religious leaders, and the MISLS personnel, together with the collective openness of the Minnesotan public, made for substantial progress over time. One might recall the mission of Spark Matsunaga from the 442nd Regimental Combat Team and the military language school to bolster the employment of Japanese Americans among the seven hundred local businesses and communities, which had up to then hired none. Beginning in late 1942, volunteers from the resettlement committee staffed a desk at the United States Employment Service (USES) office three afternoons a week to handle the employment cases of Japanese Americans. Since they had no access to the official files in their first ten months of operation, the volunteers could only contact companies that were advertising in the newspapers and talk to the employers whom they personally knew for possible placements.[7]

After December 1943, the USES office started to process Japanese American employment cases through regular channels. A 1944 committee report showed that out of 137 potential job seekers, 97 were employed—nearly half of them hired in "domestic and service occupation," about one-fifth in "clerical and sales," and the rest in "unskilled" and "semi-skilled" positions; only a few of them received "skilled" and "professional" work.[8]

The employment situation differed between the two generations of Japanese Americans. The bulk of the unskilled and manual service-oriented positions, such as laborer, janitor, dishwasher, and busboy, were held by the Issei. Clearly, their lack of formal schooling in America and English language proficiency posed an obstacle. Additionally, most of the first-generation immigrants were formerly farmers or self-employed on the West Coast before their resettlement in Minnesota, making it difficult for them, at more senior ages, to start a new business or learn a new trade in an unfamiliar environment. There were also state laws that prohibited noncitizens from entering specific professions, including civil servant, attorney, architect, pharmacist, engineer, liquor seller, poultry inspector, and certified public accountant. These fields were closed to Issei immigrants, who were not allowed to naturalize, even if they might have the background.[9]

Their wives and children did slightly better. Most Issei women were younger and possessed skills in sewing, nursery, and housekeeping that were in demand. Even more successful were their American-born offspring. Nisei were purportedly given the opportunity to compete with others on the basis of their abilities in the job market, although many of them were in school or the military.

Those Japanese Americans who were under draft age or not college-bound often worked in blue-collar positions. Take two Nisei youngsters as an example. Richard Katsumi "Kats" Okamoto came to the Twin Cities from Minidoka by himself and held a few odd jobs before being drafted into the MISLS in 1944. One of the places that hired the then teenager to work—from mopping floors to setting rooms to bartending—was the "American Legion Club" in Minneapolis. The exclusive venue was where prominent people at that time went to socialize, have a few drinks, and enjoy enter-tainment. "They would play poker most of the night," Okamoto said. The chief of the Minneapolis Police Department, Elmer Friedolph Hillner, was among the most memorable guests. "I recall that very distinctly, Chief Hillner was very nice to me," he asserted. "Drinks in those days were sixty cents; I got a dollar for each drink."[10]

Another Nisei, Hayao "Hy" Shishino, barely eighteen with only twenty-five dollars in his pocket, took the train to Minnesota as soon as he could leave the Gila River camp. The Los Angeles native signed up for a summer job at the Edgewater Beach Hotel in Detroit Lakes, later working in the kitchen at the Radisson Hotel in Minneapolis. He attributed his problem-free year and a half in Minnesota to the support of his coworkers—the Rus-sian chef, who was a "Communist" and believed "all people were created equal," as well as the German baker, a big fellow who insisted ethnicity did not matter and even converted him into a Missouri Synod Lutheran. A simple act of fairness, and perhaps a little kindness, from a colleague, an employer, or a neighbor went a long way for the Nisei.[11]

There were many capable and resourceful hands reshaping Minnesota from a place of indifference to one of tolerance and acceptance. Reverend Daisuke Kitagawa, who already appeared in Chapter Two, warrants further men-tion, as he was one of the changemakers in the Japanese American commu-nity. Born in Taihoku (Taipei, which was then a Japanese colony) in 1910, Kitagawa grew up in a missionary family affiliated with the Anglican Church in Japan. He graduated from Rikkyo University (also known as St. Paul's University) in Tokyo in 1933 and decided to immigrate to the United States in 1937 to enroll in the General Theological Seminary in New York. Upon completing his studies in 1939, he was ordained as a deacon and sent to serve a parish in Washington, where a significant number of Japanese Americans lived. In 1942, Kitagawa went with his congregation to the Pinedale Deten-tion Center near Fresno and later Tule Lake as the priest-in-charge of Epis-copalians at the camp.

The reverend first visited Minnesota in June 1943. He was then on a two-month summer tour of various cities where Japanese Americans had reset-tled to observe the supporting efforts of religious organizations that were underway. His trip took him to Chicago, Cincinnati, Cleveland, Denver, Detroit, Kansas City, Madison, St. Louis, and Minneapolis. His main purpose in going to the Twin Cities was to see the Nisei Army recruits from Tule Lake who were training at the MISLS in Camp Savage. He also had a chance to discuss employment issues with the USES office, managed by Genevieve Fallon Steefel, a volunteer representing the St. Paul Resettlement Committee.[12]

His meeting with Steefel was "eye-opening." Kitagawa was impressed by her diligence and patience, spending half a day, five days a week, at that office. "Here was a woman of ability and status—she was the wife of a professor at the University of Minnesota and mother of two children—giving generously her time and talents to help the Nisei coming to Minneapolis," he said. "She did this with a firm sense of fair play and respect for the rights of all people. . . . And behind her stood a host of religious and civic organizations working to atone in Minnesota for the errors made in California, Oregon, and Washington." The reverend asserted that knowing these empathetic partners were at work had profoundly affected him. At the same time, watching men and women, both old and young, lined up at the agency was a scene new to him.[13]

One specific problem interested Kitagawa and irritated Steefel. Apart from the regular inquiries from factories and companies for workers, many middle-class families were also eager to hire domestic servants. The trouble appeared when many of them took advantage of the situation and would pay the Nisei substandard wages. Their justification was that compared with life in camp—where they believed the Japanese Americans ought to be locked up anyway—the relocated laborers should be happy to be free and receive any sort of compensation.

A good part of Steefel's job was to refuse the requests from these prospective exploiters. She had to do so gently and in a diplomatic manner, but in a way that the ignorant inquirers might learn "the truth" about their compatriots. Her message was factual and fair. Japanese Americans were citizens, many were college students or graduates, and they came to Minnesota to make a living not through their own fault but under unfortunate circumstances over which they had no control whatsoever. To treat them as less than anyone else would be unjust and unacceptable.[14]

Kitagawa's return to Tule Lake was temporary, as he was about to em-
bark on a major career change. His summer tour had connected him with
the Federal Council of Churches, which decided to invite him to be the
field secretary for their committee on Japanese American resettlement. On
October 31, 1943, Kitagawa left Tule Lake for the East Coast. During one of
his field trips to the Midwest, he met Fujiko Sugimoto, a Nisei from San
Francisco studying at Heidelberg College in Ohio, who would later become
his wife. At the reception following their wedding in Chicago on July 1,
1944, Kitagawa received the mission to serve as chaplain for the MISLS in
Minnesota.

The news was a surprise. Since Kitagawa was a Japanese national, and
therefore an enemy alien, the idea of working with the "secretive" military
personnel sounded strange to him. It turned out that his unique background
was precisely the reason behind his appointment. Camp Savage had, in fact,
chaplains on duty, as did every other Army establishment. Worried about
the deteriorating morale of the Nisei recruits, Rasmussen, the commandant
of the school, was aware that some of the quandaries bothering his soldiers
required firsthand knowledge of not only their Japanese cultural heritage
but also the collective mentality that was prevalent among the incarcerees
behind the barbed wire. More than a religious leader in general, Rasmussen
needed a spiritual counselor who had similar lived experiences with and a
heartfelt understanding of the young Japanese American men.[15]

Kitagawa, who had visited the base earlier, naturally came to mind. Having
a strong recommendation from an old friend and teacher also helped the
reverend's case. Paul Frederick Rusch, a first lieutenant at the MISLS, knew
Kitagawa well. The American was a lay missionary of the Anglican Church
in Japan and was an instructor of economics at Rikkyo University, Kitagawa's
alma mater, before the war. As a result, Rasmussen made the unusual move
to assign the Issei clergyman as the "unofficial civilian chaplain" to the Nisei
soldiers at Camp Savage and then Fort Snelling. Kitagawa treasured this
opportunity and always remembered what Rasmussen had said to him: "My
soldiers need your ministry. Regard this school as your parish. Come here any
time of the day or night, as need arises. Be a friend and pastor to my men."[16]

Accompanied by his bride, Kitagawa began his decade-long Minnesota
chapter at the end of July 1944, a mere few weeks after he was married. The

couple arrived in Minneapolis during its annual Aquatennial Festival and stayed at the King Cole Hotel (no longer existing), overlooking Loring Park. Kitagawa started work right away with the Minneapolis Church Federation (known as the Greater Minneapolis Council of Churches since 1951), through which he concurrently served as the chaplain at the MISLS.

However, the reverend was an alien. Even basic daily activities, like going around town, could not be taken for granted. Though working with the dispersed Japanese American resettlers would take him to different parts of the state, Kitagawa recalled that the very first thing he had to do was to report to the US attorney's office in St. Paul in order to obtain a permit to travel. Legally, he needed a permit each time he went out of Minneapolis. The US attorney was sensible enough to approve his request for a renewable three-month permit that covered the entire state. In addition, military areas, such as Camp Savage and Fort Snelling, demanded special authorization for which the reverend had to apply separately.

While the stage was not yet set for his work, finding suitable housing presented another hurdle. It was seemingly a roadblock that no Japanese American could escape. After an intensive two-week search, the Kitagawas located a small three-room house at the north end of Minneapolis and paid the first month's rent as deposit. Just when the couple heaved a sigh of relief, they were told by the landlord that he had changed his mind. There was supposedly "unbearable" opposition from the neighbors. "We haven't seen any of the neighbors yet, nor have they met us. How do they know that we're objectionable to them?" Kitagawa wondered.[17]

The landlord and the Kitagawas went back and forth about a resolution, but to no avail. Recognizing that it was not a matter of rationality, Kitagawa asked the Episcopal Church bishop of Minnesota, Reverend Stephen E. Keeler, to do the persuading instead. The problem was solved after a few phone calls. Kitagawa never learned who had so intimidated the landlord.

Minneapolis was home to Kitagawa between 1944 and 1954. In return, the reverend, known by many as "Father Dai," became an influential spiritual, community, and civil rights leader, who over those ten years connected the different segments of an increasingly multicultural and multifaceted Minnesota. From his arrival in July 1944 until the MISLS relocated back to Monterey, California, in April 1946, Kitagawa offered weekly mass and moral support to its soldiers, including officiating dozens of weddings for Nisei in uniform as well as the local populace at large. Because of his religious affiliation and personal experiences, the reverend emerged as a prominent advocate for the resettlement of Japanese Americans.[18]

Kitagawa's leadership played a crucial role in helping many incarcerees successfully readjust to lives in Minnesota. The remarkable postwar growth of the Japanese American community in the Twin Cities is a testimony to his active involvement. Hatred fed off fear, and fear flourished in ignorance. An antidote to racial bigotry was simple, Kitagawa proposed: "it's just the matter of getting to know one another," not as stereotypes but as real people.[19]

The reverend came out publicly as the face of a person of Japanese ancestry and a man of God. For anyone who did not know any Japanese individuals, he appeared to be just like their neighbors, friends, and pastors. He was not only articulate but also approachable. If Kitagawa defied the wicked image of what a Japanese was supposed to be, it was because the perception was false after all. There is indeed a wide body of literature these days supporting his "contact hypothesis," which postulates cross-ethnic interactions under appropriate conditions can effectively reduce prejudice between majority and minority group members.[20]

Bringing people together across race, culture, and religion was Kitagawa's objective. "He had his earliest experiences in inter-denominational cooperation when he was appointed director of the Minneapolis Council of Churches." He was charged with "organiz[ing] the Christian church's response to the thousands of Japanese Americans who were released from various incarceration camps." He spoke about these issues before local churches, schools, industries, and community organizations. In December 1945, he worked with the St. Paul Resettlement Committee to open a hostel for Japanese American newcomers to the area. In 1946, Kitagawa sponsored the creation of the Twin Cities chapter of the JACL.[21]

That Japanese Americans found contentment and confidence in Minnesota, in effect, strengthened Kitagawa's optimistic stance on the resettlement. In 1949, he established and served as the director of the Japanese American Community Center at Twenty-Second Street and Blaisdell Avenue in Minneapolis, which quickly became a popular social space for all members of the community. The center held events for diverse groups of participants, from Native Americans to Buddhist practitioners, and from Issei elders attending the weekly Japanese language services to Nisei youth joining recreational programs like dances and parties.

Nevertheless, he did not shy away from criticizing—in interviews, speeches, and writings—the mass removal and incarceration of people of Japanese descent that had inflicted irreparable economic loss and emotional trauma upon them. With no intention of whitewashing the historical injustice, he saw the silver lining in the gloomy imprisonment, similar to those sentiments expressed by the JACL during the war. Relocating to places like the Twin Cities, and hence widening their horizons, was beneficial for Japanese Americans in the long run. Otherwise, they would have never left their insulated ethnic bubble, being easily subjected to "ghetto mentality," rather than engaging with the rest of the country.[22]

This positive take on resettlement would become a popular idea in the years before the redress movement. "Let me state publicly that the experience enriched my personal life as nothing else could have," Kitagawa said, "and I venture to think that a great number of Issei and Nisei feel the same way." Such sentiments indubitably helped to save the government from guilt and shame at the time, and paved the way for a more conciliatory discourse for the Japanese Americans to regain their admission ticket to white-dominated society.[23]

It is easy to imagine an eloquent Christian minister of color, with a brighter outlook on the Japanese American predicament, solicited by politicians to assist their handling of tricky issues. Kitagawa was a regular contributor to the state's policies on race, and consequently, he earned himself important allies in the government. In January 1949, Kitagawa authored a report on the Japanese American resettlement for then Governor Luther Youngdahl's Interracial Commission, as part of a larger survey about Asian Americans—Chinese, Filipino, and Japanese—in Minnesota.

The reverend praised the "outstanding" Nisei soldiers at the MISLS who had "won the good will of the people of Minnesota," and created an "excellent atmosphere" in the Twin Cities for Japanese Americans. He also characterized those Japanese Americans who had left Minnesota for the Western states as "steeped in the materialistic California psychology" and lacking "cultural appreciation." To some coastal returnees, what Kitagawa presented was calculated more to please the people of Minnesota than to elucidate why they would prefer to go back to their former homes.[24]

In any case, Kitagawa impressed those in power. On February 10, 1951, Minnesota Congressman Walter Henry Judd was said to have introduced a private bill that would enable Kitagawa to become a citizen, even though restrictions against the naturalization of Japanese and other Asian nationals were still in place. In February 1953, Minneapolis voters elected the reverend to be chairman of the Mayor's Council on Human Relations. During his tenure, he organized the Rainbow Club, where families of various races and ethnicities could meet, in "the hope that both children and adults would develop friendships across racial lines."[25]

Drawing on his own wartime experiences, Kitagawa turned his attention to Indigenous tribes and other populaces in Minnesota and examined how Christian organizations might assist them. The result was a public report in July 1953. He argued that relations between Caucasians and Native Americans needed a complete restructuring to overcome the animosity generated by centuries of displacement and dehumanization of the minority groups. Kitagawa's statement was issued at the same time as the Bureau of Indian Affairs (BIA) proposed its policy to terminate Native reservations. While Kitagawa did not explicitly endorse the government's plan, he referenced his time at Tule Lake as a cautionary tale of the harms that isolation and confinement could wreak and encouraged Native Americans to participate in the wider society by moving away from reservations.[26]

Kitagawa bid farewell to Minnesota in the fall of 1954, when he returned to Chicago to complete his doctoral studies at the University of Chicago. In the following decade he continued to fight for racial justice and immersed himself in the civil rights movement. In 1956, "he began the first of his two associations with the World Council of Churches (WCC) . . . as Secretary of Racial and Ethnic Relations. . . . Six years later, he was appointed the Secretary for Urban and Industrial Mission Program." He traveled throughout Africa and Asia for both his missionary work and global fellowship against racism. Kitagawa died in Geneva, Switzerland, unexpectedly in 1970, at the age of fifty-nine.[27]

The war decade, highlighted by Kitagawa's spiritual stewardship and social activism, marked the height of the Japanese American community in Minnesota. They became the largest Asian American group in the state and remained so for over twenty years, until the next wave of "resettlement" with Hmong and Vietnamese immigrants due to another disastrous war in Asia. Father Dai was not an island. Nor did he want to be one. Above all, racial harmony started with "knowing" one another beyond caricature, as the reverend had pointed out, through more personal interaction and better-informed education. "For how can one love, respect, and relate one-self to those who are nothing but samples of a group image?" Kitagawa re-capitulated. "Without opportunities to see, hear, and associate with those whose collective image haunts one, one can hardly be liberated from that image."[28]

The quest to make Minnesota a friendlier and more viable destination for ethnic minorities relied on collaborative efforts. Championed by reli-gious leaders like Kitagawa, the volunteers at the St. Paul Resettlement Committee, the MISLS, and many others, the public relations programs gradually broke down, albeit did not completely vanquish, the resistance to Japanese Americans. Noticeable results could be seen in employment. In the spring of 1944, every firm contacted by Matsunaga, who headlined the MISLS publicity campaign, either had already hired Japanese American workers or planned to do so. In the meantime, all but two major war plants in the Twin Cities had Nisei on their payrolls by the end of the war.[29]

The numbers looked reassuring. Would the individual stories behind them be as promising? To take a closer look at Japanese Americans in the workplace during the war, let's turn to three different cases, a dental techni-cian, a chicken-sexing business family, and an alumnus of a trade school, whose lived experiences were not only interesting but also illuminating.

One of the Nisei mavericks turned Minnesotan was Donald Satoshi Maeda. While his background shared many commonalities with other Japanese Americans at the time, the choices that Maeda made and the paths he took were quite unconventional. From the lumber mill to the railroad station, his immigrant father Toshishige Maeda tried his hand at many menial jobs, and at last learned the trade of and worked as a dental technician in Seattle. He wanted his children to lead an assimilated American life. Therefore, neither Maeda nor his older sister Jane Toshie Maeda attended Japanese language school. Most of their friends were white. Maeda was a high school junior when the news of Pearl Harbor arrived. His family, including his two-year-old brother, was swept away from their home into the hastily built billets at the Western State Fairgrounds and later to Minidoka.

Life in incarceration was hard. However, Maeda maintained a distinct perspective about the experience. "I didn't think it was so bad," he chuckled; "at seventeen you don't think of how terrible all this really was. . . . My sister was much more adamant about the treatment that we received. She's five years older." Instead, the teenager found a rare sense of belonging in camp. It was the first time that he had lived with people who looked like him in a community. "I fit in," he said; "I made a lot of good friends. I found out Japanese kids are more fun than white kids."[30]

Two years glided past quickly for Maeda. School was no longer meaningful at that point. Rather than continuing his education, he enrolled in a work team that shoveled, loaded, and distributed coal to all the barracks and facilities. The young man also went out with the agricultural crew, alongside Mexican laborers brought up as seasonal help, to harvest sugar beets and potatoes. When the long and laborious days of work were over, he just hung out with his friends after dinner. He played baseball during his free time and attended dances every Saturday night in the mess halls. Life was basic and simple.

Yet complications caught up with him before long. In late 1942, his sister was accepted by Hamline University in St. Paul, Minnesota, to resume her undergraduate study. His parents and his younger brother were set to join her shortly. Maeda, who had just celebrated his nineteenth birthday, learned that he was among the first group of Nisei men in Minidoka to be drafted in 1943. "But the day I was supposed to go into the service was the day my folks were scheduled to leave camp for Minnesota." Luckily, the Army was understanding and thus gave him a ninety-day extension to help his parents. The Maedas arrived in the Twin Cities on a "cold" day in March 1944. A new chapter of their lives had begun.

Little did Maeda know then that his provisional release would turn into permanent resettlement. The family of five first lodged in a rooming house near Hamline University. Assisted by the resettlement committee, his father quickly reestablished himself in St. Paul as a dental technician, a career that he

would continue for another twenty-five years. After spending three months
with his family, Maeda reported back for duty at Fort Logan, Colorado. He
did not pass the physical examination, however, due to the long-term damage he suffered from a car accident when he was six. "I was disappointed,"
he said. "Mom was relieved. This was before the end of the Pacific War."
Receiving an honorable medical discharge, Maeda found himself in Minnesota again. This time he stayed for good.[31]

The working world into which the young Japanese American entered
unveiled a different face of the state. Maeda had taken on a couple of interesting jobs even before he was called back for service. His first, also arranged
by the resettlement committee, was with Booth Cold Storage on Kellogg
and St. Peter in downtown St. Paul and involved transporting refrigerated
goods by railroad around the country. "The job was hauling these big cartons of frozen stuff . . . out of the freezer lockers into the trains," he recalled.
"I worked there for about two weeks. I wasn't strong enough to lift the heavy
cartons stacked up in the cars."[32]

His second attempt was at the Cudahy Packing Company in Newport,
across from Armour & Company on the South St. Paul side of the Mississippi River. It was then the largest industrial plant in the Twin Cities and a
major slaughtering, processing, and meatpacking hub for the nation. "The
packing house is all Mexican and African Americans, who end up in the
lower end of the job down in the cellar where the hides are dropped," he
noted. The raw and messy materials, fresh from the meat-cutting room,
were unpleasant to handle. Maeda and his coworkers had to lay down the
hides, scrape them to remove the remaining flesh and fat, and then put a
layer of rock salt to cure them before sending them off to leather makers.
"You're covered with [foulness]," he said. "I'd come home smelling like
crap, you know." Yet Maeda did not seem to mind the travails of the job and
found humor in the harsh working environment. "I thought I knew all the
bad words in the world," he laughed, "but I learned a few new [ones] down
there."[33]

Coming back to the Twin Cities after his discharge, Maeda took a chance
in the automobile business. He started at the Goodyear Tire shop on Fourth
and Washington Street in downtown St. Paul. "I was working on the service floor, and there were three of us Japanese boys there," he said. It was a

challenging time, as tires, gasoline, sugar, meat, coffee, shoes, silk, nylon, and other items were rationed during the war. "And to our knowledge we didn't have any trouble with the customers." Maeda appreciated the kindness of the manager Mr. Deindorfer, who took them in and treated them well for a year and a half before being transferred to another branch in Ohio.[34]

The new boss, Mr. Smith, was hardly the same. "The day he came, we could tell he did not like us; you could just read it in his face," Maeda asserted. A couple months later, all three Japanese American workers were dismissed on the same day. "We got to let you Jap boys go," Maeda recalled being told. "Too many customers are complaining about you Jap boys working on their cars." It was most likely a concocted excuse, Maeda thought, but there was nothing they could do. Their former supervisor at Goodyear, now working for the Jewish-owned Rosen Tire and US Oil, heard about the terminations and immediately reached out to the Nisei. "We went over and told him what happened. He hired all three of us right there," Maeda said.[35]

Although Maeda was content with changing tires, his family encouraged him to explore other options. Setting down roots in the Twin Cities, his parents sold all they had in Seattle and made a down payment on a house near Fairview and Iglehart in St. Paul in 1945. Since his father was a dental technician, such a vocational path seemed realistic and reasonable for Maeda. He referred his son to another dental technician, Ed Carlson, to be his apprentice. The working relationship lasted until Carlson's retirement in 1980. Maeda opened his own dental lab in 1981 in Roseville, where he would make crowns and bridges for the next four decades. "There are Nisei dentists here; a lot of them are retired now," Maeda noted, "but I don't really know any other Japanese dental technician here in the Twin Cities."[36]

Along with work, family was at the core of Maeda's Minnesotan story. In 1950, he married Katheryn Kubo, a medical technologist from Torrington, a small town in eastern Wyoming near the state border with Nebraska. Her farming family, who had emigrated from Japan around 1900, escaped the fate of imprisonment because of their inland location and thus was able to maintain a rather normal existence during the war. After graduating from the University of Wyoming, Kubo received her training at the Minneapolis General Hospital (now part of Hennepin County Medical Center). She then joined her friends in Baltimore for a year but decided to return to Minnesota and started working at St. Barnabas, the first hospital in Minneapolis, established by the Episcopal Church in 1871, which was closed 120 years later in 1991.

Maeda first saw Kubo at the Japanese American Community Center in Minneapolis right after the war. Reverend Kitagawa, the director of the center, frequently hosted a variety of social activities for the Issei and Nisei residents. "An offshoot of that was a youth fellowship that gathered at that center," Maeda explained; "a lot of us met our mates there." The Maedas were one of these matched couples. "I remember it was a Halloween party," he said with a smile. "She was brand new in town . . . and that's how we met. And it took off from there." Together they called Minnesota home and raised a family of five children.

Picture-perfect Minnesota certainly had its own imperfect moments. The early war years reportedly felt less friendly for the Maeda family. "I do remember I didn't have a car at first, and I'd ride on the streetcar," Maeda said. "If there was an empty seat next to me, people wouldn't sit down." He realized these Caucasian passengers would prefer standing to sitting next to a person of color. The common housing problems confronted by Japanese Americans also affected the Maedas.

When the Maedas planned to buy their own house in 1954, some properties were simply off the table because the owners would not sell to people of Japanese descent. They finally decided to move out to Roseville, then a rapidly developing area with "new little houses for the returning GIs." After consulting the neighbors if they would accept a Japanese American family, Maeda closed on a house that would remain his home from then on. He believed he was "pretty much the only Asian guy" there and enjoyed the recognition by the community as he shopped and strolled around.[37]

Likewise, his sister Jane Maeda went through some difficult times in Austin, also known as "Spam Town USA," about a hundred miles south of the Twin Cities. Her husband, George Mizuno, was a chemist and worked for the Hormel Institute, a biomedical research center that was founded by the Hormel Foods Corporation in 1942 and affiliated with the University of Minnesota and the Mayo Clinic.

Their family moved to Austin, where very few, if any, Japanese Americans, or even non-white people, resided. "It was a company town, and a lot of factory workers were rednecks from a small town," Maeda maintained; "their kids faced a lot of [discrimination], more than my children did. My sister Jane was not happy in Austin." She passed away in 1982. It was about that time Austin underwent its own demographic transformation, largely a result of the yearlong yet unsuccessful strike by union meat-packers at Hormel in 1985. Immigrant workers from Mexico, among others, were brought in by the food and processing companies to staff their plants. Now, nearly a quarter of Austin's population is composed of people of color.[38]

Change was inevitable but slow for the small town. Addressing complicated issues like race and class has never been easy, especially for those homogeneous communities with monochromatic worldviews. Perhaps no other celebrated American author wrote more critically of this than Sinclair Lewis, diagnosing the sensibilities of small-town Minnesota in the early twentieth century. His work provides some hints of the places and people then. Unlike the mythologized frontier of traditional values, moral goodness, and romantic nostalgia to which the reading public was accustomed, Lewis satirically accentuated the complacency, conformity, and narrow-mindedness of small-town life. It seems plausible that this was what a Japanese American family like Jane Maeda's might have had to put up with at the time.

If Austin had not yet embraced inclusivity and equality in the 1940s, Mankato, another city in southern Minnesota, offers a more uplifting story for Japanese Americans. It was the hometown of Carol Milford, the protagonist of Lewis's novel *Main Street* (1920), who describes Mankato, "in its garden-sheltered streets and aisles of elms" as "white and green New England reborn." Imbued with a certain East Coast outlook, Mankato was portrayed to be not as provincial and uncultured as the generic "Gopher Prairie" town.[39]

There the Saiki brothers from Fresno, California, pioneers in the "chicken sexing" industry, decided to relocate their business and rebuild their homes and lives. The story of the Saiki family in Mankato is inseparable from the history of chicken sexing in America, a phrase that outside the poultry industry is likely to elicit chuckles. A concise outline of this interesting profession and its relationship to Japanese Americans in Minnesota is thus pertinent.

Chicken sexing was a novel business back in the 1930s. Farmers only wanted to raise productive, egg-laying hens, but because the infant birds look nearly identical, they had to raise all the chicks until they could be differentiated—an expensive endeavor. A solution emerged in 1932 when a team of experts from Japan introduced an innovative technique at the World Poultry Congress in Cleveland. Developed by Tokyo Imperial University veterinary professor Kiyoshi Masui and his team, the "vent" method of identifying and sorting the sex of day-old fowl had nearly perfect accuracy and needed simply a pair of deft hands and good lighting.[40]

Many Issei at the time, deprived of the rights to own land or naturalize for citizenship, perceived this exciting development as a key to securing the prosperity of their families. Awed by the Japanese master sexers' public demonstrations between 1933 and 1934, Issei community leaders in Southern California devised a special study-abroad program to bring this "prized Japanese skill" to their American-born children.[41]

In July 1935, four Nisei men, including Kiyoto "Keek" Saiki, received full scholarships and departed for the International Chick Sexing School in Nagoya, Japan. They were enrolled in a six-month intensive education course and on-the-job training in the "science" of chicken sexing and would then bring the innovative techniques back to the States. Their plan kick-started a phenomenon. The foursome was followed by approximately a dozen learners annually until the outbreak of the war.[42]

Chicken sexing appeared to be an advanced skill that could become "a fertile vocation" for the Nisei, making it among the few trades in which Japanese Americans were essentially dominant. By 1937, the International Baby Chick Association—the leading trade organization for chicken sexers—approved the vent method and regarded it as the premier technique in the field. Despite calls from business leaders and even the federal government for "Americanization," recruiting white candidates for the job failed to gain traction and comparable outcomes. The early 1940s saw Nisei sexers in high demand by hatcheries and farms all over the country. Training schools for Japanese Americans, headed by those who had studied in Nagoya, proliferated as a result.[43]

Among the vanguard were the Saiki brothers from Fresno. Upon returning from Japan in 1936, Kiyoto Saiki became the first Nisei instructor at the

International Chick Sexing Association. This Saiki family-owned company served as not only a training school and employment agency for local Japanese Americans but also an intermediary between Nisei chicken sexers and Caucasian hatchery owners nationwide. By the late 1930s, the association had "representatives in almost every state in the union that had any poultry industry to speak of," according to George Saiki, the youngest brother of the family, who continued to run the business in Mankato after the war.[44]

The company would negotiate with hatcheries and farms to prepare work contracts on behalf of individual sexers, organize all the logistics for their service, and take a commission on their earnings, usually 10 to 15 percent. The company also provided training for interested Japanese Americans. Beginning sexers would undergo schooling from four to six months, then work through an apprenticeship that lasted about three years, before achieving the status of a fully skilled professional who could determine the sex of more than a thousand chickens per hour with close to perfect accuracy.[45]

The Saikis were a model chicken-sexing family. Emigrating from the coastal city of Hagi in Japan at the turn of the century, Rokuro Saiki and his wife, Mine Saiki, both with agricultural backgrounds, settled in central California and ran a hatchery and poultry farm in Fresno. They had six American-born children, four of whom learned the trade of chicken sexing, including their daughter Setsuko Saiki and three sons Taro "Ty" Saiki, Kiyoto Saiki, and George Saiki. They formed the International Chick Sexing Association, which was a success. Ty Saiki, who oversaw the Midwest and East Coast regions, then invited his sister Setsuko's husband, Fred Yoshio Hirasuna, to join the blossoming family enterprise.

Responding to the series of traumatic events after the Pearl Harbor attack, the Saikis relocated their operation to Mankato, where they had established contacts for several years. Prior to the war, George Saiki visited Mankato twice a year to work with hatcheries in the upper Midwest. Little did he know then that he would live there for the rest of his life. "Going back to 1938, 1939, and 1940," Saiki recalled, "the season was around February to March, and then June to July." Because daylight is crucial to stimulate egg production in hens, they lay more eggs in the spring and summer months, when the days are about fifteen hours long in the Midwest, unlike the shorter days of fall and winter.[46]

During the prime time of the hatching season, the Saiki company had crews of representatives and contracted sexers who came to service the area and then returned to California. "There would be a supervisor, say, at a station in St. Cloud, and all the different cities," he noted, "and some in St. Louis and others." His older brother Ty worked out of Minneapolis for a while but considered Mankato a more appropriate and convenient base. "It was centrally located to all the work that he had throughout the United States," Sumako "Sue" Okamoto Saiki, Ty's wife, explained. "We did come here with the intention of returning to California," she said, but the incarceration that imprisoned her "entire family" made it impossible.[47]

Mankato naturally became their safe haven. The Saikis first stayed at the Ben Pay Hotel, a famous six-story hotel in Blue Earth County that operated between 1920 and 1967, where the newly arrived Japanese American bride felt comfortable. Born in 1919 in Santa Fe Springs, California, Sue Okamoto married Ty Saiki in October 1941, and moved to Minnesota with him shortly thereafter. "We were fortunate enough to be established in business in Mankato," she said. The couple also helped with the relocation of other employees of their company during the mass incarceration. At one point, the Ben Pay Hotel accommodated about twenty-seven Japanese Americans. "The [staff] were most kind to us there, and watched out for us," Sue Saiki said. When the Saikis were expecting their first child in 1942, they rented a house on South Fourth Street, which went smoothly without any problems, although it was not quite the same when they tried to purchase one later.[48]

The younger brother George Saiki also thought the southern Minnesotan city was generally an accepting and agreeable place. "When I first came to Mankato, some of the people would break their necks when we walked by," he said. "I guess they'd never seen a Japanese." There was, of course, a Chinese family who owned a restaurant, as was always the case no matter how small a town was, he claimed. But he doubted if people could make the distinction between a Japanese and a Chinese.[49]

Saiki did not mind the curiosity, and for the most part, life in Mankato was pleasant. "One of the reasons we managed to do well was because we had a lot of sympathetic people in this area." He ascribed their positive treatment to the "German ancestry" of the residents, who had suffered from animosities and difficulties during World War I, and seemingly additional resentments in World War II. "They must have had some sympathy for us," he reckoned, "because they experienced the same thing." His brother-in-law Hirasuna, who worked and lived in Mankato for five and a half years during the war, concurred. "In our case, the German Americans were very friendly, because they knew what we were going through. They went through it themselves."[50]

Not everyone was as rational and empathetic. Being German American did not, after all, automatically translate into being a national enemy or Nazi in the public mind. Seldom did Japanese Americans receive a fair presumption of innocence. "In spite of a lot of nice people here, there were others who gave us problems," George Saiki lamented. "It is easy to understand why some of them would be upset over our presence here in Minnesota, not differentiating whether we were citizens or not, or whether we were law-abiding or not, because we looked like the enemy."[51]

For better or for worse, George Saiki did not stay in Mankato during the war. Both he and his other brother Hideyo Beck Saiki were drafted into the Army by the fall of 1941. They both entered the MISLS at Camp Savage. The two eldest Saiki brothers were exempt from the service—Ty was thirty years old then, and Kiyoto was excused for health issues. While the two younger siblings were fighting for the country in uniform, the rest of the family had to maneuver their chicken-sexing business and support the Japanese American community in an equally treacherous terrain on the home front.

Since sponsored employment was one of the three routes to free Japanese Americans from confinement, the Saikis' International Chick Sexing Association, together with other similar organizations, was important in assisting many incarcerees to leave camps and restart their lives. For young Nisei, especially those who lacked financial resources, academic aptitude, and social capital, chicken sexing was an attractive recourse, or a speedier way out of imprisonment. The associations provided one of the better and cheaper educational options for them to learn a marketable skill with an assurance of instant job offers upon training. Tuition could also be deferred on the condition that the graduates repay it by working under exclusive contracts for a given company.[52]

The opportunity was extended to women as well. Gender played no role in the trade. Women sexers were as capable and competent as men, as Setsuko Saiki proved. Nevertheless, domestic duties that fell chiefly on female family members and the frequent travel into unfamiliar places in the middle of the war deterred many Nisei women from stepping into the business. Still, it was quite common to see husbands and wives teamed up to work and travel together as partners.[53]

What seemed uncommon was the sudden appearance of all these Nisei workers in places that had barely ever seen any person of Asian descent. The sight of Japanese Americans in the small "white" towns, as George Saiki indicated, would have turned heads in ordinary days before the war. No stretch of imagination is needed to picture what the reaction might have been toward the presence of a group of Nisei traveling around during wartime.

Furthermore, the official narrative did not help clear the confusion but rather exposed the contradiction. On the one hand, people of Japanese ancestry were alleged to be nefarious actors; removing them from their West Coast homes and locking them up became a military emergency. On the other hand, the service of the sexers was so irreplaceably vital to poultry production and desperately sought by the industry that the government had little choice but to release hundreds of them to travel from hatchery to hatchery in the Midwest and on the East Coast. The War Department was even said to have authorized local Selective Service boards to grant Nisei sexers outright draft deferment.[54]

Yet the Nisei sexers were not completely free. Countermeasures kept them in check. In the early months of 1942, federal agents kept close surveillance on the chicken sexers, who were suspected of "a possible Japanese courier system due to their extensive traveling." No report of espionage or sabotage was filed. To untangle the knotty situation, the US Department of Agriculture issued a country-wide bulletin in December 1942, stressing the legitimacy of these Nisei sexers and urging all players in the business to participate in the greater seasonal leave program. Hirasuna, the executive secretary of the association at the time, emphasized: "We're chick sexers, but we are Americans." The public relations appeal along with the governmental approval might have boosted the confidence of some Nisei supporters but did not guarantee a change of heart in all skeptics.[55]

Against the backdrop of wartime hysteria, the work environment, which included extensive travel across the country, could be hostile and even dangerous for the Japanese Americans. The Saikis related that when their Nisei workers left Mankato for assignment, they were often stopped, questioned, and wrongfully arrested by the local police. "This kind of thing happened all the time during the early part of the war," George Saiki said. "In a lot of the small towns . . . in Sleepy Eye, they were thrown in jail." Some of the Japanese American sexers were halted and detained en route from California to the Midwest. Ty Saiki would then have to seek out the Mankato chief of police for assistance. "At any rate, whenever Ty got into these difficulties, he'd always ask [the police chief] to call wherever the trouble was and have them released."[56]

Sue Saiki, the wife of Ty, added: "Our chief of police, Al Salisbury, was most kind by giving us protection at all times." Because of their business, Ty Saiki often traveled around with a considerable amount of cash, and he carried a gun with him. "But that was confiscated," Sue Saiki noted. "We did give them the receipt for the gun, but for some reason, it was lost at the police station." She never heard about the gun again and counted it as "one of the unpleasantries" of her Minnesotan experience. Feeling "unprotected," she realized all they could do then was to rely on the police.[57]

If traveling to work was problematic, there was no guarantee that trouble would cease after they reached their destination. George Saiki revealed that the Japanese American sexers were regularly harassed at the workplace. The highly racialized war further exacerbated the tension. "Words would get around that there were some Japanese in town," he said. "Some folks in the hatcheries, after a couple of drinks or beers, would threaten them while they were working." He knew, many a time, that the Nisei had to "sneak outside the back door, or whatever exit that was available," and leave in a stealthy and surreptitious manner, so as to avoid making a scene. Those hatchery owners who dared to keep Japanese American sexers might also force them to work in kitchens and backrooms to ward off public attention.[58]

At that time, the opening of an International Chick Sexing Association training school on Lowry Avenue in Minneapolis in November 1944 also met with strong protests. One could deduce the severity of these challenges from newspaper headlines such as "Intolerance Here," "Neighborhood Protests Chick Sex Determination School," and "Council Fight Looms on Chicken

Sex School Pleas," in the *Minneapolis Star Journal*. One of the pieces stated that a "stormy session" with local residents cited copious opposition to the school, but solidly denied racial prejudice was a motive. However, a reporter caught a small child, playing outside the meeting, who greeted a committee member with an untutored query: "Mister, are we going to get rid of them Japs?"[59]

Backed by thirty-five complaining neighbors, the city council passed an ordinance directed at the removal of the school, whose operators, instructors, and students were all Nisei. Even without any bigoted intention, the news editor opined that the incident was "unfortunate," because "Japanese Americans, as genuine citizens of this country as any of us, learning an honest and needed skill and having their own kin in American uniforms on the world's battlefronts, have been made the conspicuous objects of what has many earmarks of racial discrimination."[60]

Within a month, the matter was resolved in the Nisei's favor. The city health commissioner quickly disclosed an inspection result that confirmed the school had "nothing objectionable from a health standpoint." About ten days later, twenty of the contesting residents withdrew their complaints. With the support of the press and state government agencies, the association obtained a permit for operation until the term finished in February 1945. The dispute ended, at least temporarily, a whirl of controversy surrounding the school in the city. Reluctantly put under the spotlight, the Saikis understood that all the attention the company received could cut both ways. There was also a difference in receptivity between urban and rural populaces. Their woes and worries were far from over.[61]

Keeping their profiles low and their heads down, as much as mastering chicken-sexing skills, became the foremost priority for the Nisei workers. The Mankato chief of police constantly reminded them how to conduct themselves and saw to it that they carried proper identification and clearances with them at all times. "That did simplify matters somewhat," Sue Saiki said. Surely, she also knew that not all unfriendly situations could be solved by documents or even rational conversations, especially if the event involved "a little too much drinking."[62]

There were also other red flags. When the Saikis had occasion to invite their Nisei friends and workers to their home, they were instructed not to draw the drapes down, lest that provoke their neighbors' suspicion that something malicious was being planned. She also noticed that Nisei men were strongly advised not to go around with, or even speak to, young Caucasian women. That included waitresses in restaurants and taverns, with whom Japanese American men must not be too familiar; otherwise, there would be resentments and repercussions. "Our chief of police did caution Ty to see that his staff were aware of the situation, and how the feelings would run," Sue Saiki remembered; "I think it was fair warning." The alert might be reasonable, but the treatment was definitely not.[63]

The burden fell on the Nisei to stay calm and turn the other cheek. "There are people who feel that our race has been responsible for all the unhappiness that existed in their families," she figured. "They just felt that they had to take it out on us." Of course, it was the minority and oppressed group that needed to show tolerance and understanding of the racial hierarchy and even bigotry. It was not the other way around. All these measures might have been sugarcoated as "protecting" the Japanese American members in the community, but the racist biases underneath them were hard to ignore. While probably compounded with other personal reasons, a number of Nisei sexers, feeling disappointed and discouraged, quit and rejoined their families in the camps instead.[64]

Sue Saiki believed that, realizing anger and pessimism would not help their cause, at least back then during the height of the war, most of them chose to swallow the bitter pill and hoped things would get better. "We tried to make it a point to get into the right places at the right times so that we would become acquainted with those who could spread the word that we weren't here to make trouble," she said. "We were just here trying to make a living and bring up our family."[65]

The Saikis' review of the postwar era was still mixed. George Saiki returned to Minnesota in 1946. He married Emi Yokoyama, raised his own family, and helped manage the chicken-sexing business in Mankato. "I spent four and a half years in the service, and we had our problems," he said. "A lot of us . . . were also pushed around, and it wasn't the easiest time of my life there." Saiki did not elaborate on his experiences in the military but offered something more general. "Even the strong oak will bend if the wind is persistent enough. And that's about it. It kind of wears on you."[66]

The Nisei veteran was confronted with the usual housing discrimination when he bought property in the "Caucasian-only" zone. However, he concluded that what his family had encountered was petty and pale in comparison to their compatriots who suffered forced displacement and confinement. "We've had our little difficulties, on account of maybe the way we look and talk, and maybe our racial background," he noted. "The great majority of people here in town have been really nice to us. I can't complain."[67]

His sister-in-law echoed the sentiment. "I have the feeling that we've been accepted so well that we couldn't feel very comfortable anywhere else," Sue Saiki said. "In time as the people got acquainted with us, they realized that there was less to fear than they thought, or no fear at all when they got to know us really well." She and her husband, Ty, had always talked about going back to California in their retirement years. "But now the grandchildren are showing up," she explained; "we are to stay here the rest of our lives." The two Saiki brothers never left Mankato after all. George Saiki passed away in 2001 and Ty in 2002.[68]

Meanwhile, the story of chicken sexing deserves an epilogue. It remained a Nisei trade for another decade after the war, and family enterprises, like the Saikis' association, maintained their role in the industry. The 1950s witnessed the gradual dissolution of the Japanese American monopoly, as the Sansei lacked interest in the profession. In addition, new techniques for breeding fowls that were more easily distinguishable in infancy, the rise of poultry conglomerates and decline of independent small farms, as well as the push from unions for diversity in the industry, all led to the Japanese American dominance of the field fading away by the 1970s.[69]

Still, chicken sexing lives on as a secretive yet "lucrative art." The vent method keeps its popularity in sorting certain stocks of egg-laying hens and turkeys to this day. The question of whether machines can substitute or surpass manual labor has been around since the inception of the profession decades ago. "People said that even when I was learning," Kiyoto Saiki said. "That's the thing I was afraid of . . . but it hasn't happened yet." It is still not the case. How an expert chicken sexer can achieve astonishing accuracy continues to be a mystery, even to cognitive scientists, although ethnicity is not a factor.[70]

For Kiyoto Saiki, Minnesota was more than a place where he took refuge and retained the family business during the war. "I received notification that my name was placed in the Congressional Records," he proudly said five decades later, "as one of the prime contributors in bringing the chick sexing industry to this country." Whereas he mastered the innovative chicken-sexing technique, which reshaped an industry, in Japan, before his arrival to the North Star State, he learned another valuable skill that helped improve his life after he came.[71]

Saiki took up a new vocation—refrigeration—in Minnesota. Upon his return to Fresno with his wife, Fumiko Nishioki Saiki, in 1946, he simultaneously rebuilt the chicken-sexing business in California and started a refrigeration company. Poultry work could be unpredictable, he explained. "Fortunately, I had developed another skill other than sexing to carry me through." Both ventures, according to him, were successful over the years, and Saiki was actively involved until he passed away in 2003. The place where Saiki learned the trade of refrigeration was the William Hood Dunwoody Industrial Institute (now Dunwoody College of Technology).[72]

Like the International Chick Sexing Association, Dunwoody provided an opportunity for Japanese Americans to train in industrial and mechanical crafts to equip themselves for professional lives ahead. For many Nisei men, as well as a few women, who had followed their families' relocations to Minnesota, the institute was a sensible stepping-stone to higher-paid and more stable jobs. Its offering of shorter programs and more practical subjects had better appeal to the working Nisei, or at the very least, provided a legitimate reason to stay around until the war ended.

Researching the students at Dunwoody puts a sharper focus on an eclectic group of Japanese Americans whose journeys to Minnesota were less intentional and structured, and hence, harder to trace and easily overlooked. Their experiences were rather different from those of the college students, cadet nurses, and MISLS soldiers, although there were overlaps—some were later drafted and sent to Camp Savage and Fort Snelling, for example. Many of them were already in the state due to a variety of reasons, mostly personal and familial, instead of coming directly from the camps.

Endeavoring to earn a living and to wait out the war, these Nisei usually were more mature and worked in blue-collar industries. Their enrollment in Dunwoody was often an expedient solution to a quandary at hand. Most of them returned to the West Coast after the war drew to a close. Kiyoto Saiki was a case in point. Even though Minnesota was not the ultimate destination for many of them, the school served its timely purpose. The institute accommodated a significant number of Nisei students—at least ninety-seven men and two women—during the war years, a total of ninety-nine Japanese Americans, despite its "almost exclusively white and male" student body throughout the last century.[73]

Dunwoody filled a gap in the emerging area of vocational education in Minnesota at the time. Both daytime and evening classes were available for not only those workers who wanted to upgrade their skills to meet present and future employment needs but also veterans who had just been discharged from the armed forces and were readjusting to civilian life. In early 1944, the school even offered free courses, under the sponsorship of the US Department of Education, to recruit and train "as quickly as possible hundreds of students" for the vacancies in the war industries. A Dunwoody course at that time normally lasted a hundred hours (about four months) and up to several months of apprenticeship in servicing, varying slightly among the fields. The popular departments among prospective students were baking, electrical, refrigeration and air conditioning, printing, building construction, radio, automobile, mechanical drafting and diesel, and sheet metal.[74]

Life at Dunwoody, because of its significant proportion of nontraditional students, presented unique challenges unlike other university campuses. Smoking was one of them. While practically all educational institutions did not permit smoking in the buildings or on the premises, Dunwoody, in "handling large numbers of mature students" and "an increasing load of veterans, many of whom had become inveterate smokers," made an exception for students over eighteen and granted them "the privilege of smoking morning, noon, and night, outside of school hours, in the students' clubroom." Regarding extracurricular activities, there were not too many but still a handful of "hobby clubs" that mirrored the general interests of the student body, such as a camera club, a radio and electronics club, a rifle club, a technical club, a glee club, and an orchestra.[75]

The less formal environment, shorter academic schedule, and more technical, skill-oriented programs of Dunwoody were exactly what Saiki was looking for during the unproductive snowy season. He began his refrigeration course the first week of November in 1944, and was immediately featured in the school newspaper, which described him as "a likable fellow" and "a credit" to the school. Saiki appeared six more times during his four-month tenure at the institute. In these short news mentions, Saiki, a "star production" man and a "competitive" worker, was careful with the machines yet playful enough to "let the gas out once in a while" to bring some lachrymatory laughter to the floor. The thirty-one-year-old Nisei and his classmates also reportedly played pool together every day during their lunch hour.[76]

Besides more mature recruits like Saiki, Dunwoody also accepted younger students, around the lower end of the military draft age, between eighteen and thirty. Jim Kirihara was one of its earliest Japanese American attendees, barely eighteen when he came to the Twin Cities in 1943. Being the son of a grocer in Oakland, California, Kirihara and his family were rounded up and sent to the Tanforan Assembly Center and then the camp in Topaz, where the teenager spent the first part of the war.

With help from a camp administrator, Kirihara was able to leave through employment. He was involved in reading thermometers and other weather

Jim Kirihara, 2015.
Courtesy of the author

instruments in the highland desert, working for an agronomist, John McComb, whose wife was from Minneapolis. "Her parents were immigrants, one was Swedish and the other Norwegian," Kirihara recalled. "He wanted me to leave camp as soon as I could." Hence, her family became his sponsor. "The couple took me in, set me up about two weeks in their home, and showed me the way of the land."[77]

They also signed up the young Japanese American for Dunwoody. "It was a famous [school for] plumbing, welding, baking, mechanics, and many trades," Kirihara said. "I wasn't to be a mechanic, but that's the first thing I did." In addition to taking classes in the evening, he worked in a couple of places during the day, a junkyard that salvaged used parts from automobiles and a restaurant that kept him in food. He soon realized being a mechanic was not meant for him and instead enrolled in a business school to learn accounting, which became his lifelong career. Kirihara was drafted in 1944 but exempted, at least for the time being, due to his poor eyesight. He was later called back and served in the 1950s.[78]

Kirihara eventually chose Minnesota to be his home, where his whole family also resettled. Although the trade he learned at Dunwoody would become neither his passion nor his profession, the institute helped the Nisei get through the difficult days and justified his remaining out of incarceration during the war. Simply having a stopgap, even if nothing more, was often crucial to the Japanese Americans' survival in the cities at the time.[79]

Longtime Bloomington resident and Minnesota Gophers sports fan Yoshimi "Matt" Matsuura, who also had a short stint at Dunwoody, had little idea about the state before he came. The story behind Matsuura's journey from the farmland in his birthplace of Fowler, California, to the incarceration camp at Gila River, Arizona, was all too familiar. The forced removal was traumatic. Not knowing what the future might hold was just as terrifying. Hence, Matsuura and his childhood sweetheart, Kazuko Kay Fujimoto, decided to get married, right before their removal from home; at least then they could face the obstacles that life threw at them together. The newlywed couple, along with their families, ended up in the harsh desert of Gila River. When the opportunity to be freed and work outside of imprisonment arose, Matsuura grabbed the chance at once. His destination turned out to be Minnesota.[80]

Matsuura was met with a rather frosty reception in Minneapolis in the summer of 1943. He was among seventy-six Nisei who joined the National Youth Administration (NYA) for its training program in the North Star State. To combat the economic hardship that hampered American youth and their families during the Great Depression, President Roosevelt had launched the NYA with his Executive Order 7086 in June 1935. The federally funded "New Deal" agency concentrated on supporting education and employment for young adults between the ages of sixteen and twenty-five, through part-time work positions, occupational training, and, particularly during the war, vocational programs related to the defense industry.[81]

When the NYA representatives recruited participants at Gila River, Matsuura signed up in an instant. "I was twenty-four," he said. "I was the daddy of the bunch." When he told his wife about leaving for the NYA training center in Shakopee, Minnesota, he was as clueless as she was about the location and what the job might involve. "Getting out of the camp was the sole reason I wanted to go," he chuckled. "When I came out there, I found out it was just a little burg outside of Minneapolis. It was like a CCC [Civilian Conservation Corps] camp, with tiny barracks, bunkbeds, and classrooms. That was it."[82]

If the crude training center was disappointing, the rude awakening the Japanese American group found was even more discouraging. The NYA Nisei, with the majority from Gila River but including other camps, started to arrive in Minneapolis at the end of May 1943 to attend the war industrial training program. They were excited to regain their freedom and to contribute to the war effort. "Everything had to do with the factory," Matsuura said, "like machine shop, drafting, foundry work, and pattern making." About two weeks later, on June 7, the NYA called a halt and ordered them out of the classroom. The reason for the abrupt cancellation was not explicitly disclosed. Since courses for other non-Japanese Americans were still open and in session, one could assume, with a certain degree of confidence, that race was the impetus behind their termination.

The *Minneapolis Star Journal* ran a piece the next day with the headline "'Breaks Against Us,' Assert Nisei Youth, Stranded in Twin Cities," which described their dilemma and decried the discrimination. It reported that these were "the much kicked around Americans with Japanese faces" whose "own country's prejudice that forced them to be penned up in the desert of Arizona had followed them to Minnesota." Most of the seventy-three Nisei men were taken to Union City Mission's farm at Medicine Lake. The three women, for the time being, could remain in the NYA resident girls' center in St. Paul. Without the government sponsorship, they were allowed to stay in Minnesota for only one week to look for jobs and accommodations on their own and otherwise had to leave town. Five men and one woman were successful, hired by a foundry and a beauty parlor, respectively. The rest planned to get part-time employment and continue training at Dunwoody or other private schools. Matsuura was one of them.[83]

Having learned that Minneapolis had a WRA office, Matsuura immediately went into town and sought assistance. Still, he remembered clearly the moment when he heard from the director who announced their dismissal. "It was dead silent. Nobody spoke up," he said. "We couldn't believe it. We were recruited, and we just got there; now they're saying we're [ousted]. We're in a strange place. Where do we go? What do we do?"

Matsuura believed that the director, who "felt that it was not right," resigned the day after. But quitting was not something that Matsuura could afford. While he acted right away, others were "numbed" by the defeat. "I told some of the people there that I'm going into Minneapolis to look around. And a lot of them . . . went directly to the lodging over at Medicine Lake. . . . They were in no mood to make any decision."

It did not take long before Matsuura and another young fellow located the WRA office, which was ready to work with them. Bad news apparently traveled fast. "We used their phone, looked through the newspaper and all kinds of listing," he noted. "I started calling." He deemed himself lucky because, after only five rejections, he found a room in North Minneapolis that would accommodate Japanese Americans. "At the time [that area] was a Jewish community," Matsuura explained; "and it was much easier for us to move in." Avoiding any type of attention, the Nisei in the cities had just one objective in mind. "We didn't want to disturb any neighborhood. We didn't want anybody to start any rumors or anything. Tried to keep it quiet and look for a job, that was our main goal, to find some employment of some kind."

This was when Dunwoody made a special appearance. "I decided to enroll at the institute . . . and I figured, the best place [for finding work] would probably be some factories," Matsuura said. "I took up machine shop." He also got a part-time janitor position, receiving thirty-five cents an hour to mop the floor in the chemistry department. Undeterred by the NYA setback, Matsuura was looking ahead, busy with job hunting all over town.

He was at Dunwoody for just a short period and did not complete the course. Instead, Matsuura was hired by a small factory that supplied dies—machine tools that were used for loading gunpowder in .50-caliber shells—to the TCOP, the large ordnance plant in Arden Hills. Other Japanese Americans also stood back up from the initial stumble. By the middle of June, all but one or two of the seventy-six Nisei had either been placed in jobs or moved to other cities. As soon as Matsuura secured employment, he sent for his wife to join him.[84]

However, both his new post and subsequent search for a place to live got off to a rocky start. Matsuura maintained that his colleagues were often verbally offensive and the environment at times hostile. "How would you like to work with a Jap boy?" was what his supervisor spread around before the Nisei arrived. Matsuura also cited one unpleasant episode when he serviced a company as a tool and die man to upgrade their equipment. "I changed some of the things and laid them out," he said. "I had one drawing all practically completed." He then went out to lunch, only to find all eyes were on him when he returned. His draft on the board was "ruined," covered with scrawls and scribbles. He felt everyone was anticipating a scene, a fit of rage or a tearful breakdown perhaps. "I just took the paper off, put a new one in, sat down, and started all over. I think I disappointed a lot of people because I didn't show any outright emotion. But why do it? That's what they wanted."[85]

Finding an apartment suitable for a married couple was another soul-crushing affair. Matsuura even had a landlady spit in his face and tell him she would never rent to "a Jap." He kept all this to himself and did not tell anyone, not even his wife, until years later. "I didn't want to talk about the humiliation; it was terrible," he said. "Experiences like that, many places I got shut down, shot down, but . . . you stomach it, and you go on." He finally rented a place, still in North Minneapolis, and the person who was willing to house them was a Swiss lady with a Greek husband.

The wartime Matsuura reunion was brief, yet their postwar residence was permanent. Just when the pair had settled down in the Twin Cities, Matsuura received the notice to "report at Fort Snelling for physical." It was the early summer of 1944. "I left her behind in camp, when I came here . . . I found an apartment, got her over here, and the army drafted me. . . . I left her behind again," he laughed. "Every time she caught up with me, I was gone." Matsuura decided to join the MISLS, for he had already lost many friends in Europe. "Camp Savage and Fort Snelling would be nine months of Japanese military language school," he thought. "And many things could happen in nine months. So, I played the odds there." After thirteen weeks of basic training at Fort McClellan in Alabama, he returned to Minnesota for the MISLS.

Minnesota would in due course become home for the Matsuuras. The newly enlisted soldier at Fort Snelling admitted that he was not a very good student, and he didn't get any promotions either. "I happened to be in the right class. None of the people in my class went beyond T-5 [Technician Fifth Grade] so that was okay," Matsuura said with a smile. "I was comfortable." He believed the schedule for his deployment was "perfect," too. The war had ended by the time he was shipped out to Manila and then Tokyo. Fortunately, his parents and in-laws had relocated to the Twin Cities in his absence. His wife was not alone. After his service in the Pacific, Matsuura rejoined his family and worked for the Warner Manufacturing Company until his retirement three decades later. He passed away in 2021 at the age of 103, "recognized by the [University of Minnesota Gophers] for being the longest season basketball ticket holder for over fifty-five years."[86]

Like many Japanese Minnesotans, the family of Bill Hirabayashi, whose words started this chapter, was intricately tied to the wartime drama that reverberated on the West Coast. The Pearl Harbor attack and its aftermath eventually led them to Minnesota. After his father, Toshiharu Hirabayashi, arrived in the Twin Cities in 1945, he started a kitchen job right away at the Nicollet Hotel in downtown Minneapolis. He worked there until he retired in his seventies. Leading a "useful" life was the philosophy that he stuck by and ingrained in his children. The motto also applied to his wife, Midori "Grace" Kitahara. Raising a family of eight in a time of chaos was an incredible feat in and of itself. Because of her sewing skills, she worked as a seamstress in a clothing factory in addition to taking care of the household. Within a few years, the sedulous family had saved enough to buy their first house, which was on Thirty-Second Street and Park Avenue. It was home for the Hirabayashis for the rest of their lives.

While there was nothing left in Washington for the Issei couple, except perhaps sad memories, their choice to resettle in the North Star State was driven by two main personal reasons. First of all, Reverend Kitagawa had been a close friend to the family for a long time, going way back to when he was the minister in Washington and then at Tule Lake. Knowing of the religious leader's move to the Twin Cities and the welcoming environment that he had helped to create brought an extra sense of comfort, confidence, and community to the Hirabayashis.

Furthermore, their second son had received training at Camp Savage and believed that Minneapolis would be an appropriate location for the family to regroup and rebound. His name was Grant Hirabayashi, one of the fourteen combat linguists in "Merrill's Marauders." The story of the Marauders, including Hirabayashi's own experiences, can be found in many books and articles. There are even two Hollywood motion pictures about their exploits; however, both films completely ignore the Japanese American contribution, and one even misidentifies the interpreter character as a Filipino.[87]

There was also another famous member in their clan. While Grant Hirabayashi demonstrated his loyalty to the country through the more conventional trajectory, his cousin Gordon Kiyoshi Hirabayashi fought for justice in the nation in what was then considered a more contentious way. He was the plaintiff in the US Supreme Court case *Hirabayashi v. United States* (1943). Along with the Nisei litigants of other similar cases, notably *Yasui v. United States* (1943) and *Korematsu v. United States* (1944), Hirabayashi challenged the legality of the restrictions and the forced removal imposed on Japanese Americans by the government. Unfortunately, they all lost. In the unanimous opinion that ruled against the Japanese Americans, the justices argued that some infringement on individual liberty was allowable in time of war, specifically with indications that a group of one national extraction might be more menacing than others.[88]

Hirabayashi never gave up throughout his ordeal. After the war, he became a professor of sociology and joined the faculty at the University of
Alberta, at Edmonton, Canada, in 1959. He taught there for the remainder
of his academic career until his retirement in 1983. It was about that time
when Aiko Herzig-Yoshinaga, the lead archival researcher of the Commission on Wartime Relocation and Internment of Civilians (CWRIC), uncovered documents that clearly indicated the War Department's misconduct in
1942. She found the sole surviving copy of John DeWitt's original report,
which revealed the government knew the exclusion order was only an alternative and not a military necessity yet deliberately withheld that information from the Supreme Court.

The new evidence played a significant role in both the *coram nobis*, or
appeal, hearings of the three Nisei cases and the Japanese American redress
movement. In September 1988, the Ninth Circuit Court of Appeals ruled in
Hirabayashi's favor and vacated his personal convictions. Robert Entenmann,
professor emeritus of Asian studies and history at St. Olaf College, recalled
when he invited Hirabayashi to give a talk on campus in 1990. "It was shortly
after the US government's official apology and the redress movement. He
was in the news at that time," Entenmann said. "People were very curious to
hear, first of all, the broad perspective on the incarceration, and also Gordon
Hirabayashi's personal experiences." Victory did come, however belatedly.
Four months after Hirabayashi passed away at the age of ninety-three in
2012, the Nisei fighter was posthumously awarded the Presidential Medal of
Freedom, the highest civilian honor, by President Barack Obama.[89]

Looking up to his brother Grant and cousin Gordon, Bill Hirabayashi took
pride in his family history. But he also knew an ideal life was one that was
lived realistically. He did not engage enemies in a dangerous jungle in a
faraway land. He did not challenge the federal government on its abuse of
power and go to prison for his beliefs. He received neither a Bronze Star for
valor nor a Presidential Medal of Freedom. While his role models wrote
two epic chapters in Japanese American history, Bill Hirabayashi furnished
yet another.

Being the fourth out of eight children, Hirabayashi had the typical traits
of a social, adaptable, and independent "middle child." Like many Japanese

American farming families, he grew up in a rural and religious setting. His gift, he believed, was not for academics or sports but people. "All I can say is . . . I am a people person. I just get along with people." Throughout grade school, he particularly enjoyed listening to the janitor in the boiler room during recesses, talking about creating new inventions and making big money. The seeds of his entrepreneurial spirit were probably sown then.[90]

Moreover, Hirabayashi loved cars, ever since his eldest brother, Martin, took him to an automobile show in Seattle when he was eight years old. He even enrolled in evening classes on mechanics and bodywork at a vocational school as a high school senior. All of these—his people skills, innovative mindset, and passion for cars—would come together years later and enable a fruitful career for him in Minnesota.

There were surely disadvantages to being middle-born though. Hirabayashi graduated from Auburn High School in late spring 1941, but his father could not afford to send him to college that fall. His two older brothers, Martin and Grant, were studying in Japan, and his older sister Helen "Kay" Hirabayashi Ujifusa was attending the University of Washington. Hirabayashi thus started working at the farm. His turn for higher education never came, and the war broke out instead.

Brimming with fear and tears in the Tule Lake camp, Hirabayashi made two bold choices fueled by his hopes and dreams. He married his childhood sweetheart, Anice E. Hirabayashi. Then the twenty-year-old couple planned to break free from imprisonment and go as far away as they could. "We wanted to prove ourselves," Hirabayashi said, "and that's how we ended up in the Chicago area." Having inundated the post office with countless résumés in search of a sponsor, he somehow caught the eye of Ernest "Ernie" Byfield, a famed hotelier and restaurateur whose establishments were frequented by screen actors and socialites of the time. In the summer of 1943, the Nisei was hired to work on an estate called Grassmere Farm, in Barrington, Illinois.

The fact that his boss was the second generation of Jewish immigrants, Hirabayashi thought, contributed to their shared experiences of racial discrimination and created mutual respect and, therefore, led to his hiring. He learned years later that his employment was also due to a postscript he had added in the application letter. "P.S: You might consider me a Jap of all trades" was what he wrote. "I used the three-letter word, but in those days, they were calling you that anyway, no matter where you went." Byfield decided that someone who could retain a sense of humor through such hardship would be capable of handling many tasks.[91]

Additionally, he arranged a deferment from military service for Hirabayashi, when Japanese Americans were reclassified to be eligible for draft. Byfield, indeed, was the boss who told the young man that supporting the war from the home front was as crucial as fighting on the battlefield. Hirabayashi was disappointed that he did not serve like his brother Grant. "But that's the way things worked out," he gathered.[92]

The whole Hirabayashi family eventually reunited in Minnesota. The Nisei couple from Barrington often visited their parents, who had resettled in Minneapolis. With close family nearby as well as a strong community under Reverend Kitagawa, Anice Hirabayashi found Minneapolis a better place to raise her son than Chicago, and they made their move to the Twin Cities. Hirabayashi joined them after Byfield passed away in 1950. They would then become proud Minnesotans.[93]

Reflecting on his job search in the postwar working world, Hirabayashi acknowledged that it was not as easy as he had expected. With experience in automobile bodywork and repair, he knocked on the door of one car dealership after another, yet all he received were rejections. The reason was that he was not a union member. Hirabayashi did not quite understand the intricacies until one of the fellows explained it to him. The Nisei was told that there was "a mafia deal" here in Minneapolis. "You don't get a job unless you have a union card." The underworld kingpin, Kid Cann, possibly the most notorious mobster in the history of Minnesota, had the city and many of its leaders—from criminals to politicians—wrapped around his fingers. Hirabayashi believed labor racketeering was a part of it.

Unions were different back then than now. Throughout the first half of the twentieth century, labor organizations across the country were mostly opposed to having immigrant workers from Asia, notably from China. That the imported and cheaper labor would undermine the economic standing and job security of Americans was one common rationale. Another argument insisted that these Asian workers, even if they were citizens, were not as readily assimilated into the mainstream culture as were Europeans, and hence, they were more problematic.[94]

The Governor's Interracial Commission of Minnesota, after checking with representatives from major industries and services, found no record of union membership on the part of anyone with Asian descent in 1949. It did reference a Chinese employee of a Minneapolis restaurant, who had once belonged to a union in Chicago. He lamented that "the organization failed to gain the same benefits for him [as] it strove to get for its white members." Hirabayashi was not alone with issues regarding the unions. For example, Yoshimi Matsuura, the Dunwoody alumnus and Gophers fan, also disclosed that he had negative encounters with union members. George Saiki, who ran the International Chick Sexing Association in Mankato, had his disconcerting story to tell, too.[95]

Being true to his optimistic character, Hirabayashi met his challenges in life with a smile. He started working in a small garage, even though he was underpaid. He knew he had better be humble about the unfair situation, for he needed a job to take care of his family. His attention to details as an auto body repairman soon earned him a reputation. His work impressed Donald Robert Skogmo, a member of the Gamble-Skogmo conglomerate who ran the auto supply stores and franchises of European cars like Jaguar and M. G. from England. When it was time for the Nisei to quit, he went straight over to Skogmo and was hired immediately.

Slowly and diligently, Hirabayashi built up a customer base, accumulated some capital, and made many friends. As his entrepreneurial spirit kicked in, he opened his own auto repair shop, eventually becoming an auto dealer for Jaguar, British Motor Corporation, Jeep, and other brands in the Twin Cities, as well as having two auto parts stores and a gas station. "Minnesota was good to me," Hirabayashi contended. "I have had several businesses here, and no matter what business I am in, the public took me on like what I am supposed to be, as if I were their [own]." In retrospect, Hirabayashi acknowledged that he was fortunate, and Minnesota had been kind to him. "People are so friendly. . . . I don't have anything to complain," he said; "if somebody cuts me off on the highway, I might be mad, but beyond that, everybody [is] such nice people in this town or this state for that matter." Such an upbeat sentiment is the perfect note to mark the end of this section.[96]

The war years in Minnesota were a transformative epoch. From Kimi Hara to Bill Hirabayashi, the working Japanese Americans broke down social barriers, begot a strong local community, and brought cultural diversity to the Twin Cities. The state had seen Asians in the local workforce before but never in the numbers or with the same visibility as they did in World War II. The MISLS, both directly and indirectly, was the catalyst. Few Nisei knew much about Minnesota prior to their arrival. To many of them, the North Star State initially served more as a convenient layover in their escape from misery than an ultimate destination for their pursuit of happiness.

The injustice of the wartime removal and incarceration, as well as the following resettlement of Japanese Americans in Minnesota, is still unfamiliar to many in the state. The topic was not a comfortable one for the Issei and Nisei to discuss outright at the time. Is it possible to hear more about these stories, even after all these years?

The window of time for such inquiries has always been short, and the odds of success low from the start. The Issei generation is gone, and many Nisei—and even their Sansei children—have also passed away. Similarly, numerous institutions have closed and disappeared. St. Mary's School of Nursing itself, for example, is now a bygone memory, having graduated its last class in June 1970. Yet, if there are common themes in all these Japanese American stories, perseverance ranks high on the list. Will there be someone, like Aiko Herzig-Yoshinaga in the Gordon Hirabayashi case, to dig out and discover new evidence decades later in a vast sea of public records, archival documents, and personal writings, that can not only restore justice but also rewrite history? Only time can tell. The chances might be slim, but, as researchers keep probing and searching while families continue tracing and sharing, the outlook needs not be grim.

8 | Resettlement and Remembrance

Connecting Wartime Japanese American Stories to Minnesota

> "I always knew my father was in the Army. He would tell me about his military work like translating and counter intelligence ... [but] I didn't appreciate it at the time, since I had no other life experience to put the facts in context.... And then I came to Minnesota.... I became more interested in what happened.... What is Camp Savage? What is Fort Snelling? ... Now it's almost like a passion for me."—KAREN TANAKA LUCAS

Sitting in her Apple Valley home one late spring afternoon, Karen Tanaka Lucas recounted the story of her Nisei father, Walter Tanaka. The search for her paternal past, which also gradually became a quest for her own identity, had been a long journey. Born on a military base in Tokyo during her father's service in Occupied Japan and growing up in Chicago where he was stationed at the Fifth Army headquarters afterward, Lucas always felt an intimate yet elusive connection with her heritage. "My siblings and I were pretty much raised in a white environment. My parents did not emphasize learning the Japanese language or culture," she said. "There was some intentionality there. My father thought all of us blend very well with our friends, our church, our school and community. We are not encouraged to show off our Japaneseness. But I do believe they take pride in the Japanese culture."

What Lucas experienced is rather common for Sansei, who encountered race as a minority when "assimilation into whiteness" was the fervent belief.

The weight of dominant cultural hegemony extended beyond the family. "Because of all the mass media, the books you read, the movies and television you watched, your mindset was very much programmed into thinking being white is normal," she continued, "but you always know you are not a part of the mainstream."[1]

Having one foot planted in white America, which she described as a wobbly rock at times, Lucas often wondered where her other foot should or could possibly land. Her life in Minnesota provided her with an answer. While she was in junior high school, her father was discharged from the Army after his last tour to Korea. He took his wife and four children back to his home state of California, where Lucas began to familiarize herself with being an Asian American. However, the Sansei did not fully reconcile with her Japanese side, including her father's legacy, until she had lived in Minnesota for two decades.

She pursued medical education at the University of Minnesota in 1970 and subsequently started her physician's career in the state. The Twin Cities were far from ethnically or culturally diverse back then. Still, she found most white Minnesotans very receptive. "I don't know whether it was the Minnesota nice or because there were very few minorities back in those days," she noted.

Nonetheless, Lucas felt invisible in a sea of whiteness. It took time for the change to come. In the 1990s, she was involved in the "Asian American Renaissance," a gathering of those in Minnesota who identified as Asian, Asian American, and Middle Eastern around literature, arts, and activism. She also joined the Twin Cities chapter of the JACL. There, she did not need to explain herself, where she came from, or how she had learned English so fluently. She had finally found a safe space in which she belonged. Lucas also thought that those who moved to Minnesota usually had parents or family members out of the state, which made the local Asian American communities their home away from home.[2]

Her link to Minnesota also became clearer as she dug deeper into her family history. Adjusting to civilian life was not particularly easy for her veteran father, and Lucas believed racial discrimination might have been a factor. Despite his extensive intelligence experience and military service, Tanaka was unable to find a job in his field, though he was glad to work for the

United States Postal Service. For twenty years, he was the reliable mailman who hauled big loads of letters, magazines, and packages, delivering them by name and not by house number, rain or shine, over the city of Santa Clara.

After his retirement, Lucas began to initiate conversations with her father whenever she visited him in California. Between 1998 and 2002, she made ten recordings. Meanwhile, Tanaka shared his stories in more official interviews with Japanese American organizations such as Densho and the Go for Broke National Education Center. Upon his death in 2012, Lucas reviewed his notes, letters, and photographs. She also retrieved documents from the National Archives about his service in the Army and her grandparents' imprisonment in Poston, Arizona. Together with her niece and siblings, she compiled these materials into a biography of Major Walter Tanaka titled *When a Tiger Dies.*[3]

Lucas was not the first in the family to live in Minnesota. Her father was among the earliest Nisei recruits of the MISLS, where he trained at Camp Savage from June to December 1942. It was a once-in-a-lifetime studying experience, according to Tanaka, that most of the Camp Savage trainees would never forget. These young Nisei men were soon shipped off to remote battlegrounds where they joined the war effort silently and stealthily. "A lot of the MIS veterans gave respect and defer to the 442nd regimental combat team," she said; "my father never bragged about himself."

Lucas believed that her father's story, in which Minnesota played a part, needed to be told. She saw herself taking on a new mission. She was a *denshosha*, a storyteller, the successor of the oral repository, and a guardian of memories. Having learned more about the Japanese American community and its history, she reckoned that the tale of her father, who might seem like just a hardworking mailman or a loving grandfather to many, not only illustrated the achievements of an individual but more significantly also testified to concrete moments in the nation's past.

For Lucas, history transformed from some distant events, abstract policies, or unknown figures in the textbook into something relatable and real. She remarked: "It takes on more meaning for me as I understand what happened to my grandfather, what happened to both of my parents' families, how my father served when they were all incarcerated, and the injustice of it all." Although Tanaka cannot talk about his experiences in person anymore,

Cp Savage, MN
16 Jul 1942

Walter Tanaka at Camp Savage, Minnesota, 1942. *Courtesy of the Tanaka Family*

his voice, images, and thoughts are preserved in interviews and his own writings, as well as his children's recollections. "I feel more responsible and more compelled to share his stories," the Sansei storyteller said, "to honor my father for one, and two, to put his life in the context of our community and the broader American history."

Behind a seemingly ordinary face may hide a surprisingly extraordinary story. That Lucas was able to connect her father to Minnesota, which she has called home for more than half a century, was an amazing revelation. And she is not alone. The donation of the forty-four diaries of Tometaro

Walter Tanaka and friends he referred to as the "rugged bunch," at Camp Savage, 1942. From left to right: Dick Hirata, George Fukuhara, Tanaka, and Kaz Tamura. *Courtesy of the Tanaka Family*

Kitagawa, a Japanese American businessman who moved to Minneapolis in 1919, to the University of Minnesota by his family in 2019 was another auspicious sign for further research. There are bound to be more discoveries like them out there. This glimmer of hope brings us to a Chicago-born marine who served in the war and would go on to be a resident of Edina for more than five decades.[4]

Piecing together the wartime relationship between Robert Edward Borchers and Japanese Americans begins with a puzzle regarding some old papers. After Borchers, a retired engineer, passed away in Roseville, Minnesota, in March 2015 at the age of ninety-three, he left behind a scrapbook containing thirteen handwritten letters and thank-you cards. They were mostly from Japanese Americans imprisoned in the camps and Nisei in the military seventy years ago.[5]

His son Bob Borchers found these personal mementos a few years earlier, after his father had moved to a nursing home. He knew his father had served

in the South Pacific and then in Occupied Japan. Other than that, the former marine seldom talked about his time in the war. Bob Borchers learned
more about his father's experiences only when he was in high school. He
was asked then by his youth group leader in Minneapolis whether he was
related to a "Robert E. Borchers" mentioned in the 1969 book *The Great
Betrayal* by Audrie Girdner and Anne Loftis. To his surprise, he was.

It turned out that his father, then a marine private first class, was court-
martialed for speaking up against the maltreatment of Japanese Americans
during the war. In late 1943, Borchers was recovering at the Naval Hospital
in Camp Pendleton, San Diego, after having contracted malaria while fighting, alongside the Nisei linguists and soldiers, in Guadalcanal. When the
twenty-two-year-old marine learned about the confinement of the Japanese
Americans on the West Coast, he was furious. As little as could he do from
his sickbed, inaction in the face of injustice was not in his nature. Borchers
decided to pen a letter to the California chapter of the American Legion, a
wartime veterans organization spouting vitriol against people of Japanese
descent; he claimed that it was "promoting a racial purge."[6]

His letter was later reprinted in a December issue of *Time* magazine in
1943. In part, Borchers wrote: "I am one of the fortunate marines who have
recently returned to this country after serving in the offensive against the
Japanese on Guadalcanal. We find a condition behind our backs that stuns
us. We find that our American citizens, those of Japanese ancestry, are being
persecuted, yes persecuted, as though Adolf Hitler himself were in charge."
The young man did not mince his words or hide his frustration. "I'm putting it mildly when I say that it makes our blood boil. . . . We will fight this
injustice, intolerance, and un-Americanism at home! We will not break faith
with those who died. . . . We have fought the Japanese and are recuperating
to fight again. We can endure the hell of battle, but we are resolved not to be
sold out at home."[7]

Apparently, his scorching critique did not go unnoticed. A backlash
in the form of court-martial charges swiftly followed. The California State
Assembly Committee on the Japanese Problem, the Gannon Committee,
questioned the patriotism of Borchers and condemned the outspoken marine
for taking such an "inflammatory" action. He was sentenced to six months
of hard labor.[8]

After an appeal, Borchers was reinstated, probably having more to do with the shortage of human power on the front lines than leniency and compassion. He was sent back to the Pacific, with a permanent mark for bad conduct. That was probably one of the reasons why he had not mentioned much about his years in uniform to his children. It might also be a generational code of honor, which many Nisei soldiers similarly observed, tending to keep their pasts to themselves.

His silence did not mean defeat or regret. On the contrary, Borchers never wavered in his beliefs and treasured his wartime memories, albeit quietly. The might of his words in fact had empowered those who most needed to hear them. Borchers received hundreds of letters from Japanese Americans behind barbed wire, expressing their gratitude for his defense of their rights that were under attack. The Nisei were counting on their fellow young citizens like Borchers who neither condescended nor tolerated but simply regarded and respected them as equals. The marine on active duty could not possibly carry all the correspondence in his seabag through trenches and across the ocean. Borchers was able to keep only some of them.[9]

Those he saved stayed with him for more than seven decades. These letters must have held special meaning to him. They "poured forth enormous and unforgettable laughter and tears" in his twilight years, according to his son, when he "read the 1940s messages again and again" to his father. Through online research, Bob Borchers was also able to connect with the descendants of a few Nisei authors of those wartime letters. He later donated the scrapbook to the Manzanar National Historic Site after his father's death.[10]

It is heartening to know, despite the unfortunate turn for Borchers himself at the time, that the American Legion posts of Minnesota did not succumb to war hysteria and betray the notion of democracy. Their 1943 state convention officially protested against their national magazine for fostering "racial discrimination and hatred in violation of the Constitution of the American Legion and of the United States." Instead, the Minnesota chapter distributed copies of its dissent with a short reading list about the Japanese Americans to serve as authoritative information and accurate "answers to distortions of fact, half-truths, and misleading statements" that were being circulated.[11]

Moreover, there were others in the military who wrote open letters that vouched for the Nisei soldiers and denounced the "radical" politicians for their vociferous persecution of the minority. It was easier to correct facts; it was much harder to correct a worldview that consistently dismissed racism and distorted the contributions of Japanese Americans. No matter how modest these attempts might have been then, they did make a difference, and the struggle for justice saw another day.[12]

These testaments to cross-racial solidarity, fighting for a common goal of combating bigotry, enrich our understanding of both the history of Japanese Americans and the scarcely known stories of Minnesotans as well. This is a point that has not been sufficiently stressed. Certainly, those who lent their hands were not limited to leaders in high places. Helpful and kind-hearted individuals can be anyone and come from anywhere. If we are to create a more complete history of Minnesota and the nation, race must be confronted without only apportioning blame, ignoring the contributions of one's fellow Caucasian citizens, or reading these accounts as white savior tales. Despite their privilege, or because of it, they stood by their fellow citizens during the maelstrom of war hysteria. The situations of many Issei and Nisei, along with those of their families, would have been far worse without their support.

The successes of the Nisei college students, combat linguists, cadet nurses, and many others are the result of the collective efforts of a multiracial America. Their stories amplify how the Japanese Americans and their allies fought together to uphold the ideals of the country, the essence of democracy, and the dignity of humanity. What we need is a more thorough and thoughtful excavation of Minnesota history, keeping our chins up and fingers crossed, which may lead to unearthing more missing links between the North Star State and the Japanese Americans' exploits.

—

The history of Minnesota might have long been imagined as a heroic narrative of European settlers, but it was and will always be, writ large, multicolor and multicultural. The actual story of the state entails messier, sadder, and uglier episodes than the sanctioned version. Fort Snelling, the first national historic landmark in Minnesota, is an excellent example. The complicated history of the area known as Bdote by the Dakota, with imprints from the Indigenous peoples, enslaved African Americans, frontier traders, and various immigrant groups, points to a diverse past beyond the fort's naming after a colonel who oversaw its construction, or its roles during the Civil War and Spanish-American War. Since the classified restriction was lifted in the 1970s, the Nisei linguists and the MISLS have also been rightfully woven into the history of Fort Snelling. Unfortunately, many Minnesotans are still oblivious to their existence or significance.[13]

Karen Lucas used to enjoy taking her out-of-town visitors to Savage and tracing the remnants of her father's time in Minnesota. The public library was one of her favorite stops. "Years ago, there were librarians who knew intimately the Asian American history. They had a section about the military intelligence school that was in Savage," she says. Then her trip with a friend in 2022 did not turn out the way she expected. "That section has shrunk to just a few books on half of a bookshelf, and that's all." She was disappointed. "The entire alcove, which used to be one wall with books about the MISLS legacy, and the other wall about the racehorse Dan Patch, is now almost all Dan Patch."

Time has changed taste, obviously. When the Sansei and her friend were taking photographs of the site where the school once stood, a neighbor came out and told them: "There used to be a military camp here; it's a prisoner of war camp for Japanese officers." Lucas was startled. "We should be so much more educated now about the truths of our country's history," she asserts; "and the person lives right there." At least for the time being, in the race for public recognition in Savage, the world champion harness horse is way ahead of the World War II veterans.

It is difficult to ascertain, though not a stretch to assume, that race might be a factor in the inconspicuous cameo of the Nisei soldiers in local memory. For the majority of non-Japanese Minnesotans, their ties to these stories, if any, seem rather indirect and inconsequential. And those tales of physical and psychological trauma surely did not evoke pride but prejudice. "I don't think we should educate people to a level of awareness that makes them feel embarrassed, ashamed, or guilty, because that's not productive," Lucas argues. Nevertheless, she also strongly believes that these stories should never be buried in history. "We cannot have an honest contemporary experience without knowing what happened in the past," she maintains, "and how we got here."

How the wartime Japanese Americans rebuilt their lives in Minnesota was in fact an intriguing story. With the founding of the military language school that brought in Nisei soldiers and their families, together with the inflow of students, nurses, and other workers, Minnesota became a popular destination for Japanese Americans. How well did the "relocation" work for them, and how smooth or tough was resettling in the north for these minority newcomers? To better comprehend what they went through, let's take a closer look at their Minnesotan experiences through two focal points— resettlement and remembrance.

The war epoch was a difficult time for all. Being the new residents, Japanese Americans had to make sure their basic needs were met, and that they could live freely and safely to pursue happiness with dignity like everybody else. For better or for worse, Japanese Americans stood out in Minnesota. Their physical features already made them different from the majority. They were warned by government officials, and by each other, that they had to manage carefully their self-presentations, to detach from the severely stigmatized "Japanese" traits, and to define themselves in exclusively "American" terms. From college students to chicken sexers, they were judged by the highest standards yet needed to keep the lowest profiles. Then, one may ask, what did resettlement in the north actually mean to the Nisei who lived through the horror of the war, and to their children, the Sansei, who were often sheltered from it all?[14]

Many Japanese Americans in Minnesota walked on a tightrope, trying to balance the pressure for assimilation on one hand, and the weight of their heritage on the other. For the wartime Nisei, assimilating to avoid racism might have seemed innocuous, but the consequence was indelible and serious. Sally Sudo, the public educator and civil rights activist, spoke of her coming of age in Minnesota during the 1940s. "All through high school, I was always aware of my own Japaneseness before anything else. Perhaps that's because I was the only person of Japanese ancestry in school." That self-consciousness was not always positive. "I felt, growing up, there must be something wrong with being Japanese, if they're going to put us in prison because of who we are," she said; "I internalized it, and therefore, you try to forget your Japaneseness... [but] how can you stop being Japanese?" Some decided to drop their birth names and deliberately changed them to more Anglo- or Christian-sounding ones. "Keiko would become Kay, or so on," Sudo said. "I think they were trying to put their Japanese heritage behind them. But when your looks give you away, what can you do?"

Bill Hirabayashi, the perpetually optimistic car dealer, also had an interesting story to tell. One of his Nisei classmates, Wales Koseki, was a gifted saxophone player, who even once got onto the *Major Bowes Amateur Hour* on the radio. It was quite an impressive feat, Hirabayashi stated, as the program was the most popular music talent show in the 1930s and 1940s. "Wales could pass as a Latino, a Polish or something like that," Hirabayashi noted, but it was the way he pronounced his surname that caught Hirabayashi off guard. Instead of Ko-se-ki, the musician introduced himself as Kose-ki. When the radio host followed up and asked about his ethnicity, the Nisei replied with "I don't know." Hirabayashi laughed. "And so that was it. No more needed to be said." All the retuning or reinvention eventually came down to the fundamental core of identity. To be or not to be identified as Japanese was the question.

The Japanese American resettlers knew that melting themselves into the pot of the white "mainstream" was the path out of suffering and toward survival. It did not make the process any easier or less excruciating, especially for their third-generation children. The Minnesota-based Sansei poet and author David Mura deconstructed such an imposing of whiteness in his formative era as a baby boomer. Looking at the incarceration that criminalized his parents and ethnicity, he writes of his younger self: "I, like my father, diligently worked to blend in with the white majority, to erase my difference. When one of my white friends said to me, 'I think of you, David, just like a white person,' I felt embraced, like I had achieved something." It would take years for Mura to unmask the conspiracy and hypocrisy of it all—how whiteness exercises supremacy, brushes off brutality against ethnic minorities in the past, and lays the foundation of systemic racism in the present.[15]

Growing up in Minneapolis was a "schizophrenic" experience, according to Stanley Kusunoki, another Sansei poet, teacher, and arts advocate.

The world of the young Kusunoki was full of contradictions and confusions. "My mother and father wanted me to be very Japanese. My dad would say: 'You must find yourself a Japanese girlfriend; you must marry a Japanese woman just like I married your mother,'" he recalled. "But at the same time, they didn't want me to be noticeably Japanese because they were afraid of the racism."

The assimilation project started the moment Kusunoki was born. "My parents even [gave me] the name Stanley, and my brother Ryan, very Anglo names, as if that would serve as a disguise," he noted. "When you look at us, it's not a very big disguise, but [they] wanted to make us as American as possible." Kusunoki used to wonder why he did not have a Japanese name. "I would like to have something that is more meaningful, and that's rooted in my culture," he said. "Japanese names are beautiful, and they have meaning. They represent something or a place, but Stanley, what is that? It's the last name of an English man." Interestingly, the surname and *kanji* character of "Kusunoki" means camphor tree, a kind of evergreen in the cypress family, which symbolizes strength and resilience in traditional Japanese culture.[16]

These attributes were much needed for the Sansei to get through childhood and adolescence. Microaggressions were commonplace in school. Kusunoki considered it part of the resettled life in a mostly white world. "It was nothing close to what my parents went through, but I did experience some racism," Kusunoki said. He had no idea why his classmates chanted "Ching Chong Chinaman," with the slanted eyes gesture, to him on the playground. He was not a Chinese. Even in the 1950s, a decade after the war, people would come up and tell him that "we won the war." The Sansei was better equipped then to deal with racial slurs and slights. "I'm an American, so what are you talking about? Yeah, we won the war," he replied with a victorious smile.

Not only did the postwar Japanese American youngsters have to swim against the current of racism, but they also needed to reach the other shore and pass the finishing line faster than their peers. "The pressure was to get good grades, not just to be an example for all of my relatives, but you also had to be almost more American than the Americans," Kusunoki explained. Exception was the rule. Yet their achievements also fed into the model minority myth, which, upon closer examination, did not signal the success of a fair and free America but quite the contrary: the struggle of an oppressed group that needed to constantly prove their worth in a harsh and hostile world. It was a brutal game of survival. Failure was not an option.

Resettling in Minnesota marked a new beginning for many Japanese Americans, but old memories refused to vanish. Hannah Semba and her family once more offered valuable insights. She has called Minneapolis home ever since she came to attend Macalester College in 1944. The Nisei resettler found that Minnesota lived up to its "nice" reputation, and people were "very helpful." However, she always knew the peace that she enjoyed was precarious. "The war had fractured our whole family," Semba maintained. "That was so humiliating. What have we done to be [treated] like this?"

The emotional toll lasts for years, if not a lifetime. Although Semba has not faced any overtly unpleasant incidents in her nearly eight decades in the state, she also never forgets "the shock of her life." Resettlement can be unsettling. "Being an Asian in a Caucasian world is different," Semba explained. "If there's a tragedy in town, like a murder, I hope that the perpetrator isn't an Asian. Because I believe for myself that I'm responsible for all the other Asian minorities." She believes her African American friends also share a similar sentiment. "White people don't have to look at things like that," she added, "[but] I want to make sure that our behavior reflects a positive note."

A self-disciplined temperament seems to run in the family. "My father wanted to make sure that we were well educated, so that we could stand on our own two feet by ourselves," Semba said. Unfrazzled by the limitations, she concentrated on her studies and was able to escape confinement by the college route. So, too, did her older sister, Mary Harue Hayano, the first St. Olaf College Nisei student. In 1945, Hayano married Noburo "Nob" Koura, who was serving in the Army at Fort Snelling, and soon followed him back to his hometown of Bainbridge Island in Washington. Meanwhile, their parents, Toraji and Tona Hayano, were the last to depart Heart Mountain in 1945 for Minnesota, where they had chosen to permanently reside. Their father was reported to be the state's first tofu maker, producing the Asian-style soybean curd in the basement of their home on Colfax Avenue South and selling groceries on the front porch at the same time.[17]

Semba's own family's story began in 1948, when she met her husband, Thomas T. Semba, a medical student at the University of Minnesota. They were wed in 1951. He became a leading pathologist and university instructor, while she worked as a dietitian in hospitals and as a nursing teacher. Just like her parents, she instilled in her children the same beliefs in hard work, academic excellence, and self-reliance. All four of them, born and raised in Minneapolis, are physicians with impressive careers.

Her older brother, Joseph Torao Hayano, also resettled in the Twin Cities. His path was slightly different though. In 1943, Hayano was allowed to leave camp for employment at a potato farm in Marengo, Illinois. Due to a tractor accident, he lost his right leg. After his recovery, he decided to join his siblings in Minnesota. He enrolled at Dunwoody to train as an auto mechanic while working as a busboy. Soon he was able to open his own service station in Minneapolis, which he later moved to St. Louis Park, where he worked for about four decades until his retirement in 1987. He married Dorothy June Varsnick, a Minnesotan from Chippewa, and started his family in 1968.

Despite all the hardship, his sense of loyalty to the country remained steadfast and strong. "He was never bitter," according to his daughter Mary J. Hayano, but became furious when she bought her first Japanese automobile. "He was so mad at me," the Sansei remembered. "He frowned on Americans buying foreign cars." It is understandable why Hayano displayed patriotism so outwardly. For the Nisei who had seen the dark side of wartime politics, loyalty to the country was a pledge that was not merely kept in their hearts but also worn on their sleeves. The effect seemed to hold out even years after the war had ended.[18]

Transcending exhaustion and dejection to rebuild a normal life after the war was easier said than done. To many Japanese Americans, those two suitcases in their two hands were all that remained. The emotional trauma was a whole different kind of baggage they had to carry. Some preferred relocating to a place where they knew no one over returning to a hometown that had stripped them of everything. This was the case not only of Hayano but also of Lucy Kirihara's family. As a fifteen-year-old high schooler, she came to St. Paul with her Issei parents because her elder sister, Esther Suzuki, was already in town as the first Japanese American student relocated to Macalester College.

"We remember the surrender. But also at the same time, we had to get out of the camp," Kirihara said. "All of a sudden . . . with two weeks' notice, we've got to get out. And we had no place to go." Her family sensed that it was "silly" to return to Portland, recalling the way people had treated them after the war started. "We didn't have any money because our bank accounts were frozen." The decision to follow her sister and resettle in Minnesota seemed logical. "My mother, fortunately, could sew, so she worked as an alterationist and cleaner. My father had to do menial jobs, as a dishwasher at Macalester College and then a gardener."[19]

Graduating from Central High School and then the University of Minnesota, Kirihara became a teacher and lifelong educator on civil rights. She first taught in Mora, a small town about eighty miles north of the Twin Cities, for a year, before she transferred back to St. Paul. She remembered her sister telling her that "half the United States is from a rural area," and it would not hurt if she had such a working experience. It turned out to be a fun adventure.

In 1955, she married Micky Kirihara, and the couple raised their family of three children in the Twin Cities. She was proud that all of them went to college with scholarships and led professional lives. In spite of running into microaggressions and housing discrimination similar to many other Japanese Americans, the Kiriharas thought Minnesota was good to them. "I think what got us through is we were optimistic, and we had a lot of hope," Kirihara said, "and particularly since by [that] time, both of my sisters are in Minnesota." It was a happy reunion. "Once we came to St. Paul. We had to stick together. I would say we got close, again."[20]

Resettlement in the north was not the plan for these Japanese Minnesotans at the beginning, although it might have been written in the stars all along. Both the Kirihara and the Hayano clans would probably have never thought of living in Minnesota if not for the war. Sitting in her residence on Minnehaha Parkway, Semba had no complaints about the North Star State, except maybe the weather. "The winters were terribly cold," she chuckled, "but it's not as cold as it was, way back."

Thanks to Semba, Sudo, Kirihara, Kusunoki, and many other Japanese American storytellers, their experiences have been passed on and preserved. Making them a part of Minnesotan history is important, though not without obstacles. The greatest adversary is time itself. Toshio Tsukahira, one of the original MISLS instructors, who recounted his mingling with the socialites of the Twin Cities earlier, stated: "I hope that there will be some value to what I said about my experience, and that it might influence or inspire somebody to do something that will benefit himself, herself or the [Japanese American] group." Every story counts. Nothing is too meager or meaningless. "It may be just a spot in the American history," he continued. "But I think it's been an honorable one, and the achievements that the pioneers, our parents, did, are still under-recognized, and they should never be forgotten."[21]

—

Attempts to remember and the act of remembering are as much about the present and the future as the past. What a nation and a people deem significant enough to commemorate and to write into history reveals the politics, priorities, and problems at hand. Societies recall or forget bygone times based on their current needs, and each generation redefines its legacy accordingly. Collective memory, hence, is an active and ongoing process, continually shaped and reshaped by governments, communities, and individuals. As a result, remembrance is both monolithic—manifested in national holidays and monuments—and multifaceted—unfolding through personal tributes and thoughts. To disentangle the intertwined strands of wartime Japanese American experiences in Minnesota is an exciting yet extensive task, and the endeavor here is only a beginning.[22]

Before traveling further down memory lane locally with Minnesotan Nisei, we should first start with how the subject of "remembrance" has emerged and evolved nationally. The "Day of Remembrance" first debuted on November 25, 1978, and was conceived by the Seattle Evacuation Redress Committee (SERC) together with other activists, like the Chinese American playwright Frank Chin. It was meant to be a gathering to discuss and even dwell on the injustices that many Japanese Americans might want to bury deep inside so they did not become their children's burden. The event took place mainly at the Puyallup Fairgrounds, which had served in 1942 as a temporary detention center for the forced removal and was disingenuously named "Camp Harmony." The Day of Remembrance has since been observed annually by members of the community all over the country.[23]

More than forty years after the first Day of Remembrance, President Joseph R. Biden issued a presidential proclamation declaring February 19, 2022, as the "Day of Remembrance of Japanese American Incarceration during World War II." He asked "the people of the United States to commemorate this injustice against civil liberties and civil rights during World War II; to honor the sacrifice of those who defended the democratic ideals of this nation; and to commit together to eradicate systemic racism to heal generational trauma in our communities." How the view of the historic day when President Roosevelt signed the Executive Order 9066 and its horrific aftermath has seemingly changed in the twenty-first century.[24]

Those eight decades in between witnessed an evolution of the Japanese American saga in the social memory of the nation. During and even years after the war, the majority of the Issei and Nisei rarely spoke about, needless to say protested against, their expulsion and imprisonment, maybe out of anger, dismay, or shame. The few who resisted like Gordon Hirabayashi were outliers and considered lawbreakers in the eyes of the legal system then. Owing to the civil rights movements of the 1960s and 1970s, the public has become more aware of its problematic record of social injustices. Asian American studies as a field of intellectual inquiry also began to appear in universities at that time. The demand for histories of people of color in the United States told from their own perspectives gained conspicuous support as a result.

The increasingly open atmosphere and progressive attitude allowed Japanese American activists to link the wartime incarceration to contemporary racist and colonial policies. In the next decade, their quest for redress in court and Congress eventually culminated in the passage of the Civil Liberties Act of 1988, signed by President Ronald Reagan, which provided a national apology and individual reparations to surviving detainees. Bill Doi, the MISLS veteran and Minnesota resident, was among those enthusiastically involved in the redress movement.[25]

Recognition of the abuses they endured from their government is a major stride for those Japanese Americans who had been affected by the war. "It was the period when the Nisei didn't have any voice," Micky Kirihara noted. "We were too young," his wife Lucy added. As time goes by and the taboo lifts, the Nisei have become more comfortable in articulating their struggles and sharing their experiences. These quiet Americans are still stoic but no longer silent. Age probably has something to do with their willingness to speak. Most have turned into seniors who realize mortality lurks not too far around the corner. Both individuals and collectives define themselves through history. The extant narrative about wartime Japanese Americans was incomplete, and many depictions were biased. They know what is not said will never be saved, and it is just a matter of time before their memories fade away.

The most concerted effort thus far to document the histories of Japanese Americans during World War II is the nonprofit organization "Densho," named after a Japanese word meaning "to pass stories to the next genera-tion." Established in 1996 by a group of Seattle volunteers, Densho uses dig-ital technology and archival practices to collect, record, and display primary sources related to the Japanese American experience in the past century. It now contains roughly two thousand hours of transcribed video interviews and eighty thousand historic photographs and materials, which this book has relied on and utilized.[26]

One of the Densho founders is Tom Ikeda. His father, Victor Ikeda, was a Nisei veteran who attended Dunwoody briefly before joining the MISLS in Minnesota. Formerly a manager at Microsoft Corporation, the third-generation Ikeda served as the executive director of the organization for more than two decades, before stepping down in 2022. "The stories Densho has collected for the past twenty years put faces, names, and emotional responses to a part of our history that many Americans would just as soon forget," he explained; it is imperative that "we remember the mistakes of the past and promote equity and justice over racism and bigotry today and in the future."[27]

Remembrance, however, is not universally embraced. As noble the cause and novel the approach of Densho, Victor Ikeda initially discouraged his son "from excavating history, saying he was going to turn up unpleasant things, rip scabs off old wounds, and rekindle friction." It took him a decade to sit for his first interview in 2007, and longer for a second one in 2022. Indeed, not until 2022 did the Sansei successfully convince his mother, Mary Kinoshita Ikeda, to talk about her Minidoka experience, including the death of her brother Francis "Bako" Kinoshita, a fallen solider from the 442nd

Regimental Combat Team. The apprehension of Ikeda's mother is not unique, echoing the story of the cadet nurse Ida Kawaguchi in the earlier chapter. Time might be the healer of all wounds, but as Ikeda and Kawaguchi show, it works not through forgetting the pain but facing the past.[28]

The past is a foreign country though. To those Japanese Americans who restarted anew in Minnesota, revisiting their old lives can be a long and difficult journey. Helen Tanigawa Tsuchiya of St. Louis Park, a former incarceree at Gila River, kept her wartime memories to herself and did not share them with the public for more than six decades. Born in Selma and raised in Parlier, California, she came to the Twin Cities in 1946 because her two uncles were serving at Fort Snelling. Tsuchiya found employment as a medical secretary, a job that she held for fifty-five years until retirement.[29]

Coming to terms with the past takes time. Tsuchiya only began to open up about her past when a golf friend, a schoolteacher, encouraged the Nisei to talk about it with her Eden Prairie fourth graders and record her story on tape. Tsuchiya, over eighty years old then, agreed; if it was not for others, she thought, it would still be good for her grandchildren to know.

The reception was overwhelmingly positive. Despite the hardship that Tsuchiya's family had suffered, there was no bitterness in her recounting of her misfortune. "I am a Buddhist. Buddhism teaches you to be compassionate and kind to people," she noted in a children's program. Her motto was the subject of a song, "Be Kind to All That Live," by Minneapolis folk singer Larry Long, and a short documentary film that celebrated her life. "Minnesota saved me," she wrote in her autobiography; "now I want to share my story with children so it will never happen again."[30]

Remembrance prompts sympathy and solidarity. The possibility that what took place during World War II might occur again, perhaps to another minority group, seems to weigh heavily on the minds of many Minnesotan Nisei. "The older I get, the sadder I get, thinking about how did all that ever happen?" Lucy Kirihara shared. "People have to know. I'd do anything just to spread the word, not to antagonize people, but it is history." Bill Doi, likewise, expressed a poignant yet pointed sentiment. "That was so, so wrong.... How this country . . . can think that it's okay to put not one or two or ten, but hundreds and thousands of people, taking their citizenship rights away, and put them in jail. [It] just doesn't seem like that could happen. But it did."[31]

Sally Sudo believes organizations like JACL play a particularly instrumental role in remembrance and thus action. Over the years, she has found the people in Minnesota generally know very little about the incarceration or even the MISLS at Camp Savage and Fort Snelling. Through the education committee of the Twin Cities JACL, Sudo and other volunteers put together teacher trainings, speaker bureaus, workshops, exhibitions, and scholarships, among other activities, to promote awareness of not only wartime Japanese American experiences but also civil rights and social justice issues.

Some immediately likened the ordeal of Muslim Americans after the terrorists struck on September 11, 2001, to that of the Japanese Americans following the attack on Pearl Harbor on December 7, 1941. Sudo was in New York City on that fateful day. "To wake up that morning, hear all the sirens, and see what's going on in the city, I was just stunned," she recalled. "I bet that's exactly what the atmosphere was like after Pearl Harbor." The first thing that dawned on her was "how super patriotic everybody became." People from all walks of life banded together and helped each other. She also could not pass through the street without seeing someone selling something red, white, and blue—a scarf, a pin, or a T-shirt.

Then fear seeped out and permeated the air. "I heard the FBI was going into some of these neighborhoods where there were large Muslim populations, and going door to door," she noted. It reminded her of what took place when she was a child. "Things are happening that happened to us. It's all starting again." She thought of what a professor once told her. "In times of war, the Bill of Rights is the first thing that goes out of the window. That's something you always have to guard against."

Accordingly, remembrance is a responsibility. War hysteria has morphed into fear tactics in racial politics these days as well. Sudo was disturbed by the government's policies toward migrants and refugees at the southern border. That many of them are children and families that are separated brings back her own grievous memories. "There are so many things that can go wrong when people are afraid," she maintained. "When people live in fear, they don't act rationally as they should."[32]

Stanley Kusunoki also noticed how his mother would become very upset whenever there was apparent discrimination in the news. Although she never explicitly talked about it, he could see her "trembles and shakes with each new story of an alleged Afghani, Arab, or Muslim detained under this suspicion or that," or "every time fingers point" to immigrants from the Somali, Southeast Asian, or Latin American diasporas for any potential misdeeds.[33]

Now is not 1942. But the similarities are hard to ignore. Tom Ikeda likes to cite a saying attributed to Mark Twain: "history may not always repeat itself, but it often rhymes." Justice need not be poetic either. This is one of the main messages of those who salvage these Japanese American stories. One must listen carefully to the metrical pattern of history and avoid the malicious echoes of the past.[34]

Remembrance, therefore, is also about reckoning. There is no higher cause than honoring the struggles and successes of those who came before by remembering them. The wartime Japanese American stories are a reminder that the fight against racism is far from complete. Keeping the Issei and Nisei memories alive, or even basic education about race and racism available, is fraught with obstacles, especially in a politically charged environment. The United States in the first two decades of the twenty-first century was driven as much by division as by marching in unison. At a time when some states are trying to wipe the histories of minority groups from textbooks, libraries, and educational curricula, diversity initiatives are increasingly under threat of erosion if not erasure.

Banning a book about the eviction and imprisonment of Japanese Americans in school is no longer a fictional scenario but a fact. The danger is clearer and closer to home than Karen Lucas expected. She was vexed by what happened in the Wisconsin Muskego-Norway School District, next to where her granddaughter and her family reside. In 2022, the school board committee decided to remove the acclaimed novel *When the Emperor Was Divine* by Julie Otsuka, which is about the incarceration experience, from its tenth-grade accelerated English class program, although there was no complaint filed by teachers, parents, or students. "The committee said because the book is too one-sided," Lucas noted in disbelief. "The whole history has been told one-sided."[35]

The argument that the novel lacks a "balanced" perspective is "deeply problematic," David Inoue, the JACL executive director, emphasized in his response. "No opposing view is not inherently racist and insensitive." Nevertheless, that fallacy has become a reality with which anyone who wishes to teach or learn about the past, in both its glory and grittiness, has to contend. Progress is seldom linear, speedy, or permanent. Nothing is guaranteed or can be taken for granted. The chords of harmony might easily fall into a cacophony of dissonance. Minnesota, fortunately, has been touched by the better angels of our nature and sung the chorus of empathy and inclusion thus far.[36]

In the end, remembrance is about the future. Determining what and how to remember is a serious bid to mold the imagination of the generations to come. Those who control the present control the past, and those who control the past control the future. It is not quite an Orwellian world today, but the ability to critically, openly, and truthfully examine the history of the nation remains a major challenge. Remembering the plight of the Issei and Nisei during the war, as all the storytellers point out, is certainly vital.

What seems slightly uncertain is its place in the future for Japanese Americans in Minnesota. Do the wartime trials, trauma, and tribulations of their forebears still hold special meaning for the progeny, who, as many indicated, have fully assimilated and are further removed from it all? What does "remembering" these stories mean to the Yonsei, and beyond?

Recounting the stories of Issei and Nisei in wartime Minnesota is not just a multiracial affair but also a multigenerational one. Important foundational work on Japanese American history in the last century has been accomplished by scholars across different ethnic lines. The next torchbearers will be even more diverse. The meaning of "Japanese American" has undergone substantial transformation in the past several decades. Jim Kirihara, the Dunwoody alumnus turned Minneapolis accountant, noted: "My three kids were intermarried. And all six grandkids of mine were biracial. That's a big change, because it was a custom for us to marry our own Japanese preferably. But this didn't happen." Karen Lucas concurred. "It's unusual to have a Yonsei or Gosei [fifth generation] not being mixed race. I think that's great," she said. "It should be the future of the world, the future of this country."[37]

The newer generations might have made the issue simpler. America was never monoethnic and always multicultural. "In a way, it is a physical manifestation of who we internally are anyway," Lucas added; "Japanese American is a hybrid culture." Though, what does hybridity look like for the Yonsei or Gosei in a predominately white Minnesota? Would their "Japaneseness," however it is defined, along with the wartime stories of their grandparents and great-grandparents, be lost in "Americanization"?

The fact that Japanese Minnesotans have increasingly trended toward interracial marriage is not an accident. One of the War Relocation Authority's main goals for imprisonment and resettlement was the reconstitution and redistribution of Japanese American communities. The predicament of race, hence, was meant to be sorted out through space. It was reported that President Roosevelt, in addition to favoring the spread of the Japanese American incarcerees around the country, even warmed up to the idea of mass intermarriage between Japanese Americans and other ethnic populaces to create a mixed "neo" race group like those in Hawai'i. This social reengineering concept was not taken seriously by any means or measure. However, it was an inevitable byproduct of geographically scattering Japanese Americans to Minnesota because of the war.[38]

For the Minnesotan Yonsei, recognizing their multicultural heritage becomes a function of self-assurance more than a form of sentimentality. "Being half Japanese, my grandmother was a big influence on my identity," T. J. Hara said of Kimi Hara, the beloved nursing instructor and community advocate. He never thought about race much when he was younger, yet he always knew that he was someone "non-descript but clearly not white." Growing up in the Twin Cities, his sister Liz Hara also recalled feeling the otherness among her classmates and friends. "I counted in my yearbook, and there were more people with the last name Anderson in my high school graduating class than there were Asians," she said; "there were definitely not a lot of *hapa* [person of mixed-race heritage] kids; we were just a fairly new phenomenon."[39]

Both siblings identify strongly with Japanese culture, and that is not necessarily by choice. "That was partly put on us," she explained. "Numerically we are fifty percent Japanese, but because people see that we are not white, it became more than fifty percent." At the same time, being close to their grandparents has made it easier for them to get in touch with their Japanese heritage. In addition to learning the language during high school,

T. J. Hara has studied Japanese sword arts for twenty years. "My grand-mother passed away in 2007, which was the last year that the Normandale Japanese Garden held the sukiyaki dinner. She got to see me perform in the festival, so that was a really nice homage," he noted. "Under her influence I got involved in the garden committee. It was the thing that I latched onto as a way to carry on her legacy."

This unique sense of ethnic connection and family history became the core building block of the Yonsei's own identity in a mainly white state. It is one of the motivations behind Liz Hara's professional efforts to raise and amplify the voices of minority groups in mass media. The award-winning writer for *Sesame Street* and the Disney Channel, now living in Los Angeles, focused on "diversity and representation" in her shows. "A large part of that is my way of carrying on grandma's legacy, because of our family's involvement in the JACL. That organization is always very important for me," she said. "There is no other real connection in the rest of life with my heritage and culture, so having the JACL and all grandma's friends is very meaningful and a reformation to my cultural identity." She also never forgot how her grandmother taught her to cook. "I got a mochi making machine from her, and I make my own fresh mochi, although they are not very good," she laughed. And she proudly keeps her grandfather's 442nd commemorative ring as a constant reminder and a lucky charm. She is a fighter, too.

Other fourth-generation Japanese Minnesotans also see the grace of their grandparents as a gravitational force in their lives. In 2011, Emily Tani-Winegarden, an eleventh grader from Eden Prairie High School, read a poem by her grandmother Yoshiko "Yoshi" Uchiyama Tani, a Seattle native who was confined in Minidoka, in the Day of Remembrance program orga-nized by the Twin Cities JACL. Tani-Winegarden is the youngest of Tani's grandchildren. The strength of her grandmother has always been her guid-ing light. "I spend so much time growing up with her, and it never feels like there is a disconnect between us," she said.[40]

Even so, connecting to her grandmother's past in the war as a young woman who was not much older than the Minnesotan teenager then, is both humbling and harrowing. After Tani graduated from Garfield High School in Seattle in 1939, her academic career at the University of Washington was interrupted by the war. "I think about what it would have been like to be incarcerated and in their situation a lot," her granddaughter stated. "I can't imagine having to leave my whole life behind without any questions."[41]

The story of the Tanis is a familiar yet no less frightful one of perseverance and resilience. The most adored family lore is the grandparents' romance. "My grandfather proposed to my grandmother in the camp," Tani-Winegarden mentioned with a smile. "He said the reason to do it was because there was nothing better to do. He just chose the most beautiful girl there." While it is a joke, the Tanis' wartime experience is a good example of the Nisei release from the camps for resettlement, namely through college, military service, and employment.

In the desolate Minidoka, Tani met her future husband, George Tadashi Tani from Oakland, California. By that time George had enrolled in the Army and was assigned to train at the MISLS. "He was sent to Minnesota because he could speak Japanese," Tani said. The two were married at the Fort Snelling Chapel in the spring of 1945. Their own parents in the camps could not attend the wedding, but Spark Matsunaga, the 442nd veteran and later senator of Hawai'i, was a guest. While the newlywed solider served in the Philippines and then Occupied Japan, his bride remained in St. Paul working at Dairy Products Laboratory. The Nisei couple would later call the Twin Cities home once and for all.

The Tanis, alongside George's mother, Moto Tani, raised a family of three children and seven grandchildren. George Tani was discharged in the fall of 1946 and went to the University of Minnesota Medical School, specializing in ophthalmology. Upon the completion of his residency at the Mayo Clinic in 1955, he opened a private practice and taught at the university for three decades before his retirement. The Tanis are a merry and multiracial family. "We all live in Minnesota," the matriarch noted. "Along with their Japanese background, our grandchildren can claim English, Irish, Danish, Swedish, Norwegian, Russian, and German ethnic heritage."[42]

Although Yoshi Tani has always been active in the local church and community, including the JACL, she was initially reserved about sharing her wartime experiences with her family. Kay Tani, the Sansei daughter and Emily Tani-Winegarden's mother, discovered her parents' story only when she was a first-year student in college. "I asked why she never told me," Kay

Yoshi Tani, 2015.
Courtesy of the author

Tani said, "and she replied something like 'well, it was in the past. Never found the need to.' So, it was a surprise."

Attending St. Olaf at that time, "which was very Lutheran Scandinavian," Kay Tani ran into "an identity crisis" as a Japanese American in Minnesota. "Learning about the camp and how they met, I wanted to delve into that a little more. That's when I took Japanese language and went to Japan for half a semester, to embrace my ancestry more and find my identity," Tani explained. "I am very proud of my parents' generation and the transition that they made."

Like her mother, Tani-Winegarden has learned to wear her unique background as a badge of honor. Growing up in Eden Prairie, she had a "pretty much white experience" during her earlier years. "The biggest thing for me is that people rather than asking what my name is, the first question they usually ask is what are you." Her response of being "half Japanese and half Norwegian German" often leads to more inquiries, such as "do you use chopsticks and eat rice, or do you speak Japanese? That's a bunch of assumptions that aren't necessarily true." Of course, she has never met anyone who probed her linguistic or cultural knowledge of Germany and Norway.

"It might not be malicious at all, but it does make you feel different," Tani-Winegarden said. She does not let these little irritants bother her, as she firmly identifies with her Japanese ancestry and her family history. After graduating from St. Olaf College, she is now a professional artist, injecting her grandparents' memories into her work. "They were dealt a horrible hand but managed to make a wondrous life together," she asserted. "They always taught me to make the most out of every situation and that is why I choose to make beautiful pottery for people to enjoy every day."[43]

Family matters. Through changing time, space, and culture, stories passing from one generation to the next, with affection and dedication, are the glue that binds the now multiracial Japanese Americans together. Still, one cannot help but wonder what remembrance might kindle in those Yonsei whose grandparents departed long before their arrival. There is no opportunity for them to spend time with their wise and loving elders. There are no tender moments of listening to and sharing their wartime encounters, engagement tidbits, or mochi recipes. Does that hereditary lineage remain meaningful? Or has their ethnic identity been reduced to simply a label?

These questions lead us back to where we started. Our journey to better understand the Japanese Americans in Minnesota during and after the war began with Yosh Murakami. It is hence appropriate to end with him as well. Sadly, he died young quite suddenly. In 1975, he passed away at the age of only forty-eight due to undiagnosed Addison's disease, before any of his grandchildren were born. What does he mean to the Yonsei generation? What can his legacy tell us about resettlement and remembrance?

⁓

Molly Murakami is a visual storyteller and illustrator from Minneapolis. She has created a four-chapter autobiographical graphic novel, *In Your Path*, that fulfilled not only the requirement for a graduate degree but also something of a more personal quest. The "your" in the title refers to her grandfather Yosh Murakami, the legendary character in her life whom she can forever wish to meet but will never have the chance. "What color were your eyes," Murakami ponders, "black like mine—the kind of brown that only glows gold in the sun?"[44]

However, what the Yonsei wants to find out is what those eyes have seen. Reckoning with family history through one's artistic expression is not unusual, and even considered natural for some, but writing about a figure who has long been deceased was more challenging than Murakami expected. Without being able to hear it firsthand from her grandfather, she relied on archival resources, old photo albums, lengthy conversations with her father, and her own imagination and self-reflection.

Her grandfather's past eventually intersected with her present. It was not planned but she finally decided to attend his alma mater. "Molly Murakami ... has followed her grandfather Yosh's path and is now a second-year studio art major at St. Olaf," a Northfield magazine remarked in 2012. Nonetheless, she had no clear idea what to make of or how to decipher this connection. "How do I follow a path so obscured by time and legend that I can't make out which footprints are yours?" she asks the faint fatherly image in her head.[45]

As Murakami learned more about her grandfather's stories, the blurry silhouette of the Nisei student who once walked through the same campus some sixty years ago slowly sharpened. The California-born Yosh was incarcerated at Manzanar, which, ironically, was listed as his hometown in his college application. He found his way out of the camp through college, joined the war effort in Army uniform, resettled in Minnesota after military service, and became a widely respected music educator in the state following the war.

Beyond his accomplishments as a teacher and choral director, the Nisei was known for filling a valuable niche in Northfield as racial tension intensified in the decade leading to the civil rights movement. Any racial minority was then a rarity in the rural town. His high school colleague believed Murakami had an open mind and did not take "ethnic jokes as an attack on his personality." Yet Murakami never shied away from race, and many saw him as a role model at a time when African Americans were confronting bigotry nationwide. "He was well accepted, and he could draw people together," a journalist reported. "To frustrated Black [Americans] he would tell about the persecution he had experienced on the West coast, yet emphasize his love of his country."[46]

Race was a tense and thorny issue then, and it continues to torture the nation to this day. Being half Japanese and half Northern European, Molly Murakami was among the very few with an Asian surname in the largely white suburbs of Bloomington and Edina. Yet she did not pay much attention to ethnic identity until she went to St. Olaf. "The grandpa" who was "laughing in his silver frame, frozen in time on the living room table," then somehow found a way to resonate with her, as she was figuring out what she could carry for him in their joint "family karma." Her senior capstone project, told from the point of view of a young woman of "mixed" heritage, was her observations on race, racism, and history through personal experiences. Upon graduation, Murakami decided to be an artist and enrolled at the Minneapolis College of Art and Design to pursue a master of fine arts degree as she tried to find her way in the Twin Cities.[47]

Her gradual evolution soon crashed into an abrupt disruption, however. The world literally changed in front of Murakami in the spring of 2020. She then had to complete her thesis, which was stressful enough for any aspirant under regular circumstances. Minnesota was anything but normal at that time. From the pandemic lockdown to the murder of George Floyd, which happened just steps away from her apartment, the Twin Cities were shaken and shocked to the core. The graphic novelist, too, was overwhelmed with anxiety, uncertainty, and misery.

Against the backdrop of lethal viruses and social injustices, Murakami once again turned to the wartime stories of her grandfather and other Japanese Americans, which helped her to fathom the indirect parallels of their sorrowful past to her own surreal present. The Yonsei was not comparing her strange reality to life in wartime incarceration. Instead, she saw positivity and possibility in how the older generations took on the direst adversity with bravery and not bitterness. "Even in the camps, people were still making art," she maintained. Creative opportunity did rise out of hindrance and hostility. It was also the catharsis she needed. Pulling herself out of mental limbo, she rolled up her sleeves and finished her thesis, a book that chronicled her putting Yosh Murakami's "life against the context of intergenerational trauma."[48]

While her grandfather is her inspiration, remembrance is her mission. The book about their spiritual interaction is only a beginning. "His story lives in me," Murakami writes. "Sharing my own experience living as a marginalized voice can be useful for someone else who is struggling with the same thoughts and inner monologue I struggle with still." Her work has drawn interest from Densho, which selected the Minnesotan cartoonist as one of the two "Artists in Residence" in 2021. She was commissioned to create artwork about Japanese American history in World War II. The result was *Tide Goes Out*, which debuted in March 2022.[49]

Considered a "companion piece to *In Your Path*," the graphic novel is partly fictional, partly biographical, recounting the lives of her great-grandparents—their early years on the Californian shores of Terminal Island, their forced removal and detention in Manzanar, and their eventual return to the Long Beach area they once called home. Preparation of the book allowed the Minnesotan Yonsei to further research her family tales and more closely bond with her relatives on the West Coast. "There's something incredibly poignant and beautiful about standing where your ancestors once stood. I felt it on the campus of St. Olaf," she asserts. "I felt it again, there on Terminal Island."[50]

Remembrance is both personal and political. "So much American history—not only Japanese American history—has been intentionally lost, razed to the ground and rarely addressed again," Murakami laments. "As I've grown—and learned who I am and where I come from—it's become increasingly important for me to be vocal about injustice, joining thousands of Japanese Americans, survivors of the camps and my fellow [Japanese American] descendants, in their calls for justice," the artist emphasizes in her book. "Omission of our Black, brown, Indigenous, queer, and disabled histories is an incredible disservice to the American people. If our leadership won't remember, then we must."[51]

Untold Histories and Unsung Heroes

Reflecting on Japanese American Stories in Wartime Minnesota

Homeless, we were once,
Forced out from our West Coast homes—
Americans, all,
But there were those who proclaimed,
We looked like the enemy.

Barbed-wire fences—
On the outside, stood armed guards—
Prisoners, were we—
Yet, we managed to survive,
Unbroken, like the bamboo.

Justice did prevail—
World War II is history,
Freedom lost, regained,
Minnesota, "Home sweet home"—
We have a story to tell.
—YOSHI UCHIYAMA TANI, "A Story to Tell"

This was the poem that Emily Tani-Winegarden read on the Day of Remembrance held in Bloomington, Minnesota, back in 2011. Her Nisei grandmother passed away eleven years later in 2022, at the age of 101. Over her century of life, Tani saw war and peace, confinement and diaspora, destruction and renewal. For nearly eight decades, she called Minnesota "home sweet home." The stories that Tani, along with many others like her, wanted to tell are what this book set out to preserve and present.

Minnesota also has a story to tell. Although the North Star State does not naturally or instantly come to mind when one talks about Japanese Americans and World War II, it played a more prominent role in this historical episode than most would expect. One reason is that colleges, universities, nursing programs, and trade schools welcomed Nisei students; another is the Military Intelligence Service Language School. Similarly, other institutions and businesses also brought Issei and Nisei from incarceration camps to the American heartland. The road to regain freedom and to rebuild a family was arduous. Although relocation to Minnesota might have been for convenience or by coincidence, and not by desire or design at first, many chose to become Minnesotans in the end.

From far away had these Japanese Americans come, but farther still is the happy ending for all. "I am living my life in a diverse urban setting with a sense of being a part of a broader ethnic community," Tani writes in her autobiography. "Winters may seem long and harsh at times, but there is a sense of satisfaction and thanksgiving when we manage to cope with adverse conditions, embraced by the warmth of our family and friends." From strangers at the gate to neighbors next door, the presence of the newcomers often requires a critical introspection of one's own preconceptions and prejudices. The reflection may prove them not as impeccable as expected.[1]

Tani was pleased that "the injustice arising from racism that the Japanese Americans endured during World War II has been addressed"; however, she worried about the incessant "racism and hate crimes," when politicians calculatingly argue that exalting the nation's "multicultural heritage of racial and ethnic pride" comes "at the expense of social cohesion." The Nisei shared her concerns in 1991, several years before her granddaughter Emily was born. "My hope is that there will be a continuing dialogue promoting the understanding of . . . racism and cultural diversity in America," she concludes; "[so] we all can more effectively strive together in creating a sense of community in a sharing and caring way." Decades have passed. Society has taken a few steps forward over the years, but a couple steps back as well. Her hope for the future remains in progress.[2]

Perhaps the predicament lies in two common misunderstandings. First, there is a perception that stories about minority groups are about them alone. They are unrelated to others, notably the mainstream populace, beyond the ethnic community involved. Second and more detrimentally, most assume when white characters appear in these narratives, they are unquestionably portrayed as the villains. Henceforth, these ethnic stories are perceived to be insignificant or irrelevant to begin with, and even worse, they make white people look bad or feel guilty. Such conventional yet unfounded beliefs uphold the "racial myths," what David Mura called "the stories whiteness tells itself." American history has long promoted only a pristine and perfect image of the nation. Stories that concern white brutality are repeatedly toned down, ignored, or erased. After all, the wrongdoings are probably the fault of specific rogue actors who might just happen to be white, and not an alarm for something deeper and more serious.

Accordingly, the country has never confronted its racist past wholeheartedly. Racism, left unchecked, is often interpreted as the natural, inevitable order of things, as it has been entrenched in the nation's systems, structures, and sensibilities. Seeing no evil, hearing no evil, and speaking no evil leads to the conclusion that there actually is no evil, or at most "necessary evil." Lessons not learned only invite mistakes to return, however. The racist ideas that caused the Japanese American incarceration "are now mirrored by present-day anti-immigrant sentiment, xenophobia, and religious bigotry," Mura observes. Such an analogue is likely neither the last nor the only one. But what can we do?[3]

Wishing upon a star is not going to solve the problem, but writing history that is honest, open, and inclusive of the viewpoints of people from minority groups can grant a promising start. From President Roosevelt to Governor then Chief Supreme Court Justice Earl Warren, one can argue that some of their decisions regarding the Japanese American incarceration were very flawed and caused immeasurable suffering for many. Their failings did not make them any less admirable in history but rather more human, and even heroic if their legacy owned up to its faults.

Moreover, to highlight the enmity instead of the empathy in the wartime stories also misses an important point. Combating the racism that the Issei and Nisei faced in the torrent of war hysteria was a collaborative effort by not only the Japanese Americans themselves but also their supporters— educators, religious leaders, politicians, military personnel, nonprofit volunteers, and numerous individuals. Their courage to go against the tide was laudable, and their help crucial. One need not fall into the trap of the white-knight complex to give credit where it is due. Regardless of racial, political, and cultural positionality, embracing the spirit of humanity, with all its splendors and shortcomings, is at the heart of the Japanese American wartime stories, and what is most needed to navigate and to repair the increasingly stratified social world.

Remembering Japanese Americans in Minnesota during World War II is an ongoing endeavor. There are now more available materials—both academic and popular works—about the wartime removal, imprisonment, and reparation afterward. Still, their lives in Minnesota, together with those who stood by them, are seldom talked about or known. The extraordinary experiences of the Japanese Americans and their allies, with more untold stories and unsung heroes on the horizon, offer an exciting perspective to revisit Minnesota's history. At a time of local and national wrestling with race, civil rights, and social justice, it is hard to see where the arc of the moral universe will bend. If what is past is prologue, let's hope for a better fate for these Japanese Minnesotan stories, that their future will never be only a footnote.

Acknowledgments

Stories have the profound ability to shape our world and are meant to be shared—passed from one person to another, from one generation to the next, and from one community to many. It is often said that it takes a village, and in this case it has taken the time and efforts of numerous individuals to bring this book to life. I extend my deepest gratitude to all the storytellers and their families who kindly shared their experiences, photographs, and personal collections with this project. Without their graciousness and generosity, this book would not have been possible. I owe special thanks to Sally Sudo, whose guidance from the outset was invaluable.

My sincere appreciation also goes to Hikari Sugisaki and Paul Sullivan, who embarked on this journey with me. Their dedication resulted in the documentary film *Beyond the Barbed Wire*, which laid the groundwork for this book. Additionally, Hikari devoted significant time helping me during the research process, and their exceptional diligence has been nothing short of remarkable. Many former students contributed in various capacities, too. I am particularly grateful to Courtney Nomiyama and Adam Weiss. Jake Caswell, Kaylar Fullington, Daniel Gaenslen, Paoge Moua, Meena Wainwright, and Jiahao Zhang deserve mention as well.

I would also like to thank the archivists and librarians whose expertise was instrumental: Angel Diaz (University of California, Santa Barbara), Candice Hart (Hamline University), Ellen Holt-Werle (Macalester College/University of Minnesota), Tom Lamb (Carleton College), Susan McElrath (University of California, Berkeley), Jeff Sauve (St. Olaf College), Jennifer

Shaw-Spence (Dunwoody College of Technology), Adam Smith (Minnesota State University, Mankato), and Virginia Wentzel (St. Mary's School of Nursing), among many others.

The support of St. Olaf College, of course, has been essential throughout this project. The Collaborative Undergraduate Research and Inquiry (CURI) program, Institute for Freedom and Community (IFC), Government, Foundation, and Corporate Relations (GFCR), Research and Instructional Technology/Digital Scholarship Center at St. Olaf (DiSCO), Rølvaag Library, and St. Olaf Archives provided crucial resources and expertise. I would like to especially acknowledge Melissa Flynn Hager for her tireless efforts in securing external grants prior to her retirement, as well as Bob Entenmann and Barbara Reed for their thoughtful reviews of the manuscript's early drafts. I am also grateful to colleagues Greta Anderson, Valeng Cha, Ed Santurri, Marci Sorter, and Helen Warren.

Moreover, I am indebted to the Minnesota Historical Society (MNHS), Stanford University East Asia Library, and Associated Colleges of the Midwest (ACM), which provided funding for different stages of my research and writing.

This book greatly benefited from the insights and contributions of many individuals. I am thankful to Shannon Pennefeather and Ann Regan at the MNHS Press for their advice along with the anonymous reviewer for their comments. Furthermore, I appreciated the help of Kathy Hara, Randy Kusunoki, Yuichiro Onishi, Brad Shirakawa, Bob Taenaka, Ellen Takayama, and Chelsey Tanaka. As always, any errors or oversights in the final work are solely my own responsibility.

Sadly, many of the storytellers who honored us with their wisdom and experiences have passed away. It is to their memory that this book is dedicated.

Appendix

List of Japanese American College Students in Minnesota by Institution during World War II (1941–1946)

Ancker Hospital (1)
Sakemi, Rose

Augsburg College (2)
Oshida, John Satoshi
Seto, Joseph Tobey

Bethel Junior College (2)
Kanno, John
Shimatsu, Kiyoo

Carleton College (18)
Akita, Jean Hanako
Akiyama, Joe
Eguchi, Hiroshi
Esaki, Aiji
Goto, Hiroshi Henry
Hamaji, Roy Shinichi
Matsumoto, Minoru Corky
Misaki, Melvin Yakio
Mori, John
Munemitsu, Saylo Seiro

Murata, Kiyoaki
Odanaka, Woodrow
Oishi, Hoshi
Sato, Hiroko
Shigemura, Masao Frank
Takeyama, Joy Margaret
Yamazaki, Louise Hana
Yoshida, John Takao

College of St. Catherine (10)
Ishikawa, Namiko
Kanegaye, Dorothy Yoshiko
Kihara, Sumiko Alyce
Kinoshita, Mary Jane
Matsuo, Ruth T.
Nara, Florence Tomiko
Nishimoto, Mary Takako
Taira, Yuri Lillian
Yoshino, Josephine Y.
Yoshino, Teresa

College of St. Teresa (1)
Yamamoto, Jane

College of St. Thomas (5)
Kawamura, Junie Joseph
Marubayashi, Stanley
Sakai, Robert Sumio
Tsuboi, Kenneth Kazutaka (later
    transferred to U of M)
Yamauchi, Thomas T.

Duluth Junior College (7)
Ishisaka, Giichi
Miyahara, Maki Hiroyuki
Mori, Atau
Morishige, Nobuo William
Sogo, Power Bunmei
Tokunaga, Katsumi
Watanabe, Shigemi Arthur

Fairview Hospital, Minneapolis (1)
Kojima, Frances Masae

Gustavus Adolphus College (5)
Kato, Akiko Penny
Kato, Masako Pat
Kitagawa, Mariko
Nishioki, Toshiko
Noma, Arthur Akitaru

Hamline University (47)
Abe, Ayako Elaine
Fujioka, James
Fujioka, June
Fukui, Takako (Ruth)

Funabiki, Claire Meiko
Funatake, Taichiro Daniel
Hakomaki, George
Hamaoka, Shigeko
Hayashi, Helen Hideko
Ikeda, Alden
Imayanagita, Osamu
Iwanaka, George Masao
Iwasaki, Kate
Jinguji, Masayoshi Jim
Jinguji, Michiko Rose
Jio, Michiko
Kamei, Michiko
Kiyokawa, Michiko
Kuratomi, Ikuko
Maeda, Jane Toshie
Matsumoto, Marie
Matsushita, Marjorie Mae
Matsuyama, Caroline K.
Miura, Marna
Miyake, Alice
Nakamatsu, William
Ogawa, Ranko
Oshiro, Janet Sakiko
Oyanagi, Kenji
Sakai, Sachiko Alice
Sameshima, Shiku Lorraine
Sasaki, Jack Shizuka
Sato, Dorothy
Sugiyama, Tadayoshi Tad
Takao, Mona
Tanabe, Grace Mieko
Terami, Dorothy S.
Tokuno, Alyce
Uchiyama, May M.

Uyehata, Viola
Uyeoka, Akimi
Uyeoka, Sierra Haruno
Watanabe, Anne
Yamamoto, Joe Yuzuru
Yamamoto, Margaret Kinuko
Yanagida, Lucy F.
Yoshimura, Shizuko

*Kahler Hospital School of
    Nursing* (15)
Fujimoto, Mie
Hatakeyama, Misa
Ino, Matsuko
Ishikawa, Ruth
Iwaki, Toshiko
Nakanishi, Masako
Nanchi, Katsuyo
Nishiyama, Masako
Nomura, Setsuko Alyce
Okamoto, Alice
Okuda, Toyo
Shimamoto, Mary
Takahashi, Geraldine
Umekubo, Irene Chizuko
Umezawa, Grace Hideko

Macalester College (20)
Furuta, Misao
Hata, Mary Masako
Ikeda, Esther
Imagawa, Tadashi David
Kadota, Emily M.
Kanow, Sinpachi
Kuranishi, Tom

Kubota, Rokurou
Makino, Kazumi Henry
Nakadegawa, Clifford Takeshi
Ochi, Midori
Ochi, Shigeru
Ogota, Dorothy
Okagaki, Ellen Yoshi
Shimotsuka, Uta
Suzuki, George M.
Takano, George Masaru
Takano, William Shigeru
Torii, Esther Mikiko
Torii, Eunice Chisaye

Minneapolis Business College (3)
Nishimoto, Patty Kimiko
Oshima, Mie Helen
Taiji, Hiroshi

*Minneapolis School of Beauty
    Culture* (1)
Tanabe, June

Minnesota State Teachers College (7)
Kaneda, Grayce Ritsu
Kawashima, Aiko
Matsumoto, Emiko Jane
Matsushita, Haruko Ruth
Miyake, Masako
Norikane, George
Tsuneyoshi, Azusa

*North Central Bible Institute &
    Business College* (3)
Kume, Cecile

Ogata, Yeiko
Okamoto, Shizuye Margaret

State Teachers College, Duluth (1)
Inouye, Lily

St. Andrew's Hospital (2)
Inouye, Anne Yasuko
Machida, Lillian Yuriko

St. Barnabas Hospital School of
Nursing, Minneapolis (3)
Hanafusa, Hiroko Deana
Kinoshita, Momoyo
Tanigawa, Grace

St. Mary's School of Nursing,
Rochester (45)
Ando, Anna Chiye
Hikida, May
Hinoki, Emiko
Hirayama, Elsie H.
Hirota, Fumiko H.
Ikeda, Hinayo
Ito, Sumiko
Iwashita, Toshiko
Izumi, Mary
Kasai, Tsuyako Margaret
Kawaguchi, Yukiye Bernadette
Kita, Grace
Koda, Florence
Kumakura, June Y.
Kumamoto, Yuriko
Mitori, June Ayako
Miyamoto, Ann

Mori, Alice
Morooka, Martha M.
Nagasawa, Tomi
Nahagawa, Yayoi
Nakamura, Dora
Nakamura, Laura
Nakamura, Yayoi Happy
Nakamura, Yukiko
Natsuhara, Maryo
Nishida, Kiyoko
Nomi, Patricia Yoshiko
Obata, Grace Aiko
Ouchi, Margaret
Sagata, Mary
Sakohira, Ida Chiyoko
Sato, Aya Cecilia Ann
Sato, Bessie Matsuye
Sato, June
Sato, Marie Shizuye
Shimidzu, Marie
Shimizu, Alyce
Tanagi, Sharon
Tokuyama, Peggy
Tsutakawa, Marion
Wada, Teruko
Yanagi, Dorothy
Yonemoto, Yoshiko Edith
Yoshida, Fumiye

St. Olaf College (11)
Hayano, Mary Harue
Kinoshita, Helen Yukiko
Kishi, Mayme Shizuyo
Murakami, Yoshiteru
Nagao, Esther

Ogata, Helen Haruyo
Oshima, Mie Helen
Sugino, Paul Seigo
Takahashi, Chiyeko
Takei, Yuki
Uyemura, Yoshino Elaine

Swedish Hospital (1)
Kitagawa, Mariko

University of Minnesota, Twin Cities
   (228)
Aisawa, Saburo
Aka, Shizu Dakuzaku
Akino, Mitsugu
Arai, Chiye
Arai, Hiroto Aaron
Araki, Kiyoko
Arao, Hideaki
Arase, Tetsuo
Bannai, Rose Sano
Deguchi, Roy
Endo, Kaoru
Fujimoto, Barbara Michiye
Fujioka, Robert Katsuto
Fujioka, Tadashi
Fujisaki, Mabel Teruko
Fujitomi, Maria
Fukui, George Masaki
Fukuto, Roy Tetsuo
Funatake, Taichiro Daniel
Furusho, Mary
Goto, Shosuke
Hakomaki, Ray
Harada, Calvin Kenichi

Harada, I. Allen
Haramaki, Chico
Hase, Momoyo Mae
Hasebe, George
Hasegawa, Hiro
Hasegawa, Yukiko Becky
Hayakawa, John Mori
Hayakawa, Toshio Harry
Hayashi, Misao
Hayashida, Stella
Higuchi, Wiley H.
Hiratsuka, Masaki
Horita, Kenji Ken
Ida, Peter M.
Iijima, Isaac
Ikoma, Gertrude Tomiko
Imagawa, Tadashi David
Imamoto, Grace Kyoko
Imamoto, Marion
Imon, Muneo Robert
Inai, Walter Tatsuto
Inouye, Oscar Kei
Isaki, Kiyoshi
Ishii, Edward Kiyoshi
Ishii, William Rin
Ito, James Sukeo
Ito, Minoru
Ito, Miyeko
Ito, Yoichi
Iwanaga, Frank Y.
Iwanaga, George Shinichi
Iwanaka, George Masao
Kajiwara, Etsue
Kami, Seiichi
Kamo, James H.

Kanegawa, Hiroshi
Kanzaki, Sekio Milton
Kasai, Amy Emi
Katagiri, George K.
Kato, Emmie
Kato, Kiku Kit
Kawahata, Kiyoshi
Kawakami, Paul K.
Kawamura, Mac
Ketagaki, Grayce Ura
Kikuchi, John Fredric
Kishaba, Thomas
Kitagaki, Grayce Chieko
Kitagawa, Kazuko
Kitahara, Toru
Kitano, Harry Haruo
Kitano, Tamio
Kiuchi, Jack Tsuneyasu
Ko, Roy
Kobayashi, Lloyd
Kohigashi, Satoru
Kojima, Frances Masae
Kono, Betty
Kono, Ruth Sachiye
Kubota, Kikuye Chrysanthia
Kumamoto, Arthur Toshio
Kuramoto, Simpey
Kurihara, Marie Mikiko
Kusaba, Jack Shigeno
Magota, Shuzi
Makino, Kazumi Henry
Marubayashi, Stanley
Matayoshi, James K.
Matsuda, Handy Hiroshi
Matsumoto, Emiko Jane

Matsumoto, Henry
Matsumoto, Kasuyuki Kay
Matsumoto, Kenzo
Matsumura, Clarence Satoru
Matsunaga, Hideo Arthur
Matsunaga, Hiroshi Thomas
Matsuoka, Rae
Mayeda, Ray
Migaki, James Tetsuo
Mirikitani, Richard Shinichi
Miyake, Tadao
Miyamoto, Yukio
Miyauchi, David Takenori
Miyauchi, Mary Tomiko
Morikawa, Frank Takayoshi
Morishige, Nobuo William
Morita, William Itsuro
Murakami, Ken
Muraki, Tom Tatsuo
Myose, Susumu
Nagano, George Kimiyoshi
Naka, Fumio
Nakagawa, Richard Manabu
Nakagiri, Ada
Nakagiri, Kay I.
Nakamura, Motoharu
Nakamura, Motozo Frank
Nakano, Isami
Nakano, Sumao Thomas
Nao, Setsu
Nazawa, Masako Martha
Nishida, George Teruo
Nishioki, Toshiko
Nitta, Hakuzo
Noma, Arthur Akitaru

Noma, Violet Sumire
Nozawa, Masako M.
Ochi, Shigeru
Ogata, Gen
Ohara, Hitoshi
Oishi, Hoshi
Oishi, Masami Mas
Okamoto, Akira
Oki, Masa
Okuma, Teruo
Okuma, Toshio
Omachi, Akira
Omata, Robert Rokuro
Omura, Shigeo
Ono, Mary Chizu
Onodera, Lily Yuriko
Oshida, John Satoshi
Ota, Alice
Ozawa, Koji
Saito, Shinobu Paul
Sakai, Alice K.
Sakai, Henry Katsumi
Sakamoto, Elton H.
Sakamoto, John
Sako, Yoshio
Sanbongi, Shigeru
Sano, Minoru
Sanui, Hisashi
Sato, Midori
Sato, Mitsuho Alvin
Sekiguchi, Nao
Semba, Thomas Tom
Seto, Joseph Tobey
Seto, Thomas Akiyoshi
Shigeki, Fuji

Shimaji, Tadashi Tom
Shimizu, George Kasuto
Shimotori, Masako
Shiraishi, Shunki
Somekawa, Carl
Sugano, Tetsuya T.
Sugiyama, Marian Haruko
Sugiyama, Tadayoshi Tad
Sumada, Tsuguo
Suyeoka, Hidetoshi
Suzuki, George
Tada, Yoko
Tahara, Marie K.
Takagi, Miyoko Len
Takahashi, Ichiro
Takamoto, Sarah Fusaye
Takano, William Shigeru
Takata, Harry H.
Takata, Ray Marcel
Takemura, George
Takemura, Henry Susumu
Takemura, Martha Masako
Takenaka, Frank I.
Tanabe, Tetsuro
Tanaka, Cherry
Tanaka, Nobu
Tanamachi, Masao
Tanbara, George Ayao
Tashiro, Gogi
Teramoto, Hagiko
Teramoto, Masakasu
Tomita, Kiku
Torii, Eunice
Tsuboi, Kenneth Kazutaka
Tsuji, Kiyoshi

Tsukuno, Kay Shida
Tsuneyoshi, Azusa
Tsunoda, William Mitsugi
Tsutsumi, Frank Akira
Uchimura, Minoru Minor
Umekubo, Robert Shoji
Umemoto, Kazuo
Umemoto, Kiyoko
Wada, Sachiko Doris
Watanabe, Clara Kimi
Yahanda, Evelyn Ayako
Yamada, Ted Tasuku
Yamaga, Kenji
Yamamoto, Chiyeko
Yamamoto, Joe
Yamamoto, Mary Shizue
Yamamoto, Yoshiyuki
Yamashita, Hisako
Yamashita, June
Yasunobu, Kerry Tsuyoshi
Yorozu, Helen Ruri
Yoshida, Makoto Mac
Yoshida, Roth K.
Yoshimori, Melvin Akira
Yoshimoto, Ray H.
Yoshimura, Kazuko
Yoshino, Kenji
Yoshioka, Shizuko
Yumibe, Toshio
Yumibe, Yukie

William Hood Dunwoody Industrial
  Institute (97)
Abe, Hirao
Aoki, Takao

Aoyaai, Harry
Fujii, Masako
Fujimoto, Fred
Fujimoto, Harold
Fukami, Frank
Hamamoto, Goichi
Hanamoto, Johnnie
Hangai, Fumio
Hayano, Torao
Hayao, Abe
Hayashi, Sakae
Hirahara, Akira
Hirano, Jiro Jack
Hoshizaki, Akira
Hoshizaki, Casey
Ikeda, Victor
Imura, Bill
Inai, Walt
Ishizaki, Hisashi
Ito, Joseph
Iwatsubo, Masaru
Kasuga, Joe
Kato, Tatsuo
Kawada, George
Kirihara, Jim
Kiyokawa, Marsh
Kiyono, Buster
Kokesh, Ruth
Koyanagi, Yasuo
Kubo, Yoshio
Kumagai, Hisahai (Hisashi)
Kurata, Mike
Magano, "Kim"
Maki, Albert
Marata, Bill

Masuda, Sadami
Matsui, George
Matsumoto, Tommy
Matsuura, Art
Matsuura, Yoshimi
Minami, Yoshimi
Miyamoto, Eddie
Mizuno, Wallace
Morikawa, George
Nakagawa, Raymond
Nakamura, (first name unknown)
Niino, Hiroshi (Hugh)
Nishiyama, S.
Nitasaka, Nobuyuki
Nogano, George
Noji, Toru "Tom"
Ohno, Joe
Okahara, Tsutomu Tom
Okamoto, Norman
Okimoto, George
Okimoto, Saburo
Okubo, Howard
Okumura, Bill
Okuye, Sam
Omori, Harry
Onishi, (first name unknown)
Rinta, Sulo
Saiki, Kiyoto
Sakaji, Haru
Shimaji, Tadashi
Shimasaki, Jimmy

Shiraishi, Shunki
Tagami, Edward
Tagami, Kakumi
Taiji, James
Takenaka, Frank
Taketa, Howard
Takeyasu, Motoi
Tamura, Oscar
Tanaka, Leo
Tanigoshi, George
Taniguchi, K.
Terada, Masateru
Togami, Frank
Tsuboi, Ted
Tsujimoto, Harold
Uchida, Masaharu
Umeda, Ben
Unemoto, (first name unknown)
Urushibata, Kunio
Utsunomiya, Tom
Uyemura, James
Yamada, Frank
Yamaguchi, Ken(ji)
Yamaguchi, Roy
Yamamoto, Edward
Yamamoto, Kiyoso
Yoshida, Makoto Mac
Yoshitsugi, Sugi
Yuyama, Kenji

TOTAL: 536

Notes

See bibliography for full source citations.

Notes to Chapter 1: Enmity and Empathy

Opening quote: Lee, "Director Yosh's Parents"; also see Hvistendahl, "Yosh Murakami," 42–45; Sauve, "Tidbits."

1. The ten incarceration camps were Gila River, Arizona; Poston, Arizona; Jerome, Arkansas; Rohwer, Arkansas; Manzanar, California; Tule Lake, California; Granada, Colorado; Minidoka, Idaho; Topaz, Utah; and Heart Mountain, Wyoming. See National Archives, "Japanese-American Incarceration."

On March 29, 1942, John L. DeWitt issued Public Proclamation No. 4, which began the forced removal and incarceration of Japanese American residents on the West Coast with only a forty-eight-hour notice. Any violation would be deemed a misdemeanor punishable by up to one year in prison and a $5,000 fine. See National Archives, "Japanese-American Incarceration." Approximately 110,000 people of Japanese ancestry on the West Coast were incarcerated the first few months following the proclamation. In addition, about 10,000 people entered the War Relocation Authority (WRA) camps after the initial roundup, including those transferred from the Department of Justice internment system, detainees from Hawai'i, and infants born in the camps during the war years. See Brian Niiya, "Ask a Historian: How Many Japanese Americans Were Incarcerated during WWII?" Densho, last modified June 2, 2021, https://densho.org/catalyst/how-many-japanese-americans -were-incarcerated-during-wwii/.

2. Hvistendahl, "Yosh Murakami," 44; Myer, *Uprooted Americans*, 111, 345. On Myer, see Shiho Imai, "Dillon Myer," Densho Encyclopedia, last modified October 16, 2020, https://encyclopedia.densho.org/Dillon_Myer/.

3. US Commission on Wartime Relocation and Internment of Civilians (CWRIC), *Personal Justice Denied*, 18. DeWitt made this comment at an off-the-record news conference on April 16, 1943. US CWRIC, *Personal Justice Denied*,

65–66; also see Brian Niiya, "John DeWitt," Densho Encyclopedia, last modified July 15, 2020, https://encyclopedia.densho.org/John_DeWitt/#cite_ref-ftnt_ref 4_4-0.

4. The entire West Coast was declared a military zone under the Executive Order 9066 that authorized the exclusion of civilians from the restricted areas. Although the language of the order did not single out any ethnic group, DeWitt of the Western Defense Command proceeded to announce curfews that included only Japanese Americans. He first urged them to voluntarily "evacuate," and about 7 percent of the total Japanese American population in these areas complied. Apparently, it was not enough. All residents of Japanese ancestry would be forcibly removed and incarcerated in the ten camps shortly. See National Archives, "Japanese-American Incarceration."

Frail, "The Injustice of Japanese-American Internment Camps." Also see US CWRIC, *Personal Justice Denied*, 3; Weglyn, *Years of Infamy*; Reeves, *Infamy*; Lee, "Director Yosh's Parents."

5. O'Brien, *The College Nisei*, 135–37; Austin, *From Concentration Camp to Campus*, 11. Also see "Total Number and Percentage Distribution," n.d., Historical Council Material (I), Box 9, NJASRC Records, Hoover Institution Archives, Stanford University (hereafter cited as Hoover Institution Archives); "Preliminary Report on the Number of American Students of Japanese Ancestry," n.d., Historical Council Material (I), Box 9, NJASRC Records, Hoover Institution Archives; Conard (Executive Secretary, Student Relocation Committee) to Deutsch, May 2, 1942, Monroe E. Deutsch (Provost, University of California, Berkeley), Box 6, NJASRC Records, Hoover Institution Archives.

6. Lee, "Director Yosh's Parents." "According to Section 60.4.21.A-C of the *WRA Administrative Handbook*, return to the camps by those who had been granted indefinite leave was allowed only with the permission of the authorities. Evacuees were encouraged not to return but could reapply for residence if they could persuade a Relocation Officer that they could not keep outside employment. Visitors to the camps were required to give up their indefinite leave permits in order to enter." James, "Life Begins with Freedom," 162, 173n16.

7. The WRA director's job was a difficult one. In his autobiography, Eisenhower wrote: "I spoke to Dillon about taking over WRA. I pulled no punches. The past three months had been the toughest of my career and I had lost a year's sleep in ninety days. I also stressed that we had turned the corner and a good strong leader could do a great deal to ensure the Japanese Americans could maintain some dignity, contribute to their own and the country's well-being, and eventually be brought back into society. [Myer] agreed to take the position the President approved." Eisenhower, *The President Is Calling*, 127–28.

8. Cosgrave, "Relocation of Japanese American Students," 2, 24, 223; James, "Life Begins with Freedom," 159, 160.

9. Provinse, "Relocation of Japanese-American College Students," 3. The best available figures suggest there were 3,530 students enrolled in college in 1941; 1,493 students in 1943; and 2,870 in 1945. See O'Brien, *The College Nisei*, 135–49.

"Only on May 5, 1942, five months after the bombing of Pearl Harbor and almost three months after President Franklin D. Roosevelt signed Executive Order 9066, did the War Relocation Authority (WRA) begin to try to get some students into colleges for the fall 1942 semester." Austin, *From Concentration Camp to Campus*, 1.

10. Daniels, "Foreword," in Austin, *From Concentration Camp to Campus*, x. There were some important works that critically examined the actions of the US government during the war. Carey McWilliams, Dorothy Thomas and Richard Nishimoto, Morton Grodzins, Jacobus tenBroek with Edward Barnhart and Floyd Matson, and Charles Allen, to name a few, wrote influential books during this period.

11. Robinson, *A Tragedy of Democracy*, 3.

12. Tsuchida, *Reflections*, xxxi. President Ronald Reagan signed the bill on August 10, 1988. As a result, a total of 82,219 former incarcerees received reparations. Alice Yang, "Redress Movement," Densho Encyclopedia, last modified August 24, 2020, https://encyclopedia.densho.org/Redress_movement/. For more information about the redress campaign, see Tateishi, *Redress*.

13. Michener, "Introduction," in Weglyn, *Years of Infamy*, 31. The US Supreme Court upheld the legality of forcible removal and detention due to "military necessity" in *Hirabayashi v. United States* (1943), *Yasui v. United States* (1943), and *Korematsu v. United States* (1944). Legal scholars do not agree unanimously whether Chief Justice John Roberts's statement actually overturned *Korematsu* or was just a "disapproving dictum" of it. These ethnically biased court cases and the ethical lapses of the government are also discussed in Chapter Seven.

14. Takei et al., *They Called Us Enemy*, 207.

15. In 1882, Congress passed an absolute ten-year ban on Chinese laborers immigrating to the United States. President Chester A. Arthur signed it into law on May 6, 1882. It was the first and only major US law to prohibit immigration for a specific nationality—Chinese workers who were defined as "both skilled and unskilled laborers and Chinese employed in mining" in this case. See "Chinese Exclusion Act (1882)," Milestone Document, National Archives, last modified January 17, 2023, https://www.archives.gov/milestone-documents/chinese-exclusion-act. Also see Lee, *At America's Gates*.

On September 2, 1885, a group of 150 white coal miners murdered twenty-eight Chinese miners and wounded another fifteen in Rock Springs, Wyoming. They also set fire to homes and drove out the rest of the several hundred Chinese in town into the desert at gunpoint. Eventually, forty-five of the white miners were fired for their roles in the massacre. However, no effective legal action was ever taken against any of the participants. See Lee, *The Making of Asian America*, 94. Also see "Chinese Miners Are Massacred in Wyoming Territory," History, last modified April 13, 2021, https://www.history.com/this-day-in-history/whites-massacre-chinese-in -wyoming-territory.

On June 19, 1982, two white men, a father and his stepson—a foreman and a laid-off auto worker in Detroit, Michigan—beat Vincent Chin, a Chinese American, to death with a baseball bat outside a McDonald's, after an argument at the nearby bar where Chin was celebrating his bachelor party. The sentence for the two assailants was a $3,000 fine each and three years of probation but no prison time. As nation-wide calls for justice grew louder, both men were indicted on federal charges for violating Chin's civil rights. However, they were eventually acquitted. For a detailed account of the murder and its aftermath, see Christine Choy, dir., *Who Killed Vincent Chin?* (Film News Now Foundation and WTVS, 1987).

In 2020, hate crimes overall increased by 2 percent, but hate crimes against the Asian American and Pacific Islander population rose by 146 percent. Center for the Study of Hate and Extremism at CSUSB, *Report to the Nation: Anti-Asian Prejudice & Hate Crime*, San Bernardino: California State University, 2021.

16. Quote from the article by Young Kim, "The Painful History of Anti-Asian Hate Crimes in America," CBS News, August 1, 2021, https://www.cbsnews.com/ news/the-painful-history-of-anti-asian-hate-crimes-in-america/.

17. In 2022, there were about 313,223 Asian Minnesotans, which was 5.4% of the state's total population of 5.7 million. Approximately 12,560 of them identified as Japanese or Japanese American. See "Asian Minnesotans," Minnesota Compass, last modified 2023, https://www.mncompass.org/chart/b14688-1/asian-minneso tans; and "Japanese Population," Minnesota Compass, last modified 2023, https:// www.mncompass.org/topics/demographics/cultural-communities/japanese.

18. Frans de Waal, "The Evolution of Empathy," Greater Good Magazine, September 1, 2005, https://greatergood.berkeley.edu/article/item/the_evolution_of _empathy.

19. During the summer of 2014, my then students—Jacob Caswell, Paoge Moua, and Meena Wainwright—and I interviewed ten Asian Americans who came from diverse ethnic backgrounds, such as Chinese, Japanese, Vietnamese, Indian, Thai, and Laotian, along with those who had worked closely with the Asian community.

20. J. Murakami, interview. The subsequent quotations from Jane Murakami come from this interview.

21. Two former students, Hikari Sugisaki and Paul Sullivan, collaborated with me on the 2015 summer project. They continued to work on it for the following few

years. We produced a website as well as a short documentary film, *Beyond the Barbed Wire: Japanese Americans in Minnesota* (2018). See "Beyond the Barbed Wire," https://pages.stolaf.edu/jam.

22. Albert, "The Japanese," 560.

23. Earlier literature, including O'Brien's count in 1949, showed twenty-two Minnesotan institutions with about four hundred Nisei students. My students and I confirmed 536 students in twenty-five higher education institutions. See the appendix for a detailed list of the schools and students.

On December 18, 1944, the US Supreme Court ruled on the *Ex parte Mitsuye Endo* case that the War Relocation Authority "has no authority to subject citizens who are concededly loyal to its leave procedure." The exclusion orders barring Japanese Americans from the West Coast were lifted on January 2, 1945, as a result. The government announced that all relocation centers would be closed by the end of 1945. The last camp to close was Tule Lake in March 1946. See O'Brien, *The College Nisei*, 123; Lee, *The Making of Asian America*, 245; Greg Robinson, "Ex parte Mitsuye Endo (1944)," Densho Encyclopedia, last modified January 5, 2024, https://ency clopedia.densho.org/Ex_parte_Mitsuye_Endo_(1944)/.

24. Peter J. DeCarlo, "Military Intelligence Service Language School (MISLS)," MNopedia, last modified April 6, 2022, https://www.mnopedia.org/group/mili tary-intelligence-service-language-school-misls.

25. B. Doi, interview; US Department of the Interior, *WRA: A Story of Human Conservation*, 109.

26. General DeWitt and his subordinates vehemently opposed the Japanese American conscription. "They argued . . . that if the government could make judgments about the loyalty of civilians in order to draft them, the whole costly evacuation program was largely unnecessary. Nevertheless, the Army announced officially in January 1943 that a special Japanese American combat unit would be formed. This became the famous 442nd Regimental Combat Team." Daniels, *Asian America*, 250.

27. For a discussion of terminology around "internment," see Daniels, "Words Do Matter," 183–207. Also see National JACL, *Power of Words Handbook*.

28. Hvistendahl, "Yosh Murakami," 44.

Notes to Chapter 2: Incarceration and Integration

Opening quote: J. Kusunoki, interview. The subsequent quotations from Jim Kusunoki come from this interview.

1. After his service in the Army, Jim Kusunoki reunited with his family, who had relocated to Chicago. He met his wife, Pearl Fujimoto, there, and they were married in 1949. In 1955, the young couple and their two sons, Stanley and Brian,

moved to the Twin Cities, and Jim continued his career in the paint and printing business. He was also committed to community service as a member of the Japanese American Citizens League and Mayflower United Church of Christ in South Minneapolis. Kusunoki passed away on June 12, 2019.

2. S. Kusunoki, interview. The subsequent quotations from Stanley Kusunoki come from this interview.

3. Sudo, interview. Subsequent quotations from Sudo come from this interview unless stated otherwise. Regarding the Ohno family, "there's a twenty-year age range from the oldest to the youngest. Takiko, being the oldest, was born in 1918 and my brother Henry, who was the youngest in the family, he was born in 1938, and I was born in 1935, so I'm next to the youngest. This is a family of seven girls and four boys." Sudo, interview by Ozone.

4. Sudo, interview by Ozone.

5. Some of the important and useful works about Issei Japanese Americans include Akemi Kikumura, *Through Harsh Winters* (Novato, CA: Chandler and Sharp, 1981), and the various books by Yuji Ichioka, a renowned historian who was an Issei himself, such as *The Issei: The World of the First Generation Japanese Immigrants, 1885–1924* (New York: The Free Press, 1988); Yasuo Sakata, Nobuya Tsuchida, and Eri Yasuhara, comps., *A Buried Past: An Annotated Bibliography of the Japanese American Research Project Collection* (Berkeley: University of California Press, 1974); and Eiichiro Azuma, comp., *A Buried Past II: A Sequel to the Annotated Bibliography of the Japanese American Research Project Collection* (Los Angeles: Asian American Studies Center, University of California, 1999). There is slightly more historical literature on the Nisei generation in the prewar years. For example: Bill Hosokawa, *Nisei: The Quiet Americans* (New York: William Morrow, 1969); Harry H. L. Kitano, *Japanese Americans: The Evolution of a Subculture* (Englewood Cliffs, NJ: Prentice–Hall, 1969/1976); S. Frank Miyamoto, *Social Solidarity Among the Japanese in Seattle* (Seattle: University of Washington Press, 1939/1981; revised ed., 1984); John Modell, *The Economics and Politics of Racial Accommodation: The Japanese of Los Angeles, 1900–1942* (Urbana: University of Illinois Press, 1977); William Petersen, *Japanese Americans: Oppression and Success* (New York: Random House, 1971); and Robert A. Wilson and Bill Hosokawa, *East to America* (New York: William Morrow, 1980).

6. Assistant Secretary of War John J. McCloy based his support for exile and incarceration on national security concerns, responding to Attorney General Francis Biddle's opposition reportedly by remarking that Biddle was "putting a Wall Street lawyer in a helluva box, but if it is a question of the safety of the country [and] the Constitution . . . Why the Constitution is just a scrap of paper to me." McCloy later testified that, given the context of the times, exile and incarceration

had been reasonable, thoughtful, and humane. The policy was, he argued forty years later, "in accordance with the best interests of the country." See Austin, *From Concentration Camp to Campus*, 186n88; Daniels, *Asian America*, 337–38; Daniels, *Concentration Camps, North America*, 55, 145.

7. Race, from the perspective of contemporary historians, anthropologists, and sociologists, is a social construct that is used to define physical differences between people, but more often than not, it has been employed as a tool for oppression and violence. More about race and Japanese American wartime experiences will be discussed in Chapter Eight.

8. See Wu, *The Color of Success*, 12.

9. Japanese American Evacuation and Resettlement Study files, 67/14, T6.10, Bancroft Library, University of California, Berkeley; also see Drinnon, *Keeper of Concentration Camps*, 55. Lee, *The Making of Asian America*, 213; also see Carter, "Memorandum on C.B. Munson's Report"; Daniels, *Prisoners without Trial*, 25–26.

10. Department of the Interior, *WRA*, 3–4. This was the final of ten reports from the WRA director.

11. Daniels, *Asian America*, 250; Department of the Interior, *WRA*, 4.

12. Okihiro, *Storied Lives*, xi.

13. See Drinnon, *Keeper of Concentration Camps*, 266–67; Wu, *The Color of Success*, 20; Semba, interview. Subsequent quotations from Semba come from this interview. For a detailed examination of Buddhism and Japanese American wartime experiences, see Williams, *American Sutra*.

14. Hayashi, "The Return of Japanese Americans."

15. *War Relocation Centers: Hearings before a Subcommittee of the Committee on Military Affairs*, 78th Cong., 1st sess., January 20, 1943 (testimony of Dillon S. Myer), 53; Lee, *The Making of Asian America*, 246; Wu, *The Color of Success*, 12–13; Robinson, *After Camp*, 15.

16. Daniels et al., *Japanese Americans*, 12. For the history of the Japanese in the United States, see Fryer, "The Japanese American Experience," 371–474.

Minnesota attracted very limited numbers of Japanese immigrants at the turn of the twentieth century. The Japanese population of Minneapolis in 1918 consisted of thirty-six adult males; all were aged between mid-twenties and mid-thirties, and just five of them were married. The Twin Cities counted only six families as late as 1934, and hence, there was hardly any sense of a Japanese community before the war. See Albert, "The Japanese," 558–59.

17. Austin, *From Concentration Camp to Campus*, 5; Daniels, *Asian America*, 134–35; Daniels, *Concentration Camps*, 6–8.

18. Daniels et al., *Japanese Americans*, 12. For the history and concept of "Yellow Peril," see John Kuo Wei Tchen and Dylan Yeats, eds., *Yellow Peril!*.

19. For more on the concept of undocumented immigrants and the making of America through mapping borders, see Ngai, *Impossible Subjects*.

20. Daniels, *The Politics of Prejudice*, 70; Steiner, *The Japanese Invasion*, v–vi, 197, 209; also see Lee, *The Making of Asian America*, 132, 133.

21. Department of the Interior, *WRA*, 7; also see Lee, *The Making of Asian America*, 132.

22. US CWRIC, *Personal Justice Denied*, 65–66; Lee, *The Making of Asian America*, 217.

DeWitt wrote to James Rowe, Assistant US Attorney General, in January 1942: "I have no confidence in their [Japanese American] loyalty whatsoever." See US CWRIC, *Personal Justice Denied*, 65–66. According to historian Erika Lee, DeWitt "saw danger everywhere and was prone to believe every sensationalist rumor that crossed his desk. DeWitt claimed, for example, that there were 'hundreds of reports' that Japanese Americans were sending signal light messages and unlawful radio transmissions to enemy surface vessels and submarines off the West Coast. However, the Federal Communications Commission reported the rumors 'without exception . . . to be baseless.'" See Lee, *The Making of Asian America*, 217.

23. US CWRIC, *Personal Justice Denied*, 64; Lee, *The Making of Asian America*, 217.

24. Daniels et al., *Japanese Americans*, 12; Department of the Interior, *WRA*, 3–4.

25. See Department of the Interior, *WRA*, 24–43, 190; Drinnon, *Keeper of Concentration Camps*, 266–67; Wu, *The Color of Success*, 12; Myer, *Uprooted Americans*, 67–80; Ngai, "An Ironic Testimony," 237–57; Simpson, *An Absent Presence*, 154; Weglyn, *Years of Infamy*, 93–102; Hosokawa, "JACL Looks Forward to Greatest Task," *Pacific Citizen*, November 26, 1942, 5.

Born in Seattle, Washington, in 1915, William "Bill" Kunpei Hosokawa was a prolific author. His better-known books include *Nisei: The Quiet Americans* (Boulder: University Press of Colorado, 1969/2002), *JACL: In Quest of Justice* (New York: William Morrow and Co., 1982), and *Colorado's Japanese Americans: From 1886 to the Present* (Boulder: University Press of Colorado, 2005).

26. Hosokawa, "JACL Looks Forward," 5; Larry Tajiri, "Nisei USA," *Pacific Citizen*, December 3, 1942, 4.

27. Dempster, *Making Home from War*, xxi; Tajiri, "Nisei USA," 4; also see Robinson, *After Camp*, 89. While all these Nisei spokespersons championed the merits of the federal resettlement in rebuilding the social status of Japanese Americans, some critics believed their community leaders had not done enough for or even failed to defend some of the most vulnerable members of their constituencies. The JACL was panned at the time for not challenging the legality of the exclusion and incarceration, but instead assisting the government intelligence agencies in

identifying "disloyal" Issei and taking a hard-line position against draft resisters in camps. See Sharon Yamato, "Carrying the Torch: Wayne Collins Jr. on His Father's Defense of the Renunciants," Discover Nikkei, October 21, 2014, https://discov ernikkei.org/en/journal/2014/10/21/carrying-the-torch/; also see Weglyn, *Years of Infamy*, 255. These issues have remained a source of division within the Japanese American community and the organization itself. Not until the dawn of the new millennium was a resolution reached, when the JACL offered a national apology to the "resisters of conscience" in 2000 and the Tule Lake resisters in 2019. Today the JACL is highly regarded as a vanguard in fighting against injustice and advocating human rights for all marginalized communities.

28. Committee on Resettlement of Japanese Americans (CRJA) et al., "Planning Resettlement of Japanese Americans"; CRJA, *Minneapolis Chapter Records*; "Introduction" (no author and undated), CRJA, *Minneapolis Chapter Records*.

29. Department of the Interior, *WRA*, 36; Report from Salt Lake Field Office, May 11, 1945, File 200, Box 24, Subject–Classified General Files, Headquarters, Records of the WRA, RG 210, National Archives. Also see Taylor, "Leaving the Concentration Camps," 188.

30. Taylor, "Leaving the Concentration Camps," 188; Department of the Interior, *WRA*, 38.

31. Department of the Interior, *WRA*, 38; Robinson, *A Tragedy of Democracy*, 182; Robinson, *After Camp*, 48; Lee, *The Making of Asian America*, 246–47. According to the WRA report in 1946, there were no major Japanese American congregations in any of the cities of the Midwest or East, such as Cleveland and New York. The exception was Chicago, where two-thirds of the 15,000 to 20,000 resettlers stayed in the area around the University of Chicago. US Department of the Interior, *People in Motion*, 167–68.

32. For example, there was the Kitagawa family, headed by Tometaro Kitagawa, who had operated a shop specializing in Japanese imports called "Japan Art Store" in downtown Minneapolis since the early twentieth century. His son Kiyoshi Kitagawa, enrolled at the Shattuck Military Academy in 1927, was its first graduate of Asian descent. He later joined the Army, serving in the 442nd Regimental Combat Team and then the MISLS in Fort Snelling. The Kitagawa daughters, including Nobuko, who was known as an accomplished young pianist, were featured in the newspaper in the 1930s more than a few times. The biographical information of Tometaro Kitagawa can be found in "Tometaro Kitagawa Papers," Immigration History Research Center Archives, University of Minnesota, Minneapolis. Also see Brown, "Diaries." Research on the Kitagawa family's history is undertaken by historian Patti Kameya.

33. Department of the Interior, *WRA*, 40.

34. Department of the Interior, *WRA*, 132.

35. Department of the Interior, *WRA*, 132.

36. Department of the Interior, *WRA*, 40.

37. Kitagawa, *Issei and Nisei*, 119. Kitagawa was an influential and inspirational figure for the local Japanese community in the Twin Cities during the war years. A more detailed profile of his work will be discussed in Chapter Seven.

38. Hanson, "St. Paul Resettlement Committee."

39. Albert, "The Japanese," 560.

40. Hanson, "St. Paul Resettlement Committee"; Tsuchida, *Reflections*, 28; Sickels, "St. Paul Extends a Hand," 1.

41. Sickels, "St. Paul Extends a Hand," 1; Albert, "The Japanese," 560. Two notable individuals who volunteered their time and efforts to the Japanese American resettlement in the Twin Cities were Genevieve Fallon Steefel and Ruth Gage-Colby, whose contributions will be discussed in Chapter Seven. The results of their work can be found in many correspondences in the Minneapolis Committee on Resettlement Papers and St. Paul Resettlement Committee Papers, both in the collection of the Minnesota Historical Society. See CRJA, "Minneapolis Chapter."

42. Albert, "The Japanese," 561; Hiner, "Narrative History," 8, 10–12; Minutes, October 31, 1945; Minutes, March 17, 1948—both in the St. Paul Resettlement Committee Papers, Minnesota Historical Society; also see Steefel to Daisuke Kitagawa, March 26, 1944, Genevieve F. Steefel Papers, Minnesota Historical Society.

43. Sickels, "St. Paul Extends a Hand," 1.

44. The autobiography of Ruth Tanbara can be found in Tanbara, "Memoirs," 1–67.

45. Tanbara, "Memoirs," 19.

46. Hanson, "St. Paul Resettlement Committee"; Tanbara, "Memoirs," 28; Sickels, *Around the World in St. Paul*, 201.

47. T. Kurihara, interview.

48. Sickels, *Around the World*, 31.

49. Department of the Interior, *People in Motion*, 8; Sickels, "St. Paul Extends a Hand."

50. Hiner, "Narrative History," 43; "400 U.S. Japs Resettled in This Area," *St. Paul Pioneer Press*, November 16, 1943; "1,369 Nisei Relocated in the State," *St. Paul Dispatch*, November 20, 1944. Also see Hanson, "St. Paul Resettlement Committee."

51. For example, many Nisei doctors and dentists in the all–Hawaiian Japanese 100th Infantry Battalion, who were then stationed at Camp McCoy near Sparta, Wisconsin, went to the Mayo Clinic for short courses before they were deployed overseas. Due to their short stay, there was no precise number as to how many of them actually came and went. See Albert, "The Japanese," 562.

52. Albert, "The Japanese," 561; Hiner, "Narrative History," 2, 8.

53. For more information on the program, see Hanson, "Festival of Nations." In 1955, Louis Warren Hill Jr., grandson of James J. Hill (1838–1916), the tycoon of the Great Northern Railway, invited Ruth Tanbara to help him start the St. Paul–Nagasaki Sister City Committee. She led six delegations from St. Paul to visit atomic-bomb victims and city leaders in Nagasaki, Japan. See Hanson, "Tanbara."

In the postwar years, Ruth Tanbara attended the University of Minnesota and received her master's degree in home economics education in 1953. She joined the YWCA World Council in 1955 and continued to work for the YWCA in St. Paul on adult education until her retirement in 1972, including teaching flower arranging and Japanese cooking classes. She was a board member of the St. Paul Council of Human Relations and a member of the Governor's Committee on Human Rights. She also served on the boards of various organizations, such as the Family Service Center of Greater St. Paul, the Minnesota Museum of Art, the International Institute, and Unity Church–Unitarian. See Hanson, "Tanbara."

54. M. Kirihara, interview.

55. Hanson, "St. Paul Resettlement Committee."

56. Robinson, *A Tragedy of Democracy*, 180; DeCarlo, "Military Intelligence Service Language School."

57. See Kenney, *Minnesota Goes to War*, 71. Author Selden Cowles Menefee wrote in 1943 that militant antisemitism appeared "to be almost entirely lacking in the Middle West . . . except for Minneapolis." See Menefee, *Assignment*, 101.

58. State Committee on Tolerance, Unity, and Loyalty (SCTUL), "An Appeal to the Citizens of Minnesota," n.d., Box 2, Miscellaneous Records, Civilian Defense Division Records, Minnesota Historical Society.

59. *Fort Snelling Bulletin*, October 27, 1945, 1. Quoted in Ano, "Loyal Linguists," 278. Also see Faster, "Newspaper Coverage," 54–55. "Army School at Savage," *Minneapolis Morning Tribune*, July 2, 1942. Also see McNaughton, *Nisei Linguists*, 94–95. Governor's Interracial Commission of Minnesota (GICM), *The Oriental in Minnesota*, 46. Also see Ruth Tanbara Papers, Box 147 G.7.3 (B), Minnesota Historical Society.

Kai Eduard Rasmussen was born in Copenhagen, Denmark, in 1902. At twenty years old, he immigrated to the United States in search of better prospects than were available in post–World War I Europe. He was rejected by both the Navy and the Marine Corps before finally joining the US Army Infantry. He was stationed stateside from 1929 to 1936, then went to the US Embassy in Tokyo, Japan, to serve as assistant military attaché until 1940. He was assigned to establish the MISLS after he returned to the United States, as he had learned Japanese during his tenure at the embassy. More about Rasmussen and the MISLS will be discussed in Chapter Five.

60. Brown, "How Japanese American Linguists Helped." Also see McNaughton, *Nisei Linguists*, 94. Nakamura, "Military Intelligence Service Language School."

61. Faster, "Newspaper Coverage," 55; Sickels, *Around the World*, 203.

62. Faster, "Newspaper Coverage," 55, 66, 69, 122, 123; Hiner, "Narrative History," 23–c. The three news articles cited are "Japs Loyal Soldiers—at Snelling," *Minneapolis Star Journal*, March 24, 1942, 15; "'Model' Soldiers Pose at Fort," *Minneapolis Morning Tribune*, May 7, 1942, 11:2; Milton Kaplan, "Snelling's Jap Language School Proves Army Opposition Wrong," *Minneapolis Morning Tribune*, October 23, 1945, 9.

The derogatory terms like "Jap" or "Nip" were rarely used to describe Japanese Americans in the local news, although both were common in headlines about people in Japan. Instead, "Nisei" was the most popular term for Japanese Americans. See Faster, "Newspaper Coverage," 59.

For a discussion of Japanese Americans and the origin of the "model minority" myth, see Wu, *The Color of Success*. Further examination of the "model minority" through John Aiso can be found in Chapter Five.

63. GICM, *The Oriental in Minnesota*, 46; also see Faster, "Newspaper Coverage," 55–56.

64. Sickels, *Around the World*, 210; Sickels, "St. Paul Extends a Hand."

65. James Tsurutani, "How Japanese American Soldier Feels About Detention Camps," *Minneapolis Sunday Tribune and Star Journal*, General News Section, July 12, 1942.

66. "Snelling Nisei Give $1,236 in Polio Fight," *Minneapolis Star Journal*, September 3, 1946, 19; Nakasone, interview. The subsequent quotations from Nakasone come from this interview unless stated otherwise.

67. Albert, "The Japanese," 558–59; also see Kenney, *Minnesota Goes to War*, 88.

68. Brown, "Japanese-Born Vet." The couple had a son in 1920, also named Edward. However, the younger Yamazaki changed his last name to the more American-sounding Evans around 1940, before he enlisted in 1941. Evans would eventually rise to the rank of major in the Air Force and retired after two decades in the military, having served during both World War II and the Korean War. See Brown, "Japanese-Born Vet."

69. "Loyal St. Paul Japs Victims of War," *St. Paul Dispatch*, December 9, 1941; also see Brown, "After the Bombing of Pearl Harbor."

70. "Nab St. Paul Japanese," *St. Paul Dispatch*, December 8, 1941; Kenney, *Minnesota Goes to War*, 87. Born in Tokyo, Japan, in 1887, Kano Ikeda came to the United States in 1904 in his late teens in hope of becoming a physician. He supported himself while in medical school at the University of Illinois by means of working as a laboratory technician. After graduation from medical school in 1914, he interned at Asbury Hospital in Minneapolis. He had a teaching fellowship in bacteriology and

pathology at the University of Minnesota from 1916 to 1918. Ikeda had since worked in pathology at the Minneapolis General Hospital, St. Luke's Hospital, and the Charles T. Miller Hospital, where he remained for the next three decades. Recognized as an expert in pathology and radiology, he later returned to teach at the University of Minnesota as well as Macalester College. He passed away in 1960. See Jarvis, "Kano Ikeda," 453–54.

71. "Japanese Gets Nod to Reopen His Restaurant," *Minneapolis Star Journal*, December 12, 1941, 7; Brown, "Japanese-Born Vet," and "After the Bombing." Also see Kenney, *Minnesota Goes to War*, 87.

72. Kenney, *Minnesota Goes to War*, 87–88.

73. Kenney, *Minnesota Goes to War*, 87.

74. Sickels, *Around the World*, 202.

75. Sickels, "St. Paul Extends a Hand"; Sickels, *Around the World*, 206–7.

76. Sickels, *Around the World*, 207.

77. "Nisei Meet Social Barriers but They Like Minneapolis," *Minneapolis Morning Tribune*, January 25, 1946. The housing story of the Tanbaras can be found in Sickels, *Around the World*, 208–9.

78. Sudo, interview by Ozone.

79. Tanbara, "Memoirs," 30.

80. "Ju Jitsu Teacher Faces Hearing on Internment Today," *Minneapolis Star Journal*, April 13, 1942, 18:2; "Minneapolis Jap Is Given Hearing by Alien Board," *Minneapolis Morning Tribune*, April 14, 1942, 2; "Ju-Jitsu Teacher May Be Interned," *Minneapolis Star Journal*, April 14, 1942, 21:1.

81. Tanbara, "Memoirs," 31.

82. Johnson and Tosdal, "A Study of the Relocated Japanese-Americans." The testimonies quoted are excerpts, with minor modifications, from this report, which does not have page numbers.

83. Johnson and Tosdal, "A Study of the Relocated Japanese-Americans."

84. GICM, *The Oriental in Minnesota*, 62.

85. Tsuchida, *Reflections*, 22.

86. "White Supremacy," *Minneapolis Morning Tribune*, January 17, 1945, 4.

87. "White Supremacy."

88. Student quoted in *Newsletter 6*, September 24, 1943, Student letters, May 25 and 29, 1944, Thomas Bodine Collection, Hoover Institution Archives. Also see James, "Life Begins with Freedom," 164.

89. L. Kirihara, interview. The house-hunting story comes from this interview.

Notes to Chapter 3: Advocates and Agencies

Opening quote: Nason, interview by Smith. The subsequent quotations from Nason come from this interview unless stated otherwise.

1. Smith, interview. The subsequent quotations from Smith come from this interview unless stated otherwise.

2. Colwell, interview. For a biography of Nason, see Colwell, *Great Purpose.* Also Austin, "John Nason." Donald J. Cowling served as the third president of Carleton College for thirty-six years, from 1909 to 1945.

3. The Foreign Policy Association is dedicated to inspiring the American public to learn more about the world and informing "citizens to make great decisions." See the FPA website (https://www.fpa.org/) for more information. Under Nason's leadership, World Affairs Councils were established in many major American cities; the public was also encouraged to debate international issues under the association's "Great Decisions" discussion programs.

4. "In 1942 more than 28 percent of the evacuated population was 15–24 years old, compared to slightly more than 17 percent of youth in the same group for the entire US population. From the rising generation of Nisei almost four thousand boys and girls had attended twelfth grade in the 1941–42 school year before being evacuated." James, "Life Begins with Freedom," 157.

5. See Austin, *From Concentration Camp to Campus,* 18; Hall, "Japanese American College Students," 158.

6. O'Brien, *The College Nisei,* 62.

7. Austin's *From Concentration Camp to Campus* provides an excellent account of the council's work and the challenges it faced during the war. Three major conferences marked the beginnings of the Student Relocation Council. The first was held on March 21, 1942, at the YMCA of the University of California. The second one was in Cleveland in April, at the State Department Conference of Advisors of Foreign Students. The third meeting was in Chicago on May 29, when the committee was formed. Invited to attend were presidents or representatives of leading national institutions of higher education, representatives of the National YMCA and YWCA, churches, government agencies, the Japanese American Citizens League, and the American Friends Service Committee. O'Brien, *The College Nisei,* 60–63.

8. Austin, *From Concentration Camp to Campus,* 24; James, "Life Begins with Freedom," 158; Robinson, *A Tragedy of Democracy,* 181.

Individual efforts along the West Coast, such as those at the University of California and the University of Washington, managed to place 216 Japanese American students, the majority of them from the University of California and the University of Washington, by the end of March 1942. See Austin, *From Concentration Camp to Campus,* 14; Hall, "Japanese American College Students," 48.

Letter from Clarence Pickett, Executive Secretary, American Friends Service Committee, to Remsen Bird, May 15, 1942, Japanese American Relocation Collection, Occidental College Library, Occidental College. The Boxer Indemnity Scholarship

Program (*Gengzi* Indemnity Scholarship) was set up in 1908 by the administration of Theodore Roosevelt Jr. for students from China to be educated in the United States, funded by the excess payment from the Boxer Indemnity, which amounted to over $17 million. President Roosevelt recognized this program as a chance for "American-directed reform in China" (which was still under Imperial Qing dynastic rule) that could potentially improve US–China relations, bridging Chinese and American culture and promoting the United States' international image. For details of the program, see Michael H. Hunt, "The American Remission of the Boxer Indemnity: A Reappraisal," *Journal of Asian Studies* 31, no. 3 (May 1972): 539–59; Weili Ye, *Seeking Modernity in China's Name: Chinese Students in the United States, 1900–1927* (Palo Alto, CA: Stanford University Press, 2001).

9. "Information Concerning American Born Japanese Facing Evacuation," University of California and S.F. Bay District, March 1942, "Historical Council Material—Volume I," Box 3, NJASRC Records, Hoover Institution Archives. Cited in Hall, "Japanese American College Students," 51–52. College students were a relatively small proportion of the total 120,000 incarcerated Japanese Americans. According to Robert W. O'Brien, there were 3,530 Nikkei students enrolled in institutions of higher learning. The initial figures later proved to be seriously underestimated. See Chapter 1, note 5 for further resources.

10. Hall, "Japanese American College Students," 51–52. Most of the three thousand-plus Nisei students on the West Coast in the 1941–1942 academic year attended large state universities. Approximately five out of eight Japanese American college students attended one of the following institutions: University of California, Berkeley (485); University of Washington (458); Los Angeles City College (265); UCLA (244); Sacramento Junior College (224); San Francisco Junior College (145); Pasadena Junior College (123); University of Southern California (113); San Jose State College (111). See Hall, "Japanese American College Students," 52.

11. When asked to explain his rationale in light of lacking evidence of actual incidents of sabotage by Japanese Americans, DeWitt later told a congressional committee that "the very fact that no sabotage has taken place to date is a disturbing and confirming indication that such action will be taken." US CWRIC, *Personal Justice Denied*, 82. Also see Lee, *The Making of Asian America*, 217. For their rationale against Japanese American conscription, see Daniels, *Asian America*, 250.

12. University of Pennsylvania was an example. See Executive Board Minutes, May 8, 1942, Trustees Minutes, Vol. 24, June 1941–August 1947, Part I and Part II, UPA 1, University of Pennsylvania Archives, Philadelphia. Also see Hall, "Japanese American College Students," 147, 148.

13. W. C. Coffey to Robert M. Hutchins, March 18, 1942, President's Papers, University Archives, University of Minnesota (hereafter cited as University of

Minnesota Archives). Also see Hall, "Japanese American College Students," 152; Okihiro, *Storied Lives*, 31. The Big Ten was made up of Illinois, Indiana, Iowa, Northwestern, Ohio State, Minnesota, Michigan, Michigan State, Purdue, and Wisconsin universities.

14. A. C. Willard to Coffey, March 20, 1942, President's Papers, University of Minnesota Archives. Also see Okihiro, *Storied Lives*, 31.

15. C. A. Dykstra to Coffey, April 2, 1942, President's Papers, University of Minnesota Archives. Also see Okihiro, *Storied Lives*, 34. Indiana University's Board of Trustees, led by Ora L. Wildermuth, decided to ban Japanese Americans from their campus. The president, Herman B Wells, and other administrators claimed the limitations on out-of-state students and military necessity as their reasons. See Langowski, "Education Denied." Also see "Japanese Students 1941–42," Herman B Wells Papers, Indiana University Archives, Bloomington. Likewise, on March 30, 1942, the executive committee of Purdue University passed a resolution that forbade Nisei students from admission. Purdue President Vivian Peterson argued that the school had already donated to the World Student Service Fund (WSSF) and was therefore indirectly assisting the cause. Purdue did not accept any Japanese American students throughout the war, even after the government lifted all restrictions. A professor of chemistry, Vivian Peterson wrote a letter to the YWCA, stating: "to quote the assistant to the president, 'We take care of our own Japs, let others take care of theirs.'" See Hans H. Jaffé to Howard Beale, October 2, 1942; and Vivian Peterson to Alice James, YWCA, Berkeley, April 21, 1942—both "Purdue University," Box 26, NJASRC Records, Hoover Institution Archives. Also see Hall, "Japanese American College Students," 152–54.

16. Hall, "Japanese American College Students," 152. Coffey, for example, was criticized for supporting the creation of the International House at the University of Minnesota in 1942, "a misnamed residence that was to exclusively house African American men in order to keep dormitories segregated." See "Walter Coffey," A Campus Divided: Documents, http://acampusdivided.umn.edu/index.php/person/walter-coffey/; "African Americans in Housing," History of the University of Minnesota in 9 Episodes, https://hist1913.umn.edu/1918-1940/african-americans-housing.

17. Okihiro, *Storied Lives*, 34. Coffey to Fred J. Kelly, April 8, 1942, President's Papers, University of Minnesota Archives.

18. *Minnesota Alumni Weekly*, June 6, 1942, "Japanese Students 1941–42," Herman B Wells Papers, Indiana University Archives. Also see Hall, "Japanese American College Students," 150, 152–53.

19. Brumbaugh to All Deans & Department Chairs, June 11, 1942, "WRA: Re: Admission of Japanese Students," Box 38, Social Sciences Division Records,

University of Chicago Library. Also see Hall, "Japanese American College Students," 150–51.

20. "Coffey Asks Jap Student Plan for 'U,'" *Minneapolis Morning Tribune*, June 2, 1942, 5; "Jap Student Plan Urged," *Minneapolis Star Journal*, June 2, 1942, 18:1. See Faster, "Newspaper Coverage," 68; "Colleges to Accept Japs Born in U.S.," *Minneapolis Star Journal*, September 17, 1942, 17.

21. Austin, *From Concentration Camp to Campus*, 27. International Student Service Executive Committee Meeting, May 20, 1942, Box 2068, Series 130, News Items, Eleanor Roosevelt Papers, Franklin D. Roosevelt Library. Also see Austin, *From Concentration Camp to Campus*, 32, 33. Provinse to Eisenhower, memo, June 5, 1942, 64.501, #1, 4–12/42; List of Persons Invited to Japanese Student Relocation Meeting Held on May 29, 1942, Chicago, Illinois, n.d., 64.501, 4–12/42; and List of Persons Who Attended the Japanese Student Relocation Meeting, Chicago, May 29, 1942, n.d., 64.501, 4–12/42—all Subject–Classified General Files, Headquarters, Records of the WRA, RG 210, National Archives. Hall, "Japanese American College Students," 167; O'Brien, *The College Nisei*, 62.

22. Dillon Myer, Press Conference, May 14, 1943, Public Statements by Director, reel 21, 33, WRA Papers, Japanese Evacuation Research Study, Bancroft Library, University of California, Berkeley; Robinson, *A Tragedy of Democracy*, 181.

23. Robinson, *A Tragedy of Democracy*, 181; Provinse to Eisenhower, memo, June 5, 1942; Austin, *From Concentration Camp to Campus*, 34. Also see Hall, "Japanese American College Students," 133.

24. Myer quoted in O'Brien, *The College Nisei*, 60. Also see Myer, *Uprooted Americans*. Austin, *From Concentration Camp to Campus*, 3; Robinson, *A Tragedy of Democracy*, 181.

25. Digest of Points Presented by Those Attending the Conference Called in Chicago for the Consideration of the Problems Connected with Relocation of the American-Born Japanese Students Who Have Been Evacuated from Pacific Coast Colleges and Universities, May 29, 1942, Barstow file, NJASRC Records, Hoover Institution Archives; Austin, *From Concentration Camp to Campus*, 34; Hall, "Japanese American College Students," 108–10; Robinson, *A Tragedy of Democracy*, 181.

26. Schauffler to Morris, Conard, Henley, Rhoades, and O'Brien, July 17, 1942, Committees and Organizations: NJASRC, Japanese-American Relocation, SIS, 1942, American Friends Service Committee Archives; Austin, *From Concentration Camp to Campus*, 51.

27. Austin, "John Nason."

28. Austin, *From Concentration Camp to Campus*, 29; Galen M. Fisher, "What Race Baiting Costs America," *Christian Century* 60 (September 8, 1943): 1009–11; James, "Life Begins with Freedom," 163. The quotes came from an editorial in the

National Legionnaire, which was cited in its entirety by Rep. Paul W. Shafer of Michigan in the Congressional Record, 78th Cong., 1st Sess., Vol. 89, Part 9, Appendix, p. A358.

29. James, "Life Begins with Freedom," 164. The best-known case was the University of Southern California's dental school, where its dean Lewis E. Ford, with the support of university president Rufus B. von KleinSmid, refused to release the transcripts of their own Nisei students. Only after repeated "sharp" exchanges with the council did the dental school send out the records, yet without granting the students' credits. Ford allegedly insisted that an incarcerated student was "equivalent to a prisoner of war," and that giving any sort of aid would "be considered as assisting him in evasion of government regulations." See Mikey Hirano Culross, "A Degree of Frustration," *Rafu Shimpo,* April 17, 2012, https://rafu.com/2012/04/a-degree-of-frustration/.

30. Austin, *From Concentration Camp to Campus,* 105; "Report of the Field Director, September 29, 1943," NJASRC–Hoover Library. Memorandum from Thomas Bodine to John W. Nason, November 7, 1943, Thomas Bodine Collection, Hoover Institution Archives; James, "Life Begins with Freedom," 167.

31. Executive Committee Minutes, May 10, 1944, Minutes, 1942–46, Box 87; and Letter to College Representatives on Council, May 1944, Box 89—both NJASRC Records, Hoover Institution Archives. Also see Austin, *From Concentration Camp to Campus,* 105.

32. John Nason, "To the Editor," February 18, 1944, John W. Nason Collection, Box 21, NJASRC correspondence; and Nason to Provinse, July 31, 1943, WRA–DC, 6/1/43–8/31/43, Box 25, NJASRC Records—both Hoover Institution Archives.

33. "N.S.R.C.: Its Purpose and Functions," May 27, 1943, Historical Council Material (II), Box 10, NJASRC Records, Hoover Institution Archives; Austin, *From Concentration Camp to Campus,* 70, 96; James, "Life Begins with Freedom," 161.

34. Nason to Myer, October 5, 1943, 64.502, #1, Subject–Classified General Files, Headquarters, Records of the WRA, RG 210, National Archives. Austin, *From Concentration Camp to Campus,* 99–100; Nason, "To the Editor."

35. Council Minutes, September 14, 1945, Minutes of Council Meetings; Executive Committee Minutes, December 19, 1945, Minutes, 1942–46; and Council Minutes, February 26, 1946, Minutes of Council Meetings—all Box 87, NJASRC Records, Hoover Institution Archives; Student Relocation Newssheet, March 1, 1946, 64.508A, #1, Subject–Classified General Files, Headquarters, Records of the WRA, RG 210, National Archives. Also see Austin, *From Concentration Camp to Campus,* 139.

36. Nason to Mai, February 24, 1944, John W. Nason Collection, Box 21, NJASRC correspondence, Hoover Institution Archives.

37. Hall, "Japanese American College Students," 153.

38. Willey to Robbins W. Barstow, September 1, 1942; and Barstow to Willey, September 5, 1942—both NJASRC Records, Box 71, Vol. I, University of Minnesota Folder, Hoover Institution Archives.

39. Coffey wrote: "We have much hoped that there would be some definite policy formulated by a responsible federal agency that would serve to guide the educational institutions with respect to the acceptance of these students." Coffey to Henry L. Stimson, September 30, 1942, President's Papers, University of Minnesota Archives; Okihiro, *Storied Lives*, 86.

John J. McCloy to Coffey, October 6, 1942; John H. Provinse to Coffey, October 9, 1942 (WRA response); and James Forrestal to Coffey, October 12, 1942—all President's Papers, University of Minnesota Archives. Also see Okihiro, *Storied Lives*, 86.

40. Okihiro, *Storied Lives*, 86, 87; Malcolm M. Willey to Coffey, October 15, 1942, President's Papers, University of Minnesota Archives.

41. Provinse to Fryer, Colleges Approved by War Department, October 31, 1942, NJASRC Records, Box 71, Vol. I, University of Minnesota Folder, Hoover Institution Archives.

42. T. E. Pettengill to Carlisle V. Hibbard, February 26, 1944; and Willey to W. Emlen, May 11, 1943—both NJASRC Records, Box 71, Vol. I, University of Minnesota Folder, Hoover Institution Archives; Willey to Provinse, October 22, 1942; Howard K. Beale to Coffey, November 22, 1942; Beale to Willey, November 22, 1942; Willey to Beale, December 1, 1942; and Beale to Willey, December 9, 1942—all President's Papers, University of Minnesota Archives.

43. Peterson to Student Relocation, November 19, 1942; Beale to Peterson, November 22, 1942; Reichard to AFSC, November 27, 1942; and Pettengill to Hibbard, February 26, 1944 —all NJASRC Records, Box 71, Vol. I, University of Minnesota Folder, Hoover Institution Archives.

44. Coffey to Forrestal, June 3, 1943, President's Papers, University of Minnesota Archives; Okihiro, *Storied Lives*, 87.

45. Forrestal to Coffey, June 14, 1943, President's Papers, University of Minnesota Archives; Okihiro, *Storied Lives*, 87.

46. Austin, *From Concentration Camp to Campus*, 74; Hibbard to Myer, June 23, 1943, WRA–DC, 6/1/43–8/31/43, Box 25, NJASRC Records, Hoover Institution Archives.

47. Nason to Provinse, July 31, 1943, WRA–DC, 6/1/43–8/31/43, Box 25, NJASRC Records, Hoover Institution Archives; Austin, *From Concentration Camp to Campus*, 76. See note 50 for Nason's response to the crisis. Coffey to Willey, June 19, 1943, President's Papers, University of Minnesota Archives; Okihiro, *Storied Lives*, 87.

48. Leeds Gulick (Director of Japanese Studies at the University of Chicago) to Hibbard, October 14, 1943, "The University of Chicago," Box 19, NJASRC Records, Hoover Institution Archives; King to Nason, June 4, 1943, "Navy," 16.382/64.505, #1, Records of the WRA, RG 210, National Archives; Hall, "Japanese American College Students," 190.

49. Daniels, *Asian America*, 247; Hall, "Japanese American College Students," 190–91; Petersen, *Japanese Americans*, 84.

50. The University of Minnesota also taught Japanese to members of the military. Most of the instructors were Nisei "of proven loyalty to this country." See James M. Sutherland, "Army Gives Public a Peek at Specialized 'U' Training," *Minneapolis Star Journal*, December 15, 1943, 21:1. Also see "'U' Center Will Resume Courses," *Minneapolis Star Journal*, January 13, 1944, 13:5; and "'U' Linguist Troop to Go to Japan," *Minneapolis Star Journal*, August 17, 1945, 9:1.

Okihiro, *Storied Lives*, 88; Willey to Commanding General, Seventh Service Command, November 4, 1943; and Rex A. Ramsay to Willey, April 1944—both President's Papers, University of Minnesota Archives.

51. Okihiro, *Storied Lives*, 88; Coffey to Pettengill, December 1, 1943, President's Papers, University of Minnesota Archives. The Law School seemed to have opened its doors earlier, in August 1943; however, the documents show some confusion regarding actual admitted and attending students. See Chuman to King, telegram, August 14, 1943, NJASRC Records, Box 71, Vol. I, University of Minnesota Folder, Hoover Institution Archives.

W. Emlen to Pettengill, December 21, 1943, NJASRC Records, Box 71, Vol. I, University of Minnesota Folder, Hoover Institution Archives.

52. Graybill to George B. Risty, June 18, 1946; and Risty to Graybill, June 15, 1946—both NJASRC Records, Box 71, Vol. III, University of Minnesota Folder, Hoover Institution Archives.

53. E. Emlen to Pettengill, December 6, 1944, NJASRC Records, Box 71, Vol. III, University of Minnesota Folder, Hoover Institution Archives.

54. See "Risty Quotation," June 8, 1944; E. Emlen to Risty, May 31, 1945; Risty to E. Emlen, June 8, 1945; Smyth to Risty, June 13, 1945; "Distribution of Scholarship Assistance Obtained for Nisei Students Attending the University of Minnesota by Source of Funds, College of Registration and Amount," June 7, 1946; Risty to Graybill, June 7, 1946—all NJASRC Records, Box 71, Vol. III, University of Minnesota Folder, Hoover Institution Archives.

55. Nason, interview by Okihiro.

Notes to Chapter 4: Ambassadors and Adversaries

Opening quote: Suzuki, "Memoirs," 101.

1. Suzuki, "Memoirs," 104.

2. Rosenberg, interview. The subsequent quotations from Rosenberg come from this interview.

3. Suzuki, "Memoirs," 126.

4. Suzuki, "Memoirs," 103–4.

5. James, "Life Begins with Freedom," 161; Nason, "To the Editor."

6. Suzuki, "Memoirs," 99.

7. Regarding funds raised for scholarships at Topaz, see *Newsletter* 6 (August 5, 1943): 2, in NJASRC Records, Hoover Institution Archives. The newsletter was prepared by NJASRC staff for student counselors in the camps. Letter from Thomas Bodine to Joseph S. Daltry, May 24, 1942, Thomas Bodine Collection, Hoover Institution Archives. Also see James, "Life Begins with Freedom," 159–60.

Eisenhower to Fryer, June 16, 1942, "U.S. Government—War Time Civil Control Administration," Box 7, NJASRC Records, Hoover Institution Archives. See Hall, "Japanese American College Students," 132; Nason to Bodine, N.S.R.C.: Its Purpose and Functions, January 13, 1943, Committees and Organizations: NJSRC-Philadelphia, Japanese-American Relocation, SIS, 1943, American Friends Service Committee Archives; Pickett to Ackerman, May 19, 1942, A-General Correspondence, Box 1, NJASRC Records, Hoover Institution Archives. Also see Austin, *From Concentration Camp to Campus*, 43.

8. Hall, "Japanese American College Students," 195–96.

9. Hall, "Japanese American College Students," 196; Robbins W. Barstow, "Japanese American Student Relocation," August 25, 1942, "Release by Barstow 8/25/42," Box 29, NJASRC Records, Hoover Institution Archives. For a synopsis of this process of student evaluation, see Cosgrave, "Relocation of Japanese American Students," 221–26. Also see Okihiro, *Storied Lives*, 39.

10. Digest of Points Presented by Those Attending the Conference Called in Chicago for the Consideration of the Problems Connected with Relocation of the American-Born Japanese Students Who Have Been Evacuated from Pacific Coast Colleges and Universities, May 29, 1942, NJASRC Records, Barstow file, Hoover Institution Archives. Also see Okihiro, *Storied Lives*, 38. "Procedure for Analysis of Student Qualifications," n.d. [stamped August 10, 1942], NJASRC, Box 35, file "Pacific Coast Branch, Japanese Situation," Hoover Institution Archives. Also see Austin, *From Concentration Camp to Campus*, 42.

Their recommendations appear to have been summarized in a document attributed to Joseph Conard, entitled "Procedure for Analysis of Student Qualifications," as his "suggestions to raters." The document stated: "We recommend that every student whose application is analyzed be given a 'rating' according to each of two types of promise, 'scholarship' and 'personal factors,' and that in addition to these two figures, there should be a composite rating which combines them." Okihiro, *Storied Lives*, 39.

11. "Students Bear a Great Burden," *Santa Anita Pacemaker,* July 11, 1942, 4; Austin, *From Concentration Camp to Campus,* 3.

12. Austin, *From Concentration Camp to Campus,* 3, 35; Digest of Points Presented by Those Attending the Conference Called in Chicago for the Consideration of the Problems Connected with Relocation of the American-Born Japanese Students Who Have Been Evacuated from Pacific Coast Colleges and Universities, May 29, 1942, NJASRC Records, Barstow file, Hoover Institution Archives. Also see Hall, "Japanese American College Students," 111; O'Brien, *The College Nisei,* 62–63; Okihiro, *Storied Lives,* 38; Provinse to Eisenhower, memo, June 5, 1942.

13. Hall, "Japanese American College Students," 198; NJASRC, "Progress Report," October 1, 1942, NJASRC, Box 36, file "Pacific Coast Branch, Japanese Situation," Hoover Institution Archives, and the pamphlet written by Thomas R. Bodine, *From Camp to College: The Story of Japanese American Student Relocation* (Philadelphia: National Japanese American Student Relocation Council, n.d.). Compare NJASRC, "Brief Report of Progress," December 24, 1942, NJASRC, Box 35, file "Pacific Coast Branch, Japanese Situation," Hoover Institution Archives, November and December 1942, 55; the box file states that 800 had been accepted and 334 attended college that fall. Also see Okihiro, *Storied Lives,* 42.

14. Okihiro, *Storied Lives,* 41.

15. Okihiro, *Storied Lives,* 41; Robbins W. Barstow to Joseph Conard, July 16, 1942, NJASRC, Box 38, file "Dr. Barstow—Philadelphia Office," Hoover Institution Archives.

16. W. Balderston to Nason, "Colorado River War Relocation Project Poston Arizona," February 12, 1943, John W. Nason Collection, Box 21, NJASRC correspondence, Hoover Institution Archives; Barstow to Conard. Also see Okihiro, *Storied Lives,* 41.

17. NJASRC, "Progress Report."

18. Okihiro, *Storied Lives,* 40; NJASRC, "Procedure Concerning Community Acceptance," July 24, 1942, NJASRC, Box 35, file "Pacific Coast Branch, Japanese Situation," Hoover Institution Archives.

19. NJASRC, "Brief Report of Progress," December 24, 1942, NJASRC, Box 35, file "Pacific Coast Branch, Japanese Situation," Hoover Institution Archives; Barstow to Ruth T. Forsyth (Secretary to the President, Oberlin), August 20, 1942, NJASRC, Box 75, Oberlin File, Hoover Institution Archives. Also see Austin, *From Concentration Camp to Campus,* 58.

20. King to Ogata, July 20, 1943, NJASRC Records, Box 53, Ancker Hospital Folder, Hoover Institution Archives.

21. Suzuki, "Memoirs," 104.

22. *The Mac Weekly,* December 10, 1943, Macalester College Library.

23. George Lindbeck to Barstow, August 24, 1942, NJASRC Records, Box 64, Gustavus Adolphus College Folder, Hoover Institution Archives.

24. *The Mac Weekly*, December 3, 1943; November 10, 1944, Macalester College Library.

25. *The Mac Weekly*, March 24, 1944; October 1 and October 22, 1943; April 20, 1945, Macalester College Library.

26. Suzuki, "The Good Lives On," 23.

27. Oliver, interview.

28. Oliver, interview.

29. Suzuki, "Memoirs," 105, 123–24; Suzuki, "The Good Lives On," 22.

30. *The Mac Weekly*, November 5, November 12, December 3, 1943; and January 14, February 11, February 25, March 3, March 24, 1944, Macalester College Library.

31. Suzuki, "Memoirs," 112, 123–24.

32. Jon Halvorsen, "Esther Torii Suzuki '46," in *Macalester Today* (November 1999): 22.

33. Halvorsen, "Esther Torii Suzuki," 22.

34. Suzuki, "Memoirs," 122; Frank Joseph, "Esther Suzuki Will Be Missed," *Asian Pages* (January 14, 2000): 3.

35. Halvorsen, "Esther Torii Suzuki," 21; Suzuki, "Memoirs," 106; Joseph, "Esther Suzuki," 3. Also see Okihiro, *Storied Lives*, 62–63.

36. David Mura and Esther Torii Suzuki, *Internment Voices*, Theater Mu at Intermedia Arts, South Minneapolis, June 4–21, 1998.

37. *The Echo Newspaper*, March 24, 1944, Augsburg University Archives, Augsburg University.

38. Christensen to Myer, July 23, 1943; and Bodine to Fredrik A. Schiotz, September 19, 1942—both NJASRC Records, Box 54, Augsburg College Folder, Hoover Institution Archives. The three individuals eventually chose the University of Nebraska–Lincoln (UNL) over attending Augsburg. On the UNL's list of Nisei students, their names are spelled slightly differently compared to the letter from Bodine. See "Nisei Experience at UNL," Archives of the University of Nebraska–Lincoln, https://archives-spec.unl.edu/nisei/nisei-experience-at-unl.

39. Quanbeck to Hibbard, November 1, 1943; and Beale to Quanbeck, May 11, 1943—both NJASRC Records, Box 54, Augsburg College Folder, Hoover Institution Archives.

40. Seto, interview. The subsequent quotations from Seto come from this interview.

41. *The Echo Newspaper*, March 24, April 21, May 19, October 26, November 22, December 13, 1944; and March 2, April 27, May 28, 1945, Augsburg University Archives, Augsburg University.

42. *The Echo Newspaper*, March 24, 1944. There was a third accepted student, George K. Kawaguchi from Minidoka, on record for fall 1943. However, he was unable to attend because of financial reasons. See George K. Kawaguchi index card, NJASRC Records, Box 117, Student Name Index Cards Ho-Ka, Hoover Institution Archives. Quanbeck to NJASRC, October 1, 1943, NJASRC Records, Box 54, Augsburg College Folder, Hoover Institution Archives.

43. *The Echo Newspaper*, March 24, 1944; Permit Dept. to Oshida, March 25, 1944, NJASRC Records, Box 71, Vol. II, University of Minnesota Folder, Hoover Institution Archives.

44. NJASRC Questionnaire for Colleges—Gustavus Adolphus College; and Donald Wilson to NJASRC Eastern Branch, August 31, 1942—both NJASRC Records, Box 64, Gustavus Adolphus College Folder, Hoover Institution Archives.

45. Lindbeck to Barstow, August 24, 1942, NJASRC Records, Box 64, Gustavus Adolphus College Folder, Hoover Institution Archives.

46. Barstow to Lindbeck, August 31, 1942; and Barstow to Wilson, September 2, 1942—both NJASRC Records, Box 64, Gustavus Adolphus College Folder, Hoover Institution Archives.

47. Walter A. Lunden to Barstow, September 18, 1942; and Curtis to Barstow, September 14, 1942—both NJASRC Records, Box 64, Gustavus Adolphus College Folder, Hoover Institution Archives.

48. Wilcher to Lunden, January 14, 1943; and Kirchhoefer to O'Brien, February 26, 1943—both NJASRC Records, Box 64, Gustavus Adolphus College Folder, Hoover Institution Archives.

49. Kirchhoefer to W. Emlen, July 31, 1943; and Hall to Kirchhoefer, August 10, 1943—both NJASRC Records, Box 64, Gustavus Adolphus College Folder, Hoover Institution Archives.

50. King to Kirchhoefer, January 4, 1944, NJASRC Records, Box 64, Gustavus Adolphus College Folder, Hoover Institution Archives.

51. Harry to E. Emlen, December 23, 1944, NJASRC Records, Box 64, Gustavus Adolphus College Folder, Hoover Institution Archives; *Gustavian Weekly*, December 22, 1943; June 14, 1944, Gustavus Adolphus College Archives, Gustavus Adolphus College.

52. Schiotz to J. Jörgen Thompson, August 24, 1942, St. Olaf Archives, St. Olaf College.

53. Thompson to Lindbeck, August 27, 1942; Thompson to Thorlaksson, October 6, 1942; Schiotz to Thompson, September 2, 1942; and Myer (WRA) to Boe, November 9, 1942—all St. Olaf Archives, St. Olaf College.

54. Schiotz to Thompson, October 3, 1942, St. Olaf Archives, St. Olaf College.

55. Thompson to Thorlaksson, October 6, 1942, St. Olaf Archives, St. Olaf College.

56. It was a poignant moment and poetic justice that in 1992 Hayano was invited back by her high school's senior class to march in their graduation ceremony and walked up to receive her diploma to a standing ovation. Semba, too, enjoyed a similar and surprising reception in 2021, seventy-seven years later, when her son took her back for a visit. Kera Wanielista, "77 Years Later, Mount Vernon High School Student Receives Diploma," *Go Skagit*, May 3, 2021, https://www.goskagit.com/news/education/77-years-later-mount-vernon-high-school-student-receives-diploma/article_1bf2d3fc-1977-5d39-880a-5a478034c0f9.html.

57. Scardigli to Bly, December 1, 1942; Bodine to Bly, January 14, 1943; and Bly to Beale, June 15, 1943—all NJASRC Records, Box 79, St. Olaf College Folder, Hoover Institution Archives.

58. Hilleboe to E. Emlen, March 16, 1944, NJASRC Records, Box 79, St. Olaf College Folder, Hoover Institution Archives.

59. Bly to NJASRC, July 25, 1944; Swan to Paul, July 28, 1944; and Paul to Swan, August 1, 1944—all NJASRC Records, Box 79, St. Olaf College Folder, Hoover Institution Archives. Joseph M. Shaw, *History of St. Olaf College, 1874–1974* (Northfield: St. Olaf College Press, 1974).

60. Hayano to L. D. Stiefel, October 7, 1943, Mary Hayano, St. Olaf College, Box 2, Minnesota Historical Society.

61. Hayano to Stiefel, September 13, 1943, Mary Hayano, St. Olaf College, Box 2, Minnesota Historical Society; Executive Board Minutes, May 8, 1942, Trustees Minutes, Vol. 24, June 1941–August 1947, Part I and Part II, UPA 1, University of Pennsylvania Archives; Hall, "Japanese American College Students," 147.

62. St. Olaf Chapel Sermon by Evelyn Zakarison, March 4, 1944, St. Olaf Archives, St. Olaf College.

63. Adjusted for inflation, $100 in the 1940s is equal to about $2,200 in 2020s. Annual inflation over this period was 3.75 percent. Harry to E. Emlen, May 9, 1944; Nason to Bly, October 24, 1944; and E. Emlen to Gertrude Hilleboe, January 29, 1944—all NJASRC Records, Box 79, St. Olaf College Folder, Hoover Institution Archives.

64. Hilleboe to E. Emlen, April 18, 1944, NJASRC Records, Box 79, St. Olaf College Folder, Hoover Institution Archives.

65. Hilleboe to E. Emlen, December 16, 1943, NJASRC Records, Box 79, St. Olaf College Folder, Hoover Institution Archives.

66. Hayano to Stiefel, October 31, 1943, Mary Hayano, St. Olaf College, Box 2, Minnesota Historical Society. More about her brother, Joseph Torao Hayano, can be found in Chapter Eight.

67. Hilleboe to E. Emlen, April 18, 1944, NJASRC Records, Box 79, St. Olaf College Folder, Hoover Institution Archives.

68. Hayano to Stiefel, September 13, 1943, Mary Hayano, St. Olaf College, Box 2, Minnesota Historical Society.

69. Hilleboe to E. Emlen, March 16, 1944, NJASRC Records, Box 79, St. Olaf College Folder, Hoover Institution Archives.

70. Hilleboe to E. Emlen, April 18, 1944; Graybill to Hilleboe, September 11, 1946; and Beldin (E. Emlen) to Hilleboe, August 14, 1944—all NJASRC Records, Box 79, St. Olaf College Folder, Hoover Institution Archives. 1945 St. Olaf College Viking Yearbook and 1946 St. Olaf College Viking Yearbook, St. Olaf College Archives and Special Collections.

71. Bly to Takasugi, May 28, 1946, NJASRC Records, Box 79, St. Olaf College Folder, Hoover Institution Archives.

72. Hilleboe to E. Emlen, March 16, 1944; and Hilleboe to Graybill, May 18, 1946—both NJASRC Records, Box 79, St. Olaf College Folder, Hoover Institution Archives.

73. Hvistendahl, "Yosh Murakami," 43.

74. Hvistendahl, "Yosh Murakami," 43, 44.

75. Lee, "Director Yosh's Parents."

76. Conard to Director of Carleton, August 26, 1942, NJASRC Records, Box 56, Carleton College Folder, Hoover Institution Archives.

77. Donald J. Cowling to Barstow, June 26, 1942; and NJASRC Questionnaire for Colleges—Carleton College, August 5, 1942—both NJASRC Records, Box 56, Carleton College Folder, Hoover Institution Archives.

78. Barstow to Cowling, June 30, 1942; Crandall to Barstow, July 29, 1942; Barstow to Cowling, August 5, 1942; and Conard to Director of Carleton, August 26, 1942—all NJASRC Records, Box 56, Carleton College Folder, Hoover Institution Archives.

79. Robert E. Allen to O'Brien, March 24, 1943, NJASRC Records, Box 56, Carleton College Folder, Hoover Institution Archives.

80. Allen to Hibbard, April 7, 1943, NJASRC Records, Box 56, Carleton College Folder, Hoover Institution Archives.

81. Allen to E. Emlen, July 7, 1943, NJASRC Records, Box 56, Carleton College Folder, Hoover Institution Archives.

82. Mildred D. Babcock to Lindsey Blayney, March 27, 1943, Carleton Library Archives, Carleton College.

83. Blayney to Richard L. Koselka, January 13, 1945; and Blayney to Williamson, February 23, 1945—both Carleton Library Archives, Carleton College.

84. Comments on Japanese American Students, ca. August 1944, NJASRC Records, Box 56, Carleton College Folder, Hoover Institution Archives.

85. Murata talks about his wartime experience in America in one of his books. See Kiyoaki Murata, *An Enemy Among Friends* (Tokyo: Kodansha International, 1991).

86. The Shigemura story presented in this segment is greatly informed by two articles that were published in 1950: George Grim, "A College, a Solider, a Gift—and a Surprise Ending," *Minneapolis Sunday Tribune*, May 7, 1950; "We Deeply Feel Honored," Newspaper Human-Interest Award of the Month, *Reader's Digest*, September 1950.

87. Blayney to the Adjutant General of the Army, n.d./ca. 1944, Carleton Library Archives, Carleton College.

88. For the history of the "Lost Battalion," see Abbie Grubb, "Rescue of the Lost Battalion," Densho Encyclopedia, last modified October 16, 2020, https://encyclo pedia.densho.org/Rescue_of_the_Lost_Battalion/.

89. *Carletonian*, September 23, 1950, 3, Carleton Library Archives, Carleton College.

90. Grim, "A College, a Solider, a Gift"; "We Deeply Feel Honored."

91. "The Shigemuras visited Carleton over Thanksgiving in 1951, when they met the first scholarship recipient, Annie (Kaneshiro) Yamada '52, the daughter of a Japanese farmer in Hawai'i. 'They were very courteous, dignified, and quiet,' recalls Yamada, now a retired counselor living in Hawai'i. 'They were so grateful to Carleton, and I was humbled by the whole thing.'" Cornell, "Honor Bound," 36–37.

92. Cornell, "Honor Bound," 36, 37; Fred Hagstrom, *Deeply Honored* (St. Paul: Strong Silent Type Press, 2010).

93. Hvistendahl, "Yosh Murakami," 43.

Notes to Chapter 5: Courage and Combat

Opening quote: P. Doi, interview.

1. Normandale Japanese Garden was built by the Bloomington Affiliated Garden Clubs, led by Bunnie Aaze and Yvonne Bublitz, among others. The concept and design of the garden was by chief architect Takao Watanabe, a professional garden architect from Tokyo. The founding members of the Normandale Japanese Garden Committee formed in June 1980 were Bunnie Aaze, Kaye Blatz, Yvonne Bublitz, Chester Fujino, Kimi Hara, Dale Lorenz, Mary Ness, Sandra Schley, Sondra Simonson, May Tanaka, and Frank Yanari. The history of the garden can be found in Kenney, *Normandale Japanese Garden*.

2. Nakatsu, "The Nisei Soldiers," 76.

3. Mashbir, *I Was an American Spy*, 242; MacArthur quoted in Charles Hillinger, "Secret Weapon: Japanese-American Soldiers Saved Time and Lives in World

War II," *Tampa Tribune-Times*, July 15, 1982; Nakamura, "They Are Our Human Secret Weapons," 54.

4. McNaughton, "Nisei Linguists and New Perspectives"; City of Savage, "History: World War II Camp Savage," last modified December 20, 2022, https://www .cityofsavage.com/our-city/about-savage/history#ad-image-1.

Former structures of the MISLS, such as its headquarters (Building 57), the infantry barrack that once housed the classrooms and the library (Buildings 101, 102, 103), and gymnasium (Service Club) still stand today, although they are all empty buildings, boarded off and inaccessible for visitors. Others, like the "Turkey Farm," the baseball stadium and athletic fields, and the hospital ward, no longer exist. For a more detailed and descriptive tour of the MISLS at Fort Snelling, see Minnesota Historical Society, "Military Intelligence Service Language School Tour: Nisei Linguists at Fort Snelling," July 2020, https://www.youtube.com/watch?v=SMaYsz BpyC8. The quote is from Kimmy Tanaka, Site Supervisor of Historic Fort Snelling, in this video. Collaborating with the Twin Cities Japanese American Citizens League, the University of Minnesota offers a virtual tour of one of the barrack buildings (103) through a digital project, https://historyxr.umn.edu/projects/vir tual-misls.

5. Nakatsu, "The Nisei Soldiers," 77. Harry Truman reportedly called the Nisei linguists "our human secret weapons." Charles Hellinger, "The Secrets Come Out for Nisei Soldiers: Japanese-American Role in Military Intelligence Service Finally Told," *Los Angeles Times*, July 20, 1982, V, 1.

6. Nakatsu, "The Nisei Soldiers," 76. See the National WWII Museum New Orleans, "American Indian Code Talkers," https://www.nationalww2museum.org/ war/articles/american-indian-code-talkers. Also see Chester Nez and Judith Schiess Avila, *Code Talker: The First and Only Memoir by One of the Original Navajo Code Talkers of WWII* (New York: Berkely Caliber, 2011); Smithsonian, National Museum of the American Indian, *Native Words, Native Warriors*, https://ameri canindian.si.edu/nk360/code-talkers/.

7. Nakamura, "They Are Our Human Secret Weapons," 55.

8. Roy Uyehata, a 1942 graduate of MISLS at Camp Savage, compiled a list of 102 units in which the linguists served during World War II. Also see Japanese American Veterans Association, "Background of the Presidential Unit Citation for MIS," www.javadc.org/background_of_the_presidential_u.htm.

Nakatsu, "The Nisei Soldiers," 77. For example, in the process of connecting with the Veterans Administration early in 2018 to seek available services for her MIS veteran father, Shunso Frank Watanabe, Alysa Sakkas discovered that Watanabe's Army personnel records had been destroyed in a 1978 fire. See "MIS Veteran Posthumously Receives Congressional Gold Medal," *Pacific Citizen*, September 13,

2019, https://www.pacificcitizen.org/mis-veteran-posthumously-receives-congres
sional-gold-medal/.

9. Sterner, *Go for Broke*, 125; Takemae, *Inside GHQ*, 21.

10. Nakatsu, "The Nisei Soldiers," 77.

11. Since the 1970s, many accounts of the MIS have greatly informed the public about its little-known history. They also provide valuable sources for this chapter. The first important book was Harrington's *Yankee Samurai*, in which the term "Yankee Samurai" for the MIS veterans was coined. Coming nearly three decades later, McNaughton's *Nisei Linguists* was another seminal work that details the exploits of the military intelligence soldiers. Moreover, the MIS stories can be found in books compiled by the alumni themselves, such as *John Aiso and the M.I.S.*, edited by Ichinokuchi and Aiso, and Ishimaru's *Military Intelligence Service Language School*. Documentaries, too, feature the insights of the veterans and scholars in interviews, such as *Honor and Sacrifice: The Roy Matsumoto Story* (Stourwater Pictures 2013) and *Proof of Loyalty: Kazuo Yamane and the Nisei Soldiers of Hawai'i* (Stourwater Pictures, 2017), both directed by Lucy Ostrander and Don Sellers; *MIS: Human Secret Weapon*, directed by Junichi Suzuki (UTB, 2012); *The Registry*, directed by Bill Kubota and Steve Ozone (PBS, 2020); *Uncommon Courage: Patriotism and Civil Liberties*, directed by gayle yamada (Bridge Media, 2001); and *Armed with Language*, directed by Katie O'Rourke (TPT, 2021). Finally, digital databases and archives provide easily accessible sources for the public, including Densho Encyclopedia, Go for Broke National Education Center, Minnesota Historical Society, and Veterans History Project from the Library of Congress.

12. See Jesse Lee, "An Awe-Inspiring Chapter of America's History," The White House: President Barack Obama, October 5, 2010, https://obamawhitehouse.ar chives.gov/blog/2010/10/05/awe-inspiring-chapter-americas-history. Also see Congressional Record, Vol. 156, Issue 129, September 23, 2010.

13. McNaughton, *Nisei Linguists*, 27. The two Caucasians selected for the first class were Dempster Dirks and Victor V. Belousoff (who later changed his name to Bell). Both had lived in Japan for a time and spoke some colloquial Japanese. McNaughton, *Nisei Linguists*, 28n81.

14. Selective Service System, *Selective Service as the Tide of War Turns*, Third Report of the Director of Selective Service, 1943–1944 (Washington, DC: Selective Service System, 1945), 241–43; also see McNaughton, *Nisei Linguists*, 49. Weckerling argues that "[t]he implementation of this policy would have vitiated the only feasible plan to provide qualified interpreters and translators for the Pacific theatre and would have thoroughly frustrated the efforts of the field intelligence agencies." Weckerling, "Nisei at War," 44.

15. Kai E. Rasmussen, speech, DLIFLC, Monterey, CA, June 25, 1977, printed in *DLIF LC Forum* (November 1977); also see McNaughton, *Nisei Linguists*, 51. "Nisei Soldiers Removed from Western Zone," *Pacific Citizen*, June 11, 1942. When the ban was lifted, there were approximately five thousand Nisei serving in the United States armed forces: see Uyeda and Saiki, *The Pacific War and Peace*, 13; also see McNaughton, *Nisei Linguists*, 56.

16. Ano, "Loyal Linguists," 278.

17. Rasmussen quoted in Ano, "Loyal Linguists," 278; *Fort Snelling Bulletin*, October 27, 1945, 1. Also see Faster, "Newspaper Coverage," 54–55. *The Oriental in Minnesota*, 46; *Minnesota Valley Sun* [Apple Valley, Eagan, Savage], April 28, 1976, 28.

The exact number of students that began with the first Savage class varies from one source to another. One report from the Western Defense Command (WDC) and Fourth Army states that there were 22 officers (2 Nisei, 18 Caucasians, 2 Chinese Americans) and 160 enlisted men (149 Nisei, 10 Caucasians, 1 Chinese American), another report lists 9 officers and 174 enlisted men altogether, and a third one claims 12 officers (Caucasian) and 200 enlisted men (192 Nisei and 8 Caucasians). Other sources, like the *MISLS Album*, note that there were 200. Some of the discrepancies might be due to the counting of overhead personnel or students who reported after June 1, 1942. See McNaughton, *Nisei Linguists*, 49.

18. Ichinokuchi, *John Aiso*, 2.

19. Ichinokuchi, *John Aiso*, 1, 2.

20. McNaughton, *Nisei Linguists*, 9. In 1952, Aiso was appointed commissioner of the Los Angeles superior court. A year later, he became a judge of the Los Angeles municipal court, then of the Los Angeles County superior court. In 1968, Aiso was appointed an associate justice to the California court of appeals for the second appellate district, where he remained until his retirement in 1972.

Aiso passed away December 29, 1987, from a head injury sustained in an attempted mugging. He was filling his car at a Hollywood gas station when he was attacked and knocked to the pavement. He died two weeks later in a Burbank hospital. See Pat Morrison and Santiago O'Donnell, "John Aiso, Prominent Nisei and Jurist, Dies After Mugger's Attack," *Los Angeles Times*, December 31, 1987.

21. For more details about Aiso's stories in high school, see Hosokawa, *Nisei*, 167.

22. Yano, "Participating in the Mainstream," 7.

23. The meeting most likely took place in late September or early October 1941. It is recounted in multiple sources, including many interviews Aiso gave later in the 1970s and '80s. See McNaughton, *Nisei Linguists*, 34n2; Harrington, *Yankee Samurai*, 20–21; Yano, "Participating in the Mainstream," 15.

24. Harrington, *Yankee Samurai*, 20–21; McNaughton, *Nisei Linguists*, 34. Weckerling ordered Aiso to discharge from the Enlisted Reserve Corps and hired him as a civilian for the language school. One of the first things that Aiso did right then was to set a wedding date, which fell on his birthday, December 14, before the Christmas holidays. See McNaughton, *Nisei Linguists*, 34. Also see Harrington, *Yankee Samurai*, 32; Yano, "Participating in the Mainstream," 16.

25. Kihara, "That Day," 206.

26. Kihara, "That Day," 207; Harrington, *Yankee Samurai*, 105–6.

27. Aiso, "Observations of a California Nisei."

28. Hosokawa, *Nisei*, 494. In Warren's posthumously published *The Memoirs of Chief Justice Earl Warren* (Garden City, NJ: Doubleday, 1977), he finally acknowledged his error, stating that he "since deeply regretted the removal order and my own testimony advocating it, because it was not in keeping with our American concept of freedom and the rights of citizens. . . . Whenever I thought of the innocent little children who were torn from home, school friends, and congenial surroundings, I was conscience-stricken. . . . It was wrong to react so impulsively, without positive evidence of disloyalty." See G. Edward White, "The Unacknowledged Lesson: Earl Warren and the Japanese Relocation Controversy," *Virginia Quarterly Review* (Autumn 1979): 613–29.

29. McNaughton, *Nisei Linguists*, 94.

30. Yamashita, interview; Harrington, *Yankee Samurai*, 130; Oguro, *Senpai Gumi*, 13. Nisei solider Terry Takahashi said, "Dickey painted a rosy picture," which implied Savage "would be like West Point." He said, "I got the impression I'd be part of an elite program, and that all graduates would get commissions." Quoted in Harrington, *Yankee Samurai*, 8.

31. Harrington, *Yankee Samurai*, 8; Bradsher, "The Beginnings of the United States Army."

32. Ano, "Loyal Linguists," 281.

33. MISLS Album Staff, *MISLS Album*, 62–65; Ano, "Loyal Linguists," 281; Nakasone, interview by Hawkins et al.

34. MISLS Album Staff, *MISLS Album*, 62–65; Ano, "Loyal Linguists," 281; Nakasone, interview by Hawkins et al. Also see Tad Ichinokuchi's description of the "Turkey Farm" as "the tar paper shacks," in Ichinokuchi, "Montage of Scenes," 36.

35. MISLS Album Staff, *MISLS Album*, 74; McNaughton, *Nisei Linguists*, 313. From the winter of 1941 to the summer of 1944, both the Army language school in California and the MISLS at Camp Savage produced five classes of students in two and a half years. In the year between August 1944 and July 1945, Fort Snelling held six regular classes along with six classes for officer candidates and other special groups in approximately 125 classrooms. See McNaughton, *Nisei Linguists*, 313.

36. Bray, "75th Anniversary Special"; McNaughton, *Nisei Linguists*, 315; Nakamura, "Military Intelligence Service Language School."

37. The explanation was popularized by the film *Go for Broke!*, directed by Robert Pirosh (Metro-Goldwyn-Mayer, 1951). Also see Bosley Crowther, "'Go for Broke!,' Tribute to War Record of Nisei Regiment, Opens at the Capitol," *New York Times*, May 25, 1951.

38. Harrington, *Yankee Samurai*, 135; Sterner, *Go for Broke*, 21.

39. Nakamura, "John Aiso."

40. MISLS Album Staff, *MISLS Album*, 11; McNaughton, *Nisei Linguists*, 109, 110.

41. MISLS Album Staff, *MISLS Album*, 13. Also see McNaughton, *Nisei Linguists*, 417.

42. Falkand Tsukahira, *MIS in the War against Japan*, 10. MISLS was among the first institutions to use the "immersion method" for second language acquisition, which has been continued in the Defense Language Institute in Monterey. The practice was then introduced for "regular" language students in 1965 in Canada, for English-speaking students to learn French in Quebec. The first adaptation in an American setting took place in California in 1971, for English and Spanish instruction. See Fred Genesee, "Second Language Learning through Immersion: A Review of U.S. Programs," *Review of Educational Research* 55, no. 4 (Winter 1985): 541–56.

43. The summary of the daily routine is adapted from Ishimaru, *Military Intelligence*.

44. Doi, interview; Ichinokuchi, "Montage of Scenes," 36.

45. McNaughton, *Nisei Linguists*, 101.

46. Doi, interview by Hawkins; Matsui, interview by Uratsu and Otake. Gene Uratsu, a student and enlisted instructor at Camp Savage, recalled students and staff jokingly referring to Aiso as "Der Hitler," but Uratsu also realized how difficult it must have been for the Nisei director to run the school under such extreme wartime circumstances. See McNaughton, *Nisei Linguists*, 100n23.

47. Matsui, interview; McNaughton, *Nisei Linguists*, 100.

48. Doi, interview by Hawkins; MISLS Album Staff, *MISLS Album*, 80.

49. MISLS Album Staff, *MISLS Album*, 80–82; Doi, interview by Hawkins. Also see Peggy Doi, "Saburo 'Bill' Doi" Presentation," March 22, 2021, Twin Cities JACL.

50. Doi, interview by Hawkins.

51. Umeda, interview.

52. MISLS Album Staff, *MISLS Album*, 37; also see Crost, *Honor by Fire*, 25. Doi rekindled his passion for art after the war. He graduated from the Minneapolis College of Art and Design in 1950 and worked in graphic design and advertising until his retirement. Doi, interview.

53. Acknowledging the request of some Native Americans, the MISLS veteran groups stopped using the logo in the 1990s. See McNaughton, *Nisei Linguists*, 112n62.

54. Ichinokuchi, "Montage of Scenes," 36; MISLS Album Staff, *MISLS Album*, 38; Doi, interview by Hawkins.

The Planning Committee, headed by Marian Deininger, was responsible for the many USO activities since beginning operation in April 1943. Representatives from both the hostesses and companies of the MISLS worked together to bring entertainment and enhance students' extracurricular life. Among those who served on this committee were Edwin Kawahara, Shiro Omata, Adela Shiraishi, Corrine Peterson, Jeanne Bettinger, Opu Sugihara, Chuck Tatsuda, Lois Hansen, Irene Ekre, Eerna Peterson, Mas Horiuchi, Bernice Volbruck, Mae Kuroda, Toy Shindo, Yoshida Doi, Sachi Akimoto, Charmion Heath, Edna Modene, Bill Doi, Betty Gummeson, Mildred Zollars, Fred Chino, and Erna Wallin. See Kishi, "Thrice Told Tales," 51.

Besides the Minneapolis–St. Paul YWCA, USO, and the Red Cross, some of the principal groups included the International Institute of St. Paul, the Minneapolis Defense Council, the St. Paul Chapter of the Daughters of the American Revolution, and the Council of Jewish Women, as well as many churches and religious institutions. Doi, interview by Hawkins; Ishimaru, *Military Intelligence*.

55. Kishi, "Thrice Told Tales," 38–39, 48. For the second "Birthday Ball," the door count of attendance reached 953.

56. Nakasone, interview by Saylor; Edwin Nakasone, "Thanks to Fort Snelling, I've Become Minnesotan All the Way Through," *St. Paul Pioneer Press*, May 15, 2016, https://www.twincities.com/2016/05/15/edwin-nakasone-thanks-to-fort-snelling -ive-become-minnesotan-all-the-way-through/.

57. J. Oda, interview.

58. G. Hara, interview; Umeda, interview.

59. Ishimaru, *Military Intelligence*; Gideon Seymour, "Address to the Graduating Class, Camp Savage, Minn., Jan. 15, 1944," in *Senpai Gumi*, 217. For the work of the Tanbaras and Reverend Kitagawa, see Chapter Two.

60. Matsunaga, interview.

61. Matsunaga, interview.

62. In a letter to Rasmussen on May 8, 1945, Mrs. William Quist, special assistant in charge of the Mobile Unit, wrote: "The Red Cross Blood Donor Service, and in particular the Minneapolis Center and its Mobile Unit, are deeply appreciative of the contribution you and the men and officers under your command have made to the Blood Donor Service. Every visit to your group, both at Camp Savage and at Fort Snelling, have resulted in whatever quota we requested, and several emergency visits arranged on short notice to fill in cancellations, maintained our quota." Quoted in Ishimaru, *Military Intelligence*.

63. Ishimaru, *Military Intelligence*.

64. Abe, interview.

65. Harrington, *Yankee Samurai*, 129.

66. Abe, interview.

67. Oguro, *Senpai Gumi*, 14.

68. Nakasone, interview by Hawkins.

69. "Masao 'Harold' Onishi: Former Instructor Shares Memories," *Hawaii Herald*, July 2, 1993. Also see McNaughton, *Nisei Linguists*, 139.

70. Hawley, interview by Asaka; Oguro, *Senpai Gumi*, 14; Ano, "Loyal Linguists," 280.

71. Ouchida, interview. The subsequent quotations from Ouchida come from this interview.

72. The story about a Nisei soldier hiding the Japanese radish was told by Joseph James Milanoski, a Polish American soldier from Seattle. Milanoski was one of only three non-Japanese Americans in Barracks 7, Company F—the other two were a Jewish American and a Chinese American. See Milanoski, "Camp Savage Memories," 58.

73. Tsukiyama, "Dr. J. Alfred Burden, Col.," 52–54; Kai E. Rasmussen to John A. Burden, August 10, 1943, Box 1, John A. Burden Papers, Hoover Institution Archives.

74. Commanded by and named after Major General Frank D. Merrill, "Merrill's Marauders," also called Unit Galahad (though officially the 5307th Composite Unit [Provisional]), was a special operations unit jungle warfare that operated in the China-Burma-India Theater (CBI). There were fourteen Nisei linguists who served with Merrill's Marauders: Howard Furumoto, Henry Gosho, Grant J. Hirabayashi, Robert Y. Honda, Calvin T. Kobata, Russell K. Kono, Roy H. Matsumoto, Edward H. Mitsukado, Herbert Y. Miyasaki, Roy K. Nakada, Ben S. Sugeta, Thomas K. Tsubota, Jimmy Yamaguchi, and Akiji Yoshimura. They were led by Captain William A. Laffin, who was born in Yokohama, Japan, to a Japanese mother and a Caucasian seaman father. He was a Savage graduate in July 1943. Sadly, Laffin was killed in action in 1944 in Myanmar with the Marauders. Various books and articles have documented their history, such as Center of Military History, *Merrill's Marauders: February–May 1944* (Washington, DC: United States Army, 1945/1990); Charlton Ogburn Jr., *The Marauders* (New York: Overlook Press, 1959/2002), which won the National Book Award for Nonfiction in 1959; and Gavin Mortimer, *Merrill's Marauders: The Untold Story of Unit Galahad and the Toughest Special Forces Mission of World War II* (Kenilworth, NJ: Zenith Press, 2013).

The "Dixie Mission," or the US Army Observation Group, marked the first mission sent out to gather intelligence and make contact with the Chinese Communist Party (CCP) and the People's Liberation Army. The mission, with five Nisei linguists among a team of eighteen military and diplomatic personnel led by Colonel

David D. Barrett, began on July 22, 1944, and concluded on March 11, 1947, when the last member left China. They worked in the city Ya'an in Shaanxi, China, with CCP leaders such as Mao Zedong and Zhou Enlai. The first two Nisei on the team were Sho Nomura and George Itsuo Nakamura. In the fall of 1944, a psychological warfare specialist by the name of Koji Ariyoshi joined the group, then, shortly following the end of the Pacific War, Jack Togo Ishii and Toshi Uesato. The history of the mission can be found in the following: David D. Barrett, *Dixie Mission: The United States Army Observer Group in Yenan, 1944* (Berkeley: Center for Chinese Studies, University of California, 1970); Carolle J. Carter, *Mission to Yenan: American Liaison with the Chinese Communists, 1944–1947* (Lexington: University of Kentucky Press, 1997); and John P. Davies Jr., *Dragon by the Tail: American, British, Japanese, and Russian Encounters with China and One Another* (New York: W. W. Norton, 1972).

75. Tsukahira, interview. The subsequent quotations from Tsukahira come from this interview.

76. Sakamoto, interview.

77. The Tsukahiras appear twice in Lewis's diary between 1942 and 1946—the dinner at his house on November 10, 1942, and an earlier gathering for tea on October 10, 1942. The meetings also included two other MISLS members, Faubion Bowers and Thomas Sakamoto. See Sinclair Lewis, *Minnesota Diary 1942–46*, ed. George Killough (Moscow: University of Idaho Press, 2000), 159, 165.

78. See Okamoto, *The Man Who Saved Kabuki*.

79. Leiter, "Faubion Bowers," 314; Okamoto, *The Man Who Saved Kabuki*, 4.

80. Okamoto, *The Man Who Saved Kabuki*, 4.

81. Okamoto, *The Man Who Saved Kabuki*, 8. Also see Leiter, "Faubion Bowers," 315. Bowers, "The *Hakujin* Experience," 11.

82. Bowers, interview.

83. Ariyoshi, *From Kona to Yenan*, 82. From 1942 to 1946, the US Department of State chartered *Gripsholm*, a Swedish ocean liner, as an exchange and repatriation ship, carrying Japanese and German nationals to exchange points where it then picked up US and Canadian citizens (and British married to Americans or Canadians) to bring them home to the United States and Canada. See Elleman, *Japanese-American Civilian Prisoner*, 31.

84. Oda, interview; Harrington, *Yankee Samurai*, 63.

85. Bowers, "The *Hakujin* Experience," 11–12; Ariyoshi, *From Kona to Yenan*, 82.

86. Bowers, "The *Hakujin* Experience," 11–12.

87. Okamoto, *The Man Who Saved Kabuki*, xv, 10, 14–15; Leiter, "Faubion Bowers," 315.

88. Okamoto, *The Man Who Saved Kabuki*, xv; Leiter, "Faubion Bowers," 317.

Earle Ernst was in the class of April 1945 at Fort Snelling. Like Bowers, Ernst had deep admiration for Asian theater. Born in Mifflintown, Pennsylvania, in 1911, he graduated from Gettysburg College in 1933. In 1940, he earned a PhD in theater from Cornell University and was immediately hired by the University of Hawaiʻi to teach courses on Shakespeare. The attack on Pearl Harbor was a turning point for his career. The thirty-one-year-old college instructor volunteered for the Army and its Japanese-language training. He was one of those Caucasian officer candidates who transferred from the University of Michigan's intensive program to Minnesota before their assignments in the Pacific. He was sent to Tokyo in November 1945. He was placed in charge of the CCD at the Theater Censorship Section in MacArthur's headquarters. As soon as his demobilization came in May 1947, Ernst handed the head censor torch to Bowers and returned to his professorship in Honolulu. His service at the University of Hawaiʻi at Mānoa spanned more than three decades. He was credited for establishing Asian theater as a legitimate field of academic study in the United States, among many other achievements. He passed away in 1994.

Bowers used his power in the military and provided foodstuffs as well as other necessities for his actor and theater friends during this period. See Leiter, "Faubion Bowers," 315. For the story of censoring Kabuki and traditional Japanese theater during the occupation period, see James R. Brandon, "Myth and Reality: A Story of *Kabuki* during American Censorship, 1945–1949," *Asian Theatre Journal* 23, no. 1 (Spring 2006): 1–110; Okamoto, *The Man Who Saved Kabuki.*

89. See Leiter, "Faubion Bowers." The last writing of Ernst is a novel titled *Finding Monju*, posthumously published in 2000. The author explains that *Monju* is the Japanese deity for men who love other men, and the fiction depicts the lives of occupying American soldiers in war-ravaged Japan. In Ernst's portrayal, the repressed gay American military men found the chance to finally open up and enjoy same-sex relationships in the faraway land; the protagonist says, "in this wretched feudal country I'd found freedom I'd never known in the victorious land of the free." Earle Ernst, *Finding Monju* (Key West: Eaton Street Press, 2000), 96. At the same time, Edward Seidensticker, a student from the Navy officer program who later also became a famed Japanese professor, writes in his memoir that he sensed a governmental "witch-hunting" in which bachelors were subjected to "peculiar rumors" as well as skeptical and surveilling eyes. See Seidensticker, *Tokyo Central: A Memoir* (Seattle: University of Washington Press, 2002), 57.

In the 1940s, homosexuality was classified as a mental illness by the medical community. Mental illness was one condition that disqualified young people from service, and therefore, American service members would be given a Section 8 "blue discharge" for being homosexual. For a detailed history, see Allan Bérubé, *Coming*

Out under Fire: The History of Gay Men and Women in World War II, twentieth-anniversary edition (Chapel Hill, NC: The University of North Carolina Press, 2010). Also see Randy Shilts, *Conduct Unbecoming: Gays and Lesbians in the U.S. Military* (New York: St. Martin's Press, 1993).

90. For the history of women in the US military, see "Women in the Army" online exhibit and historical resource portal from the US Army website, https://www.army.mil/women/index.html. For further information, see "History of the WAC and Army Women," Women's Army Corps Veterans' Association—Army Women United.

The WAC members were the first non-nurse women within the ranks of the Army. They undertook a variety of noncombat job positions, including switchboard operators, postal clerks, typists, stenographers, mechanics, and drivers. Another hundred thousand women served as Navy WAVES (Women Accepted for Volunteer Emergency Service), while others joined the WASP (Women Airforce Service Pilots), the Marines, and the Coast Guard. By the end of the war, nearly five hundred Nisei women had served the country in uniform in various roles.

91. Treadwell, *The Women's Army Corps*, 589; also see McNaughton, *Nisei Linguists*, 143. For the slander against the WAC in 1943, see Leisa D. Meyer, *Creating GI Jane: Sexuality and Power in the Women's Army Corps during World War II* (New York: Columbia University Press, 1996), 47–51; Bettie J. Morden, *The Women's Army Corps, 1945–1978* (Washington, DC: US Government Printing Office, 1990), 10–11. Moore, *Serving Our Country*, 19.

92. Eleanor Roosevelt, "To Undo a Mistake Is Always Harder Than Not to Create One Originally," May 1943, in Burton, ed., *Confinement and Ethnicity*, 19–24. Also see McNaughton, *Nisei Linguists*, 144, 144n43, 224. Treadwell, *The Women's Army Corps*, 435.

93. Fujitani, *Race for Empire*, 192–93; Hirose, "Japanese American Women," 17–22; Japanese American Veterans Association, "Japanese American Women." There were five training centers that included the WAC during the war period—Daytona Beach, Florida; Fort Oglethorpe, Georgia; Fort Des Moines, Iowa; Camp Ruston, Louisiana; and Fort Devens, Massachusetts.

94. Go for Broke, "Japanese American Women in Service," Go for Broke Education Center, https://goforbroke.org/history/unit-history/japanese-american-women-in-service/. From the start, the MISLS did not allow women instructors not merely "because of inadequate administrative facilities" but also due to the belief "that Military Japanese could best be taught by men." The school might have tried to recruit Nisei women as instructors in early 1943, but none were hired. See McNaughton, *Nisei Linguists*, 116; Moore, *Serving Our Country*, 92.

The eleven Nisei WACs were Harriet Hirakawa, Chito Isonaga, Matsuko Kido, Edith Kodama, Mickey Minata, Atsuko Mori, Mary Nakamura, Terry Nakanishi, Fumiko Segawa, Sue Shinagawa, and Miwako Yanamoto. The Chinese American was Bertha Chin, and the Caucasian American was Rhoda Knudten.

Ruth Fujii was the only Nisei woman to be sent to the Asiatic-Pacific Theater during the war. For a wartime story on Fujii, see "Recruiting of WACs in Hawaii Will Start at Armory Today," *Honolulu Advertiser*, October 2, 1944.

95. Nakayama, "Momma Wore Combat Boots," 10; Kato, interview. The subsequent quotations from Kato come from this interview.

The first Nisei woman to become a member of the WAC was Frances Iritani from Colorado, inducted on November 10, 1943, in Denver. Iris Watanabe was the first Nisei incarceree to join the WAC. Margaret K. Fukuoka of Newcastle, California, followed several weeks later, having enlisted from Manzanar. The other two were Bette Nishimura of Rocky Ford, Colorado, and Sue S. Ogata (Kato) of Greeley, Colorado. See Moore, *Serving Our Country*, 95.

96. Nakayama, "Momma Wore Combat Boots," 10.

97. Kato's scrapbook items include Women's Army Auxiliary Corps pamphlets, newspaper and magazine clippings, correspondence, photographs, and other ephemera, which she donated to the California State University. See the California State University Dominguez Hills Photograph Collection, https://cdm16855.contentdm.oclc.org/digital/collection/p16855coll4/id/39413/rec/1.

98. "Nisei in Rochester WRA Office Leaves for WAC Training," *Pacific Citizen*, May 12, 1945.

99. Inefuku, "Story of a WAC in MIS"; Lam, "The Nisei WACs."

100. Kono, interview. Also see Katherine Fecteau, "Alice Tetsuko Kono: Wise, Well-Traveled, WAC," August 4, 2016, National Museum of American History Behring Center, https://americanhistory.si.edu/blog/alice-tetsuko-kono.

101. Hurt, interview. The subsequent quotations from Hurt come from this interview. Haruko Sugi Hurt was born in Parlier, California, in 1915, but her family moved to Gardena shortly, where she also retired in 1995 at the age of seventy.

102. "Haruko Sugi Hurt," Japanese American Military Experience Database, Discover Nikkei, https://www.discovernikkei.org/en/resources/military/113/.

103. "Haruko Sugi Hurt." Hurt met her husband at the University of Southern California, and they were married in 1949. They stayed in Los Angeles and raised a family with two adopted children. Hurt worked in social work and education-related fields, including for the Girl Scouts and an adult learning school as an English teacher. The Hurts were divorced in 1984. She returned to Gardena then and lived there until she passed away in 2012.

104. P. Doi, interview.

105. "Japanese Garden," Normandale Community College website, https://www.normandale.edu/why-normandale/community/japanese-garden/index.html. See Kenney, *Normandale Japanese Garden*, and note 1 for this chapter.

106. Kenney, *Normandale Japanese Garden*, 21. More than three hundred plants, shrubs, and trees have been planted in the Normandale Japanese Garden. Because of climate differences, they are not plants that would be used in gardens in Japan. The architect and gardeners chose plants hardy enough to survive Minnesota's extremely cold winters. Normandale Community College, "Japanese Garden."

107. Kenney, *Normandale Japanese Garden*, 21, 34.

Notes to Chapter 6: Compassion and Commitment

Opening quote: Amemiya, Dahlman, Hara, Lee, and Lee, interview. The subsequent quotations from Hara came from this interview.

1. According to Hara, the doctor was Ed Banick.

2. Tad Vezner, "Kimi Hara, 91, Japanese-Americans' Advocate," *St. Paul Pioneer Press*, January 17, 2007; Haras, interview.

3. Born in 1926 in Seattle, Reiko Taguchi Sumada was the youngest of five children in the Taguchi family. Her eldest sister was Kimi Taguchi Hara. She continued her education and completed high school in Rochester. She met her future husband, Tsuguo Sumada, while attending the University of Minnesota. They were married in 1951 and raised their family in St. Louis Park. She worked as a science paraprofessional at Westwood Junior High School until her retirement. Like her sister, Sumada was active in the Japanese American Citizens League. She passed away in March 2019.

4. Born in 1910 on Bainbridge Island in Washington state, Sam Hara graduated from West Seattle High School in 1928. The Great Depression forced the Nisei to answer the call of the contract recruiter and go to Alaska for job opportunities. For two years, he worked in a cannery on Kodiak Island, across the Shelikof Strait, and later in the 1930s, he became a commercial tuna fisherman. Hara was in California in September 1940 when his draft notice arrived. By the time he completed basic training in 1941, he was already thirty-one years old, and thus was put into a standby Army reserve category. He was called back to duty after the attack on Pearl Harbor. In late 1942, he was transferred to Fort Snelling, as a mechanic for the motor pool for a transportation company. In early 1944, he volunteered for the 442nd, and he sailed off to Italy in early June of 1944. He saw combat in northern Italy and France and was wounded in November that year. He then flew back to the United States and stayed at the Percy Jones Hospital in Battle Creek, Michigan, for rehabilitation. He returned to Minnesota and found employment as a diesel engine

mechanic in an outlet of the White Motor Company. He worked there for thirty-four years, until he retired in 1980. He passed away in 1983.

5. Haras, interview.

6. Haras, interview; Tsuchida, "Preface," in *Reflections*, ix.

7. Tsuchida, "Preface," in *Reflections*, ix; Haras, interview.

8. Vezner, "Kimi Hara"; Haras, interview. Thomas I. Hara was born in 1946 at the Fort Snelling Station Hospital in Minneapolis, where his mother Kimi Hara worked.

According to T. J. Hara, the grandson of Kimi Hara and a lead committee member of the Normandale Japanese Garden Festival in 2014, the last time the campus held a sukiyaki dinner was in 2007. Renovations in the student center the next year made the fundraising go on a hiatus. Then changes in the college regulations no longer permitted outside organizations and volunteers to prepare food in a campus kitchen. Instead, the committee opted to expand the entertainment portion of its dinners into a day of various performances, such as music, dances, martial arts, Taiko drumming, and Japanese sword and archery demonstrations, becoming the Normandale Japanese Garden Festival.

9. Amemiya, Dahlman, Hara, Lee, and Lee, interview.

10. Dahlman, "Questionnaire." The subsequent quotes from Dahlman come from this questionnaire unless stated otherwise.

11. See the appendix for the names of the cadet nurses in both programs. Also see Robinson, "Distribution of Nisei Cadet Nurses"; Robinson, *Nisei Cadet Nurse*, 127.

12. "The United States Cadet Nurse Corps Service Recognition Act of 2023" is the latest federal legislative attempt to acknowledge the work of the estimated 120,000 cadet nurses who served in World War II. See Senator Elizabeth Warren, sponsor, "S.1633—United States Cadet Nurse Corps Service Recognition Act of 2023," May 17, 2023, https://www.congress.gov/bill/118th-congress/senate-bill/16 33. Although "the bill authorizes DOD [Department of Defense] to produce a service medal or other commendation, memorial plaque, or grave marker to honor the individuals," the legislation "would not provide still-living Cadet Nurses with Veterans Affairs pensions, healthcare benefits, or other privileges afforded to former active-duty service members, such as burial benefits in Arlington Cemetery."

13. Threat, *Nursing Civil Right*, 13, 20; Federal Security Agency, *The U.S. Cadet Nurse Corps*, 11. It was not until 1955 that the Army Nurse Corps allowed male nurses into its ranks. Lieutenant Edward T. Lyon, an anesthetist, became the ANC's first male nurse. For more information about male nurses, see Liz Lotts, "Men in Nursing: History, Stereotypes, and the Gender Pay Gap," Online FNP Programs, https://www.onlinefnpprograms.com/features/men-in-nursing/.

14. Federal Security Agency, *The U.S. Cadet Nurse Corps*, 7, 15–20; Petry, "U.S. Cadet Nurse Corps," 704–5. When the United States entered World War I, there were only 403 Army nurses on active duty. By November 1918, the number rose to 21,480, with 10,000 serving overseas. See Federal Security Agency, *The U.S. Cadet Nurse Corps*, 7.

15. Federal Security Agency, *The U.S. Cadet Nurse Corps*, 97; Robinson, *Nisei Cadet Nurse*, xi.

16. Kalisch and Kalisch, *From Training to Education*, 111–14; Robinson, *Nisei Cadet Nurse*, 110.

17. For more information about the Nisei nursing students at the University of Colorado, see Hamilton, *Becoming a Presence Within Nursing*, 56–57. Also see Beaton, *Colorado Women*, 200–203.

Carr argued that Colorado should accept its share of the Japanese American incarcerees and treat them respectfully. He also underscored the broader context of war against several enemy countries in order to downplay the struggle with Japan that could easily be seen as a racial conflict. Even after he lost his Senate election to the Democratic incumbent Edwin Carl Johnson, Carr did not waver in his position. See Wei, *Asians in Colorado*, 208–9. "The Japanese in Our Midst" [brochures from the Council of Churches, 1943], Thomas Bodine Collection, Hoover Institution Archives.

Alumna Mae Kashiwagi Nishitani wrote in a letter published in the *University of Washington Alumni Magazine* in 2006: "When the evacuation notice was going to take place [the University of Washington School of Nursing Dean] made arrangements to transfer three of the Japanese American students to the University of Colorado School of Nursing in Denver.... We felt very fortunate to be able to continue our studies instead of going to camp." Quoted in David Kelly, "Former Nursing Dean Honored for Shielding Japanese-Americans," *University of Colorado Anschutz Medical Campus News*, September 11, 2013.

18. Whelan and Dacy, *The Little Book of Mayo Clinic*, 46; Wentzel, *Sincere et Constanter*, 55–56.

19. Wentzel, *Sincere et Constanter*, 56. Information about admitting Nisei women to St. Mary's can be found in the entry "American-Japanese Students" in the *Annals of Saint Mary's Hospital* (1943). Cited in Whelan and Dacy, *The Little Book of Mayo Clinic*, 46.

20. See Letter to Dr. Thomas Parran, Surgeon General USPHS, August 19, 1943, from Walter Godfrey, the American Friends Manuscript Collection (ca. 1942–1945), University of Washington Library, Seattle.

21. See Letter to Walter Godfrey, August 31, 1943, from Lucile Petry, Director, Division of Nurse Education, USPHS, the American Friends Manuscript

Collection (ca. 1942–1945), University of Washington Library. Also see Robinson, *Nisei Cadet Nurse*, 114.

22. Robinson, *Nisei Cadet Nurse*, 59. According to a 1943 report, only 84 Japanese American women out of 371 had been able to finish their course in nursing that year due to the war. Besides the University of Colorado that initially took in several Japanese American women, other schools enrolled merely a few Nisei students at most. For example, only one small Catholic school of nursing in Nebraska accepted Japanese American students. The St. Joseph's School of Nursing in the western part of the state admitted one Nisei woman in 1944 and a second in 1945. See American Journal of Nursing editorial, "The Problem of Student Nurses," 895; Brueggemann, "The U.S. Cadet Nurse Corps."

Other reasons for refusal included: "the school had refugee students, and it was not felt that those of Japanese ancestry could be admitted" and "facilities for students were already crowded in order to accommodate local applicants of non-Japanese ancestry." See American Journal of Nursing editorial, "The Problem of Student Nurses," 895–96. Also see Robinson, *Your Country Needs You*, 94.

23. American Journal of Nursing editorial, "The Problem of Student Nurses," 896.

24. Wentzel, *Sincere et Constanter*, 67.

25. Robinson, *Nisei Cadet Nurse*, 60.

26. Whelan and Dacy, *The Little Book of Mayo Clinic*, 44–45.

27. Whelan and Dacy, *The Little Book of Mayo Clinic*, 44–45.

28. Amemiya, Dahlman, Hara, Lee, and Lee, interview.

29. F. Lee, "Questionnaire." The following quotes from Lee come from this questionnaire unless stated otherwise.

30. Amemiya, Dahlman, Hara, Lee, and Lee, interview.

31. Aburano, "Questionnaire." Also see Robinson, *Nisei Cadet Nurse*, 132. According to Aburano, her father was picked up by the FBI in February 1942, as were most Issei businessmen. Associated Press, "Internments Still Spark Painful Memories," *Deseret News*, January 26, 1992, https://www.deseret.com/1992/1/26/18964153/internments-still-spark-painful-memories-br.

Born in 1922, Frank Shigeo Tanagi grew up in Seattle with his two sisters. In 1942, he was studying health sciences at the University of Washington. His education was, of course, interrupted by the war. He was imprisoned at Minidoka along with his mother and younger sister, Aburano. From camp, he was drafted into the Army and was assigned to the Military Intelligence Service. After his training at the MISLS in Minnesota, Tanagi served in the Pacific Theater, including the Philippines, Japan, and Korea. After his military service, he picked his education back up at Washington State University and obtained a BS in pharmacy. He settled down in

Seattle with his own family and worked at Pay N' Save (a popular drugstore chain in Seattle during the 1940s until its closing in 1992) for thirty-five years. He passed away in June 2020.

32. Aburano, interview. The subsequent quotations from Aburano come from this interview unless stated otherwise.

33. Robinson, *Nisei Cadet Nurse*, 129; Morooka, "St. Mary's School of Nursing." Born in Long Beach, California, in 1921, Martha Masako Morooka graduated from Long Beach Poly High in 1939 and was incarcerated from 1942 to 1943 in Gila River, Arizona, where she received acceptances to become a nursing student at three institutions. Her parents encouraged her to attend St. Mary's, the well-known "Mayo Clinic" facility, instead of the nursing schools at Arizona State University and Temple University. She started her training in Rochester on September 7, 1943, and graduated from the Cadet Nurse Corps in 1945. After the war, she returned to California, where she held several positions over the years: at Long Beach Community Hospital, various companies around Los Angeles, and the US Customs Service. She passed away in 2012.

In 2002, Morooka wrote in a letter to the alumni association: "One of the highlights of our school was the nursing school choral group which many of us joined. The chorale was led by one of our classmates, Alice Brown French. She was a talented, marvelous director. Alice coaxed music out of us, and we enjoyed her expertise. Subsequently, we put on several concerts." Morooka, "St. Mary's School of Nursing."

Born in 1925 on Terminal Island in Los Angeles, California, Mary Izumi Tamura spent her childhood in the fishing community, which had about three thousand Japanese Americans until the war started. Her family, like many others, was forcibly removed from their home and incarcerated in Gila River. In camp, the eighteen-year-old Tamura decided to join the US Cadet Nurse Corps. She was accepted by St. Mary's School of Nursing in 1944 and then graduated in 1947. She counted meeting Helen Keller and taking care of Harry Hopkins, the eighth United States Secretary of Commerce and an adviser to President Franklin Roosevelt, as highlights of her tenure in Rochester. She later went to New York, met her husband, and married there in 1950. In 1954, the Tamuras returned to Los Angeles. She continued to be a nurse for four decades until her retirement in 1989. She was then involved in the "Terminal Island Life History Project" by the Japanese American National Museum in Los Angeles, California. Tamura shared her story with the Go for Broke National Education Center. See Mary Tamura, "WWII Cadet Nurse Corps, Discusses Her Training at St. Mary's School of Nursing," July 28, 2022, Go for Broke National Education Center. She also did a podcast interview, from which the quote originates. See Melissa Ritz, "Special Edition: WWII Nisei Cadet Nurse Mary Tamura," *Served:*

Military Women's Stories, August 25, 2021, https://served.podbean.com/e/special
-edition-wwii-nisei-cadet-nurse-mary-tamura/. Tamura and other Nisei cadet nurses
also appear in a Go for Broke National Education Center video, "Heroes Among
US—U.S. Cadet Nurse Corps," March 27, 2023, https://www.youtube.com/
watch?v=Yew2Oobpuy4.

34. Robinson, *Nisei Cadet Nurse*, 129.

35. Robinson, *Nisei Cadet Nurse*, 131.

36. Born in Sebastopol, California, in 1923, Paul Aburano was the second of
four sons in the Aburano family. His family had an apple-dehydrating plant, where
he worked with his parents, Seijiro and Fusa. He graduated from Analy High
School; the start of the war soon forced the whole family to Camp Amache in Colorado. Shortly after the incarceration, he entered military service, at one point being
stationed in Occupied Japan. Once he returned after the war, he first went to Albion
College and later received an electrical engineering degree from the University of
Michigan in 1949. He relocated to Seattle subsequently and met his wife, Sharon
Tanagi, through church. Aburano began his engineering career at the Boeing Com-
pany and stayed there for thirty-five years. They had two sons, Brian and Richard.
Aburano passed away in 2014 at the age of ninety-one.

37. Kawaguchi, "Questionnaire." The subsequent quotes from Kawaguchi come
from this questionnaire unless stated otherwise.

38. According to Kawaguchi, "Gila River Relocation Center had two camps,
one was the Canal Camp and the other camp was called Butte Camp, which was
located a few miles away and operated as a separate camp. They had a larger hospital than Canal. We were paid $16.00 a month, and the doctors and all professional
workers were paid a significant sum of $19.00 a month."

39. Todd Sakohira was later brought home to rest in the cemetery in Fowler,
California.

40. Todd Sakohira was inducted on June 17, 1943, and joined the new, segregated
all–Japanese American 442nd Regimental Combat Team. He "was posthumously
awarded the Purple Heart Medal; Bronze Star Medal; Combat Infantryman Badge;
Distinguished Unit Citation; the American Campaign Medal; the European-African-
Middle Eastern Campaign Medal; Good Conduct Medal; and the World War II
Victory Medal." Mits Kojimoto and Kuniko Shimoguchi, "Echoes of Silence,"
Americans of Japanese Ancestry World War II (AJA WWII) Memorial Alliance,
http://www.nvcfmemorialwall.org/profile/view/654.

41. Harry Sakohira earned the Silver Star for gallantry in action in Italy on April 23,
1945. See "Harry Torao Sakohira, U.S. Army—442nd R.C.T. World War II," NVC
Foundation Japanese American Memorial Wall, http://www.nvcfmemorialwall
.org/profile/view/653.

For more information about the "Lost Battalion," see Abbie Salyers Grubb, "Rescue of the Lost Battalion," Densho Encyclopedia, last modified October 16, 2020, https://encyclopedia.densho.org/Rescue_of_the_Lost_Battalion/; for more details of the rescue, also see Franz Steidl, *Lost Battalions: Going for Broke in the Vosges, Autumn 1944* (Novato, CA: Presidio Press, 1997).

42. Over the years, about a dozen Nisei cadet nurses at St. Mary's, approximately one-third of the total number, wrote or were interviewed in detail about their wartime experiences. Besides those mentioned in this chapter, other St. Mary's alumnae include Grace Aiko Obata Amemiya and Yoshiko "Edith" Yonemoto Ichiuji. Their stories can be found in Robinson, *Nisei Cadet Nurse*, 137–42 and 118–20, respectively. Yuriko "Judy" Kumamoto Ishii, June Yoshiko Momoda, and Margaret Miye Ouchi also wrote back and contributed to the "Questionnaire from the Nursing History/Mayo Medical Center History Project" in 2002.

For the story of Teruko Wada Tanaka, see Robinson, *Nisei Cadet Nurse*, 6–11.

Notes to Chapter 7: Risks and Rewards

Opening quote: B. Hirabayashi, interview. Subsequent quotes from Bill Hirabayashi are taken from this interview unless stated otherwise.

1. Hiner, "Narrative History," 43.

2. J. L. Anderson, "Introduction," in *The Rural Midwest Since World War II* (DeKalb: Northern Illinois University Press, 2014), 3; see Cathy Wurzer, "Minn. Companies Helped Fight WWII in Surprising Ways," MPR News, June 16, 2010, https://www.mprnews.org/story/2010/06/15/minn-companies-helped-fight-wwii -in-surprising-ways.

3. See Jade Ryerson, "Twin Cities Ordnance Plant: Integrating the WWII Workforce," National Park Service, https://www.nps.gov/articles/000/twin-cities-ord nance-plant-integrating-the-wwii-workforce.htm.

4. "Executive Order 8802: Prohibition of Discrimination in the Defense Industry (1941)," issued on June 25, 1941, National Archives, https://www.archives.gov/ milestone-documents/executive-order-8802; see Ryerson, "Twin Cities Ordnance Plant." Also see Cecil E. Newman, "Industrialist Charles Horn Changed Employment Patterns Here by Job Democracy," *Minneapolis Spokesman*, February 27, 1953; previously published in *Opportunity Magazine* (April–June 1944), Minnesota Digital Newspaper Hub.

5. Minnesota Division of Employment and Security, *Summary of Twin Cities Labor Market Area Survey*, September 1941, Box 3, Miscellaneous Records, Civilian Defense Division Records, Minnesota Historical Society. Also see Kenney, *Minnesota Goes to War*, 70–71.

6. See Ryerson, "Twin Cities Ordnance Plant." Both stories are cited in Kenney, *Minnesota Goes to War*, 93.

7. During 1943 the Minneapolis Settlement Committee subcommittee on employment made 7 domestic placements and 136 non-domestic. See GICM, *The Oriental in Minnesota*, 51.

8. GICM, *The Oriental in Minnesota*, 51–52.

9. GICM, *The Oriental in Minnesota*, 54.

10. Okamoto, interview.

11. Shishino, interview.

12. Kitagawa, *Issei and Nisei*, 124. Genevieve F. Steefel was the wife of Lawrence Dinkelspiel Steefel, a history professor from the University of Minnesota. She was a leader in numerous Minnesota and Minneapolis religious, cultural, social welfare, and human rights organizations. Documents, notes, and correspondences related to Steefel's work can be found in the Genevieve F. Steefel Papers, 1923–1962, at the Minnesota Historical Society.

13. Kitagawa, *Issei and Nisei*, 127.

14. Kitagawa, *Issei and Nisei*, 126–27.

15. Kitagawa, *Issei and Nisei*, 163–64.

16. Kitagawa, *Issei and Nisei*, 164. For more details about Rusch, see Elizabeth Hemphill, *The Road to KEEP: The Story of Paul Rusch in Japan* (New York and Tokyo: John Weatherhill, 1969).

17. Kitagawa, *Issei and Nisei*, 165–66.

18. Kitagawa even had the ear of the government. As the West Coast reopened to Issei and Nisei in the early summer of 1945, the reverend penned a report to the WRA, after a field investigation in Washington state, confirming that the former residents would be welcomed back to the area despite its wartime hostility. He credited the change to the many Christian leaders who helped convince the doubters and correct the state's course.

19. Kitagawa, *Issei and Nisei*, 166.

20. See Gordon W. Allport, *The Nature of Prejudice* (Cambridge: Perseus Books, 1954); Rupert Brown and Miles Hewstone, "An Integrative Theory of Intergroup Contact," in *Advances in Experimental Social Psychology*, vol. 37, edited by Mark P. Zanna (San Diego: Elsevier Academic Press, 2005), 255–343.

21. Archives of the Episcopal Church, "The Reverend Daisuke Kitagawa, 1910–1970," *The Church Awakens: African Americans and the Struggle for Justice*, Online Exhibition, https://episcopalarchives.org/church-awakens/exhibits/show/leadership/clergy/kitagawa; Krista Finstad Hanson, "St. Paul Resettlement Committee Helped Bring Japanese Americans to Minnesota in Wake of World War Two Camp Policy," *MinnPost*, March 26, 2018, https://www.minnpost.com/mnopedia/2018/

03/st-paul-resettlement-committee-helped-bring-japanese-americans-minnesota
-wake-world/.

22. Kitagawa, *Issei and Nisei*, 137, 169.

23. Jonathan van Harmelen, "Daisuke Kitagawa: Civil Rights and Anti-Racism Activist—Part 2," Discover Nikkei, May 9, 2022, https://discovernikkei.org/en/journal/2022/5/9/daisuke-kitagawa-2/; Kitagawa, *Issei and Nisei*, 168.

24. GICM, *The Oriental in Minnesota*, 46; see Edward M. Kitazumi, "Report on Minnesota," *Pacific Citizen*, February 12, 1949, 6. Also see van Harmelen, "Daisuke Kitagawa."

25. Archives of the Episcopal Church, "The Reverend Daisuke Kitagawa." The reverend also appeared briefly before the President's Commission on Immigration and Naturalization in October 1952 to communicate a statement on behalf of the Twin Cities JACL in support of the McCarran-Walter Act that allowed for people of Asian descent to immigrate and to become citizens. See van Harmelen, "Daisuke Kitagawa."

26. Archives of the Episcopal Church, "The Reverend Daisuke Kitagawa"; Van Harmelen, "Daisuke Kitagawa."

27. Van Harmelen, "Daisuke Kitagawa"; Archives of the Episcopal Church, "The Reverend Daisuke Kitagawa." What was paramount in the reverend's concern was how the Christian church, still engraved with the image of the "white race" with a long history of exploitation, suppression, and discrimination against peoples of color, could continue to be the church in the contemporary world, in which racism happened to be one of the most crucial factors. He believed the church thus far, in the early 1960s, had not yet come to grips with the racial problems. See Daisuke Kitagawa, *Race Relations and Christian Mission* (New York: Friendship Press, 1964).

28. Kitagawa, *Issei and Nisei*, 169.

29. Kenney, *Minnesota Goes to War*, 93.

30. Maeda, interview. The following quotes from Maeda come from this interview unless stated otherwise.

31. LaVenture, "Don Maeda."

32. LaVenture, "Don Maeda."

33. LaVenture, "Don Maeda."

34. LaVenture, "Don Maeda."

35. LaVenture, "Don Maeda."

36. LaVenture, "Don Maeda."

37. LaVenture, "Don Maeda."

38. The Hormel strike received national attention at the time. A documentary feature, *American Dream*, directed by Barbara Kopple (Prestige Films, 1990), was filmed during the conflict, and won the Best Documentary Feature at the Academy

Awards in 1991. See Elizabeth Baier, "25 Years Ago, Hormel Strike Changed Austin, Industry," MPR News, August 17, 2010, https://www.mprnews.org/story/2010/08/17/austin-hormel-strike.

According to the 2020 US Census, the largest ethnic groups in Austin are White alone (67.1%), Hispanic (16.9%), Asian (7.3%), Black or African American (5.4%), Two or more races (6.5%), Native American (0.2%). See US Department of Commerce, QuickFacts, Austin City, Minnesota, https://www.census.gov/quickfacts/fact/table/austincityminnesota/LND110210.

39. Sinclair Lewis, *Main Street & Babbitt* (New York: The Library of America, 1992), 10.

40. See K. Masui, J. Hashimoto, and I. Ono, "The Rudimental Copulatory Organ of the Male Domestic Fowl, with Reference to the Difference of the Sexes in the Chick" [in Japanese with English summary], *Animal Science Journal* 1 (1925): 153–63; also see Sue Kunitomi Embrey, "Nisei Pioneer U.S. Chick-Sexing Industry," *Pacific Citizen*, December 20, 1957, B-13. "Chick Sexing Is Big Business: Nisei Pioneer a New Industry," *Pacific Citizen*, December 31, 1949, 2.

41. Azuma, "Race, Citizenship," 250.

42. Azuma, "Race, Citizenship," 250n17. The first group of four Nisei pioneers who went to Nagoya to learn chicken sexing included Clyde Goto, George Hayashi, Benny Ishikura, and Kiyoto Saiki. Only Goto and Saiki remained in the chicken-sexing business after the war. See Embrey, "Nisei Pioneer U.S. Chick-Sexing Industry."

43. "Japan Chick Sex Experts in California," *Kashu Mainichi* [Japan-California Daily], April 4, 1934; also see "Chick Sexing Is Big Business," 2; Jonathan van Harmelen, "Chick Sexing," Densho Encyclopedia, last modified September 2, 2022, https://encyclopedia.densho.org/Chick_sexing/; see Azuma, "Race, Citizenship," 254–55. Also see W. E. Schultz, "Shortage of Sexors," *Hatchery Tribune* 16 (September 1942): 28–35; "Japanese Help," *Business Week*, December 12, 1942, 63; Clark Holtzman, "Shortage of Chick Sexors?," *Hatchery Tribune* 16 (November 1942): 58.

Shigeru John Nitta of San Pedro, California, started the American Chick Sexing Association (AmChick) in 1937, which moved to Lansdale, Pennsylvania, in the spring of 1942, just before the forced removal of people of Japanese ancestry on the West Coast. Other organizations followed suit, moving their operations to locations such as Illinois and Georgia.

44. G. Saiki, interview, 3–4.

45. Hirasuna, interview.

46. G. Saiki, interview, 3–4.

47. S. Saiki, interview, 4.

48. S. Saiki, interview, 5.

49. G. Saiki, interview, 2, 12, 14.

50. G. Saiki, interview, 2; Hirasuna, interview.

51. G. Saiki, interview, 2.

52. Azuma, "Race, Citizenship," 257–58.

53. Azuma, "Race, Citizenship," 258.

54. Azuma, "Race, Citizenship," 256.

55. Azuma, "Race, Citizenship," 252–53. The US Department of Agriculture statement read in part: "Use of American-born Japanese is wholly proper in all parts of the United States except the restricted zones set up by the military authorities. American-born Japanese are encouraged to seek employment outside the relocation centers. Every one of them is thoroughly investigated before being permitted to accept employment." Quoted in Azuma, "Race, Citizenship," 256.

The ad was taken out in *Hatchery Tribune* 17, February 1943; Fred Hirasuna, "Life History," June 1, 1998, Japanese American National Museum, 32. Also see Azuma, "Race, Citizenship," 266–67.

56. G. Saiki, interview, 2, 3.

57. S. Saiki, interview, 7.

58. G. Saiki, interview, 3; Azuma, "Race, Citizenship," 253.

59. The reporting on the incident includes the following: "Intolerance Here," *Minneapolis Star Journal*, November 14, 1944, 8:1; William Thorkelson, "Neighborhood Protests Chick Sex Determination School," *Minneapolis Star Journal*, November 14, 1944, 11:1; "Council Fight Looms on Chicken Sex School Pleas," *Minneapolis Star Journal*, November 15, 1944, 13:6; "Chick Sexing Permit Ok'd," *Minneapolis Star Journal*, November 24, 1944, 1:7.

The residents opposing the school, for example, complained on the grounds of hygiene. However, the health commissioner reported that chickens "killed in teaching sexing are placed in a tightly covered garbage can and are removed every day. He said there was no evidence rats would be attracted to the school." See "Council Fight Looms on Chicken Sex School Pleas," 13:6.

60. "Intolerance Here," 8:1.

61. "Council Fight Looms on Chicken Sex School Pleas," 13:6. The permit was issued to Fred Y. Hirasuna, executive secretary of the association. See "Chick Sexing Permit Ok'd," 1:7.

62. S. Saiki, interview, 7.

63. S. Saiki, interview, 7.

64. S. Saiki, interview, 7; S. John Nitta, "Terminal Island Life History Project" (Los Angeles, ca. 1994), Japanese American National Museum, 14. Also see Azuma, "Race, Citizenship," 253.

65. S. Saiki, interview, 12–13.

66. G. Saiki, interview, 14, 18.

67. G. Saiki, interview, 20–21. Saiki recalled the incident when he bought his house on Woodshire Drive, which remained his residence for the rest of his life. "That was quite a controversy when they found out that I had bought the lot to build up there. In fact, it's right in the title, that's one of the clauses, that you had to be Caucasian. . . . It's right on one of the conditions of a restricted area. And I don't know who it was initiated it, maybe the neighbors. . . . They let us build in the area. . . . But I think these restrictions have all been outlawed . . . in the last few years." G. Saiki, interview, 20.

68. S. Saiki, interview, 7, 14.

69. There has been a marked increase of Korean and Mexican immigrants accepting the jobs. The Sundance Festival Award–winning film *Minari* (dir. Lee Isaac Chung, 2020), for example, features a South Korean immigrant couple who engaged in the chicken-sexing profession in Arkansas as part of their pursuit of the American dream in the 1980s. Both South Koreans and Mexicans are new labor forces in the field of chicken sexing. Also see Azuma, "Race, Citizenship," 268–72.

70. McWilliams, "The Lucrative Art"; K. Saiki, interview.

71. K. Saiki, interview.

72. The William Hood Dunwoody Industrial Institute was founded with a gift of $3 million from the Minneapolis businessman William Hood Dunwoody upon his death in 1914. In 2003, it merged with NEI College of Technology of Columbia Heights, Minnesota, and was renamed Dunwoody College of Technology.

73. "Until two years ago, [Dunwoody]'s student body was almost exclusively white and male." See Art Hughes, "Tech College Sees Future of Minnesota Work Force in Minority Students," MPR News, January 31, 2007.

74. *The Dunwoody News*, March 17, 1944, vol. 22, no. 27, 1; *The Dunwoody News*, September 15, 1944, vol. 23, no. 3, 1; *The Dunwoody News*, September 1, 1944, vol. 23, no. 1, 1.

75. *The Dunwoody News*, October 27, 1944, vol. 23, no. 9, 1; *The Dunwoody News*, October 13, 1944, vol. 23, no. 7, 2.

76. *The Dunwoody News*, November 3, 1944, vol. 23, no. 10, 2; *The Dunwoody News*, January 5, 1945, vol. 23, no. 17, 3. In addition to his first appearance on November 3, 1944, Kiyoto "Keek" Saiki was mentioned on November 10 and 17 as well as December 1 and 15 in 1944, and on January 5 and 19 in 1945.

77. J. Kirihara, interview.

78. J. Kirihara, interview.

79. Kirihara talked about the relocation of his family to Minnesota: "My dad was in the grocery business; he got a job downtown [in] a big grocery store. He worked in the produce section and [got] stuff ready to sell. And then he finally got

a job in a frame company in the Northeast Minneapolis. My mother was a tailor. She knew something about clothing alteration and stuff. She got a job right away, so we were able to buy the house. My uncle opened a restaurant in Dinkytown, a Japanese restaurant." Kirihara had been an accountant since 1949. He passed away in 2018. See J. Kirihara, interview. Moreover, his younger brother Mikio "Micky" Kirihara, whose story appeared in Chapter Two, also came to Minnesota as a high school student.

80. Born in Fowler, California, to Issei parents from Hiroshima, Japan, Yoshimi Matsuura was the third son of six children in a farming family. He graduated from high school in 1936 and started helping out on the family farm. Matsuura thought Fowler was good in general, and "everybody minded their own business until the war broke out. . . . All of a sudden, as far as they were concerned, we were 'Japs.' Well, that's the way it went." His father was taken away by the FBI for no particular reason that Matsuura could think of, probably because he was involved in the local Japanese community. The rest of the family, including his mother and siblings, along with his wife and her family, were sent to Gila River. See Matsuura, interview.

81. From the creation of the NYA on June 26, 1935, to its official end on January 1, 1944, the organization helped over 4.5 million American youths. For the establishment and work of the NYA, see Federal Security Agency, War Manpower Commission, *Final Report of the National Youth Administration: Fiscal Years 1936–1943* (Washington, DC: Government Printing Office, 1944); Betty G. Lindley and Ernest K. Lindley, *A New Deal for Youth: The Story of the National Youth Administration* (New York: Viking Press, 1938).

82. Matsuura, interview. The subsequent quotations from Matsuura come from this interview unless stated otherwise.

Being a part of President Roosevelt's New Deal, the Civilian Conservation Corps (CCC) was a voluntary government work relief program for unemployed and unmarried men ages seventeen to twenty-eight. It employed them in manual labor jobs related to the conservation and development of natural resources in rural lands owned by federal, state, and local governments. It ran from 1933 to 1942. For more information, see John A. Salmond, *The Civilian Conservation Corps, 1933–1942: A New Deal Case Study* (Durham, NC: Duke University Press, 1967).

83. William Thorkelson, "'Breaks Against Us,' Assert Nisei Youths, Stranded in Twin Cities," *Minneapolis Star Journal*, June 8, 1943, 17.

84. "Stranded Nisei Now Has Jobs," *Minneapolis Star Journal*, June 23, 1943, 2.

85. Matsuura also believed that the hostility might have something to do with his not being a union member. Matsuura, interview.

86. "Yoshimi 'Matt' Matsuura," Obituaries, Minneapolis *Star Tribune*, October 3, 2021.

87. See G. J. Hirabayashi, interview by Shima. His story is also featured in Henderson, *Bridge to the Sun*, 24–39, 139–51, 203–217, 342–44.

The two Hollywood films about the Marauders are *Never So Few*, directed by John Sturges (Metro-Goldwyn-Mayer, 1959) and *Merrill's Marauders*, directed by Sam Fuller (Warner Bros., 1962). Neither mentions the Japanese American linguists, and the latter features an interpreter character, "Taggy," who is a Filipino solider played by a Filipino actor.

88. For a detailed biography of Gordon Hirabayashi, see G. K. Hirabayashi et al., *A Principled Stand*. See Brian Niiya, "Hirabayashi v. United States," Densho Encyclopedia, last modified October 8, 2020, https://encyclopedia.densho.org/Hirabayashi_v._United_States/.

Yasui v. United States (1943) was a US Supreme Court case regarding the constitutionality of curfews used during World War II. On March 28, 1942, an Oregon native, Minoru Yasui, deliberately broke the curfew in Portland by walking around the downtown area and then presenting himself at a police station after 11:00 p.m. to test the legality of the curfew. In its decision, the Supreme Court held that the application of curfews against citizens is constitutional. See *Minoru Yasui v. U.S.*, 320 U.S. 115 (1943), https://caselaw.findlaw.com/court/us-supreme-court/320/115.html; Brian Niiya. "Yasui v. United States," Densho Encyclopedia, last modified October 5, 2020, https://encyclopedia.densho.org/Yasui_v._United_States/. Also see Stephanie Bangarth, *Voices Raised in Protest: Defending Citizens of Japanese Ancestry in North America, 1942–49* (Vancouver: UBC Press, 2008).

In *Korematsu v. United States* (1944), the US Supreme Court upheld the exclusion of Japanese Americans from the military area on the West Coast during World War II. It was brought to the court by a twenty-three-year-old Californian Nisei man, Fred Korematsu, who refused to leave the exclusion zone and instead challenged the order on the grounds that it violated the Fifth Amendment. The case is often cited as one of the worst Supreme Court decisions of all time. However, it was not overturned until 2018, when Chief Justice John Roberts repudiated the Korematsu decision in his majority opinion in the case of *Trump v. Hawai'i*. See *Korematsu v. United States*, 323 U.S. 214 (1944), Library of Congress, https://www.loc.gov/item/usrep323214/; Shiho Imai, "Korematsu v. United States," Densho Encyclopedia, last modified July 29, 2020, https://encyclopedia.densho.org/Korematsu_v._United_States/.

89. See Hirabayashi et al., *A Principled Stand*, 181; Entenmann, interview.

90. B. Hirabayashi, interview; B. Hirabayashi, interview by Asaka.

91. B. Hirabayashi, interview by Asaka.

92. B. Hirabayashi, interview.

93. Hirabayashi recalled his wife said, "'I don't want to raise Ron [their eldest son] in Chicago. We need to go, like, out in Minneapolis where people are so nice and things are a lot different.' This is why we came up, and she came ahead of me and stayed with my parents 'til she could find a house to buy. And we bought our first house in Richfield." B. Hirabayashi, interview.

94. GICM, *The Oriental in Minnesota*, 22.

95. GICM, *The Oriental in Minnesota*, 22; Matsuura, interview. See the court case *Ty Saiki and George Saiki, a Partnership Doing Business Under the Trade Name and Style of International Chick Sexing Association, Appellants, v. United States of America, Appellee*, 306 F.2d 642 (8th Cir. 1962). See G. Saiki, interview, 5–9.

96. B. Hirabayashi, interview; B. Hirabayashi, interview by Asaka.

Notes to Chapter 8: Resettlement and Remembrance

Opening quote: Lucas, interview. The subsequent quotations from Lucas come from this interview unless stated otherwise.

1. Mura, *The Stories Whiteness Tells Itself*, 2.

2. In 1992, Asian American Renaissance (AAR) began as a coming together of artists, writers, and community activists of Asian and Middle-Eastern descent in the Twin Cities, which helped to inspire succeeding generations of Asian American artists in the upper Midwest. It became the anchor for various Asian and Asian American communities in Minnesota. Through the AAR rose many Asian American art organizations that are known today, including the Theater Mu. David Mura was one of the founders of AAR and its first artistic director. For more information about the organization, see Coalition of Asian American Leaders, Episode 2.1: "Don't Give Power to People Who Cannot See You," *MinneAsian Stories Podcast*, https://caalmn.org/podcast/s2e1-david/.

3. Tanaka did two interviews at the turn of the millennium. See Tanaka, interview by yamada; and Tanaka, interview by Hawkins.

The Tanaka family published a book titled *When a Tiger Dies: The Life of Walter Tanaka*, edited by Chelsey Tanaka, his granddaughter, along with a committee that includes Lucas and her siblings, Wesley Tanaka, Terri Tanaka Koike, and the late Patricia Tanaka Martin's husband, Dave Martin. The author is grateful for a copy gifted by Lucas.

4. "Tometaro's granddaughter, Marilyn Lauglo, donated the 44 pocket-sized diaries to the Immigration History Research Center Archives at the U in 2019. Her cousin, Kiyoshi's daughter Sharon Kitagawa, has painstakingly transcribed them." Curt Brown, "Diaries through Four Decades Tell Story of Japanese Immigrant Family in Minneapolis." Research of the Kitagawa family history is undertaken by St. Paul historian Patti Kameya. Biographical information of Tometaro Kitagawa

can be found in "Tometaro Kitagawa Papers," Immigration History Research Center Archives, University of Minnesota, https://archives.lib.umn.edu/repositories/6/resources/7870.

5. The Borchers story is based upon the following two articles: Susie Ling, "A Father's Letters: The Story of Nisei and U.S. Marine Robert Borchers," *Rafu Shimpo*, June 19, 2015; Rocío Gomez, "Manzanar: Lasting Remnants and Reflections on an American Injustice," *History in the Making* 11, no. 12 (2018): 194–98.

6. Borchers, "From a Veteran," 1.

7. Borchers, "From a Veteran," 1.

8. See Jonathan van Harmelen, "Gannon Committee," Densho Encyclopedia, last modified October 8, 2020, https://encyclopedia.densho.org/Gannon_Committee/.

9. For example, one of the letters from Taeko Omori of Poston High School read: "I am more than grateful because I am one who is living in a relocation center, shut away from my dear friends and not free to my unalienable rights. I am an American citizen, and I surely think that I am privileged to my liberties, don't you?" Another letter signed "A Reader" from Idaho Falls noted: "We are fighting for the same freedom as you and other Americans. We are doing everything we can to prove our loyalty to America—to prove that we are real Americans." There were hundreds of others, including Tomiko Sakita at "Rivers, Arizona," Roy Nakabayashi at USAFISPA (United States Armed Forces in South Pacific Area) in San Francisco, Shuichi Ogura at Camp Shelby, who also wrote letters to thank Borchers for his letter to the American Legion. See Ling, "A Father's Letters"; Gomez, "Manzanar."

10. Borchers connected with Karl and Elaine Yoneda's son Tom Yoneda, Arlene Eddow Kishi, and a cousin of Taeko Omori. See Ling, "A Father's Letters."

11. Sickels, *Around the World*, 211.

12. The Department of the Interior, which coincidentally was also the department that oversaw the War Relocation Authority, published a booklet titled *What We're Fighting For* that included nineteen letters written by servicemen expressing great discontent in the government's treatment of Japanese Americans. Borchers's letter was the first in the collection.

13. The fort was named after Colonel Josiah Snelling, who was its first commander between 1820 and 1827 and responsible for the initial design and construction of the fort. See Minnesota Historical Society website on Historic Fort Snelling, https://www.mnhs.org/fortsnelling.

14. Robinson, *After Camp*, 5.

15. Mura, *The Stories Whiteness Tells Itself*, 2, 17.

16. Stanley Kusunoki wrote a poem titled "In a Name," which, in part, reads: "I am the only one in my family with my name / It has not been passed down / through generations / I am nobody's namesake / I have a made up name / It would give my ancestors fits / Su-tan-ran-nee / As close as they could get / Mouths straining to pronounce / Consonants in conjunction / Sounds that do not exist in their world." Shared with the author in the interview.

17. Curt Brown, "77 Years After Family Was Sent to Prison Camp, Minneapolis Woman Gets Diploma," Minneapolis *Star Tribune*, May 15, 2021.

18. Ben Cohen, "Despite WWII Internment, Hayano 'Was Never Bitter,'" Minneapolis *Star Tribune*, January 15, 2008.

19. M. and L. Kirihara, interview.

20. L. Kirihara, interview by Ozone.

21. Tsukahira, interview.

22. Wong, *Visions of a Nation*.

23. The first Day of Remembrance was organized by the SERC with cosponsors such as the JACL, churches, veterans' groups, and other social organizations. See Jennifer Ott, "First Day of Remembrance Is Held at the Puyallup Fairgrounds on November 25, 1978," History Link, August 23, 2010, https://www.historylink.org/File/9464. Also see Young, *Tom Ikeda*, 2.

24. The White House, "Day of Remembrance of Japanese American Incarceration during World War II," February 18, 2022, https://bidenwhitehouse.archives.gov/briefing-room/presidential-actions/2022/02/18/day-of-remembrance-of-japanese-american-incarceration-during-world-war-ii/.

25. Regarding the redress movement, see US CWRIC, *Personal Justice Denied*; also see Leslie T. Hatamiya, *Righting a Wrong: Japanese Americans and the Passage of the Civil Liberties Act of 1988* (Stanford, CA: Stanford University Press, 1993); Mitchell T. Maki, Harry H. L. Kitano, and S. Megan Berthold, *Achieving the Impossible Dream: How Japanese Americans Obtained Redress* (Urbana and Chicago: University of Illinois Press, 1999); Alice Yang Murray, *Historical Memories of the Japanese American Internment and the Struggle for Redress* (Stanford, CA: Stanford University Press, 2007); Yasuko I. Takezawa, *Breaking the Silence: Redress and Japanese American Ethnicity* (Ithaca, NY: Cornell University Press, 1995).

26. See "Densho History," Densho website, https://densho.org/about-densho/densho-history/.

27. Japanese American National Museum, "Tom Ikeda, Founders' Award," *Gala Dinner Journal* (Los Angeles: Japanese American National Museum, 2017), 20.

28. Young, *Tom Ikeda*, 16. Also see V. Ikeda, interview by T. Ikeda and Yasui.

29. Tsuchiya, interview by Asaka.

30. See Tsuchiya, interview by Asaka; also see Ben Petry, "Minnesota's Greatest Generation: Helen Tanigawa Tsuchiya," *Minnesota History* 61, no. 4 (Winter 2008/2009): 130; Tsuchiya, "Helen Tsuchiya"; see Larry Long, "Be Kind to All That Live," https://www.larrylong.org/product/be-kind-to-all-that-live/. Also see https://www.youtube.com/watch?v=0p0QsdAtQJw; Helen Tsuchiya and Larry Long, "Beyond the Barbed Wire," *Teaching Tolerance* (Spring 2010), https://www.learningforjustice.org/classroom-resources/texts/beyond-the-barbed-wire; Petry, "Minnesota's Greatest Generation," 130.

31. B. and P. Doi, interview.

32. Clarissa Baker, "Why a Smithsonian Exhibit on Japanese-Americans and World War II Is Coming to Stearns," *St. Cloud Times*, August 23, 2019, https://www.sctimes.com/story/news/local/2019/08/23/why-smithsonian-exhibit-japanese-americans-and-world-war-ii-coming-stearns-museum-history-minnesota/2055670001/.

33. The quotes are taken from the poem "Chills" by Kusunoki, who shared it with us in the interview about his mother's reaction. S. Kusunoki, interview.

34. Young, *Tom Ikeda*, 28.

35. See Julie Otsuka, *When the Emperor Was Divine* (New York: Knopf Doubleday, 2003). The short novel focuses on the forced removal and incarceration of a Japanese American family in 1942 from Berkeley, California, loosely based on the experiences of the author's mother, to the camp in Topaz, Utah, as well as their return to their home after the war.

For the details of the Muskego-Norway School District case, see Bill Lueders, "When a 'Diverse' Book Ban Goes Awry," *The Bulwark*, June 22, 2022, https://www.thebulwark.com/when-a-diverse-book-ban-goes-awry/.

36. See David Inoue, "JACL Letter to Muskego Norway School District," Japanese American Citizens League, June 13, 2022, https://jacl.org/blog/jacl-letter-to-muskego-norway-school-board.

37. J. Kirihara, interview.

38. See Robinson, *After Camp*, 26. The source of these alleged comments by President Roosevelt can be found in Hung Wai Ching, "Visit to White House for Conference with President F.D. Roosevelt, May 9, 1943," Hung Wai Ching File, Morale Committee Files, Box 1, Romanzo Adams Social Research Laboratory Papers, Special Collections, University of Hawai'i, Mānoa.

39. Haras, interview.

40. Tani, "Yoshi Uchiyama Tani," 127–53. The Twin Cities JACL's Day of Remembrance observation event, titled "Looking Forward by Looking Back," was held on February 12, 2011, at the Transfiguration Lutheran Church in Bloomington.

It featured seventeen youth, including Emily Tani-Winegarden, and was attended by over two hundred people. See Twin Cities JACL, *The Rice Paper*, April 2011.

41. Tani-Winegarden, interview; Y. and K. Tani, interview.

42. Tani, "Yoshi Uchiyama Tani," 148.

43. Emily Tani-Winegarden, "Living in the World of the Wondrous," on the mission page on her professional website, https://www.wondrouscrane.com/about-mission.

44. Murakami, *In Your Path*, 16.

45. Hvistendahl, "Yosh Murakami," 45.

46. An anecdote went something like this. When Yosh Murakami was in a blood bank one day, "a nurse asked him the usual question whether he had ever suffered from jaundice. When he, in feigned innocence, asked what the symptoms were, she explained that the skin often turns yellow." Murakami humorously responded: "I've had it all my life!" Hvistendahl, "Yosh Murakami," 45.

47. Murakami, *In Your Path*, 70, 97, 115; Andy Steiner, "Uncharted Waters," *St. Olaf Magazine* (Summer 2020), July 19, 2020, https://wp.stolaf.edu/news/uncharted-waters.

48. Steiner, "Uncharted Waters"; Murakami, "Foreword," *In Your Path*, n.p.

49. Murakami, "Foreword," *In Your Path*, n.p.

50. Murakami, *Tide Goes Out*, back cover, 140.

51. Murakami, *Tide Goes Out*, 140.

Notes to Chapter 9: Untold Histories and Unsung Heroes

Opening quote: Tani, "A Story to Tell," cited in Tsuchida, ed., *Reflections*, xli.

1. Tani, "Yoshi Uchiyama Tani," 153.

2. Tani is concerned by "[t]he July 8, 1991 issue of the *TIME* magazine [that] posed the questions: 'Who are We?' and 'Whose America?' The lead statement was, 'A growing emphasis on the nation's multicultural heritage exalts racial and ethnic pride at the expense of social cohesion.'" Tani, "Yoshi Uchiyama Tani," 151.

3. Paula A. Braveman, Elaine Arkin, Dwayne Proctor, Tina Kauh, and Nicole Holm, "Systemic and Structural Racism: Definitions, Examples, Health Damages, and Approaches to Dismantling," *Health Affairs* 41, no. 2 (2022): 172. See Bryan Armen Graham, "Tom Cotton Calls Slavery 'Necessary Evil' in Attack on *New York Times*' 1619 Project," *The Guardian*, July 26, 2020, https://www.theguardian.com/world/2020/jul/26/tom-cotton-slavery-necessary-evil-1619-project-new-york-times. Mura, *The Stories Whiteness Tells Itself*, 2.

Bibliography

Aburano, Sharon Tanagi. "Questionnaire from the Nursing History/Mayo Medical Center History Project," March 8, 2002. Unpublished data. St. Mary's School of Nursing Alumni Association, Rochester, Minnesota.

Albert, Michael. "The Japanese." In *They Chose Minnesota: A Survey of the State's Ethnic Groups*, edited by June Drenning Holmquist, 558–71. St. Paul: Minnesota Historical Society Press, 1981.

American Journal of Nursing editorial. "The Problem of Student Nurses of Japanese Ancestry." *The American Journal of Nursing* 43, no. 10 (October 1943): 895–96.

Ano, Masaharu. "Loyal Linguists: Nisei of World War II Learned Japanese in Minnesota." *Minnesota History* 45, no. 7 (Fall 1977): 273–87.

Ariyoshi, Koji. *From Kona to Yenan: The Political Memoirs of Koji Ariyoshi*. Edited by Alice M. Beechert and Edward D. Beechert. Honolulu: University of Hawaii Press, 2000.

Austin, Allan W. *From Concentration Camp to Campus: Japanese American Students and World War II*. Urbana: University of Illinois Press, 2004.

Austin, Allan W. "John Nason." Densho Encyclopedia. Last modified June 24, 2020. https://encyclopedia.densho.org/John_Nason/.

Azuma, Eiichiro. "Race, Citizenship, and the 'Science of Chick Sexing': The Politics of Racial Identity among Japanese Americans." *Pacific Historical Review* 78, no. 2 (May 2009): 242–75.

Beaton, Gail M. *Colorado Women in World War II*. Louisville: University Press of Colorado, 2020.

Borchers, Robert E. "From a Veteran of Guadalcanal." In *"What We're Fighting For": Statements by United States Servicemen about Americans of Japanese Descent*. Washington, DC: War Relocation Authority, 1944.

Bowers, Faubion. "The Hakujin Experience." In *MIS in the War against Japan*, edited by Stanley L. Falk and Warren M. Tsuneishi, 11–12. Washington, DC: Japanese American Veterans Association, 1995.

Bradsher, Greg. "The Beginnings of the United States Army's Japanese Language Training: From the Presidio of San Francisco to Camp Savage, Minnesota 1941–1942." *The Text Message* (blog). National Archives, December 19, 2017. https://text-message.blogs.archives.gov/2017/12/19/the-beginnings-of-the-united-states-armys-japanese-language-training-from-the-presidio-of-san-francisco-to-camp-savage-minnesota-1941-1942/.

Bray, Patrick, ed. "75th Anniversary Special: The Savage and Snelling Years." Article composed of excerpts from *MISLS Album, 1946*. Defense Language Institute Foreign Language Center News, August 9, 2016. https://www.dliflc.edu/75th-anniversary-special-the-savage-and-snelling-years/.

Brown, Curt. "After the Bombing of Pearl Harbor, St. Paul Family Was Exiled by Country, Not Community." Minneapolis *Star Tribune*, June 16, 2018.

Brown, Curt. "Japanese-Born Vet Edward Yamazaki a Rarity at Fort Snelling National Cemetery." Minneapolis *Star Tribune*, October 21, 2021.

Brown, Curt. "Diaries through Four Decades Tell Story of Japanese Immigrant Family in Minneapolis." Minneapolis *Star Tribune*, June 3, 2023.

Brown, Jessica Wambach. "How Japanese American Linguists Helped the U.S. Army Fight Japan." HistoryNet, July 9, 2018. https://www.historynet.com/japanese-american-linguists-in-army.htm. First published in *World War II*, August, 2018.

Brueggemann, David. "The U.S. Cadet Nurse Corps 1943–1948: The Nebraska Experience." MA thesis, University of Nebraska Omaha, 1991.

Burton, Jeffery F., ed. *Confinement and Ethnicity: An Overview of World War II Japanese American Relocation Sites*. Tucson, AZ: Western Archeological and Conservation Center, National Park Service, 1999.

Carter, John Franklin. "Memorandum on C.B. Munson's Report 'Japanese on the West Coast.'" Commission on Wartime Relocation and Internment of Civilians. November 7, 1941. Densho Digital Repository. https://ddr.densho.org/ddr-densho-67-11/.

Colwell, Bruce William. *Great Purpose: The Life of John W. Nason. Philosopher, President and Champion of Liberal Learning*. Northfield: Carleton College, 2023.

Commission on Wartime Relocation and Internment of Civilians (CWRIC). *Personal Justice Denied: Report of the Commission on Wartime Relocation and Internment of Civilians*. Washington, DC: US Government Printing Office, 1983.

Committee on Resettlement of Japanese Americans (CRJA). *Minneapolis Chapter Records, 1942–1944*. St. Paul: Minnesota Historical Society, n.d.

Committee on Resettlement of Japanese Americans (CRJA). "Committee of Resettlement of Japanese Americans, Minneapolis Chapter: An Inventory of Its Records at the Minnesota Historical Society." Minnesota Historical Society, n.d. http://www2.mnhs.org/library/findaids/01311.xml.

Committee on Resettlement of Japanese Americans (CRJA), the Federal Council of the Churches of Christ in America, the Home Missions Council of North America, and the Foreign Missions Conference of North America. "Planning Resettlement of Japanese Americans." Pamphlet. July 1943.

Cornell, Tricia. "Honor Bound." *Carleton College Voice* 77, no. 2 (Winter 2012): 34–37.

Cosgrave, Margaret. "Relocation of Japanese American Students." *Journal of the American Association of Collegiate Registrars* 18 (April 1943): 221–26.

Crost, Lyn. *Honor by Fire: Japanese Americans at War in Europe and the Pacific.* Novato, CA: Presidio Press, 1994.

Dahlman, Sumiko Ito. "Questionnaire from the Nursing History/Mayo Medical Center History Project," February 20, 2002. Unpublished data. St. Mary's School of Nursing Alumni Association, Rochester, Minnesota.

Daniels, Roger. *The Politics of Prejudice: The Anti-Japanese Movement in California and the Struggle for Japanese Exclusion.* 2nd ed. Berkeley: University of California Press, 1978.

Daniels, Roger. *Concentration Camps, North America: Japanese in the United States and Canada during World War II.* Malabar, FL: Robert E. Krieger Publishing, 1981.

Daniels, Roger. *Asian America: Chinese and Japanese in the United States Since 1850.* Seattle: University of Washington Press, 1988.

Daniels, Roger. *Prisoners without Trial: Japanese Americans in World War II.* New York: Hill and Wang, 1993.

Daniels, Roger. "Words Do Matter: A Note on Inappropriate Terminology and the Incarceration of the Japanese Americans." In *Nikkei in the Pacific Northwest: Japanese Americans and Japanese Canadians in the Twentieth Century,* edited by Louis Fiset and Gail M. Nomura, 183–207. Seattle: University of Washington Press, 2005.

Daniels, Roger, Sandra C. Taylor, and Harry H. L. Kitano, eds. *Japanese Americans: From Relocation to Redress.* Seattle: University of Washington Press, 1992.

DeCarlo, Peter J. "Military Intelligence Service Language School (MISLS)." MNopedia. Published May 13, 2015. Last modified April 6, 2022. https://www.mnopedia.org/group/military-intelligence-service-language-school-misls.

Dempster, Brian Komei. *Making Home from War: Stories of Japanese American Exile and Resettlement.* Berkeley, CA: Heyday, 2011.

Drinnon, Richard. *Keeper of Concentration Camps: Dillon S. Myer and American Racism*. Berkeley: University of California Press, 1987.

Eisenhower, Milton S. *The President Is Calling*. Garden City, NY: Doubleday, 1974.

Elleman, Bruce. *Japanese-American Civilian Prisoner Exchanges and Detention Camps, 1941–45*. New York: Routledge, 2006.

Falk, Stanley L., and Warren M. Tsuneishi, eds. *MIS in the War against Japan*. Washington, DC: Japanese American Veterans Association, 1995.

Faster, Karen E. "Newspaper Coverage and Cultural Representations of Racial and Ethnic Groups in Minneapolis, 1941–1971." PhD Diss., University of Wisconsin–Madison, 2003.

Federal Security Agency. *The U.S. Cadet Nurse Corps, 1943–1948*. Washington, DC: US Government Printing Office, 1950.

Fiset, Louis, and Gail M. Nomura, eds. *Nikkei in the Pacific Northwest: Japanese Americans and Japanese Canadians in the Twentieth Century*. Seattle: University of Washington Press, 2005.

Fisher, Galen M. "Our Two Japanese-American Policies." *Christian Century* 60 (August 25, 1943): 961–63.

Fisher, Galen M. *Public Affairs and the Y.M.C.A., 1844–1944, with Special Reference to the United States*. New York: Association Press, 1948.

Frail, T. A. "The Injustice of Japanese-American Internment Camps Resonates Strongly to This Day." *Smithsonian Magazine*, Jan/Feb 2017. https://www.smith sonianmag.com/history/injustice-japanese-americans-internment-camps-reso nates-strongly-180961422/.

Fryer, Heather. "The Japanese American Experience: History and Culture." In *Asian American History and Culture: An Encyclopedia*, edited by Huping Ling and Allan W. Austin, 371–474 (e-edition). New York: Routledge, 2015.

Fujitani, Takashi. *Race for Empire: Koreans as Japanese and Japanese as Americans during World War II*. Berkeley: University of California Press, 2011.

Girdner, Audrie, and Anne Loftis. *The Great Betrayal: The Evacuation of the Japanese-Americans during World War II*. New York: The Macmillan Company, 1969.

Governor's Interracial Commission of Minnesota (GICM). *The Oriental in Minnesota: A Report to Governor Luther W. Youngdahl*. St. Paul: GICM, 1949.

Hall, Jenness Evaline. "Japanese American College Students during the Second World War." PhD Diss., Indiana University, 1996.

Hamilton, Diane B. *Becoming a Presence within Nursing: The History of the University of Colorado School of Nursing, 1898–1998*. Denver: University of Colorado School of Nursing, 1999.

Hanson, Krista Finstad. "St. Paul Resettlement Committee Helped Bring Japanese Americans to Minnesota in Wake of World War Two Camp Policy." *MinnPost*,

March 26, 2018. https://www.minnpost.com/mnopedia/2018/03/st-paul-reset
tlement-committee-helped-bring-japanese-americans-minnesota-wake-world/.

Hanson, Krista Finstad. "Festival of Nations." MNopedia. Published May 1, 2019. Last modified February 16, 2021. https://www.mnopedia.org/event/festival -nations.

Hanson, Krista Finstad. "Tanbara, Ruth Nomura (1907–2008)." MNopedia. Published June 11, 2018. Last modified April 5, 2022. https://www.mnopedia.org/person/tanbara-ruth-nomura-1907-2008.

Harrington, Joseph. *Yankee Samurai: The Secret Role of Nisei in America's Pacific Victory.* Detroit: Pettigrew Enterprises, 1979.

Hayashi, Kristen. "The Return of Japanese Americans to the West Coast in 1945." The National WWII Museum: New Orleans. Last modified March 26, 2021. https://www.nationalww2museum.org/war/articles/return-japanese-ameri cans-west-coast-1945.

Henderson, Bruce. *Bridge to the Sun: The Secret Role of the Japanese Americans Who Fought in the Pacific in World War II.* New York: Alfred A. Knopf, 2022.

Hiner, James H. Jr. "Narrative History: War Relocation Authority, Minneapolis District 1942–1946." Minnesota Ethnic History Project, 25 box 14. Minnesota Historical Society.

Hirabayashi, Gordon K., James A. Hirabayashi, and Lane Ryo Hirabayashi. *A Principled Stand: The Story of* Hirabayashi v. the United States. Seattle: University of Washington Press, 2013.

Hirabayashi, James A. "Four Hirabayashi Cousins: A Question of Identity." In *Nikkei in the Pacific Northwest: Japanese Americans and Japanese Canadians in the Twentieth Century*, edited by Louis Fiset and Gail M. Nomura. Seattle: University of Washington Press, 2005.

Hirose, Stacey Yukari. "Japanese American Women and the Women's Army Corp, 1935–1950." MA thesis, University of California, Los Angeles, 1993.

Hosokawa, Bill. *Nisei: The Quiet Americans.* New York: William Morrow, 1969.

Hvistendahl, Susan. "Yosh Murakami: Beloved Northfield Vocal Music Teacher." *Northfield Entertainment Guide,* June 2012.

Ichinokuchi, Tad. "Montage of Scenes from Fort Snelling." In *John Aiso and the M.I.S.: Japanese-American Soldiers in the Military Intelligence Service, World War II,* edited by Tad Ichinokuchi and Daniel Aiso, 36–41. Los Angeles: MIS Club of Southern California, 1988.

Inefuku, Rodney. "Story of a WAC in MIS: Miwako Yanamoto." *Nisei Veteran Committee Foundation Newsletter* 68, no. 9 (October 2018): 10.

Ishimaru, Stone S. *Military Intelligence Service Language School, U.S. Army, Fort Snelling, Minnesota.* Los Angeles: TecCom Production, 1991.

James, Thomas. "'Life Begins with Freedom': The College Nisei, 1942–1945." *History of Education Quarterly* 25, no. 1/2 (Spring–Summer 1985): 155–74.

Japanese American Veterans Association. "Japanese American Women in World War II." http://www.javadc.org/AJA%20women_in_wwII.htm. First published in *Echoes of Silence: The Untold Stories of the Nisei Soldiers Who Served in WWII*, Americans of Japanese Ancestry (AJA) World War II Memorial Alliance. Montebello, CA: AJA, 1999. CD-ROM.

Jarvis, Charles W. "Kano Ikeda, M.D.: 1887–1960." *American Journal of Clinical Pathology* 35, no. 5 (May 1961): 453–54.

Johnson, Audrey, and Barbara Tosdal. "A Study of the Relocated Japanese-Americans in Minneapolis." Unpublished sociology class report, University of Minnesota, n.d.

Kalisch, Philip A., and Beatrice J. Kalisch. *From Training to Education: The Impact of Federal Aid on Schools of Nursing in the United States during the 1940's.* Vol. 1 of Final Report of NIH Grant NU 00443, December 1974: 111–14.

Kawaguchi, Ida C. "Questionnaire from the Nursing History/Mayo Medical Center History Project," March 12, 2002. Unpublished data. St. Mary's School of Nursing Alumni Association, Rochester, Minnesota.

Kenney, Dave. *Minnesota Goes to War: The Home Front during World War II.* St. Paul: Minnesota Historical Society Press, 2005.

Kenney, Dave. *Normandale Japanese Garden: Celebrating a Dream.* Minneapolis: Nodin Press, 2014.

Kihara, Shig. "The Day Will Be Long Remembered." In *John Aiso and the M.I.S.: Japanese-American Soldiers in the Military Intelligence Service, World War II*, edited by Tad Ichinokuchi and Daniel Aiso, 205–8. Los Angeles: MIS Club of Southern California, 1988.

Kishi, Stella. "Thrice Told Tales: Turning Back the Clock on Our U.S.O." In *John Aiso and the M.I.S.: Japanese-American Soldiers in the Military Intelligence Service, World War II*, edited by Tad Ichinokuchi and Daniel Aiso, 48–53. Los Angeles: MIS Club of Southern California, 1988.

Kitagawa, Daisuke. *Issei and Nisei: The Internment Years.* New York: Seabury Press, 1967.

Lam, Samantha. "The Nisei WACs: The Combination of a Japanese Linguist and an American Soldier." Pacific Atrocities Education, July 10, 2019. https://www.pacificatrocities.org/blog/the_nisei_wacs.

Langowski, Eric. "Education Denied: Indiana University's Japanese American Ban, 1942 to 1945." *Indiana Magazine of History* 115, no. 2 (June 2019): 65–115.

LaVenture, Tom J. "Don Maeda Still Making Crowns at 86." *Discover Nikkei*, June 30, 2011. https://discovernikkei.org/en/journal/article/4057/. First published in *Asian American Press*, June 12, 2011.

Lee, Erika. *At America's Gates: Chinese Immigration during the Exclusion Era, 1882–1943*. Chapel Hill: The University of North Carolina Press, 2003.

Lee, Erika. *The Making of Asian America: A History*. New York: Simon and Schuster, 2015.

Lee, Fumiye Yoshida. "Questionnaire from the Nursing History/Mayo Medical Center History Project," April 9, 2002. Unpublished data. St. Mary's School of Nursing Alumni Association, Rochester, Minnesota.

Lee, Maggie. "Director Yosh's Parents Brought to Northfield." *Northfield News*, May 23, 1968.

Leiter, Samuel L. "Faubion Bowers." *Asian Theatre Journal* 28, no. 2 (Fall 2011): 314–21.

Mashbir, Sidney Forrester. *I Was an American Spy*. New York: Vantage Press, 1953.

McNaughton, James C. "Nisei Linguists and New Perspectives on the Pacific War." Paper presented at the 1994 Conference of Army Historians, Washington, DC, June 13–16, 1994.

McNaughton, James C. *Nisei Linguists: Japanese Americans in the Military Intelligence Service during World War II*. Washington, DC: Department of the Army, 2006.

McWilliams, James. "The Lucrative Art of Chicken Sexing." *Pacific Standard*, December/January 2018.

Menefee, Selden Cowles. *Assignment: U.S.A.* New York: Reynal and Hitchcock, 1943.

Milanoski, Joe. "Camp Savage Memories." In *John Aiso and the M.I.S.: Japanese-American Soldiers in the Military Intelligence Service, World War II*, edited by Tad Ichinokuchi and Daniel Aiso, 54–59. Los Angeles: MIS Club of Southern California, 1988.

MISLS Album Staff. *MISLS Album*. Minneapolis: Military Intelligence Service Language School, 1946.

Moore, Brenda L. *Serving Our Country: Japanese American Women in the Military during World War II*. New Brunswick, NJ: Rutgers University Press, 2003.

Morooka, Martha Masako. "St. Mary's School of Nursing 2006—One Hundredth Anniversary Celebration," March 2002. Unpublished letter. St. Mary's School of Nursing Alumni Association, Rochester, Minnesota.

Mura, David. *The Stories Whiteness Tells Itself: Racial Myths and Our American Narratives*. Minneapolis: University of Minnesota Press, 2023.

Murakami, Molly. *In Your Path: Letters to My Grandfather*. Minneapolis: Molly Murakami Comics and Illustration, 2020.

Murakami, Molly. *Tide Goes Out*. Seattle: Densho, 2022.

Myer, Dillon S. *Uprooted Americans: The Japanese Americans and the War Relocation Authority during World War II*. Tucson: University of Arizona Press, 1971.

Nakamura, Kelli Y. "'They Are Our Human Secret Weapons': The Military Intelligence Service and the Role of Japanese-Americans in the Pacific War and in the Occupation of Japan." *The Historian* 70, no. 1 (Spring 2008): 54–74.

Nakamura, Kelli Y. "John Aiso." Densho Encyclopedia. Last modified July 14, 2020. https://encyclopedia.densho.org/John_Aiso/.

Nakamura, Kelli Y. "Military Intelligence Service Language School." Densho Encyclopedia. Last modified October 16, 2020. https://encyclopedia.densho.org/Military_Intelligence_Service_Language_School/.

Nakasone, Edwin M. *Japanese American Veterans of Minnesota*. White Bear Lake, MN: J-Press Publishing, 2002.

Nakatsu, Dan. "The Nisei Soldiers of U.S. Military Intelligence: America's Superb Secret Weapon of World War II." In *John Aiso and the M.I.S.: Japanese-American Soldiers in the Military Intelligence Service, World War II*, edited by Tad Ichinokuchi and Daniel Aiso, 76–84. Los Angeles: MIS Club of Southern California, 1988.

Nakayama, Takeshi. "Momma Wore Combat Boots." *The Rafu Magazine*, December 18, 1993.

National Archives. "Japanese-American Incarceration during World War II." Educator Resources. Last modified January 24, 2022. https://www.archives.gov/education/lessons/japanese-relocation.

National Japanese American Citizens League, Power of Words II Committee. *Power of Words Handbook: A Guide to Language about Japanese Americans in World War II; Understanding Euphemisms and Preferred Terminology*. San Francisco: JACL, 2013.

Ngai, Mae M. "'An Ironic Testimony to the Value of American Democracy': Assimilationism and the World War II Internment of Japanese Americans." In *Contested Democracy: Freedom, Race, and Power in American History*, edited by Manisha Sinha and Penny Von Eschen, 237–57. New York: Columbia University Press, 2007.

Ngai, Mae M. *Impossible Subjects: Illegal Aliens and the Making of Modern America*. Princeton, NJ: Princeton University Press, 2014.

O'Brien, Robert W. *The College Nisei*. Palo Alto, CA: Pacific Books, 1949.

Oguro, Richard S., ed. *Senpai Gumi*. Honolulu: MIS Veterans of Hawai'i, 1982.

Okamoto, Shirō. *The Man Who Saved Kabuki: Faubion Bowers and Theatre Censorship in Occupied Japan*. Translated by Samuel L. Leiter. Honolulu: University of Hawai'i Press, 2001.

Okihiro, Gary Y. *Storied Lives: Japanese American Students and World War II*. Seattle: University of Washington Press, 1999.

Petersen, William. *Japanese Americans: Oppression and Success.* New York: Random House, 1971.

Petry, Lucile. "U.S. Cadet Nurse Corps: Established under the Bolton Act." *The American Journal of Nursing* 43, no. 8 (August 1943): 704–8.

Provinse, John H. "Relocation of Japanese-American College Students: Acceptance of a Challenge." *Higher Education* 1, no. 8 (April 16, 1945): 1–4.

Reeves, Richard. *Infamy: The Shocking Story of the Japanese American Internment in World War II.* New York: Henry Holt and Co., 2015.

Rhude, Kristofer. "Buddhism in Japanese-American Internment Camps." *Buddhism Case Study–Minority in America* (2018). Harvard Divinity School. https://rpl .hds.harvard.edu/religion-context/case-studies/minority-america/buddhism -japanese-american-internment-camps.

Robinson, Greg. *A Tragedy of Democracy: Japanese Confinement in North America.* New York: Columbia University Press, 2009.

Robinson, Greg. *After Camp: Portraits in Midcentury Japanese American Life and Politics.* Berkeley: University of California Press, 2012.

Robinson, Thelma M. "Distribution of Nisei Cadet Nurses 1944–1946 by Region, States, City and Schools of Nursing," 2001. Unpublished data. Nisei Cadet Nurse Project, Boulder, Colorado.

Robinson, Thelma M. *Nisei Cadet Nurse of World War II: Patriotism in Spite of Prejudice.* Boulder, CO: Black Swan Mill Press, 2005.

Robinson, Thelma M. *Your Country Needs You: Cadet Nurses of World War II.* Bloomington, IN: Xlibris, 2009.

Sauve, Jeff. "Tidbits from the Archives: Nisei Oles." St. Olaf College Archives, May 18, 2006. https://wp.stolaf.edu/archives/tidbits-from-the-archives-nisei-oles/.

Sickels, Alice L. "St. Paul Extends a Hand," n.d. California State University Japanese American Digitization Project, California State University-Dominguez Hills. https://cdm16855.contentdm.oclc.org/digital/collection/p16855coll4/id/ 8466.

Sickels, Alice L. *Around the World in St. Paul.* Minneapolis: University of Minnesota Press, 1945.

Simpson, Caroline Chung. *An Absent Presence: Japanese Americans in Postwar American Culture, 1945–1960.* Durham, NC: Duke University Press, 2001.

Steiner, Jesse Frederick. *The Japanese Invasion: A Study in the Psychology of Interracial Contacts.* Chicago: A. C. McClurg and Co., 1917.

Sterner, C. Douglas. *Go for Broke: The Nisei Warriors of World War II Who Conquered Germany, Japan, and American Bigotry.* Clearfield, UT: American Legacy Historical Press, 2015.

Suzuki, Esther Torii. "The Good Lives On." *Friends Journal* 38, no. 11 (November 1992): 22–24.

Suzuki, Esther Torii. "Memoirs." In *Reflections: Memoirs of Japanese American Women in Minnesota*, edited by John Tsuchida, 89–126. Covina, CA: Pacific Asia Press, 1994.

Takei, George, Justin Eisinger, Steven Scott, and Harmony Becker. *They Called Us Enemy: Expanded Edition.* Marietta, GA: Top Shelf Productions, 2020.

Takemae, Eiji. *Inside GHQ: The Allied Occupation of Japan and Its Legacy.* Translated by Robert Ricketts and Sebastian Swann. New York: Continuum, 2002.

Tanaka, Chelsey, et al. *When a Tiger Dies: The Life of Walter Tanaka.* Tanaka Family, 2023.

Tanbara, Ruth Nomura. "Memoirs." In *Reflections: Memoirs of Japanese American Women in Minnesota*, edited by John Tsuchida, 1–67. Covina, CA: Pacific Asia Press, 1994.

Tani, Yoshi Uchiyama. "Yoshi Uchiyama Tani." In *Reflections: Memoirs of Japanese American Women in Minnesota*, edited by John Tsuchida, 127–53. Covina, CA: Pacific Asia Press, 1994.

Tateishi, John. *Redress: The Inside Story of the Successful Campaign for Japanese American Reparations.* Berkeley, CA: Heyday, 2020.

Taylor, Sandra C. "Leaving the Concentration Camps: Japanese American Resettlement in Utah and the Intermountain West." *Pacific Historical Review* 60, no. 2 (May 1991): 169–94.

Tchen, John Kuo Wei, and Dylan Yeats, eds. *Yellow Peril! An Archive of Anti-Asian Fear.* New York: Verso, 2014.

Threat, Charissa J. *Nursing Civil Rights: Gender and Race in the Army Nurse Corps.* Chicago: University of Illinois Press, 2015.

Toyoda, Sus. "MISLS Camp Savage, Minnesota." Japanese American Veterans Association. http://www.javadc.org/camp_savage%20life%20toyoda.htm.

Treadwell, Mattie E. *United States Army in World War II: The Women's Army Corps.* Washington, DC: Office of the Chief of Military History, 1954.

Tsuchida, John, ed. *Reflections: Memoirs of Japanese American Women in Minnesota.* Covina, CA: Pacific Asia Press, 1994.

Tsuchiya, Helen. "Helen Tsuchiya." Elders' Wisdom, Children's Song. Community Celebration of Place. https://www.communitycelebration.org/elder/tsuchiya.

Tsukiyama, Ted T. "Dr. J. Alfred Burden, Col." In *Secret Valor: M.I.S. Personnel, World War II, Pacific Theater, Pre-Pearl Harbor to Sept. 8, 1951*, edited by Ted T. Tsukiyama et al., 52–54. Honolulu: Military Intelligence Service Veterans Club of Hawaii, 1993.

US Commission on Wartime Relocation and Internment of Civilians (US CWRIC). *Personal Justice Denied.* Washington, DC: Civil Liberties Public Education Fund; Seattle: University of Washington Press, 1997.

US Department of the Interior. *WRA: A Story of Human Conservation.* Washington, DC: US Government Printing Office, 1946.

Uyeda, Clifford, and Barry Saiki, eds. *The Pacific War and Peace: Americans of Japanese Ancestry in Military Intelligence Service 1941 to 1952.* San Francisco: Military Intelligence Service Association of Northern California and the National Japanese American Historical Society, 1991.

War Agency Liquidation Unit. *People in Motion: The Postwar Adjustment of the Evacuated Japanese Americans.* Washington, DC: US Department of the Interior, 1947.

Weckerling, John. "Nisei at War." In *Senpai Gumi,* edited by Richard S. Oguro. Honolulu: MIS Veterans of Hawaiʻi, 1982.

Weglyn, Michi Nishiura. *Years of Infamy: The Untold Story of America's Concentration Camps.* 3rd ed. Seattle: University of Washington Press, 1996/2003.

Wei, William. *Asians in Colorado: A History of Persecution and Perseverance in the Centennial State.* Seattle: University of Washington Press, 2016.

Wentzel, Virginia Simons. *Sincere et Constanter 1906–1970: The Story of Saint Mary's School of Nursing.* Rochester, MN: Scientific Publications, 2006.

Whelan, Ellen, and Matthew D. Dacy. *The Little Book of Mayo Clinic Values: A Field Guide for Your Journey.* Rochester, MN: Mayo Foundation for Medical Education and Research, 2017.

White, G. Edward. *Earl Warren, a Public Life.* Oxford: Oxford University Press, 1982.

Williams, Duncan Ryūken. *American Sutra: A Story of Faith and Freedom in the Second World War.* Cambridge, MA: Belknap Press of Harvard University Press, 2019.

Wong, Ka F. *Visions of a Nation: Public Monuments in Twentieth-Century Thailand.* Bangkok: White Lotus, 2006.

Wu, Ellen D. *The Color of Success: Asian Americans and the Origins of the Model Minority.* Princeton, NJ: Princeton University Press, 2014.

Yano, Kiyoshi. "Participating in the Mainstream of American Life Amidst Drawback of Racial Prejudice and Discrimination." In *John Aiso and the M.I.S.: Japanese-American Soldiers in the Military Intelligence Service, World War II,* edited by Tad Ichinokuchi and Daniel Aiso, 4–35. Los Angeles: MIS Club of Southern California, 1988.

Yoneda, Elaine B. "Statement to the Commission." In *Only What We Could Carry: The Japanese American Internment Experience,* edited by Lawson Fusao Inada, 153–72. Berkeley, CA: Heyday Books, 2000.

Yonemoto, Karen. "Paul M. Nagano." Densho Encyclopedia. Last modified March 19, 2013. https://encyclopedia.densho.org/Paul_M._Nagano.

Young, Bob. *Tom Ikeda: Things They Left Behind*. Seattle: The Washington Office of the Secretary of State, 2021.

Original Interviews

Colwell, Bruce. "Interview." Interview by the author and Hikari Sugisaki, September 10, 2018.

Doi, Bill, and Peggy Doi. "Interview." Interview by the author, Hikari Sugisaki, and Paul Sullivan, July 1, 2015.

Entenmann, Robert. "Interview." Interview by the author, Hikari Sugisaki, and Paul Sullivan, July 22, 2015.

Hara, Thomas, T. J. Hara, and Elizabeth Hara. "Interview." Interview by the author, March 5, 2023.

Hirabayashi, Bill. "Interview." Interview by the author, Hikari Sugisaki, and Paul Sullivan, July 9, 2015.

Kirihara, Jim. "Interview." Interview by the author, Hikari Sugisaki, and Paul Sullivan, July 9, 2015.

Kirihara, Mikio "Micky," and Lucy Torii Kirihara. "Interview." Interview by the author, Hikari Sugisaki, and Paul Sullivan, June 30, 2015.

Kurihara, Thomas. "Interview." Interview by the author, September 23, 2023.

Kusunoki, Jim. "Interview." Interview by the author, Hikari Sugisaki, and Paul Sullivan, June 22, 2015.

Kusunoki, Stanley. "Interview." Interview by the author, Hikari Sugisaki, and Paul Sullivan, July 10, 2015.

Lucas, Karen Tanaka. "Interview." Interview by the author, May 16, 2023.

Murakami, Jane. "Interview." Interview by the author, Jacob Caswell, Paoge Moua, and Meena Wainwright, June 26, 2014.

Nakasone, Edwin. "Interview." Interview by the author, Hikari Sugisaki, and Paul Sullivan, October 23, 2015.

Rosenberg, Brian. "Interview." Interview by the author and Hikari Sugisaki, September 25, 2018.

Semba, Hannah Hayano. "Interview." Interview by the author, Hikari Sugisaki, Paul Sullivan, and Jiahao Zhang, October 6, 2015.

Smith, Bardwell. "Interview." Interview by the author, Hikari Sugisaki, and Paul Sullivan, July 2, 2015.

Sudo, Sally. "Interview." Interview by the author, Hikari Sugisaki, and Paul Sullivan, June 18, 2015.

Tani, Yoshi, and Kay Tani. "Interview." Interview by the author, Hikari Sugisaki, and Paul Sullivan, November 14, 2015.

Tani-Winegarden, Emily. "Interview." Interview by Hikari Sugisaki and Paul Sullivan, June 15, 2015.

Other Interviews

Abe, Toshio. "Interview." Interview by Thomas Saylor, March 1, 2002, Minnesota Historical Society Oral History Collection.

Aburano, Sharon Tanagi. "Interview." Interview by Tom Ikeda and Megan Asaka, April 3, 2008, Densho Visual History Collection, Densho Digital Repository.

Aiso, John F. "Interview." Interview by Marc Landy, July 23, 1970, Oral History Program, University of California, Los Angeles.

Amemiya, Grace Obata, Sumiko Ito Dahlman, Kimi T. Hara, Amemiya Lee, and Fumiye Yoshida Lee. "Interview." Interview by Virginia Wentzel, August 25, 1996, "Oral History of Nursing," St. Mary's Hospital, Rochester, Minnesota.

Bowers, Faubion. "Interview." Interview by Beate Gordon, 1960, Columbia Digital Library Collections, Columbia University Libraries.

Doi, Saburo Bill. "Interview." Interview by Richard Hawkins, June 26, 2005, Japanese American Military History Collective.

Hara, George. "Interview." Interview by Loen Dozono, February 5, 2003, Oregon Nikkei Endowment Collection, Densho Digital Repository.

Hawley, Grace Sugita. "Interview." Interview by Megan Asaka, June 3, 2009, Densho Visual History Collection, Densho Digital Repository.

Hirabayashi, Bill. "Interview." Interview by Megan Asaka, June 16, 2009, Twin Cities JACL Collection, Densho Digital Repository.

Hirabayashi, Grant J. "Interview." Interview by Terry Shima, June 29, 2005, Veterans History Project, Library of Congress.

Hirasuna, Fred. "Interview." Interview by Larry Hashima and Cherry Kinoshita, September 12, 1997, Densho Visual History Collection, Densho Digital Repository.

Hurt, Haruko. "Interview." Interview by Jim Gatewood, February 28, 1998, REgenerations Oral History Project: Rebuilding Japanese American Families, Communities, and Civil Rights in the Resettlement Era, University of California.

Ikeda, Mary. "Interview." Interview by Tom Ikeda and Barbara Yasui, April 28, 2022, Densho Visual History Collection, Densho Digital Repository.

Ikeda, Victor. "Interview." Interview by Tom Ikeda and Barbara Yasui, February 11, 2022, Densho Visual History Collection, Densho Digital Repository.

Kato, Sue. "Interview." Interview by Corinne Akahoshi, June 17, 2006, Go for Broke National Education Center Oral History Project.

Kirihara, Lucy. "Interview." Interview by Steve Ozone, October 13, 2009, Twin Cities JACL Collection, Densho Digital Repository.

Kono, Alice Tetsuko. "Interview." Interview by James Tanabe and Yoshie Tanabe, March 18, 2004, Veterans History Project, American Folklife Center, Library of Congress.

Maeda, Don. "Interview." Interview by Carolyn Nayematsu, October 13, 2009, Twin Cities JACL Collection, Densho Digital Repository.

Matsui, Mitsue. "Interview." Interview by Marvin Uratsu and Gary Otake, December 12, 1997, National Japanese American Historical Society Collection, Densho Digital Repository.

Matsunaga, Spark. "Interview." Interview by Loni Ding, April 17, 1987, Loni Ding Collection, Densho Digital Repository.

Matsuura, Yoshimi. "Interview." Interview by Tom Ikeda, June 17, 2009, Twin Cities JACL Collection, Densho Digital Repository.

Nagano, Paul. "Interview." Interview by Stephen Fugita and Becky Fukuda, May 25, 1999, Densho Visual History Collection, Densho Digital Repository.

Nakahara, Peter. "Interview." Interview by Robert Horsting, Stephanie Tanaka, and David Yonishige, March 23, 2002, Japanese American Military History Collective, Go for Broke National Education Center.

Nakano, Lillian. "Interview." Interview by Megan Asaka, July 8, 2009, Densho Visual History Collection, Densho Digital Repository.

Nakasone, Edwin. "Interview." Interview by Richard Hawkins, Lisa Sueki, and Steve Itano Wasserman, June 8, 2010, Go for Broke National Education Center Oral History Project.

Nason, John W. "Interview." Interview by Carleton College Oral History Program, August 12, 1992, Carleton College.

Nason, John W. "Interview." Interview by Gary Y. Okihiro, June 9, 1994, Gary Y. Okihiro Papers, Japanese American National Museum.

Nason, John W. "Interview." Interview by Bardwell Smith, April 15, 2000, Carleton College.

Oda, James. "Interview." Interview by Diane Tanaka, November 13, 1999, Go for Broke National Education Center Oral History Project.

Okamoto, Katsumi. "Interview." Interview by Richard Potashin, November 7, 2007, Manzanar National Historic Site Collection, Densho Digital Repository.

Oliver, Jean. "Interview." Interview by Laura Zeccardi, June 20, 2007, Macalester Oral History Project, Macalester College.

Ouchida, Bennie. "Interview." Interview by Stephan Gilchrist, September 13, 2004, Oregon Nikkei Endowment Collection, Densho Digital Repository.

Saiki, George. "Interview." Interview by Karin Thiem, February 10, 1975, Blue Earth County Historical Society, *Wholesale and Retail Businesses of Mankato Since 1900*, Memorial Library, Minnesota State University, Mankato.

Saiki, Kiyoto, and Fumiko Nishioki Saiki. "Interview." Interview by Yoshino Hasegawa, August 27, 1980, *Success Through Perseverance: San Joaquin Valley Japanese Americans in WWII*, California State University, Fresno.

Saiki, Sue. "Interview." Interview by Karin Thiem, February 25, 1975, Blue Earth County Historical Society, *Wholesale and Retail Businesses of Mankato Since 1900*, Memorial Library, Minnesota State University, Mankato.

Sakamoto, Thomas. "Interview." Interview by Richard Hawkins, June 3, 2001, Japanese American Military History Collective, Go for Broke National Education Center.

Seto, Joe. "Interview." Interview by Erin Brasfield, July 10, 2006, Manzanar National Historic Site Collection, Densho Digital Repository.

Shishino, Hy. "Interview." Interview by Sharon Yamato, January 31, 2012, Densho Visual History Collection, Densho Digital Repository.

Sudo, Sally. "Interview." Interview by Steve Ozone, October 12, 2009, Twin Cities JACL Collection, Densho Digital Repository.

Tanaka, Walter. "Interview." Interview by gayle k. yamada, October 20, 2000, gayle k. yamada Collection, Densho Digital Repository.

Tanaka, Walter. "Interview." Interview by Richard Hawkins, June 1, 2001, Japanese American Military History Collective, Go for Broke National Education Center.

Tsuchiya, Helen Tanigawa. "Interview." Interview by Megan Asaka, June 16, 2009, Twin Cities JACL Collection, Densho Digital Repository.

Tsukahira, Toshio. "Interview." Interview by Dennis Yamamoto, March 25, 2000, Japanese American Military History Collective, Go for Broke National Education Center.

Umeda, Harry. "Interview." Interview by Tom Ikeda, June 18, 2009, Twin Cities JACL Collection, Densho Digital Repository.

Yamashita, Nobuo. "Interview." Interview by Diane Tanaka, October 6, 2001, Japanese American Military History Collective, Go for Broke National Education Center.

Index

Note: Photographs in the text are indicated here in *italics*.